THE
GREAT LAKES
DIVING
GUIDE

THE
GREAT LAKES
DIVING
GUIDE

CRIS KOHL

West Chicago

DEDICATION:

TO THOSE WHO EXPLORE, APPRECIATE AND RESPECT
THE BEAUTIFUL, INCREDIBLE AND UNIQUE GREAT LAKES
AND TO THE MEMORY OF MY FRIEND
DON EDWARDS
WHO DID ALL OF THOSE.

THE GREAT LAKES DIVING GUIDE
BY CRIS KOHL

COPYRIGHT © 2001 SEAWOLF COMMUNICATIONS, INC.

ALL RIGHTS RESERVED

ISBN 0-9679976-2-3

LIBRARY OF CONGRESS CARD NUMBER: 2001095489

SEAWOLF COMMUNICATIONS, INC.
PO BOX 66
WEST CHICAGO, IL 60186
USA

Tel: (630) 293-8996   Fax: (630) 293-8837
www.seawolfcommunications.com

NOTE: Photo credits are shown in terms of the author's source for the photograph rather than a specific photographer who might have taken it, except where the photographer is known and specifically named. All maps are by Cris Kohl, unless otherwise indicated, and are © Seawolf Communications, Inc. Artwork © artists as indicated. Underwater photos © photographers as indicated, excluding Cris Kohl, whose photos are © Seawolf Communications, Inc.

Printed and bound in the United States of America

FIRST EDITION: OCTOBER, 2001

5   4   3   2   1

FRONT COVER PHOTO: Only in the Great Lakes can a scuba diver explore an incredibly preserved wooden shipwreck that is about 150 years old. The brigantine, *Sandusky,* an eight-year-old vessel that sank in 1856 in the Straits of Mackinac, which connects Lakes Michigan and Huron, offers the visiting diver many fascinating glimpses of material history from a long-gone era. Joan Forsberg studies the unique figurehead, in the shape of a ram's head, at a depth of 75' at this popular central Great Lakes location. For more information about this site, see page 254.   PHOTO BY CRIS KOHL

BACK COVER PHOTO: Diver Joan Forsberg navigates over the boiler of the shipwreck, *Columbus,* in Lake Superior's Gargantua Harbour, Ontario. For more information about this site, see page 394. PHOTO BY CRIS KOHL

INTRODUCTION

The growing interest in scuba diving as a recreational activity has produced large numbers of scuba-certified people searching for new dive sites. This book provides them with over 900 places to go diving in the Great Lakes.

I wrote my first book about scuba diving in the Great Lakes 16 years ago out of frustration at what I was seeing: men and women taking scuba courses in the Great Lakes region, then using their certification cards only for their annual winter trip down to warm tropical waters. They were totally missing out on what we have in our own back yards! I also saw "old pros" make the claim that they had seen and done everything when it came to Great Lakes scuba diving. It was a shame to see them hang up their fins because they had run out of dive sites or because they felt that the Great Lakes offered no more challenges.

To all of those people, I say, "READ MY BOOKS."

This is my ninth book about scuba diving and/or shipwrecks and the Great Lakes. Obviously I still wasn't satisfied that I had done everything I could to let the world know that what we have here in our freshwater seas is unique and worthy of aquatic exploration. Even I have ventured considerably into tropical waters all around the world. Each place has its notable attributes. However, with all that I have experienced, I maintain that the best shipwreck diving lies in our five Great Lakes. And we also have other types of excellent freshwater diving as well: caverns, quarries, lakes, rivers, old docks, etc.

Right here in the middle of the continent, straddling the two great nations of the United States and Canada, lie the massive and scuba-underrated bodies of water which store the best preserved shipwrecks in the world. Unlike that incorrectly labeled "Shipwreck Capital of the World" over in Asia, Truk Lagoon, which offers only one type of shipwreck (steel war machines) from only one point in history (the year 1944) in one small quantity (50 shipwrecks), the varied types of, and eras represented by, the approximately 1,000 Great Lakes shipwrecks located to date, take one's breath away in their epic and substantial scope.

This book offers suggestions and descriptions of where to go scuba diving in the Great Lakes region. Through its advertisements, this book also becomes a clearinghouse for scuba or scuba-related businesses. This book puts divers and non-divers seeking Great Lakes services in touch with those who provide those services.

Since no book is perfect (I like to say that my books provide something for everyone --- and some people are always looking for mistakes!), I welcome your comments, corrections, additions, and suggestions. For example, if I missed mentioning someone who located a shipwreck, please send me your information (photocopied newspaper articles, or whatever, no matter how old), so I can give credit where credit is due. I can be reached at: Cris Kohl, c/o Seawolf Communications, P.O. Box 66, West Chicago, IL 60186, or telephone (630) 293-8996, or check out our website at www.seawolfcommunications.com. I will send you a copy of the next edition of *The Great Lakes Diving Guide* in appreciation for usable items.

I hope this book brings people (back) into Great Lakes scuba diving.

Cris Kohl,
High Lake, Illinois
August, 2001

ACKNOWLEDGEMENTS

No book is the product of a single writer without access to human resources and/or material research facilities. The author's sincere THANK YOU goes out to the following for their help in the massive undertaking of this book's production:

For providing artwork: Robert McGreevy, Peter Rindlisbacher, Tim Reed, Douglas King, Sr., Adam Henley, Chuck and Jeri Feltner, Pat Stayer, Valerie Olson-van Heest, Pat Labadie, Jeff Gray (Wisconsin State Underwater Archaeologist), Russ Green and the State Historical Society of Wisconsin, Save Ontario Shipwrecks, the Underwater Archaeological Society of Chicago, the Michigan Maritime Museum, Daniel Lenihan and the staff of the National Park Service (Submerged Cultural Resources Unit), Scott Anfinson and the Minnesota Historical Society, and Ken Merryman and the Great Lakes Shipwreck Preservation Society.

For providing additional underwater images: Peter Tomasino, Jon Zeaman, Mike Williams, Joyce Hayward, Jim & Pat Stayer, David Ostifichuk, Jim Jarecki and Joe Lark.

For underwater modeling: Joan Forsberg, Roy Pickering, Winston Smith, Brian Roffel, Doug Pettingill, James Taylor, Marcy McElmon, Barb Marshall, Jim & Pat Stayer, Frank Troxell, Sharon Troxell, Joyce Hayward, the late Don Edwards, Jennifer Elcomb, Art Vermette, Christoff Kohl, Greg Schieman, Joe Drummond, Alan Armbruster, Joe Corsaro, Tim Philp, Karen Della-Mattia, Ryan LeBlanc, Sean Moore, Steve Whitman, Bill Atkins and Dan Perry.

For providing information or other assistance: the former Institute for Great Lakes Research, Bowling Green State University, Bowling Green, Ohio (recently absorbed into the Archival Collections of Bowling Green State University, which I also thank wholeheartedly), Robert Graham of the Center for Archival Collections, Bowling Green State University, Bowling Green, Ohio, the Ontario Archives in Toronto, the Public Archives of Canada in Ottawa, the Great Lakes branch (in Chicago) of the National Archives, the Great Lakes Marine Collection of the Milwaukee Public Library/Wisconsin Marine Historical Society and Paul Woehrmann and his excellent staff, the Great Lakes Historical Society, Vermilion, OH, and its superb staff, the Marine Museum of the Great Lakes, Kingston, ON, the Metropolitan Toronto Public Library, Erika Wetzel, Rev. Peter Van der Linden, Ralph Roberts, Dennis Hale, Dean Ziegler, Brian Jackson, Kent Divers Association (of Chatham, ON), Peter Vanoutsos, Ed Fabok, Greg Millinger and Aqua Vision Research, John Halsey (Michigan State Historian), Brendon Baillod, Kimm Stabelfeldt, David Trotter, Peter Rijnieks, Hugh Wyatt, Jean Edwards, Susan Yankoo and George Wheeler, John Steele, Paul Ehorn, Jim Brotz, George West, Claude Jewell, Tom Farnquist, Capt. Jerry Guyer, Capt. Roy Pickering and Capt. Jim Stayer. Personal THANKS also to Jim Herbert of Osprey Charters, Barcelona, NY, to Jeff Omstead of Waruwanago Charters, Wheatley, ON, and to Lara Hernandez;Corkrey, my hardworking stepdaughter who will someday be a famous writer.

To all of the advertisers in this first edition of this book: THANK YOU for believing in a product sight unseen and in me.

An intensely heartfelt THANK YOU to Jim and Pat Stayer for their assistance, artwork, modeling, underwater images, computer training sessions and patience. Without them, a book of this caliber would simply not have been possible.

My apologies to anyone I may have inadvertently overlooked.

The largest THANK YOU goes to my patient wife, Joan Forsberg, who, besides tolerating long days of my absence and seclusion necessitated by this work and providing me with strong coffee and the world's best meals, worked enthusiastically as my proofreader, editor, research assistant, underwater model, travel buddy and believer. She's the best.

CONTENTS

FEATURES

HOW TO USE THIS BOOK

These 416 pages, a "where to" rather than a "how to" book on scuba diving in the Great Lakes, are divided into 50 chapters, each covering one, small geographical area of the vast Great Lakes system. Basically, the chapters begin at the extreme eastern end of this region, and head west, concluding in the Lake Superior area.

I have attempted as often as possible to divide this book into geographic areas rather than political ones, and in large part I been able to avoid those human delineations in favor of the natural ones. It makes no sense to divide Lake Michigan, for example, into four areas, each under the jurisdiction of Michigan, Indiana, Illinois, and Wisconsin, and to ignore the natural divisions and subdivions provided by nature. Lake Michigan is Lake Michigan; one simply has to look at it to see what its real boundaries happen to be. The state lines of Michigan, Indiana, Illinois and Wisconsin, even extending out over the waters, are manmade and, theoretically, alterable at the stroke of a pen. Writers in the past, myself included with my *Dive Ontario!* books, have been guilty of this "political limitation" which implies that the waters they are writing about end in the middle of the lake where that invisible boundary line has been set. I shake my head over "Great Lakes" travel books (and there are many) which exclude New York and Pennsylvania because they are considered Atlantic Ocean, East Coast states, in spite of the fact that those two states have many miles of Great Lakes shoreline. Is the vast Ontario portion of the Great Lakes non-existent simply because it's on the other side of that political line which separates Canada from the United States? A few so-called "Great Lakes" travel books would have you believe that. It makes no sense to me (but then again, I have long felt that the Great Lakes and the land 100 miles around them, all the way east to the Atlantic Ocean, should be their own single country, the "Empire of the Great Lakes," if you will. I am not holding my breath for that to happen soon). For this book, think more in terms of geography than politics.

This book is mostly about shipwrecks because shipwrecks are the mainstay of scuba diving in the Great Lakes. Remove the shipwrecks, or the access to them, and you kill the scuba industry here. The **names of shipwrecks** appear in *italic type*. If the ship was named after a human being, I have indexed it under its surname (to quote what the late Dr. Richard Wright of the Institute for Great Lakes Research at Bowling Green State University in Ohio told me in early 1986, "Do we call that famous, big ship the *'Fitzgerald'* or the *'Edmund'?*" Take it from there.)

The site co-ordinates are given, if known or required to find the site, in both the gradually outgoing LORAN-C system and in the latitude and longitude of the newer GPS (Global Positioning System). A few latitute/longitude locations are given in the old, traditional system of having only 60 seconds in a minute and, of course, 60 minutes in a degree. Today's electronic method of showing latitude/longitude eliminates "seconds" completely in favor of three decimal places following the minute number.

For example,

LAT 45° 02′ 59″   LON 074° 37′ 18″

is the old, traditional method of giving latitude/longitude. The last two numbers in each set indicate "seconds," of which there could never be more than 59 before the "minute" number ahead of it moved up to the next one.

Today's GPS latitude/longitude reads like this:

LAT 45° 16.798'   LON 083° 31.942'

where the last three numbers are a decimal point fraction in thousandths of a whole minute.

Some LORAN-C units can convert their TD (Time Differential) numbers to latitude / longitude, but these are rarely the same as the latitude/longitude reading you would get from a GPS unit at the same location. However, my experience has been that there is a difference of usually no more than 400 feet in the distances given by two such readings. If the co-ordinates in this book place you within 400 feet of a shipwreck, and you still can't find it, then you shouldn't be out there on your own boat. Take a charter.

The dive site **depth** is usually given as its deepest point, but sometimes there is a range, indicating the distance which the shipwreck rises off the lake bottom (e.g. "59 to 74 feet" for the *Admiral* on page 125), or the depth range of an underwater slope (e.g. "25 to 115 feet" for the *Keystorm* on page 44).

The **level** of diver experience is explained in the section called "Some Notes of Diving Safety" on pages 21 and 22.

The **dimensions** of a ship before it became a shipwreck are given as a set of three numbers, in feet and inches, in brackets after the vessel's name in the body of the description, for example

(343'4" x 43'8" x 22'8")

where the first measurement is the ship's length, the second is the ship's beam, or width, and the third is the ship's draft, or depth from the waterline. If only two sets of numbers are given, then the ship's draft was unknown. If a ship was rebuilt during its career and its dimensions changed, the vessel's dimensions at the time of loss are given. A metric conversion chart is on the right; this chart can also be applied to dive site depths, which are also given in feet.

The **maps** in this book, which were drawn by Cris Kohl and are © Seawolf Communications, Inc., are not to be used for navigation, as they omit information which is vital to the safe operation of a boat. Regulations require vessels operating in Great Lakes waters to carry the latest, best scale, corrected charts for their area of operation.

I have used a number of **short-forms** to credit the main institutions which provided the many archival images in this book. They are:

METRIC CONVERSION CHART

FEET	METERS
1	0.3
2	0.6
3	0.9
4	1.2
5	1.5
6	1.8
7	2.1
8	2.4
9	2.7
10	3
20	6
30	9
40	12
50	15
60	18
70	21
80	24
90	27
100	30
200	60
300	90
400	120
500	150
1000	300

GLHS = The Great Lakes Historical Society, Vermilion, Ohio.

IGLR = Institute for Great Lakes Research, Bowling Green State University, Bowling Green, Ohio. In 1997, the IGLR was was incorporated into Bowling Green State University's Center for Archival Collections. Any images credited to IGLR were purchased for publication through that institution prior to its absorption.

MPL/WMHS = The Great Lakes Marine Collection of the Milwaukee Public Library/ Wisconsin Marine Historical Society, Milwaukee, Wisconsin.

OA = The Ontario Archives in Toronto, Ontario.

PAC = The Public Archives of Canada, Ottawa, Ontario.

Lastly, don't forget that there is a list of emergency telephone numbers on the last page of this book.

Regional Maps
for the Great Lakes
as Found in
the Chapters of This Book

GREAT LAKES
DISTANCE
CHART

Road distances, in miles, are calculated by the shortest or quickest routes from town or city center to center. Factors such as weather, road conditions, construction, detours and traffic may affect the time in which any given distance may be traversed.

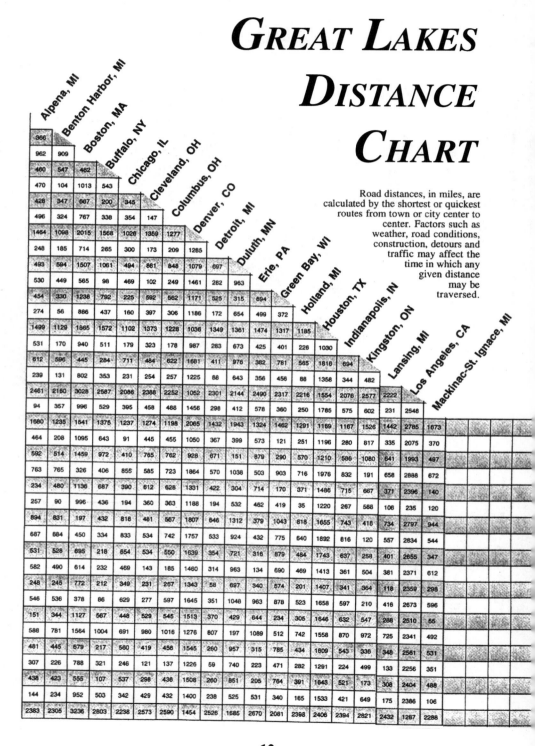

Distance chart with origin cities along the diagonal: Alpena, MI; Benton Harbor, MI; Boston, MA; Buffalo, NY; Chicago, IL; Cleveland, OH; Columbus, OH; Denver, CO; Detroit, MI; Duluth, MN; Erie, PA; Green Bay, WI; Holland, MI; Houston, TX; Indianapolis, IN; Kingston, ON; Lansing, MI; Los Angeles, CA; Mackinac-St. Ignace, MI.

Alpena, MI	Benton Harbor, MI	Boston, MA	Buffalo, NY	Chicago, IL	Cleveland, OH	Columbus, OH	Denver, CO	Detroit, MI	Duluth, MN	Erie, PA	Green Bay, WI	Holland, MI	Houston, TX	Indianapolis, IN	Kingston, ON	Lansing, MI	Los Angeles, CA	Mackinac-St. Ignace, MI
366																		
962	909																	
460	547	482																
470	104	1013	543															
428	347	667	200	345														
496	324	767	338	354	147													
1464	1098	2015	1568	1026	1359	1277												
248	185	714	265	300	173	209	1285											
493	594	1507	1061	494	661	848	1079	697										
530	449	565	98	469	102	249	1461	282	963									
454	330	1238	792	225	592	562	1171	525	315	894								
274	56	886	437	160	397	306	1186	172	654	499	372							
1499	1129	1865	1572	1102	1373	1228	1036	1349	1361	1474	1317	1185						
531	170	940	511	179	323	178	987	283	673	425	401	226	1030					
612	596	445	284	711	484	622	1681	411	976	382	781	565	1816	694				
239	131	802	353	231	254	257	1225	88	643	356	456	88	1358	344	482			
2461	2160	3028	2587	2086	2388	2252	1052	2301	2144	2490	2317	2216	1554	2076	2577	2222		
94	357	996	529	395	458	488	1456	298	412	578	360	250	1785	575	602	231	2548	
1680	1235	1541	1375	1237	1274	1198	2065	1432	1943	1324	1462	1291	1169	1167	1526	1442	2785	1673
464	208	1095	643	91	445	455	1050	367	399	573	121	251	1196	280	817	335	2075	370
592	514	1459	972	410	765	762	928	671	151	879	290	570	1210	586	1080	641	1993	497
763	765	326	406	855	585	723	1864	570	1038	503	903	716	1976	832	191	658	2888	672
234	480	1136	687	390	612	628	1331	422	304	714	170	371	1486	715	667	371	2396	140
257	90	996	436	194	360	363	1188	194	532	462	419	35	1220	267	588	106	235	120
894	831	197	432	818	481	567	1807	646	1312	379	1043	818	1655	743	418	734	2797	944
687	684	450	334	833	534	742	1757	533	924	432	775	640	1892	816	120	557	2834	544
531	528	695	218	654	534	550	1639	354	721	316	879	484	1745	637	258	401	2655	347
582	490	614	232	469	143	185	1460	314	963	134	690	469	1413	361	504	381	2371	612
248	245	772	212	349	231	267	1343	58	697	340	574	201	1407	341	364	118	2359	298
546	536	378	86	629	277	597	1645	351	1048	963	878	523	1658	597	210	416	2673	596
151	344	1127	567	448	529	545	1513	370	429	644	234	305	1646	632	547	288	2510	55
588	781	1564	1004	691	980	1016	1276	807	197	1089	512	742	1558	870	972	725	2341	492
481	445	679	217	580	419	456	1545	260	957	315	785	434	1609	543	336	348	2561	531
307	226	788	321	246	121	137	1226	59	740	223	471	282	1291	224	499	133	2256	351
438	423	555	107	537	298	438	1508	260	851	205	764	391	1643	521	173	308	2404	488
144	234	952	503	342	429	432	1400	238	525	531	340	165	1533	421	649	175	2386	106
2383	2305	3236	2803	2238	2573	2590	1454	2526	1685	2670	2081	2398	2406	2394	2821	2432	1287	2288

Quick Glance Map of the Great Lakes

MILES	KMS.
1	1.6
5	8.0
10	16
20	32
30	48
40	64
50	80
100	160
200	320
300	480
400	640
500	800
1000	1600

Diagonal city labels (top-left to bottom-right): Miami, FL · Milwaukee, WI · Minneapolis, MN · Montreal, QC · Munising, MI · Muskegon, MI · New York, NY · Ottawa, ON · Parry Sound, ON · Pittsburgh, PA · Port Huron, MI · Rochester, NY · Sault Ste. Marie, MI · Thunder Bay, ON · Tobermory, ON · Toledo, OH · Toronto, ON · Traverse City, MI · Vancouver, BC

1341																	
1802	336																
1676	955	1196															
1813	275	403	740														
1326	285	604	739	400													
1347	907	1218	346	1068	840												
1636	771	1050	124	615	663	455											
1786	745	825	392	412	507	650	267										
1248	589	880	617	752	474	392	551	450									
1490	453	759	515	438	224	644	439	283	375								
1380	751	405	350	736	522	362	257	304	295	298							
1730	355	533	819	120	289	1015	495	292	665	355	653						
2140	596	348	1052	501	726	1452	929	715	1102	792	1059	437					
1692	627	931	513	671	457	649	404	205	434	233	303	516	953				
1373	350	656	715	491	226	602	595	413	248	117	407	408	848	318			
1564	637	948	367	549	432	496	249	140	337	190	822	429	863	182	297		
1681	446	579	782	246	154	928	652	455	556	268	589	163	600	498	308	476	
3498	2164	1791	2939	1989	2432	3082	2819	2616	2694	2679	2889	2324	1887	2840	2484	2753	2487

BORDER CROSSING

INFORMATION

Thousands of scuba divers from both the United States and Canada have found visits to their neighbor's Great Lakes dive sites to be interesting and fun, and it's a nice experience to be able to visit a foreign country once in a while and still be close to home.

To make the border crossings easier, for both leaving and returning, do this:

1. If you are taking your scuba gear with you, as you likely would be if you are driving across the border, make certain that, for every item of gear that has a serial number on it (tanks, regulators, dive computers, B.C.'s, etc.) you either have a receipt for it to prove that it was purchased in your country (and any receipts have to bear that item's serial number to be recognized as legitimate), or you need to register your equipment by taking it to any Customs Office in your country prior to your departure. (Don't forget your C cards, either.)

2. Be prepared to state politely to the Customs Officer of the country that you are visiting what your citizenship is (and have proof of citizenship handy if asked to see it), exactly how long and where you will be staying in that country, what goods you are bringing into the country, and what goods will be staying in that country. One concern is that you are crossing the border with scuba equipment which you intend to sell or give as a gift, which is illegal unless you explicitly state that you are taking goods into that country for resale or as gifts, and go through the necessary paperwork and pay any taxes, duties or fees applicable.

3. Remember that it is virtually impossible to enter Canada with any type of firearm or dangerous weapon. Leave the spearguns and shark knives at home.

DISCLAIMERS

Firstly, the maps in this book (all of which are © Seawolf Communications, Inc.) are not suitable for navigation. To locate the majority of the sites in this book, you must have the most up-to-date navigation charts available issued by the proper authorities.

Secondly, every effort has been made to make this book accurate, informative, and useful. However, the information presented in *The Great Lakes Diving Guide* is not infallible. There may be errors, but we are certainly not aware of them.

Thirdly, boating to these Great Lakes destinations is not always a simple task. Readers must be confident that they have the skills required to safely enjoy their exploration of these waterways, or at least they must be travelling with someone who does. When going to these sites, you do so at your own risk.

Lastly, and most importantly, scuba diving is a potentially dangerous activity. The author and publisher do not endorse or encourage specific practices, nor is this book meant to be a substitute for proper training, education, and personal dive site and self-skills evaluation. The author and publisher accept no liability for the diving practices or judgments of the readers of this book. You're on your own.

Introduction
to Great Lakes Diving

First, the lay of the land (or the water).

The Great Lakes, lying between the United States and Canada in nearly the middle of the North American continent, form the largest group of lakes in the world. the Great Lakes proper, extending from east to west, are Lakes Ontario, Erie, Huron, Michigan and Superior. The lakes are all connected to form a single drainage system which discharges down the St. Lawrence River into the Atlantic Ocean. The combined shorelines of the five lakes are an enormous 7,870 miles long and enclose a water surface of 95,170 square miles, of which 60,960 square miles are in the United States and 34,210 square miles are in Canada. The shallowest Great Lake is Erie (maximum depth, 210 feet) and the deepest is Lake Superior (maximum depth, 1,333 feet). Lake Superior, at the head of this vast system, stands at an altitude of 600 feet above sea level, and it's downhill from there all the way to the Atlantic Ocean 2,340 miles away.

The Great Lakes are so vast that one could spend a lifetime scuba diving in them and not see the same site twice.

◆　　◆　　◆　　◆　　◆　　◆　　◆　　◆　　◆

The Great Lakes hold approximately 5,000 shipwrecks, a staggering number unknown even to many longtime residents of the region. Because of their location near the middle of a continent which is a producer of heavy commodities, the Great Lakes have historically provided the transportation system for enormous quantities of bulk freight, such as iron ore, lumber, coal and grain. Florida and other tropical areas had the gold-laden galleons; the Great Lakes swarmed with the workhorses.

The shipwrecks in the Great Lakes are, as I explained earlier, the best preserved shipwrecks in the world. Some of the elements which promote this preservation are the same which add challenges to scuba diving:

1. Cold water was invented in the Great Lakes.

The water in the Great Lakes, below a depth of 100 feet, remains almost steady at about 39 degrees fahrenheit (surface temperatures generally warm up to the high 50's or as high as the low 70's in the southern areas by summer's end). Usually it is the shipwrecks which lie in deeper water that have remained in the most pristine condition, enjoying the preserving powers of this ice water, as well as being situated too deep to suffer from the damaging effects of ice, waves

Scuba diving in the Great Lakes is quite gear-intensive compared to warm-water locations. PHOTO BY CRIS KOHL

15

and wind.

Scuba divers in the Great Lakes require some sort of thermal protection, such as good wetsuits or, even better, drysuits accompanied by thick, woolen underwear. Regardless of your choice, it is still a shock when that cold water hits one's face!

2. The Great Lakes are freshwater lakes. Called the "sweetwater seas" by early explorers, these bodies of water lack the saltwater organisms which destroy wood almost instantly. This fresh water, with its low temperature and lack of oxygen, preserves our shipwrecks.

3. The deeper you go, the darker it gets. This darkness also helps preserve the shipwrecks in the Great Lakes, and it sells a lot of dive lights. However, a couple of the best-preserved and most frequently visited Great Lakes shipwrecks, the *Bermuda* and the *Sweepstakes*, lie in only 20 to 30 feet of water and are blessed with an abundance of natural light. If you dive near the middle of the day, when the sun is at its highest point, even the deeper sites will receive a fair amount of ambient light available to help you see all the wonderful sights.

4. The visibility in the Great Lakes can range from 70 feet on a good day in Lake Superior down to one foot in the St. Clair River after a heavy rainfall. Generally, poor visibility results from millions of suspended particles in the water, usually caused by strong weather churning up the lake bottom. It usually requires at least a couple of days for heavily disturbed water to settle.

In 1988 I was fortunate enough to be scuba diving in New Zealand. The divemaster on our charterboat, a robust, young Australian named Mark, chatted up each of the 16 divers who were going to be under his care once our large boat reached the island of our destination.

Mark got to me and casually asked, "And where do you do most of your diving, mate?"

"In the Great Lakes," I replied.

"Well, we won't have to worry about you then," was his immediate response. He was evidently aware of the fact that scuba diving in the Great Lakes is tougher than diving in the tropics.

That's a trade-off that thousands of scuba divers who explore the Great Lakes are willing to make, as evidenced by the fact that there are over 300 scuba dive shops, as

Scores of charter boats take divers to many of the best-preserved shipwrecks in the world. PHOTO BY CRIS KOHL

well as over 100 charter boats and over 170 dive clubs, all around the Great Lakes, all of them promoting local diving.

While not exactly the waters of Bonaire or Key Largo, the Great Lakes offer many opportunities for underwater exploration and enjoyment, similar to diving conditions in the waters of New England, the Pacific Northwest, British Columbia, and the British Isles (except for the fact that our waters are fresh).

Besides seeing shipwrecks the likes of which are not available anywhere else on the planet, visitors to Great Lakes waters are indulging in an even more adventurous form of an already exciting activity.

ELEVEN FISH A SCUBA DIVER MIGHT ENCOUNTER IN THE GREAT LAKES

(In alphabetical order. Sizes are not to comparative scale.)

BASS -- This popular game fish is often seen by divers in streams, ponds, rocky lake areas and shallow water shipwrecks.

BLUEGILL -- This fish is commonly seen by scuba divers on shallow shipwrecks and especially in quarries. They are usually no long than 8 inches and weigh 0.5 pound.

BURBOT -- Also called ling, lingcod, or "lawyer fish," the burbot is seen on most Great Lakes shipwrecks, even deeper ones, and is easily recognized by the barbel at the tip of the jaw and its "eel-like" tail. Shunned as a food-fish due to its appearance and texture, it predaciously feeds upon smaller fish and may reach 4 feet in length.

CARP -- Viewed as a delicacy by some who know how to prepare it, and as a junk fish by others, the carp is a bottom feeder which can grow to a maximum length of 3 feet and a weight of 50 pounds.

CATFISH --Considered an active game fish and, by some, fine eating, in spite of the fact that they are bottom feeders, catfish can reach a maximum length of four feet and a maximum weight of 55 pounds, but they are usually much smaller.

MUSKY (MUSKELLONGE) -- This fierce game fish, which has teeth like a small barracuda and sometimes the temper to match, is rarely seen or caught today. Large ones could reach 6 feet in length and weigh 90 pounds.

PERCH -- Its white flesh is valued as one of the best food fish in the Great Lakes, and many people enjoy it as a sport fish. Although the record perch weighed over 4 pounds, most are just under one pound, with an average length of 10 inches.

PIKE -- Although usually found in the northern Great Lakes regions, pike, a fighting game fish, are occasionally seen and caught in the southern portions as well. They reach a length of 3.5 feet.

SMELT -- Smelt runs along shorelines in the spring (usually late April) were very popular with net fishermen wearing waders, but smelt numbers have decreased alarmingly in recent years. The average length of this small fish is 6 to 9 inches.

STURGEON -- This migratory fish has occasionally been caught by sportsfishermen; in the 1980's, a five-footer was "captured" by a young man when he saw it basking near the

surface of the St. Clair River. He jumped in and dragged it, alive and kicking, ashore. Their once-vast numbers have been so decimated that they now need our help to replenish.

WALLEYE (also called PICKEREL) -- This fish, like the perch, is one of the most important game and food fish in the Great Lakes. The large ones will be 2 feet in length and weigh as much as 14 pounds.

Freshwater Versus Saltwater Scuba Diving

My scuba dive buddies have come in many varieties, ranging from the weather-beaten, long-time Great Lakes diver clad in thick, wooly underwear and a dry suit that requires 30 pounds of lead weight for proper buoyancy (why not just strap an old transmission to your stomach?), to those bikinied novice divers in the tropics who are unknowingly (or knowingly) imitating Jacqueline Bissette in "The Deep" (am I giving away my age with that reference?). There must be a reason that I wrote this book about the Great Lakes instead of applying my research and writing abilities to an easier, smaller, more managable, more laid back, warmer and, one would think, more enjoyable subject like scuba diving in Bonaire or the Florida Keys or Fiji.

Here are the reasons I prefer scuba diving in the Great Lakes:

Firstly, the Great Lakes are freshwater and the tropics are saltwater. If you have ever accidentally swallowed a mouthful of saltwater while you were diving, you may have cut your dive short because it made you sick. Great Lakes divers, on the other hand, often take their regulators out of their mouths and suck in a bit of cool fresh water to rinse off their dry tongues (this is generally not done in the waters off Cleveland or Toronto, and don't even think about Detroit).

Of course, post-diving activities in the tropics include the mandatory and completely thorough rinsing of all dive equipment in fresh water to remove that nasty salt. Any hurried diver who has ended up throwing his gear into his dive bag and forgetting about it for a few days will know, from the cloud of salt dust that he kicks up when he yanks his gritty equipment out of that white bag that used to be blue, that his last dive was definitely not done in Lake Superior.

In the Great Lakes after a dive, we get out of our wetsuits or drysuits and jump overboard for a refreshing swim. The only salt we have to wash off is the sweat we worked up from the surface swim back to the boat (that distance varies with one's ability to find the anchor line at the end of the dive.) In the tropics, taking a dip off the back of the boat to rinse off the salt isn't going to work, no matter how many times you make the jump.

If salt corrodes your scuba equipment like that, can you imagine what it does to your hair, your skin, your fingernails and other parts we don't dare mention?

Secondly, I like diving in the Great Lakes because no matter how long I stay in the water, there is nothing in there that can eat me. The same can't be said for the tropics. I remember Easter Sunday, 1988. I was in Tahiti, the French divemaster was my dive buddy, we were the last ones left in the water and we were making an extra-long safety stop because this was our second deep dive of the day. We hung off, back-to-back, while a half dozen black-tipped sharks steadily circled us. On the first dive that day, a huge moray eel had tried to eat my camera. I was glad to get back to the Great Lakes, where we're not afraid to turn out backs on burbots, and zebra mussel shell cuts are the closest we'll come to losing life or limb to some critter.

Thirdly, no matter where I do my scuba diving, I prefer to photograph shipwrecks. However, that is often a difficult thing to do in the tropics because I have to kick all those fish out of the way so I can get my picture. I don't have that problem in the Great Lakes.

Reason number four for loving the Great Lakes: when the weather kicks up, the waves rarely exceed the height of your boat, and it's over in a few hours. No matter how wet I get on board, it's always freshwater wet. In the tropics, when the weather kicks up, it lasts for four months (they call it the hurricane season) and the wind and the waves yank out palm trees and flatten houses. When I get wet in the tropics, it's saltwater wet (review reason number one above).

Fifthly, I prefer our more adventurous Great Lakes scuba diving to that easy stuff in the tropics. I enjoy being in that no-man's-land zone between the surface and the bottom and not being able to see either one. I welcome all those opportunities to practice my underwater navigation, and I thrill at that rush of adrenalin when I wonder exactly where the heck my boat is. In the tropics, all I have to do is look up and I can see the bottom of my dive boat, even when I'm in 100 feet of water. Now what fun is that?

Lastly, I dive the Great Lakes for their shipwrecks, which, regardless of age, are fabulously preserved in our cold, fresh waters. Saltwater does nasty things to wood, metal, in fact, almost everything (review reason number one above). Scuba divers enjoy shipwreck diving a lot more when the wrecks still resemble ships. It's hard to imagine a pile of ballast stones as a ship, and it's impossible to convince people back home that that pile of rocks in tropical waters once conveyed people and cargoes across oceans. It really stretches the imagination. Not so in the Great Lakes (have you been on the *Dunderberg* yet? Or the *Annie Falconer*? Have you seen the *George A. Marsh*? Or the hundreds of others?)

But things are not perfect in our Great Lakes paradise. We don't have everything here. I understand that the tropics have some exotic beaches frequented by scuba divers, mostly Europeans, with a proclivity for eliminating tan lines and being transformed into bronze gods and goddesses. Perhaps it would be worthwhile to investigate the possibility of importing that custom and attitude and physical transformation capability to our inland seas.

But then again, it wouldn't work. We palefaces would just end up having to kick those people out of our way as we, in our full drysuits, schlepp our small mountain of dive gear down to the beach to do a shore dive. But at least it's in fresh water.

Some Notes on Diving Safety

This is not a "how to" book about scuba diving, but rather a "where to" guide to dive sites in the Great Lakes.

Regarding scuba safety, these statistics might offer some insight: in the U.S.A. in one recent year, the following activities had these death rates per 100,000 people participating in that activity -- mountain climbing, 599; hang gliding, 114; parachuting, 24; snowmobiling, 13; mountain hiking, 6.4; scuba diving, 2.9.

Scuba diving is one of the safest activities a human being can enjoy.

♦   ♦   ♦   ♦   ♦   ♦   ♦   ♦   ♦

I have identified each of the dive sites as suitable for novice, intermediate, advanced or technical divers, or midway points in between each of these designations. I thank Joyce Hayward and the Bay Area Divers of Ohio for their assistance:

A novice dive:
a) is less than 60 feet in depth.
b) is suitable for a newly-certified or infrequent diver.
c) has no or very little current.
d) has good visibility.
e) may include wreck diving with no penetration.

An intermediate dive:
a) is suitable for more experienced divers.
b) may reach depths between 60 and 100 feet.
c) may include wreck diving with no penetration.
d) may involve some current or waves.
e) may involve open water sites with boat entries.
f) has good to moderate visibility.
g) may have other conditions that may warrant more experience.

An advanced dive:
a) may reach depths between 100 and 130 feet.
b) is suitable for very experienced divers.
c) may involve limited wreck penetration where there are multiple, visible exits, or swift or variable current diving, or very cold water diving.
d) may have extremely limited or zero visibility.
e) may require special skills such as navigation, rescue, cavern diving, or special equipment.

A technical dive:

a) may reach depths in excess of 130 feet.

b) may do deep shipwreck penetration, or cave diving, or ice diving, or any type of diving where there is an overhead environment blocking direct and immediate access to the surface.

c) may involve the use of any gas that is not compressed air, including nitrox.

Regarding safety during scuba diving: use common sense and neither forget nor neglect nor ignore your training. Keep these pointers in mind:

When using a diveboat, keep a lookout aboard at all times. Fly both the swallowtail, blue-and-white alpha flag (it means that the boat has limited maneuverability) and the red-and-white dive flag from your boat when divers are actually in the water. The passing boater who may fail to recognize one flag may respond to the other.

Use a dive flag any time you are scuba diving, whether from a boat or from shore.

Never dive with your diveboat unattended. Should an emergency occur below, or should the exhausted divers be unable to climb back on board the boat, an assistant who stays on the boat is always helpful.

An obvious bit of advice, yet on occasion ignored, is to avoid diving in front of freighters which require great distances to make even slight turns. If you do end up with one passing immediately over you, hug the bottom of the river or the lake. If necessary, sink your dive knife into the bottom to act as a holding post. Don't do anything that may force you to make an emergency ascent. While you're on the bottom, with the water, sand, silt and other debris swirling madly all around you from the freighter's propeller, ask yourself how you got into that situation in the first place. Then, don't do it again.

Current, or swiftwater, diving requires special training and practice; begin with a mild current before you take on one of the "rush" dives in the St. Lawrence River or at the mouth of the St. Clair River.

Make sure that you have a sharp dive knife with you just in case you get caught in some of the old fishing nets on shipwrecks, or in the miles of monofilament fishing lines around docks and in river debris.

Never, ever dive alone.

Beware of concrete buoy anchors and submerged cribs or posts which may suddenly appear from the edge of visibility in any current. These things could frighten a novice diver. Obviously, divers should not hit these obstructions or snag any of their gear on them.

Don't scuba dive in a busy harbor or in or near canals. Harbormasters, boaters and lockmasters would find scuba divers to be a potentially dangerous (mostly to the person of the diver) nuisance.

Dive only when weather and water conditions permit. For example, the *City of Superior* shipwreck at Copper Harbor, Michigan, from shore on a calm day will create fond memories, but when the waves are pounding, you might end up remembering this site from a hospital bed.

Lastly, don't forget that there is a list of emergency telephone numbers on the last page of this book.

Safe diving!

St. Lawrence River: Area 1

The steamer, *Fred Mercur*, was destroyed by fire in the St. Lawrence River in 1925.
AUTHOR'S COLLECTION.

1. *Fred Mercur*
2. Aultsville
3. Dickinson's Landing
4. *Cornwall*
5. Mille Roches Power House
6. Sheik Island dam
7. "Belly Dumper" wreck
8. Swing bridge
9. Lock 21
10. Chrysler Park wreck
11. *Eastcliffe Hall*

1. FRED MERCUR

> **LORAN: 98765.45/45678.32   LAT 45° 02′ 03″ LON 074° 37′ 18″**
> **DEPTH: 3 to 45 feet   LEVEL: Novice-Intermediate**

LOCATION: You'll need a boat to take you over to the west side of Stanley Island in the St. Lawrence River near Cornwall, Ontario.

The wooden propeller, *Fred Mercur,* (232′ x 35′5″ x 18′2″), burned to a total loss after she was beached in a bed of rushes off Stanley Island on July 3, 1925. A nearby cottager saved the entire crew in six round-trips with his rowboat. Built at Buffalo in 1882, the *Mercur* sailed under U.S. registry until being sold to Canadian interests in 1919.

See page 23 for an archival photograph of the steamer, *Fred Mercur.*

The bow reaches to within a few feet of the surface and is often marked with a jug by local divers. Numerous fish and American eels inhabit this site, with most of the hull intact and on a slope to 45′. Coal cargo can be seen inside the hull, while a rudder and propeller grace the stern. A tractor that went through the ice rests in about 25′ just off the bow. Beware of a moderate current and the silt bottom, which is quick to stir up and affect visibility.

2. AULTSVILLE

> **LORAN: LAT   LON**
> **DEPTH: To 70 feet   LEVEL: Novice-Intermediate**

LOCATION: Off Cornwall, Ontario. Accessible from shore, but a boat is needed to reach the more distant and more interesting parts of this site.

This village was totally flooded during the construction of the St. Lawrence Seaway in the 1950's. One of the oldest pottery works in Ontario was located at this site, and, in 1987, a crock was recovered from the 60′ depth by government divers for analysis in Ottawa.

When water levels drop late in the year, parts of this submerged village can be explored without getting wet. Reportedly the best areas for diving are along the old shoreline by the former town pier and ferry landing, because bottles are common there.

3. DICKINSON'S LANDING

> **LORAN: LAT   LON**
> **DEPTH: To 65 feet   LEVEL: Novice-Intermediate**

LOCATION: Near Cornwall, Ontario.

Dickinson's Landing was formerly a small village which existed mainly to service the locks of the old St. Lawrence River canal system. The village, like most of the old locks in this region, is now totally submerged as part of the St. Lawrence Seaway project connecting the Great Lakes with the Atlantic Ocean and the rest of the world. Local divers placed ropes on the underwater locks as guides for visiting scuba divers. Use wise judgment with the variable visibility at this site, and beware of depth/time limitations.

4. CORNWALL

> **LORAN: LAT   LON**
> **DEPTH: 60 feet   LEVEL: Advanced**

LOCATION: This site is off the south side of Machinette Island (Island 17) near Cornwall, Ontario. A boat is necessary.

The old schooner-barge, *Cornwall,* rests upright in 60′ of water, with the bow fairly intact, but the stern somewhat disintegrated. Be cautious of the boating traffic here, as well as variable visibility, depth/time limitations, and the 2-3 knot current.

5. MILLE ROCHES POWER HOUSE

LORAN:	LAT	LON
DEPTH: 35, 55, and 75 feet	LEVEL: Intermediate-Advanced	

LOCATION: From Highway 401's exit #778 (Moulinette Road), head east on Moulinette Rd. towards Cornwall for about three miles until you reach Guindon Park. The park offers a boat launch ramp, changing and restroom facilities, and picnic tables for meals and post-diving festivities. The site, usually buoyed in season, is 0.5 nautical mile away on a heading of 183° magnetic from the tip of Guindon Park.

The Mille Roches Power House, built in 1900-1901 by the St. Lawrence Power Company, was part of the former town, now submerged, named Mille Roches. The plant operated until 1955, and in 1958, the roof and walls of the building were removed in preparation for the St. Lawrence Seaway flooding.

Although the roof, walls and generators were removed, two 35-inch Samson water turbines remain intact, as well as a wheel chamber, exciter reservoirs, and other items of interest. The intake gate mechanisms lie at a depth of 35', while the power house floor is

Drawings by Nick Baets for Save Ontario Shipwrecks

Intake gate mechanisms

Flume or wheel chamber

35 Inch Samson turbines

Exciter reservoirs

▽ 35'
▽ 55'
▽ 75'

Water release pit

Tailrace

N.BAETS

situated at 55', and the water release pits and tailrace are at 75'. Bring a dive light for viewing the deepest remains, but penetration is only for the trained and prepared.

Boating traffic here can be a problem, especially on summer weekends; use a dive flag as one precaution. The one-to-two-knot current is not usually a problem, and is noticeable only during your descent and ascent. On the deepest level, beware of time/depth limitations.

6. SHEIK ISLAND DAM

LORAN:	LAT	LON
DEPTH: 30 to 65 feet	LEVEL: Advanced	

LOCATION: Near Long Sault, Ontario, St. Lawrence River.

The flooding of the St. Lawrence River lowlands in the late 1950's for the Seaway project created numerous submerged sites that scuba divers are exploring to this day.

A boat is necessary to reach the Sheik Island Dam, which is similar to another nearby site, Lock 21 (see site #10 in this section). Boating traffic, current, dark waters, and depth can make this a challenging divesite.

7. "BELLY DUMPER" WRECK

LORAN:	LAT	LON
DEPTH: 65 to 92 feet	LEVEL: Advanced	

LOCATION: In the Long Sault area, near the Mille Roches Power House.

This unidentified steel barge, used in the St. Lawrence Seaway construction in the late 1950's, was located by Bob Dumond in 1991. This shallow vessel rests on an incline and has three compartments which were used for gravel or other bulk materials. One door is fully open on the bottom of one compartment, while the other two are only half so.

Beware of boating traffic, some current, and depth/time limitations.

8. SWING BRIDGE (MOULINETTE)

LORAN:	LAT	LON
DEPTH: 30 to 65 feet	LEVEL: Advanced	

LOCATION: Just west of the Mille Roches site (see site #5 in this section).

The small farming town of Moulinette disappeared completely in the flooding which was necessary for the creation of the St. Lawrence Seaway. The swing bridge itself is no longer there, but its old stone pillars remain submerged. There are six pillars total, with the swivel mechanism still in place on the center one. For this dive, you should have some experience in current diving. Besides the current, there is some boating traffic, depth/time limitations, and occasional low visibility.

9. LOCK 21

LORAN: Shore dive	LAT	LON
DEPTH: 40 to 60 feet	LEVEL: Advanced	

LOCATION: From either Ingleside or Long Sault, Ontario, take Highway 2 to the Long Sault Parkway (entrance fee) to Macdonell Island. Past picnic areas, restrooms and snackbars, at the southwestern end of the island, you will find ropes that run from shore to the site.

Lock 21, which was built in 1885-86 as part of the second enlargement of the old St.

Lawrence River canal system, is 270' long between the gates, 45' wide, and has 14' of clearance over the sill. It was flooded as part of the St. Lawrence Seaway system in 1958.

From shore, the upstream rope takes the diver to the site and the downstream one leads back to shore. Following the rope system, the diver will see the weir and sluice gates, as well as concrete walkways, a bollard, and chain-wells. The current is fairly strong (2-3 knots), the visibility can be low, and the bottom is 60' down. On land, watch your step. Canada geese and their droppings abound.

10. CHRYSLER PARK WRECK

LORAN:	LAT 44° 56' 03" LON 075° 03' 43"
DEPTH: 65 feet	LEVEL: Advanced

LOCATION: Northeast of Morrisburg, Ontario, off Chrysler Memorial Park. From the park, you can look across the waters of the St. Lawrence River to Wilson Hill Island, which is part of the USA. Between these two points, and just inside the Canadian side of the international boundary, is this shipwreck.

This small wooden propeller is a mystery wreck, but some people believe it is the *Chippewa,* which sank in this area on August 12, 1920. It is approximately 65' in length and rises off the bottom about 18'. Boating traffic is heavy since this site lies right in the middle of the main shipping channel, meaning that huge freighters traverse these waters. A strong current flows through this site as well. For these reasons, this site is not very popular and little survey work has been done in an effort to identify the shipwreck.

11. *EASTCLIFFE HALL*

LORAN:	LAT 44° 55' 29" LON 075° 06' 04"
DEPTH: 40 to 65 feet	LEVEL: Advanced

LOCATION: Near Morrisburg, Ontario, with relatively easy boat launch and access from Chrysler Marina, just east of Upper Canada Village. The wreck lies just inside the Canadian border in the busy St. Lawrence River shipping channel. Beware of boating traffic!

The *Eastcliffe Hall* (343'4" x 43'8" x 22'8"), a bulk freight motor vessel built in Montreal in 1954, struck a shoal and the concrete buoy abutment at Chrysler Shoal at 3:00 AM on July 14, 1970, and sank on a slope with the tragic loss of nine lives. She carried pig-iron.

The shallow bow points into the current. Even with her superstructure dynamited off due to being a hazard to navigation, this is an interesting site. Her bow cabins and open holds are inviting, but wreck penetration is for the ultra-experienced only! The stern is a labyrinth of tangled steel ideally avoided (both props were salvaged). With the current stronger than usual (3 to 6 knots), this is a challenging dive,

Eastcliffe Hall. AUTHOR'S COLLECTION.

Artwork ©Adam Henley

and, at times, poor visibility causes disorientation. Use an anchor line to descend, and remember where it is for your return!

St. Lawrence River: Area 2

Scuba divers, their vehicles parked in a long line along the slim, riverfront roadway, prepare to dive the *Conestoga* from shore. PHOTO BY CRIS KOHL.

1. Iroquois Beach
2. Seaway barge graveyard
3. *Conestoga*
4. *Wee Hawk* and Lock 28
5. Channel barge
6. *Fleur Marie*
7. Windmill site and wreck
8. Prescott ferry docks
9. Prescott u/w park
10. *Rothesay*
11. "Loblaw's" wreck

1. IROQUOIS BEACH

LORAN: Shore dive	**LAT**	**LON**
DEPTH: To 40 feet	**LEVEL: Novice-Intermediate**	

LOCATION: At the village of Iroquois, Ontario, near the Iroquois Locks, along the St. Lawrence River.

This site, accessible from shore just west of the actual beach, has a sandy bottom, some submerged cribs (rocks inside square timber frames used as bases for docks), an old anchor and a wooden-hulled sailboat about 15′ in length.

Stay aware of your underwater location so that you don't drift out into the shipping channel. The backwash current can make returning to shore confusing, so take a compass along to find your way back.

2. SEAWAY BARGE GRAVEYARD

LORAN:	**LAT**	**LON**
DEPTH: To 30 feet	**LEVEL: Novice-Intermediate**	

LOCATION: A boat is required to take you to the old canal wall just a few miles downstream from Cardinal, Ontario. One abandoned wooden barge rests alongside the wall, while the remains of two more lie inside the old canal. These sites offer "Kodak moments" for the underwater photographer as well as opportunities to view fish life.

3. *CONESTOGA*

LORAN: Shore or boat dive	**LAT 44° 46′ 46″**	**LON 075° 23′ 36″**
DEPTH: 28 feet	**LEVEL: Novice-Intermediate**	

LOCATION: From the intersection of Highway 2 and Road No. 22 in Cardinal, Ontario, proceed along Road No. 22 towards the river. At the bottom of the hill, turn right and follow the unserviced (bumpy) dirt road along the narrow causeway for about 0.6 mile. The large upper portion of the vessel's 1878 Cuyahoga Iron Works steeple compound engine seems intent on exhibitionism as it flashes out from the river and reveals the underwater resting place of the rest of this ship about 80′ from shore. There is a small, narrow parking area at the site.

Left: The top of the *Conestoga's* engine reveals the wreck's location. PHOTO BY CRIS KOHL. *Below:* The *Conestoga* worked on the Great Lakes for over 40 years. GREAT LAKES HISTORICAL SOCIETY, VERMILION, OH.

Conestoga's propeller. PHOTO BY CRIS KOHL.

The wooden combination passenger and package steam freighter, *Conestoga* (253′ x 36′ x 16′3″), launched at Cleveland on July 6, 1878, caught fire and sank with 30,000 bushels of wheat outside Lock 28 of the Galop Canal on May 22, 1922. No lives were lost, and much of the cargo was salvaged, but the ship was a total loss.

The wooden hull, pointing upstream, is still in very good condition, although the fire (and ice in subsequent winters) took their toll on the superstructure. A windlass and anchor chain adorn the bow, near a Dake steam winch. The enormous, upright engine makes for fascinating exploration, while the rudder lies flat off the stern. The usually mild current is strongest at the bow. Fly the divers down flag because of the boating traffic.

4. *WEE HAWK* AND LOCK 28

LORAN: Shore dive	LAT	LON
DEPTH: 18 feet	LEVEL: Novice-Intermediate	

LOCATION: The abandoned hull of the old steel ferry, *Wee Hawk*, lies about one-quarter mile upstream (that is, to the west) of the *Conestoga* site. Lock 28 has gained popularity in recent years as a picnic site. The best diver access is to the east of the wreck at the closed lock gate. A popular drift dive takes divers through the old gates, ending up just upstream of the *Conestoga*. Warning: Do not penetrate this old, steel hull unless properly trained and prepared, as the silt reduces visibility to zero easily.

5. CHANNEL BARGE

LORAN:	LAT	LON
DEPTH: 50 feet	LEVEL: Advanced	

LOCATION: Access to this site is by boat from Johnstown, Ontario. A wooden barge approximately 60′ long with a beam of 20′ was located in 1995 in front of Chimney Island at the head of the Galop Rapids.

Because of the fast current, this is an exhilarating dive for experienced divers only.

6. FLEUR MARIE

LORAN:	LAT 44° 42.987′ LON 75° 28.578′
DEPTH: 52 feet	LEVEL: Intermediate-Advanced

LOCATION: Taking a boat from Ogdensburg, NY, or Prescott, ON, will get you to this site just inside the US border near the middle of the river.

Originally constructed as a brigantine at Lanoraie, Quebec, in 1850, the *Fleur Marie* (92′5″ x 20′1″ x 8′7″) aged quickly into a decrepit hulk and was scuttled in 1884.

A strong current flows above this shipwreck, but diminishes considerably at the bottom, so the challenging part of the

Fleur Marie. PHOTOS BY CRIS KOHL.

dive is at the beginning getting down and at the end getting up. Visibility in recent years has been up to 35′ because of filter-feeding zebra mussels, and the water temperature has reached 70 degrees by the end of summer.

Most of the ship's framing, beams and conterboard box remain explorable, with an ornate stern undercut by the current. The rudder, unfortunately, is missing, perhaps carried downstream by these fast waters long ago when the ship sank. The river bottom consists mainly of clean sand and millions of tiny, white seashells, offering a soft bottom for this ship and its artifacts. You'll find fish galore! Numerous bass, sunfish, pickerel and the odd carp greet visiting divers. Boating traffic can be hectic on summer weekends; use caution.

7. WINDMILL SITE AND WRECK

LORAN: Shore or boat dive	LAT	LON
DEPTH: 0 to 30 feet	LEVEL: Novice-Intermediate	

LOCATION: East of Prescott, Ontario.

This windmill played a significant role in the Upper Canada Rebellion of 1838 when Canadian refugees and American sympathizers launched an attack on Prescott from the U.S. side. After a seven-day fiasco, most of the 300 invaders were captured.

Dive directly below the old windmill. To the left (east) of the windmill, a set of wooden stairs and a path lead to a picnic table positioned on a flat rock at the water's edge. It's an ideal place to suit up. Enjoy the underwater sights of rubble from the old mill and American eels. In about 60' of water near the red buoy on the Canadian side lie the remains of a small, unidentified wooden vessel, only about 35' long and consisting mainly of ribs and planks.

8. PRESCOTT FERRY DOCKS

LORAN: Shore dive	LAT	LON
DEPTH: To 55 feet	LEVEL: Intermediate-Advanced	

LOCATION: Just to the east of the town of Prescott, Ontario.

Long a favorite location for drift diving the St. Lawrence River, this site also offers small, unidentified shipwrecks. Two lifeboats, in very poor shape, lie at a depth of about 55' approximately 300' and 350' off shore.

9. PRESCOTT UNDERWATER PARK

LORAN: Shore dive	LAT	LON
DEPTH: To 40 feet	LEVEL: Novice-Intermediate	

LOCATION: This popular site is located off the town docks right in the heart of downtown Prescott, Ontario.

Used frequently as a training site by scuba instructors and their students, a large parking lot right next to the river helps make parking and suiting up as easy as the access. Reportedly ice boom anchors lie scattered on the bottom in front of the Coast Guard Station.

10. *ROTHESAY*

LORAN: Shore dive	LAT 44° 41' 58" LON 075° 31' 40"
DEPTH: 20 to 30 feet	LEVEL: Novice-Intermediate

LOCATION: An historic marker commemorating Loyalist Justus Sherwood stands just southwest of Prescott, Ontario. Park your car on the grass strip there, carry your dive gear down the wooden stairs to the water's edge and suit up at the picnic tables.

Launched in 1868 at St. John, New Brunswick, the wooden sidewheel passenger steamer, *Rothesay* (193' x 28'8" x 7'9"), sank in a collision with the tug *Myra* on September 12, 1889, killing two of the latter's crew. Ottawa scuba divers located the wreck in 1964.

The paddlewheeler, *Rothesay,* before the collision. AUTHOR'S COLLECTION.

The best visibility is found in the spring; sometimes the early fall can also be good. Two buoys mark the route to the wreck: one about 100′ off shore and the other placed right on the wreck about 300′ out. A rope strung along the river's bottom from shore can be used as a guideline. Impressive sights include the smokestack, boilers, walking beam, paddlewheels, and rudder. The wreck was dynamited for target practice in 1901, so not much of the middle remains intact.

Only bare planking remains where a porthole once hung, and massive bow-wood dwarfs a diver. PHOTOS BY CRIS KOHL.

SAVE ONTARIO SHIPWRECKS

Rothesay

Rope to shore marker

Float

Bow undercut by collision

Hatch

End of decking at bow

Boilers

Smoke stack

Starboard wheel

End of all decking

Decking beams broken up

Aft cabin footing

Stem post

Carrick bitts

Rudder

SOS Plaque

DEBRIS FIELD

Hawse pipe

Chain locker

Hold

Cleat

Walking beam

Cleat Cleat Rudder post

Portwheel

Scale:
0 1 2 3 4 5   10m

N. Baets

CURRENT

NOTE: This drawing shows the wreck in rather good condition
Actually it is quite broken, especially in the centre

11. "LOBLAW'S" WRECK

LORAN:	LAT	LON
DEPTH: 52 feet	LEVEL: Intermediate	

LOCATION: If you take a boat halfway between the wreck site of the *Rothesay* and the Canadian Coast Guard Station, and line up directly in front of a huge brick chimney over in Ogdensburg, this unidentified wreck lies south of the downstream channel.

This wooden ship sits upright in the firm clay, rising about eight feet off the bottom. The vessel's dimensions appear to be approximately 130′ x 24′ x 8′, and there is evidence that the vessel burned to the waterline. It is usually buoyed with some sort of marker.

St. Lawrence River: Area 3

1. *Muscallonge*
2. Brockville wall dive
3. *Robert Gaskin*
4. Mahogany launch
5. Two unidentified hulls
6. Unidentified motor vessel
7. Narrows current "rush"
8. MacDonald's Point
9. *John B. King*
10. *Lillie Parsons*
11. Needle's Eye "rush"
12. *Sam Cooke*
13. 3 Molly's Gut wrecks

1. MUSCALLONGE

LORAN:	LAT 44° 36.245′ LON 75° 39.213′
DEPTH: 99 feet	LEVEL: Advanced

The huge tug, *Muscallonge,* worked on inland waters for 40 years. GREAT LAKES MARINE COLLECTION OF THE MILWAUKEE PUBLIC LIBRARY/WISCONSIN MARINE HISTORICAL SOCIETY.

LOCATION: Three miles east of Brockville, Ontario; 1.5 miles downstream from Blockhouse Island.

The wooden tug, *Muscallonge* (128′ x 24′5″ x 12′), launched as the *Vigilant* at Port Huron, Michigan, on April 23, 1896, received her name change when Canadian owners purchased the ship in 1913. On August 15, 1936, while towing a barge to Toronto, the *Muscallonge* caught fire near Brockville. Captain F. Ahern ran his doomed ship aground, where it broke in two as it slid into deep water. No lives were lost in this mishap.

In spite of its land proximity (it's about 300′ off shore), the *Muscallonge* is a boat dive. The main portion of the ship sits in 90′ to 100′ of water, with much to see for the visiting scuba diver: winches, the scotch boiler, the engine, the starboard side and numerous other ship's parts. The stern and props have reportedly been located across the channel on the U.S. side. How they got there is anyone's guess. Local divers try to keep this main site buoyed throughout the dive season. It is well away from the main shipping channel, but small boat traffic can be heavy during summer.

2. BROCKVILLE WALL DIVE

LORAN:	LAT	LON
DEPTH: To 100 feet	LEVEL: To Advanced	

LOCATION: Three-quarters of a mile downstream from Blockhouse Island, these underwater walls are halfway between the wrecks of the *Muscallonge* and the *Robert Gaskin*.

The advantage of this site is that it provides varying levels of difficulty (or "challenges") for any scuba diver, and the diver can stay shallow or go deep within a very short distance from shore. Absolutely use a dive flag on a float above you as you drift downstream. Keep track of where you are heading, as the current varies in places and can provide casual slow drifting or a thrilling, fast ride downstream. Things to look for as you drift along are sturgeon (apparently increasing numbers have made this unusual type of fish a regular sight for divers), milk cans, and old vehicles on the river bottom. Reportedly illicit booze from the Prohibition days of the 1920's can also be encountered here. Good luck!

3. ROBERT GASKIN

LORAN:	LAT 44° 35.359′ LON 75° 40.625′
DEPTH: 55 to 70 feet	LEVEL: Intermediate-Advanced

LOCATION: This is a boat dive about 2,500′ downstream from the pier at Brockville.

The *Robert Gaskin* (132′6″ x 26′3″ x 11′3″), launched as a triple-masted, iron-rigged, wooden barque on April 21, 1863, at Kingston, Ontario, but later altered to a work barge, had an impressive carrying capacity of 20,000 bushels. However, that did not save her from

Artwork ©Adam Henley

sinking not once, but a total of three times in late 1889 while salvaging the train ferry *William Armstrong*. First, on September 18, 1889, a salvage pontoon broke loose and put a hole into the *Gaskin*. She ended up sinking on top of the vessel she was trying to salvage! On November 11, 1889, when the *Gaskin* was nearly raised, she dropped to the bottom again when a hose coupling broke. Twelve days later, the *Gaskin* was again raised and towed about 600' before sinking for the third and final time after a rear pontoon tore her stern away. Ironically, the *William Armstrong* was successfully raised and returned to service.

Long a favorite divesite, the *Robert Gaskin* sits with her bow in 55' of water, while what is left of her stern rests in 70'. Her bow faces downriver, parallel to the shore. Many interesting items appear on the deck, such as chains and a kingpost, while cargo holds can be cautiously penetrated for those trained and prepare for such diving. Do not destroy your visibility by disturbing the silt in the holds, one of which contains two steel barrels full of rivets and chain links. A large anchor sits about 40' off the bow towards shore. Local divers usually keep this site buoyed.

4. MAHOGANY LAUNCH

LORAN:	LAT	LON
DEPTH: 70 feet	LEVEL: Advanced	

LOCATION: Brockville, just off the "Sabre Jet" memorial on Blockhouse Island.

A motor vessel, 22' in length, complete with engine and wheel still in place, reportedly sits in the midst of this busy (boatwise) waterfront. Do not do this as a shore dive; use boat access. This little wreck, supposedly sunk after a collision with a yacht, rests in about 70' of water on a clay bottom. Make sure you utilize a divers down flag here.

5. TWO UNIDENTIFIED HULLS

LORAN:	LAT	LON
DEPTH: 32 feet and 82 feet	LEVEL: Intermediate/Advanced	

LOCATION: In front of the bandshell, Hardy Park, Brockville, Ontario.

The ribs of two old, wooden vessels, a small one (approximately 40' x 15') in 32' of water, the other larger one (estimated at 130' x 25') in 82' of water, remain a mystery.

6. UNIDENTIFIED MOTOR VESSEL

LORAN:	LAT	LON
DEPTH: 60 feet	LEVEL: Intermediate-Advanced	

LOCATION: Smith Island (drifting from the southeast corner), near Brockville.

Besides a wooden vessel about 35′ long sitting upright at a depth of 55′-60′, this fun drift dive in good visibility shows the visitor a couple of old garbage dump sites from back in the environmentally worry-free days when people got rid of their garbage the easy and most immediate way. Today, the occasional old bottle can still be found. It is possible to explore all around this small island on a single dive. Use a dive boat and a divers down flag in this high boating traffic area.

7. NARROWS CURRENT "RUSH"

LORAN:	LAT	LON
DEPTH: 100 feet	LEVEL: Advanced	

LOCATION: Upstream of the Brockville waterfront.

This site is only for divers experienced in swiftwater diving! Similar to the speedy mouth of the St. Clair River at the Bluewater Bridge in Sarnia/Port Huron, this site whisks the diver along an "express current" producing quite a "rush." Slower speeds can be found along the wall or at the bottom at a depth of 100′. A boat is necessary to take you out there; good island access points are off the west end of McCoy or Conran/Refuge Islands. You'll need a boat to pick you up. Avoid drifting downstream from Royal Island, as the very strong current will push you out into the open shipping channel through a narrow cut at Heathers Point. Having been in a strong current which seems to press the diver down and away from shore, I can vouch that there are better ways of having fun. Some "rushes" you don't need.

8. MacDONALD'S POINT

LORAN:	LAT	LON
DEPTH: 30 to 100 feet	LEVEL: Intermediate-Advanced	

LOCATION: Southwest of Brockville. Launch your boat at Brockville; MacDonald's Point is privately owned and there is no place to park unless you know a cottage owner.

An old dump site is located about 200′ west of the end of MacDonald's Point, right against the shore, which drops off steeply. Ten feet out, the diver will be in 30′ of water; 20′ out and the water is 60′ deep, while 30′ from shore, the diver will be in 100′ of water. Old bottles and even a model T automobile have been located here.

Be cautious with depth and the rather strong current. If done properly, the current will take the divers round the point into calm water, but if they attempt to surface earlier, they will likely encounter a strong downdraft current from the slight whirlpool effect at the end of the point, a frightening encounter if unprepared for it. Save plenty of air for surfacing.

9. JOHN B. KING

LORAN:	LAT 44° 33.747′ LON 75° 42.693′
DEPTH: 90 feet	LEVEL: Advanced

LOCATION: Upstream from Brockville, Ontario, about 80′ downstream from the number "143 A" flashing green light buoy, just west of Cockburn Island.

One of the St. Lawrence River's worse loss-of-life marine accidents occurred off the northeast point of Cockburn Island on June 26, 1930. The 140′ wooden drill scow, *John B. King*, with a large crew of 41 men on board, was busily placing underwater charges while at anchor in the main shipping channel. A summer thunderstorm suddenly developed, and lighting struck just as the vessel was pulling away from the dynamite-laden site. All the submerged charges, as well as the dynamite still on board, detonated. The massive explosion rocketed wreckage a couple of hundred feet into the air, and a few seconds later, when the

miniature atomic-like mushroom cloud began to dissipate, the ship was gone, along with 30 of the crew. The U.S. Coast Guard cutter, *Succor,* almost a mile upstream, responded to the frightening sound and was able to rescue eleven survivors at the tragic site.

The wreck site consists of heavily twisted metal lying scattered on the deep bottom. This is a very challenging (read

The tragic drill barge, *John B. King*. EVERRIT SNYDER COLLECTION.

"dangerous") dive. The St. Lawrence River currents are strong at this point, and the depth of 90′ makes it a deep, dark dive. The strong current could sweep you off this site into the deeper channel (155′ deep). Maintaining a boat anchorage near this site is also difficult.

10. LILLIE PARSONS

LORAN:	LAT 44° 33.377′ LON 75° 43.150′
DEPTH: 42 to 83 feet	LEVEL: Advanced

LOCATION: Along Sparrow Island, southwest of Brockville, Ontario.

Launched on September 5, 1868, at Tonawanda, NY, the two-masted, fore-and-after,

centerboard schooner, *Lillie Parsons* (131′ x 26′ x 12′), was loaded with 500 tons of coal when she encountered disaster. Sailing from Black Rock, NY, to Brockville, ON, on August 5, 1877, the *Lillie Parsons* plowed headstrong into a violent squall which heeled her onto her beam ends and shifted her cargo. Just after the crew escaped to safety, the ship struck a rock, filled with water, and sank on a relatively shallow shoal. The swift current in the treacherous Brockville Narrows gradually worked the *Lillie Parsons* into deeper water.

This shipwreck lies just off the northwest corner of Sparrow Island, which is about two miles southwest of Brockville, Ontario. The Brockville Parks Department operates this island's facilities: with prior permission and fee payment, one may camp upon the island, which offers docks, outhouses, picnic tables, and firewood.

The anchor and chain from the *Lillie Parsons* are on land display on Sparrow Island, with the anchor chain trailing down into the water and extending to the wreck itself, thus making it easy for divers to locate this

Hardware such as a double-sheave block remains attached to the *Lillie Parson's* main boom.   PHOTO BY CRIS KOHL.

site. The chain ends at the intact hull, which lies upside-down, enabling divers to explore the hull and keel areas. Other interesting parts of this wreck are the rudderhead, stern deadwood, bowsprit, and the keelson with stanchions still attached. The masts jut out from beneath the overturned hull, and a huge rudder can be viewed at the ship's square stern.

The ever-present and variable current runs between 2.3 and 3.6 knots, so this site is recommended only for very experienced swiftwater divers. Totally deflate your BCD and maintain as low a profile as possible while hugging the rocks. Penetration of the wreck is

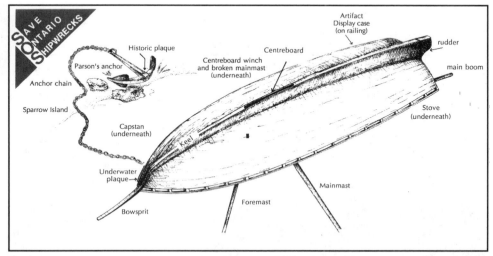

possible, although not recommended because of the potential difficulties or problems. Cave and ice diving techniques prevail when shipwreck penetration is done. There is boating traffic above, so the use of a divers down flag is recommended. The wreck is gradually slipping off the ledge where she currently rests, so make certain that you are not inside or under her when she finally does slide off.

11. NEEDLE'S EYE "RUSH"

LORAN:	LAT	LON
DEPTH:From 30 to 100 feet	LEVEL: All levels	

LOCATION: Between the mainland of Ontario and Needle's Eye Island, just across the channel from the *Lillie Parsons* wreck site.

Drop from the dive boat into the current at the west entrance and enjoy the ride (the south side of the island seems to provide the zestiest run). Going further west along the shoreline will take divers deeper (50' to 100'), yet keep them close to shore. Divers down flags are vital.

12. SAM COOKE

LORAN:	LAT 44° 33' 11" LON 075° 43' 34"
DEPTH: To 60 feet	LEVEL: Advanced

LOCATION: On the west side of Battersby Island, which lies between Black Charlie Island and Picnic Island.

Divers have long been aware of the remains of a wooden vessel, seemingly constructed in the mid-nineteenth century, and, it appears, at least partially salvaged, which have rested in the strong currents at the upstream side of Battersby Island for some time.

Still referred to occasionally as the "Battersby Island Wreck," these remains may be those of the three-masted schooner, *Sam Cooke*. Constructed at Oswego, New York, in 1873, the *Sam Cooke's* anchor failed to catch during a sudden strong breeze out of the north on July 6, 1882, and she was blown onto Battersby Island. The ship and her iron ore cargo sank, but no lives were lost. Subsequent salvage removed most of the cargo and virtually all of the ship's fittings and rigging.

The very strong currents at this site demand that only properly trained and fully prepared scuba divers attempt to explore this area.

13. THREE MOLLY'S GUT WRECKS

LORAN:	LAT	LON
DEPTH: To 20 feet	LEVEL: Novice-Intermediate	

LOCATION: On the west side of Molly's Gut, southwest of Brockville, Ontario.

Three abandoned wooden hulls lie in shallow water in this quiet backwater area, accessible by boat. This is a good place to go snorkeling or shallow water scuba diving, or to capture impressive underwater images on film or videotape.

One of the hulks is possibly the small steamer, *Roosevelt,* built in 1906 and burned to a total loss on October 7, 1936, at Edgewood Park, Alexandria Bay, New York. The other two hulls remain unidentified.

St. Lawrence River scenes from advertising flyers, late 1800's. AUTHOR'S COLLECTION

St. Lawrence River: Area 4

1. *Henry C. Daryaw*
2. *"Eel City"*
3. **Indian Chief Island and Shoal**
4. *America*
5. *Keystorm*
6. **S E Grenadier Island wrecks**
7. *Clara White*
8. *Kingshorn*
9. **Rockport wall**
10. *Sophia* (?)
11. *Catherine*
12. *Islander*
13. *Roy A. Jodrey*
14. *Sir Robert Peel*
15. *Iroquois*
16. *Oconto*
17. *A. E. Vickery*
18. *Raymond*
19. *Dauntless*
20. *Squaw*
21. *Maggie L.*
22. **Gas launch**
23. *Julia*
24. **Bateau Channel wreck**
25. **Howe Island wrecks**
26. **Holliday Point wreck**
27. *Lewiston*
28. *Harvey J. Kendall*
29. *St. Louis*
30. *Arizona*

1. HENRY C. DARYAW

LORAN:	LAT 44° 31.567′ LON 75° 45.754′
DEPTH: 55 to 85 feet	LEVEL: Advanced

PUBLIC ARCHIVES OF CANADA

Artwork ©Adam Henley

LOCATION: About six miles west of Brockville, Ontario, at Buoy Shoal (the wreck is marked on C.H.S. Chart #1418) about one-quarter mile off shore.

Divers hover at one of the *Daryaw's* propellers. PHOTO BY MIKE WILLIAMS.

The steel freighter, *Henry C. Daryaw* (219′2″ x 35′ x 13′2″), built in France in 1919, tore a huge gash in her starboard side when she ran aground in a dense fog near Brockville on November 21, 1941 with the loss of one life.

The hull lies upside-down, with the bow aimed into the current, while the stern is wedged against a bank. Bow anchors and the hull gash that caused her sinking can be seen. The current is strong, so use a solid anchor line for the descent and ascent. The current poses another problem as there are no handholds on the smooth hull. It often gets dark beyond the hull, so bring a light. Avoid getting wedged between the ship's stern and the bank.

2. "EEL CITY"

LORAN:	LAT	LON
DEPTH: To 40 feet	LEVEL: Novice-Intermediate	

LOCATION: Off the shores of Crossover Island.

A boat is required to reach Crossover Island, where, in recent years, scuba divers have noticed an unusually large number of American eels thriving in these waters. If it's Great Lakes sub-aquatic wildlife you wish to see and possibly photograph, this site is for you.

3. INDIAN CHIEF ISLAND AND SHOAL

LORAN:	LAT	LON
DEPTH: To 60 feet	LEVEL: Intermediate	

LOCATION: This island and shoal lie across the main channel and Chippewa Point.

Scuba divers have reported locating pieces of a shipwreck off Indian Chief Shoal (possibly portions of the *Persia,* which hit a rock, lost her rudder, and was carried by the current to this shoal, where she broke up), but nothing large enough to be identifiable.

Relaxing scuba diving can be enjoyed around off Indian Chief Island, and further downstream from Bilberry Island, Big Island, Robinson Island and Ingal Island, as well as at Blind Bay. Beware of small craft boating, as there are marinas in this region.

4. *AMERICA*

LORAN:	LAT 44° 27.018′ LON 75° 48.590′
DEPTH: 78 feet	LEVEL: Advanced

LOCATION: Between Brockville and Mallorytown, Ontario, a few hundred yards off the southwest side of Singer Castle Island. Sometimes a buoy line is established just east of black buoy #167 on the shipping lane's downstream side. The wreck lies just inside Canada near the international boundary in the busy shipping channel, and therefore makes access dangerous for divers and boaters. Never leave a boat unattended! Check for oncoming ships!

America. AUTHOR'S COLLECTION.

Artwork ©Adam Henley

The steel drill barge, *America* (sometimes also referred to as *American*), worked at dynamiting shoals when an explosion on board sank the vessel on June 20, 1932. She lies upside-down, with the four bracing posts, or retractable legs, which kept her anchored at a site, now helplessly aimed upwards. Experienced divers can view the twin propellers at a depth of 55′, as well as the twin rudders. Trained and experienced divers exploring underneath the wreck will see winches, a brick oven or kiln, and a jumble of wire rigging. Don't get lost inside! The deck cabin appears on the stern end, but inside it, too, is a tangled clutter of equipment (remember that this wreck is upside-down).

A small, wooden barge which accompanied the *America* lies off her stern.

5. KEYSTORM

LORAN:	LAT 44° 25.785' LON 075° 49.390'
DEPTH: 25 to 115 feet	LEVEL: Advanced

LOCATION: East of Mallorytown, Ontario, and south of the shipping channel, at Outer Scow Island Shoal.

The steel canaller, *Keystorm* (250' x 42'5" x 17'5"), built in England in 1910, sank on a foggy night two years later on October 26, 1912, when she ran aground at Scow Island Shoal, Chippewa Point, St. Lawrence River. Her crew escaped and, after five hours

Artwork ©Adam Henley

AUTHOR'S COLLECTION

aground, the ship slid off into deep water. Her coal cargo was salvaged in 1919.

The *Keystorm* is one of the most exciting and visited shipwrecks in the St. Lawrence River. Lying on her starboard side, her bow reaches within 25' of the surface and her propeller

Scuba divers explore the bridge of the *Keystorm*. PHOTO BY MIKE WILLIAMS.

rests in 115'. In between are an intact forward superstructure, a pair of freight masts and booms, and huge cargo holds. Four-inch cable double-wrapped at 20' intervals are remnants of failed salvage efforts (a blessing for today's scuba divers!). The gash in the ship's port bow area is quite evident. Swimming a bit off-site at midship will often reveal an impressive panoramic view of the entire shipwreck.

Usually local charter operators maintain a buoy at the bow and another at midship. Beware of boating traffic, which can be heavy, and use precaution in the usually moderate current at this site. Penetration requires special training and preparation.

6. SOUTHEAST GRENADIER ISLAND WRECKS

LORAN:	LAT 44° 24′ 14″ LON 075° 53′ 13″
DEPTH: To 18 feet	LEVEL: Novice-Intermediate

LOCATION: Grenadier Island, near Mallorytown, Ontario. The locations of these shipwrecks are marked on Canadian Hydrographic Service chart #1418 off the southeast part of Grenadier Island.

This unidentified wooden wreck was likely abandoned for age at a spot along Grenadier Island where it would be out of the way and not interfere with navigation. The wreck lies broken and scattered on a sandy bottom in about 18′ of protected water, offering a refuge for fish, usually found in large numbers at this site. Two other shallower and less interesting wrecks lie at **LAT 44° 24′ 57″   LON 075° 53′ 00″**.

7. CLARA WHITE

LORAN:	LAT LON
DEPTH: To 25 feet	LEVEL: Novice

LOCATION: Off the north side of Bloomfield Island, south end of Grenadier Island.

Built in 1871, the small, two-masted, 63-ton, carvel style schooner, *Clara White* (79′ x 18′5″ x 6′), caught fire (a cook stove accident) on November 11, 1889, while moored for the night. She burned to a total loss with her bow in close to shore and the stern in slightly deeper water. Early divers called her the "Clay Pipe Wreck " because of the many clay pipes found at the site.

8. KINGSHORN

LORAN:	LAT 44° 22.616′ LON 75° 55.818′
DEPTH: 92 feet	LEVEL: Advanced

LOCATION: Rockport, Ontario, directly in front of the Customs Office and the marina.

Located in 1995 by Ron McDonald with research assistance from Deb Ring, this schooner-barge, about 130′ long, sits upright and incredibly intact in a busy small boat shipping channel. Plates found on the wreck were manufactured only during a six-year period in the 1890's; this fact helped establish the probable identity of the wreck as the *Kingshorn*, one of seven wheat-laden schooner-barges being towed by the powerful tug, *Hiram A. Walker,* on April 27, 1897, bound for Montreal. A storm sank three of the barges, with the *Kingshorn* leaking so badly that she eventually sank just before the tug captain could reach Rockport.

This fascinating shipwreck sports a rarity: a ship's wheel! Also at the stern, the broken-off rudder lies flat while a windlass adorns the bow area. Three bilge pumps, one mounted just forward of each of the three cargo holds, add to the unique nature of this shipwreck. Anchor chain lies on the forward deck, and authorities are still searching for the divers who removed the anchor in 1997.

The *Kingshorn's* wheel. PHOTO BY MIKE WILLIAMS.

9. ROCKPORT WALL

LORAN: Shore dive	LAT	LON
DEPTH: To 90 feet	LEVEL: Advanced	

LOCATION: Off the town of Rockport, Ontario.

Ask permission at the restaurant along the river to dive off their huge dock. Just downstream (east) of the dock is a large rock. Divers have customarily suited up at the dock and swum over to the rock to make their descent along the Rockport wall there.

This wall dive is a popular checkout site for advanced courses because of its shore proximity and good visibility. Boating traffic can be heavy during summer, so use a divers down flag. Don't forget to account for the current and the depth. Go only as deep as your experience and training will allow.

10. *SOPHIA* (?)

LORAN: Shore dive	LAT	LON
DEPTH: 65 feet	LEVEL: Advanced	

LOCATION: Off the government dock at Rockport, Ontario, across the bay on the west wall of the harbor.

This shipwreck, in poor condition, may be that of the *Sophia* (82′ x 18′ x 8′), a two-masted schooner built in Kingston, Ontario, in 1844. The site lies in a busy pleasure craft channel which must not be blocked. Use care and discretion about diving here.

11. *CATHERINE*

LORAN:	LAT	LON
DEPTH: 60 feet	LEVEL: Advanced	

LOCATION: This schooner lies downstream from Alexandria Bay, New York, between Sunken Rock Island and Sunken Rock Shoal.

12. *ISLANDER*

LORAN:	LAT	LON
DEPTH: 15 to 60 feet	LEVEL: Novice-Intermediate	

LOCATION: On the shoreline of Alexandria Bay, New York, north of the hospital.

Built in Rochester, New York, in 1871, and originally named the *James H. Kelly,* the 118-gross-ton sidewheel steamer, *Islander* (125′ x 20′ x 7′), operated as a mail boat between Clayton and Alexandria Bay, New York, as well as an island and river excursion ship, until she burned to a total loss at Alexandria Bay on September 16, 1909.

Divers park in the town lot in front of the pavilion in Alexandria Bay to the west of the

AUTHOR'S COLLECTION

hospital, where they suit up before walking across to the east end of the pavilion and down the hill to the dock, the entry point. The wreck site is between 100′ and 150′ downstream of this dock. The wreck's downstream starboard side is a bit lower than the port side, offering an unecessary shield from the slight current. The stern sits in 15′ of water, while the intact bow is settled deeper in 60′. The considerable boating traffic warrants using a dive flag.

13. ROY A. JODREY

LORAN:	LAT 44° 36.245′ LON 75° 39.213′
DEPTH: 140 to 242 feet	LEVEL: Technical

LOCATION: Off the Coast Guard Station on the south shoreline of Wellesley Island.

The freighter, *Roy A. Jodrey*, is a very deep shipwreck site for technically-trained divers only. This site is deeper than the recommended sport diving limit.

REV. PETER VAN DER LINDEN COLLECTION

The Algoma Central Railway motor vessel, *Roy A Jodrey* (640′6″ x 72′ x 40′), carried over 20,000 tons of iron ore pellets towards Detroit when she struck Pullman Shoal near Wellesley Island and sank at 3:00 A.M., November 21, 1974, with no loss of life. The nine-year-old freighter, named after one of Algoma's directors (who lived from 1888 until 1973), was almost 90′ shorter than the famous *Edmund Fitzgerald,* the Great Lakes system's largest shipwreck, which sank in Lake Superior with the loss of 29 lives a year after the *Jodrey* went down. The *Fitzgerald* also carried iron ore pellets when she sank. Perhaps these resemblances to the *Edmund Fitzgerald,* which lies virtually unreachable in 529′ of water, make the *Jodrey* a symbolic, acceptable, and attainable substitute among technical divers.

The *Jodrey's* bow lies in about 140′ of water, her wheelhouse is in about 155′, and her stern rests in 242′. The extreme depth, the fast current, and the high volume of boating traffic make this an extremely formidable site, well beyond the realm of sport diving.

14. SIR ROBERT PEEL

LORAN:	LAT 44° 18.040′ LON 075° 59.175′
DEPTH: 80 to 135 feet	LEVEL: Advanced

LOCATION: Just upstream from the 1000 Islands Bridge.

The small sidewheel passenger steamer, *Sir Robert Peel*, built at Brockville, Upper Canada (today Ontario) in 1837, had a short life. On May 29, 1838, during the tumultuous Upper Canada Rebellion, a rebel named "Pirate" Bill Johnston and his followers, some dressed as Indians, decided to steal the *Sir Robert Peel*. After removing the crew and the 60 passengers when the ship stopped at the Wellesley Island refueling station, Johnston and his men, unable to start the ship which they had appropriated, set it on fire.

Today the burned out remains of this historic vessel rest with her stern in 135′, the bow in 95′, and the boiler in 80′. Beware of the current, depth and boating traffic at this site.

15 . IROQUOIS

LORAN:	LAT 44° 17.238′ LON 76° 00.324′
DEPTH: 65 to 80 feet	LEVEL: Advanced

LOCATION: Near the foot of Niagara Shoal, 150′ south of the green buoy.

Built in 1759 by the French and sunk after striking a shoal in 1763, only the fragile ribs remain of the oldest known wreck site in the Great Lakes. Please do not disturb the remains.

16. OCONTO

LORAN:	LAT 44° 17.005′ LON 076° 00.972′
DEPTH: 175 to 200 feet	LEVEL: Technical

Oconto, before she slid deep.
AUTHOR'S COLLECTION.

LOCATION: Across the channel from the *A.E. Vickery* (see site #17), at light #214 south of Thousand Island Park on Wellesley Island and west of the Thousand Island Bridge.

In July, 1886, the steamer, *Oconto,* struck a boulder in mid-channel and sank with her bow out of the water. During salvage operations several weeks later, the ship suddenly slid down the embankment into deep water. Today, the wreck lies beyond sport diving range in a dangerously swift current in 175′ to 200′ of water. Technical divers usually reach this site by anchoring their boat in shallow water next to the concrete light abutment (#214) and descending along the drop-off to 175′.

17. A. E. VICKERY

LORAN:	LAT 44° 16.820′ LON 076° 01.183′
DEPTH: From 65 to 118 feet	LEVEL: Advanced

LOCATION: Off Rock Island Shoal, about four miles southwest of Alexandria Bay, New York, west-south-west of the Ivy Lea Bridge.

The schooner, *A.E. Vickery* (136′2″ x 26′2″ x 10′8″), launched as the *J.B. Penfield* in July, 1861, and renamed in 1884, struck a shoal on August 16, 1889, and sank. Her entire crew escaped uninjured, but the pilot was almost murdered by the angry Captain Massey, who shouted profanities and pointed a revolver at the old river guide who had steered him wrong in the night. The ship's mate, a brother of the captain, pitched the revolver overboard at an opportune moment, in all likelihood saving the pilot's life. Like the *Oconto*, the *A.E. Vickery* slipped off the shoal and into deep water before she could be salvaged.

This popular site, usually buoyed, has a strong surface current. Once the upright wreck is reached at 65′, the angled bow, which sports a photogenic windlass, shields the diver from most of the current. In the hold, a huge centerboard box can be studied by careful divers experienced in wreck penetration. The rudder is in place at a depth of 118′.

18. RAYMOND

LORAN:	LAT	LON
DEPTH: 25 feet	LEVEL: Novice-Intermediate	

LOCATION: This wreck lies midway between the east end of Round Island and Irwin Point on the mainland.

The *Raymond* was a 40′, two-masted sailing yacht which burned to the waterline.

19. DAUNTLESS

LORAN:	LAT	LON
DEPTH: 50 feet	LEVEL: Intermediate	

LOCATION: Midway between Washington Island (near Clayton) and Round Island.

This double-ender wreck, with scroll work near the bow, much decking, and hatches still in place, shows evidence of a fire. With the engine missing, she may have been scuttled.

20. SQUAW

LORAN:	LAT	LON
DEPTH: 60 feet	LEVEL: Intermediate	

LOCATION: About halfway between the public docks at Clayton, New York, and the wreck of the *Maggie L.* This motorized workboat, about 35′ in length, sits on a hard sand bottom. The wheel, deck hardware (e.g. cleats), and the engine are still in place on this boat.

21. MAGGIE L.

LORAN:	LAT	LON
DEPTH: 75 feet	LEVEL: Advanced	

LOCATION: In the shipping channel between the public docks at Clayton, New York, and Governors Island. A steel freighter plowed into the small schooner, *Maggie L.*, as the latter was heading for Clayton in June, 1927. The stern portion is located in 75′ of water, while divers are still searching for the bow section.

22. GAS LAUNCH

LORAN:	LAT	LON
DEPTH: 30 feet	LEVEL: Novice-Intermediate	

LOCATION: Just north of Quebec Head on the eastern tip of Wolfe Island.
Reputedly this 30′ long motor launch utilized the first gas-powered engine on the St. Lawrence River. The small boat burned to a total loss in 1912.

23. JULIA

LORAN:	LAT	LON
DEPTH: 20 feet	LEVEL: Novice-Intermediate	

LOCATION: On the east tip of Wolfe Island halfway between Brakey Bay and Quebec Head. The 108-ton schooner, *Julia,* burned to a complete loss on February 25, 1895.

24. BATEAU CHANNEL WRECK

LORAN:	LAT 44° 15′ 53″ LON 076° 20′ 23″	
DEPTH: To 18 feet	LEVEL: Novice-Intermediate	

LOCATION: Just off the north side of Howe Island. About 60′ long, this wreck may be the ferry vessel, *Amherst Islander I.* You will find mild current and abundant fish life here.

25. HOWE ISLAND WRECKS

LORAN:	LAT	LON
DEPTH: To 12 feet	LEVEL: Novice-Intermediate	

LOCATION: In shallow water on the northwest end of Howe Island.

The westernmost wreck has considerable chain strewn about the limestone and sand bottom, but the two wrecks in the eastern corner of the bay are more lackluster.

26. HOLLIDAY POINT WRECK

LORAN:	LAT	LON
DEPTH: 17 to 46 feet	LEVEL: Novice-Intermediate	

LOCATION: Just off Holliday Point on eastern Wolfe Island, Ontario.

This unidentified wooden sailing vessel, because of her position in the shallows, is broken up except for the relatively intact bow section.

27. *LEWISTON*

LORAN:	LAT	LON
DEPTH: To 20 feet	LEVEL: Novice-Intermediate	

LOCATION: In the Hinckley Flats off the south side of Wolfe Island.

The *Lewiston,* a wooden propeller barge built in 1864, lies abandoned in shallow water at the entrance to Button Bay. This broken-up wreck is marked on the chart.

28. *HARVEY J. KENDALL*

LORAN:	LAT	LON
DEPTH: 7 to 18 feet	LEVEL: Novice-Intermediate	

LOCATION: In Button Bay, on the southwest side of Wolfe Island.

The wooden steam barge, *Harvey J. Kendall* (141'7" x 31' x 9'2"), was launched at Marine City, Michigan, on April 10, 1892. This ship was abandoned for age in 1932.

29. *ST. LOUIS*

LORAN:	LAT	LON
DEPTH: 40 feet	LEVEL: Novice-Intermediate	

LOCATION: Close to shore at the east end of Cape Vincent, New York.

This large barge, built in 1864, sank on February 18, 1914. Today, the *St. Louis* is popular as a dive training site.

30. *ARIZONA*

LORAN:	LAT 44° 06.55' LON 076° 24.38'	
DEPTH: 25 feet	LEVEL: Novice-Intermediate	

LOCATION: Southwest of the ferry landing on the south shore of Wolfe Island near the red buoy. The oak-built wooden steamer, *Arizona* (201' x 32'6" x 14'3"), launched at Cleveland in 1868, caught fire at Cape Vincent, New York, on December 1, 1922. Since no adequate firefighting equipment was available, the blazing ship was towed 1.5 miles upstream, where she was scuttled. She carried no cargo at the time of her loss.

Divers can explore the hull (which rises 12' off the bottom) and framing, the shaft, a portion of the propeller and the fallen rudder at the stern, plus a huge winch and considerable chain at the bow.

5. Kingston

ONTARIO

KINGSTON

1. *Wolfe Islander II*
2. *Prince Regent* and *Psyche*
3. Marine Museum dock
4. *St. Lawrence*
5. Anchors and stacked hulls
6. The *K.P.H.* wreck
7. *"Titanic"*
8. *Munson*
9. *William Jamieson*
10. *Aloha* and *Effie Mae*
11. *George T. Davie*
12. *Comet*
13. *George A. Marsh*
14. *Cornwall*
15. *Mapleglen*
16. *Glendora*
17. *Simla*
18. *Varuna*
19. *Frontenac*
20. *City of Sheboygan*
21. Scuttled deep hulls

Kingston and Lake Ontario

Kingston, Ontario, nestled nicely in the northeast corner of Lake Ontario at the point where the lake tries to empty itself into the St. Lawrence River, is rich in history, particularly maritime history. The Kingston site is the location that was chosen by the explorer LaSalle for an important meeting between the Governor of New France, Frontenac, and the Iroquois chiefs in 1673, as well as for the construction of a fort in 1675 named Fort Frontenac. In the 1700's, the site served as a defended port of trans-shipment, handling supplies heading to the western forts and furs brought up in canoes and lake schooners from the frontier regions. In 1783, the site was settled by United Empire Loyalists from New York State, who renamed it Kingston in honor of King George III. By 1793, Kingston was chosen as the chief naval base for Lake Ontario, the establishment of which was crucial later during the War of 1812 with the United States. The Kingston stockyard became furiously engaged in a shipbuilding race with the American Lake Ontario base at Sackets Harbor. Ships the size of those which were sailing across the oceans of the world at that time were constructed at Kingston. The fort which had been built at Point Henry during the War of 1812 to protect the dockyard was rebuilt on a larger scale in 1823-36 (this is the present Fort Henry which serves as a public attraction). Shipping traffic from the west increased steadily, and the harbor at Kingston enjoyed boom times until the rise of the railways. The last regularly-scheduled passenger steamer called at Kingston in 1951.

What all of this means to the average scuba diver is that this area has a high concentration of shipwrecks! Kingston is considered by many to be one of the top two scuba diving destinations in the huge province of Ontario. The shipwrecks at Kingston range from sailing vessels to sidewheelers, from War of 1812 naval ships to 20th century ferryboats.

Non-shipwreck shore dives can also be done; in the mid-1980's, we explored the area along the Maritime Museum's waterfront, and found charred remains of a ship, chain twisted by the flames' heat, old embossed bottles located beyond elbow depth in the muck, and a lawn chair in superb condition!

The area around old Fort Henry still, on occasion, yields items of historical interest, and in late November, 1985, two divers doing routine maintenance on the 139-year-old Martello tower in Kingston's Confederation Basin found fifteen 32-pound cannonballs, which Parks Canada refurbished for display at historic sites across Canada.

I have seen the number of scuba charter boats at Kingston increase from three to 15 since the early 1980's; that should give any aquatic visitor a good idea of the dramatically increasing popularity of Kingston as a Great Lakes scuba diving destination! Enjoy!

1. *Wolfe Islander II*

LORAN: 15639.2/60051.06	LAT 44° 13' 55" LON 076° 24' 98"
DEPTH: 40 to 85 feet	LEVEL: Intermediate-Advanced

LOCATION: Three miles east of Kingston, Ontario.

Built at Collingwood, Ontario, 1946, the *Wolfe Islander II* (144'3" x 43'1" x 8') plied the waters between Wolfe Island and Kingston for almost 30 years, carrying tourists, cars, trucks, and future divebook writers. After sitting idle for ten years, she became the very first commercial vessel to be scuttled in the Great Lakes (on September 21, 1985) for the express purpose of creating a scuba dive site. The ship was sunk in a protected "all weather" area three miles east of Kingston. Since 1985, the *Wolfe Islander II* has become the most visited shipwreck in Lake Ontario!

The ship sits upright in 85' of water, with the superstructure starting just 40' below the surface. Visiting divers can explore her open deck area, complete with davits, bollards, dorades, smokestack, railings galore, a motorcycle and other items too numerous to mention. Divers trained in shipwreck penetration can also explore her interior, including the engine

Artwork ©Adam Henley

Clockwise from upper right: a plaque mounted on the bridge names those who arranged the scuttling, piping in the engine room, a diver-instructor (Marcie McElmon) poses in a dorade, and later at the propeller. PHOTOS BY CRIS KOHL.

room. But don't get lost below deck! All doors and hatches have been removed for diver safety, but she's a big ship. Keep track of your depth and bottom time, since a diver can get carried away while exploring the many wonderful nooks and crannies at this site. It takes at least two scuba dives at this site to become comfortably familiar with the vessel.

2. _PRINCE REGENT_ AND _PSYCHE_

LORAN: Shore dive	LAT 44° 13′ 00″ LON 076° 27′ 13″
DEPTH: 12 to 20 feet	LEVEL: Novice-Intermediate

LOCATION: In Deadman Bay, east of Fort Henry, Kingston.

The 1,294-ton _Prince Regent,_ built completely at Kingston in 1813-14, carried 58 cannons and was heavily involved in the War of 1812 in its final year. After the war and several years of inactivity, the huge ship sank in the bay. The _Psyche_, transported in pieces from England and assembled at Kingston, was completed right when the war ended, and was eventually abandoned in the bay.

The _Prince Regent_ is located in about 20′ to 25′ of water about

Prince Regent

Public Archives of Canada

300′ from the shore opposite Cartright Point. The *Psyche* is located in shallower water (about 12′) at the end, or the head, of the bay. the wrecks can be done as a shore dive from Arrowhead Point. The keels and ribs are virtually all that remain of these two old, historic shipwrecks lying in a shallow, sand-and-silt-bottom bay.

3. MARINE MUSEUM DOCK

LORAN: Shore dive	LAT	LON
DEPTH: To 50 feet far offshore	LEVEL: Novice-Intermediate	

LOCATION: Behind the Maritime Museum of the Great Lakes, Kingston, Ontario.

This local favorite offers sights common to the waters off old shipbuilding yards: ship timbers, old bottles, and fish. Scuba instructors take their students here for checkouts, and sometimes night dives, with perch, pike, burbot, and salamanders, attract other divers.

4. ST. LAWRENCE

LORAN: Shore dive	LAT	LON
DEPTH: 5 to 10 feet	LEVEL: Novice-Intermediate	

METROPOLITAN TORONTO LIBRARY

LOCATION: The *St. Lawrence* is marked on Canadian Hydrographic Service chart #1459 as lying just east of the Kingston Penitentiary, in a little bay at the foot of Morton Street. A city-owned park is adjacent to this site, and divers can suit up and wade in there.

The *St. Lawrence* is considered the mightiest sailing war vessel ever seen on the Great Lakes. Constructed at Kingston for use in the War of 1812, the ship ironically took most of the war to construct. When she finally did sail across Lake Ontario to do battle, no enemy ship was sighted! Canadian historian Pierre Berton described the *St. Lawrence* as a ship "too precious to be risked in battle and too grand to be used as transport." The war ended two months after her maiden voyage, and this 2,304-ton vessel was stripped of her cannons and masts and towed to Morton's distillery, where her broken remains lie to this day. The few remaining planks of the *St. Lawrence* are scattered along the bottom of this shallow bay quite close to shore. Silt is easily stirred and visibility is usually poor.

5. ANCHORS AND STACKED HULLS

LORAN: Shore dive	LAT	LON
DEPTH: To 50 feet	LEVEL: Novice-Intermediate	

LOCATION: Portsmouth Olympic Harbour, near the Coast Guard Station at the corner of the government dock.

There is a line (rope) starting from shore to the site of the anchors. From there, a second line runs out about 600′ to the remains of a couple of stacked ship's hulls. Although it is a long swim, the scenery is well worth it. Use a divers down flag to let boaters know that you are there, and keep an eye on your air supply. Respect the rights of local private residence owners.

6. THE *K.P.H.* WRECK

LORAN:	LAT 44° 12.42' LON 076° 31.46'
DEPTH: 65 feet	LEVEL: Intermediate-Advanced

LOCATION: This unknown wreck is situated off Olympic Harbour in front of the Kingston Psychiatric Hospital (the K.P.H., from which the site takes its name).

This unidentified flat barge, 135' long, is steel-framed, wood-sheathed, wood-decked, and has 6'-8' of height when exploring below deck (use caution!). There are two boilers inside this wreck, as well as other numerous internal details like coal chutes, piping and machinery. The stern is completely broken open, with loose boards littering the area. Steel beams supporting the decking make penetration safer than one might expect it to be. The rudder appears to be missing, but a four-bladed propeller is still intact. Right at the stern, the steering post, resembling a funnel or smokestack, stands upright off the bottom. The heavy amount of silt at this site makes it too easy to destroy your visibility, especially inside the wreck. Use cave diving swimming techniques and plenty of caution! This site is usually buoyed.

Inside the *K.P.H.* wreck.
PHOTO BY CRIS KOHL.

7. *"TITANIC"*

LORAN: 15740.4/60027.1	LAT 44° 08.33' LON 076° 37.20'
DEPTH: 75 feet	LEVEL: Intermediate-Advanced

LOCATION: To the west of Kingston, Ontario.

This unidentified vessel is a huge, intact barge with two large boilers and enormous anchor chain. This wreck may be penetrated by more experienced and trained divers. This site is usually buoyed by local divers in the spring.

8. *MUNSON*

LORAN: 15701.4/60016.0	LAT LON
DEPTH: 93 to 111 feet	LEVEL: Advanced

LOCATION: About six miles west of Kingston, just off Lemoine Point, near Kingston Airport.

On the last day of April, 1890, the dredge, *Munson,* having completed the most significant dredging job of its career (that of ensuring that the largest sailing ship ever built on the Canadian side of the Great Lakes, the *Minnedosa,* would have adequate depth for its upcoming launch at Kingston), was being towed back to Rossmore, Ontario, when it

A dredge similar to the *Munson.* AUTHOR'S COLLECTION.

leaned to one side and, within a few minutes, vanished beneath the waves. The three *Munson* crew were saved. A hardhat diver later inspected the dredge and proclaimed the vessel to be unrecoverable.

The dredge, *Munson,* sits upright in 111′ of water, and experienced scuba divers can penetrate her basic, skeletal layout, and appreciate the distinctive crane and bucket features. On the upper deck, divers have placed an interesting collection of plates, bottles and other artifacts in one area for easy viewing. Below deck, on a workbench, are laid out many of the original 1890 ship's tools. Please do not remove any of these items. Besides their removal being illegal, they mean much more at the shipwreck site than they do as souvenirs to you. Sometimes the site is dark, even at midday; take a light with you!

Artwork ©Adam Henley

The gears of the *Munson's* long-armed bucket are amazing to behold, while, below deck, the ship's tools are carefully laid out on a work-bench. PHOTOS BY CRIS KOHL.

9. WILLIAM JAMIESON

LORAN: 15781.55/59986.62	LAT	LON
DEPTH: 80 feet	LEVEL: Advanced	

LOCATION: Off the north shore of Amherst Island, west of Emerald, Ontario.

Left: The aging schooner, *William Jamieson.* INSTITUTE FOR GREAT LAKES RESEARCH, BOWLING GREEN STATE UNIVERSITY, BOWLING GREEN, OHIO. *Right:* A diver closely examines a fallen *Jamieson* deadeye. PHOTO BY CRIS KOHL.

The two-masted schooner, *William Jamieson* (100′ x 25′4″ x 8′6″), built by Mr. William Jamieson at Mill Point (Deseronto), Ontario, and named after himself, was launched on July 3, 1878. On May 15, 1923, the 45-year-old ship showed her age when she opened her seams during a severe storm. The crew abandoned the doomed vessel just before she hit the bottom with her hard anthracite coal cargo. Much silt rests on this site, but, with a bit of buoyancy skill and consideration, the visibility can remain quite good. The wreck is intact with some of her rigging and bow pumps still in their original positions.

10. *ALOHA* AND *EFFIE MAE*

LORAN: 15715.2/60034.3	LAT 44° 09′ 00″ LON 076° 34′ 07″
DEPTH: 55 feet	LEVEL: Novice-Intermediate

LOCATION: Off Nine Mile Point, Simcoe Island, west of Kingston, Ontario.

The schooner-barge, *Aloha* (128′5″ x 24′5″ x 12′5″), built in Mt. Clemens, Michigan, in 1888, began to leak in a gale on October 29, 1917, and foundered with her aging captain and her load of coal several hours later. The rest of the crew survived the sinking.

Clockwise from upper left: The schooner-barge, *Aloha* (1888-1917). INSTITUTE FOR GREAT LAKES RESEARCH, BOWLING GREEN STATE UNIVERSITY, BOWLING GREEN, OHIO. Diver Marcie McElmon exmines Roman numeral draught markings at the bow. A diver explores *Effie Mae's* cabin. *Effie Mae* afloat in the mid-1980's. PHOTOS BY CRIS KOHL.

Most of the hull is intact, although she was divested of the majority of her small artifacts years ago by early divers. Anchor chain sits on the bow attached to a windlass, and divers can see the original coal cargo by carefully descending into the holds. At the stern, in the sand, lie a capstan, steering quadrant, and rudder post. The Roman numeral depth markings at the bow are also interesting.

In the early 1990's, when owners of the popular, old scuba charter boat, *Effie Mae* (39′10″ x 13′ x 3′3″), could find no buyer for her, they donated their vessel to a local marine conservation group, consisting mostly of divers, who cleaned her up and decided that the old *Aloha* needed some company. They scuttled the *Effie Mae* right next to the old schooner-barge on October 17, 1993, and they lie within easy underwater swimming distance of each other. Yes, it does feel strange to be exploring, underwater, the dive boat that used to take me (and thousands of other scuba divers over the years) to so many wonderful shipwrecks. The former dive boat, ever faithful, continues to practice her calling (in a slightly different way) of providing a service to visiting scuba divers.

11. GEORGE T. DAVIE

LORAN:	LAT 44° 06.815′ LON 076° 34.804′
DEPTH: 105 feet	LEVEL: Advanced

LOCATION: Approximately three miles southwest of Nine Mile Point, Simcoe Island, less than two miles south of the *Comet* (see site #12) and almost one-and-a-half miles southeast of the *George A. Marsh* (see site #13).

PUBLIC ARCHIVES OF CANADA

The composite bulk freight barge, *George T. Davie* (186′ x 35′ x 12′5″), built in Levis, Quebec in 1898 by the George T. Davie & Sons Company, worked on fresh water for 47 years before foundering in heavy seas on April 18, 1945. All four men who had been on board were rescued, but the ship and the more than 1,000 tons of hard coal cargo were lost.

The *George T. Davie* rests on her starboard side with most of her coal cargo spilled out of her five hatches. The ship's wheel, a type utilizing steam-powered assistance, remains at the stern, while the crane (which had been salvaged from the wreck of the *Henry C. Daryaw* in the St. Lawrence River in 1941 -- see page 42) lies parallel to the starboard side, with a photogenic lifeboat lying between the hull and the crane's arm. A windlass adorns the bow, while an anchor hangs off the bow's port side.

12. COMET

LORAN: 15732.7/60036.2	LAT 44° 08.350′ LON 076° 35.070′
DEPTH: 90 feet	LEVEL: Advanced

LOCATION: The wreck lies two miles off Nine Mile Point on Simcoe Island.

The elegant sidewheel steamer, *Comet* (174′8″ x 23′5″--or 45′ with sidewheels--x 10′), was built at Kingston in 1848, but sank 13 unlucky years later after a collision with the American schooner, *Exchange,* on May 15, 1861, with the loss of three lives. Kingston scuba divers located this shipwreck in October, 1967.

As with about 20 other shipwrecks in the Kingston area, the *Comet* is buoyed annually by a marine conservation group named Preserve Our Wrecks (P.O.W.). The vessel's bow and stern have collapsed, but her distinctive sidewheels are still intact and tower about 25′ off the lake bed. The rocker arms and walking beam are also clearly visible. Remnants of

Art courtesy of the Metropolitan Toronto Library.

her railing, doors and smokestacks can be seen along the east side, and portions of her farm implements cargo are scattered around the site. Experienced divers may penetrate below deck and study the ship's boiler. Beware of depth/ time limitations and of disturbing the silt.

Above: Exploring between paddle-wheel spokes. *Right:* The *Comet* sports tall, breathtaking structures, such as the engine and paddlewheels. *Below:* A pair of 1840's procelain doorknobs lie among the wreckage. PHOTOS BY CRIS KOHL.

13. GEORGE A. MARSH

LORAN: 15744.2/60034.8	LAT 44° 07.690' LON 076° 36.260'
DEPTH: 70 to 85 feet	LEVEL: Advanced

LOCATION: About three miles off Nine Mile Point, Simcoe island.

The three-masted schooner, *George A. Marsh* (135'x 27' x 9'3"), named after a Great Lakes lumber magnate when the ship was launched in 1882 at Muskegon, Michigan,

The schooner, *George A. Marsh*. GREAT LAKES MARINE COLLECTION OF THE MILWAUKEE PUBLIC LIBRARY/WISCONSIN MARINE HISTORICAL SOCIETY. The tragic loss of life made front page news in every Kingston area newspaper. One even published a photo of the mast portions seen above water. AUTHOR'S COLLECTION.

VOL. 53.   BELLEVILLE, O

TWELVE LIVES LOST WHEN SCHOONER SANK

SAD TRAGEDY ON LAKE ONTARIO

SCHOONER GEORGE A. MARSH, OF BELLEVILLE, FOUNDERED YESTERDAY THIRTY MILES FROM KINGSTON—LIFEBOAT CAPSIZED—TWELVE WERE DROWNED—ONLY TWO SURVIVORS—MARSH WAS OWNED IN BELLEVILLE AND WAS TAKING A CARGO OF COAL TO KINGSTON—SEVEN LITTLE CHILDREN AMONG THE VICTIMS.

(Special to The Intelligencer.)

KINGSTON, Aug. 9.—The Sewards Coal Company, of this Sy. has been officially notified of the sinking of the schooner George A. Marsh, of Belleville, between Nine Mile Point and Pidgeon Island, on Lake Ontario, yesterday morning. The Marsh had on 450 tons of coal from Oswego for the Sewards Company. There were fourteen people on board, and out of that number eleven were drowned and one died from

foundered in a furious storm with a cargo of coal from Oswego, New York, on August 8, 1917. Reportedly 12 of the 14 people on board drowned, including Captain Smith, his new wife, and five of his children from a previous marriage (although recent information indicates the captain may have secretly survived the sinking of the *George A. Marsh* and, in his grief and shame, fled to Nebraska to begin life anew).

The wreck sits deep in silt that is easily disturbed. Be aware that there are probably divers coming down the line not too far behind you, and they, too, will want to be impressed by this beautiful shipwreck site. Don't muck it up for them. Learn buoyancy control!

This shipwreck is almost 100% intact! Besides the many deadeyes, blocks

SAVE ONTARIO SHIPWRECKS

Transom Wheel Capstan Boiler Life boat Chain locker Windlass Bowsprit

Depth 80'

SOS Credit:
Research: Jeff Nelson
Drawing : Nick Baets

George A. Marsh
L 44° 7.55' N
Lo 76° 36.16' W

A diver is silhouetted with the *Marsh's* magnificent bowsprit, while another diver takes a close look at a pair of deadeyes along the port rail. *Below:* The ship's wheel is the focal point of any vessel. PHOTOS BY CRIS KOHL.

and belaying pins, there is the ship's wheel and a stove, complete with cooking utensils in place, on the deck. Also look at and appreciate the ship's rigging, lifeboat, bowsprit and pottery artifacts. It is easy to see why Kingston divers are proud and protective of this, and the other, shipwrecks. Charter boat operators, whose livelihood depends upon the continued integrity of these incredibly preserved shipwreck sites, will hand over to the police any diver who removes anything from any of the area's shipwrecks. In some cases, anyone caught desecrating these shipwreck sites by removing even so little as a nail would have a long swim back to shore -- before being tarred and feathered!

14. *CORNWALL*

LORAN: 15742.2/60028.5	LAT 44° 08.02' LON 076° 37.05'
DEPTH: 73 feet	LEVEL: Advanced

The wrecking tug, *Cornwall.* AUTHOR'S COLLECTION.

LOCATION: About seven miles west of Kingston, Ontario.

This iron-hulled sidewheeler, launched in 1855 at Montreal, worked for more than 70 years on the Great Lakes under a variety of names: *Kingston* (1855-1873), *Bavarian* (1873-1895), *Algerian* (1895-1906), and finally, *Cornwall* (1906-1928). The *Cornwall* (176'6" x 27'1" x 9'9") was a wrecking tug, outfitted with an A-frame derrick, clamshell outfit, steam pumps, air compressor and other equipment used in the salvage business. In 1928, the vessel had outlived its usefulness, and was towed to the ship graveyard off Amherst Island and dynamited.

The wreck sits upright in 73' of water. Her engine was removed before scuttling, but the two large boilers are in place, as are the ten-bladed, 20-foot-diameter paddlewheels. Scattered around the site are woodwork, a windlass, a ladder, barrels, pipes and tools.

The author thanks Josephine Donnelly Cole of Kingston for information which she mailed to him about the *Cornwall* (her family had owned it) and its discovery in 1989.

Artwork ©Adam Henley

Diver Doug Pettingill examines the secondary boiler mounted atop one of the larger ones on the scuttled tug, *Cornwall*. PHOTO BY CRIS KOHL.

15. *MAPLEGLEN*

LORAN:	LAT	LON
DEPTH: 78 feet	LEVEL: Advanced	

LOCATION: In the Amherst Island ships' graveyard, about seven miles west of Kingston.

The wooden package freighter, *Mapleglen* (241' x 39'9" x 14'6"), built in Buffalo, New York, in 1887 and launched as the *Wyoming,* had outlived her usefulness by 1920 and was sold inexpensively to Canadian interests, who renamed her *Mapleglen.* On June 19, 1925, the old and, by now, unreliable, ship was towed out into Lake Ontario and scuttled.

This vessel sits upright on a muddy bottom. The decking and hull have collapsed and are in great disarray, with frames, planking, hanging knees and other wood aiming in all directions. It is possible to explore under portions of the decking. The boilers and the four-bladed propeller are definitely the highlights. Bass, perch, burbot (ling cod) and American eels can be seen, particularly around the boilers. The intact bow area is worth viewing, but plan your bottom time well. This is a big wreck!

GREAT LAKES MARINE COLLECTION OF THE MILWAUKEE PUBLIC LIBRARY/WISCONSIN MARINE HISTORICAL SOCIETY.

A diver explores the upper portion of one of the *Mapleglen's* boilers. PHOTO BY CRIS KOHL.

Artwork ©Adam Henley

16. *GLENDORA*

LORAN:	LAT 44° 08′ 50″ LON 076° 37′ 00″
DEPTH: 75 feet	LEVEL: Advanced

LOCATION: In the ships' graveyard about seven miles west of Kingston.

The *Glendora* was one of several abandoned vessels scuttled off Amherst Island in 1925 by the Donnelly Wrecking Company. The ship was stripped of any useful machinery before she went to the ships' graveyard. All of her fittings and machinery, except for the 12′ high rudder and four-bladed propeller, were removed. The bow was extensively damaged in the scuttling. A couple of large holds allow easy access for divers to the below deck area. The stern rail, perfectly intact a few years ago, was torn apart in the late 1980's by anchors from visiting boats, a graphic example of the need for the type of permanent mooring lines set up by Preserve Our Wrecks (P.O.W.) just off most of the shipwrecks in the Kingston area. A dive light is necessary for exploring the holds. Try not to stir up the silt.

Artwork ©Adam Henley

17. SIMLA

LORAN: 15745.9/60046.1	LAT	LON
DEPTH: 90 feet	LEVEL: Advanced	

LOCATION: In the ships' graveyard about seven miles east of Kingston, Ontario.

The oak-hulled, propeller-driven bulk freighter, _Simla_ (225'6" x 34'8" x 15'), launched at Garden Island just off Kingston, Ontario, on May 9, 1903, was one of the last steamers built of wood on the Great Lakes. The ship sat idle at Kingston for years before finally burning and sinking in 1926. These sunken remains were raised and towed out into Lake Ontario to be scuttled on September 6, 1927. The large propeller is the most impressive part of this site. Take an underwater light along, as this location is frequently dark.

The _Simla_ was one of the last wooden steamers built on the Great Lakes. AUTHOR'S COLLECTION.

18. VARUNA

LORAN:	LAT	LON
DEPTH: 67 feet	LEVEL: Advanced	

LOCATION: In the ships' graveyard about seven miles west of Kingston, Ontario.

This small, 72-ton, steam-powered passenger and freight ferry was built in Picton, Ontario, in 1880 and, after more than 40 years of service, the old ship was scuttled off Amherst Island in the 1920's. Several hatches on this wreck offer divers huge entry points for shipwreck penetration, but with the amount of silt in the hold, this may not be advisable.

19. FRONTENAC

LORAN:	LAT 44° 01.128' LON 076° 36.164'
DEPTH: 100 to 115 feet	LEVEL: Advanced

LOCATION: The wreck lies to the west-northwest of Pigeon Island.

The wooden tugboat, _Frontenac_ (89' x 22'), launched at Garden Island immediately opposite the city of Kingston, Ontario, in 1901, was returning from a wrecking job on December 11, 1929, when she began taking on water. She sank within ten minutes, with her crew escaping to another tugboat just in time. Spencer Shoniker, acting on a fisherman's tip, located the _Frontenac_ in September, 1995.

This site offers many visual treats: porcelain plates, cups and saucers still sit in their boxes. The large four-bladed propeller and the rudder are still upright and in place. There are also the ship's anchors, a huge winch fully loaded with braided steel cable, fallen dorades, chain running down the bow, the ship's wheel and, at last report, the ship's compass. As with all Great Lakes shipwrecks, please leave every item in place for the next divers to see.

The tug, _Frontenac,_ in drydock. MARINE MUSEUM OF THE GREAT LAKES AT KINGSTON

The _Frontenac_ reportedly will be buoyed some time in 2001.

Exploring the *Frontenac* is a thrill a minute, which is a good thing because, at that depth, you don't have too many minutes. The tug's bow rises majestically from the lake bottom, while numerous items like wooden crates intrigue visiting divers. Braided steel cable is still coiled around the winch. PHOTOS BY CRIS KOHL.

20. CITY OF SHEBOYGAN

LORAN: 15805.2/60016.6	LAT 44° 04′ 56″ LON 076° 44′ 04″
DEPTH: 90 to 105 feet	LEVEL: Advanced

LOCATION: Southwest of Amherst Island, near Nut Island, west of Kingston.

The three-masted schooner, *City of Sheboygan* (135′2″ x 27′4″ x 10′), was launched at Sheboygan, Wisconsin, on July 5, 1871. The ship's career spanned almost 45 years on the Great Lakes until she foundered in a violent storm on September 25, 1915. Helpless fishermen on Amherst Island gazed in silent horror as the captain and the crew of four drowned. The wreck is deep, and hence well-preserved and mostly intact. The ship's wheel and an anchor are the only items that have been removed, and they are on exhibit at a local museum. Her masts, rigging and most other items, including deadeyes, are present. The depth, the cold and the dark (take along a light) are inhibiting factors at this site.

Left: City of Sheboygan. INSTITUTE FOR GREAT LAKES RESEARCH, BOWLING GREEN STATE UNIVERSITY, OHIO. *Right:* A diver approaches machinery and a mast rail on the *City of Sheboygan.* PHOTO BY MIKE WILLIAMS.

Artwork ©Adam Henley

21. SCUTTLED DEEP HULLS

LOCATION: In the Upper Gap off the northwest corner of Amherst Island.

At least two (and possibly three) scuttled hulls have been located in about 230′ of water in an oddly deep section of one of the relatively narrow passages between the islands and the mainland. These wrecks may be developed as an attraction for technical divers.

6. Point Traverse

Doug Pettingill and James Taylor head to a Point Traverse shipwreck site. PHOTO BY CRIS KOHL.

1. **Cabin cruiser & habitat**
2. *Echo*
3. *Banshee*
4. *Florence*
5. *Annie Falconer*
6. *Katie Eccles*
7. *China*
8. *Alberta*

9. *Fabiola*
10. *Manola*
11. *Olive Branch*
12. *Oliver Mowat*
13. *John Randall*
14. *Atlasco*
15. *R. H. Rae*
16. *Ocean Wave*

1. CABIN CRUISER AND HABITAT

LORAN: Shore dive	LAT	LON
DEPTH: To 30 feet	LEVEL: Novice-Intermediate	

LOCATION: Behind Ducks Dive Shop at Point Traverse.

The purposely sunk 30-foot-long wooden Owen cabin cruiser just offshore is usually marked with a buoy, as is the underwater habitat, which is the original "Sublimnos" built in the late 1960's by Dr. Joseph McGinnis for experiments in Georgian Bay near Tobermory.

Simply enter the water from the beach and surface swim to the left (northern) marker; this is the cabin cruiser, which sits upright and is intact and penetrable. You can certainly get to the underwater habitat from the surface, but you're good if you can do it underwater from the cabin cruiser. Both sites can easily be done on a single tank of air.

The underwater habitat.
PHOTOS BY CRIS KOHL.

2. *ECHO*

LORAN:	LAT 43° 56' 19" LON 076° 49' 54"
DEPTH: 22 feet	LEVEL: Novice-Intermediate

LOCATION: One-half mile off Gull Bar near False Duck Island.

This Canadian "fore-and-after" (meaning it was a two-masted schooner; a "three-and-after" was marine slang for a three-masted schooner) sank on October 11, 1861, with a load of barley. The entire crew was saved. This broken up shipwreck in shallow water was located on September 17, 1967 by members of the Quinte Aqua Divers of Belleville, Ontario.

3. *BANSHEE*

LORAN: 15904.2/60020.4	LAT 43° 56' 14" LON 076° 50' 04"
DEPTH: 18 feet	LEVEL: Novice-Intermediate

LOCATION: The wreck lies between Timber Island and the Duck Islands, not very far from the wreck of the *Echo*.

The 400-ton wooden propeller, *Banshee* (119' x 18' x 8'), carried a cargo of 6,000 bushels of wheat, 250 barrels of flour and 300 kegs of butter from Port Stanley on Lake Erie towards Montreal when she sank in a nefarious storm after her engine expired and she drifted into the shallow waters of Gull Shoal. One life was lost from the 18 that were on board. Members of the Quinte Aqua Divers of Belleville, Ontario, located these badly broken up shipwreck remains in late 1967.

4. *FLORENCE*

LORAN: 15892.7/60019.4	LAT 43° 57' 49" LON 076° 49' 00"
DEPTH: 40 to 50 feet	LEVEL: Novice-Intermediate

LOCATION: About 300 feet off Timber Island, off Point Traverse.

The wooden tugboat, *Florence* (91' x 19'8" x 9'), built at Levis, Quebec, in 1885, worked in Quebec, New Brunswick and the Windsor, Ontario, area before springing a leak and sinking at this site on November 14, 1933, with no loss of life. Salvage attempts moved the ship from her original depth of 80' to shallower water, and her engine and propeller were salvaged. The bow and boiler, plus a hatch ladder and several other items, are intact, but much of the vessel is broken up from the salvage efforts plus the shallow water conditions.

The tugboat, *Florence*, plied both fresh and salt waters for nearly half a century. GREAT LAKES MARINE COLLECTION OF THE MILWAUKEE PUBLIC LIBRARY/WISCONSIN MARINE HISTORICAL SOCIETY. A diver takes a close look at chain and the upper portion of the boiler on the *Florence*. PHOTO BY CRIS KOHL.

5. ANNIE FALCONER

LORAN: 15882.20/60015.06	LAT 45° 58′ 10″ LON 076° 48′ 28″
DEPTH: 67 to 78 feet	LEVEL: Intermediate-Advanced

LOCATION: The wreck lies 1.5 miles north of the False Duck Island lighthouse.

The two-masted schooner, *Annie Falconer* (108′ x 24′ x 9′), named after the first owner's wife who had died seven years before her namesake vessel was built, is one of the best and most popular shipwreck dives in the area. The vessel, built at Kingston and launched on May 22, 1867 (just a few weeks before Canada became a country!) foundered in a violent storm on November 12, 1904, with a cargo of soft coal. The crew of seven reached Amherst

The schooner, *Annie Falconer*, from a painting by Gibbons. Diver and marine historian/artist Pat Stayer approaches the precariously-perched port bow anchor to get a closer look at it; two weeks later, the anchor fell off the rail to the lake bottom. Pat claims she didn't do it. PHOTO BY CRIS KOHL.

Island in the ship's yawl boat "after hours of suffering and hardship" (*The Daily British Whig*, Kingston, November 14, 1904), but the first mate, James Sullivan, died of exposure shortly thereafter when he wandered away from the rest of the crew.

Barbara Carson, Audrey Rushbrook and Doug Pettingill located the wreck of the *Annie Falconer* in 1975. The wreck sits upright on a mud bottom, and is well-preserved, with deadeyes, anchors, blocks, chain and the ship's wheel in place. Her stern broke off, but it lies within visible range at an angle to the main hull. Limited shipwreck penetration is possible in the forward portion. There's lots to see at this incredible site!

The wheel is a ship's usual focal point, being examined here by diver, marine historian and shipwreck hunter Doug Pettingill. Many visiting divers have taken turns "steering the *Annie*." PHOTO BY CRIS KOHL.

6. KATIE ECCLES

LORAN: 15843.18/60028.99	LAT	LON
DEPTH: 102 feet	LEVEL: Advanced	

LOCATION: The wreck lies to the northeast of Timber Island. The small, graceful 122-ton schooner, *Katie Eccles* (95' x 24'6" x 9'6"), was built in 1877 by William Jamieson (see pages 56-57) at Mill Point (now Deseronto), Ontario. On November 26, 1922, the ship left Oswego, New York, with 300 tons of hard coal and made it to Timber Island without her rudder, which she had lost outside Oswego. After dropping anchor, the crew rowed to Timber Island, but that night, the anchor chain cut through the vessel's planking, and she foundered in deep water. The wreck is upright and intact.

The gaff-rigged schooner, *Katie Eccles*. GREAT LAKES MARINE COLLECTION OF THE MILWAUKEE PUBLIC LIBRARY/WISCONSIN MARINE HISTORICAL SOCIETY.

7. CHINA

LORAN:	LAT 43° 58.331' LON 076° 46.342'
DEPTH: 104 feet	LEVEL: Advanced

LOCATION: The wreck lies northeast of False Duck Island.

The propeller-driven steamer, *China*, was accidentally located in the 1970's by divers seeking the schooner, *Annie Falconer* (see pages 68-69). This is a badly-burned, quiet wreck sitting in deep, dark waters. This 130-foot-long, 333-ton ship burned to a complete loss in October, 1872, the same year she was launched at Kingston. She carried a load of pig iron and general merchandise, and her explorable remains include a steeple compound engine, a boiler, and a four-bladed propeller. Take a dive light along, as it gets dark down there.

8. ALBERTA

LORAN: 15828.6/59974.6	LAT 44° 05.822' LON 076° 53.054'
DEPTH: 106 feet	LEVEL: Advanced

LOCATION: This wreck lies opposite Prinyer's Cove, east of Picton, Ontario.

The flat barge, *Alberta* (not to be confused with the wooden steamer, *Alberta,* which burned to a complete loss at nearby Trenton, Ontario, on October 8, 1902) was a 62-ton, 65-foot-long paddlewheeler built at Deseronto, Ontario, in 1888. She sank on July 21, 1899.

This flat barge-type boat with a single paddlewheel in the middle of it lies upside-down. The bay waters here are quite dark, so take along a dive light and do your dive only if you feel secure about it. This is a deep dive, so watch your depth and time.

9. FABIOLA

LORAN: 15889.8/60031.3	LAT 43° 56' 52" LON 076° 47' 38"
DEPTH: 55 feet	LEVEL: Novice-Intermediate

Doug Pettingill explores the bow of the *Fabiola* and later stops at a local museum to see the ship's wheel. Bass are often found on Great Lakes shipwrecks; notice the freshwater sponges growing on the *Fabiola's* railing in the background. PHOTOS BY CRIS KOHL.

LOCATION: Off the southeast corner of False Duck Island.

The two-masted schooner, *Fabiola* (95' x 22'4" x 9'), was launched at Oakville, Ontario, under the name *Red Oak* in 1852 (her name was changed to *Fabiola* in 1876). She was an old, twice-rebuilt vessel when she was lost on October 23, 1900, while downbound from Oswego, New York, with a cargo of coal. The bow, with its windlass and capstan, is quite intact, but the stern has collapsed. This is usually a relaxing dive in good visibility, a sandy bottom, and no current.

10. MANOLA

> LORAN: 15907.5/60046.7   LAT   LON
> DEPTH: 45 to 82 feet   LEVEL: Intermediate-Advanced

LOCATION: Southeast off False Duck Island, eastern Lake Ontario.

The large steel freighter, *Manola*. GREAT LAKES MARINE COLLECTION OF THE MILWAUKEE PUBLIC LIBRARY/WISCONSIN MARINE HISTORICAL SOCIETY.

The wreck's co-discoverer, Doug Pettingill, approaches the *Manola's* port anchor. PHOTO BY CRIS KOHL.

The steel steamer, *Manola* (282'4" x 40'3" x 21'2"), launched on January 21, 1890 at Cleveland, Ohio, was needed for overseas service during World War I. However, to get such a long ship out of the upper Great Lakes through the Welland Canal required cutting her in half. The stern half was towed safely across Lake Ontario, while the bow half sank during a snowstorm on December 3, 1918, taking the lives of all 11 men who were on her. Ironically, World War I had just ended, and the ship was no longer needed to win the war.

The wreck was located in 1976 by Barbara Carson and Doug Pettingill. Diving on this enormous bow half of a ship is exhilarating, even though it lies upside-down. Both bow anchors hang down impressively, while a spare anchor can be seen below the wreck. Brass portholes are situated along the bottom portion of the vessel. The wooden bulkhead where the ship was torched in two is of interest. A variety of pulleys and other marine parts litter the lake bottom. Penetration is possible, but confusing due to the upside-down nature of the wreck and the many corridors; this should be left to the trained and prepared experts!

The orphaned stern half was given a new bow half and renamed the *Mapledawn*, which sank in Lake Huron five years later (that story and site description are also in this book).

11. OLIVE BRANCH

> LORAN: 15885.11/60047.79   LAT 43° 55' 00" LON 076° 44' 37"
> DEPTH: 90 to 101 feet   LEVEL: Advanced

The *Olive Branch's* wheel. PHOTO BY CRIS KOHL.

LOCATION: Southeast off False Duck Island.

The small schooner, *Olive Branch* (92' x 22' x 8'), sank in a storm on September 30, 1880, with the loss of all five people on board. The uninsured ship (her insurance had expired just two weeks earlier!) had been constructed in 1871 in nearby Picton, Ontario. The wreck is intact, resting upright at the base of a shoal down which she seems to have slid (the original account put the wreck in 70' of water, but she now sits in about 100'). Most of her original equipment remains on board, including a windlass, deadeyes, blocks, a standing

The schooner, *Olive Branch*

capstan, a pump, hinged catheads (the starboard one holds a steel-stock fluke anchor), a Quebec stove, a fallen mast with wire rigging, a collapsed bowsprit, and the ship's wheel. The depth and occasional low visibility can make this a challenging dive.

Artwork ©Adam Henley

The schooner, *Oliver Mowat*. INSTITUTE FOR GREAT LAKES RESEARCH, BOWLING GREEN STATE UNIVERSITY, OHIO.

12. OLIVER MOWAT

LORAN:	LAT 43° 55′ 40″ LON 076° 44′ 05″
DEPTH: 105 feet	LEVEL: Advanced

LOCATION: To the southeast of False Duck Island.

The 295-ton schooner, *Oliver Mowat* (116′ x 23′8″ x 9′8″), sank after the steel freighter, *Keywest,* struck it midship on September 1, 1921, with the loss of three of the five lives on board the schooner. The *Oliver Mowat* had been built in 1873 at Mill Haven, near Kingston. Her masts were dynamited, as they presented a menace to navigation. This wreck was located in the early 1960's and many of her artifacts were removed by divers, as was the accepted practice in those early days. The damage which sank her can clearly be seen on her hull.

13. JOHN RANDALL

LORAN:	LAT	LON
DEPTH: 20 feet	LEVEL: Novice-Intermediate	

LOCATION: This shipwreck lies in School House Bay at Main Duck Island.

The wooden steamer, *John Randall* (104′4″ x 22′5″ x 7′7″), built in Kingston in 1905, encountered a severe storm on November 16, 1920, while hauling a cargo of coal from Oswego, New York, towards Belleville, Ontario. Captain Harry Randall (John was his father) steered his ship towards shelter at School House Bay at Main Duck Island, where the vessel sank. The entire crew safely reached the island and stayed as guests of the lighthouse keeper for nine days before word of their survival reached the outside world. A year

The steamer, *John Randall*. AUTHOR'S COLLECTION.

later, Capt. Harry Randall perished when the ill-fated steamer, *City of New York,* sank on Lake Ontario with all eight hands.

The *John Randall* lies broken and scattered around the waters of the bay, and is an excellent site for novice scuba divers and for snorkelers.

Left: School House Bay at Main Duck Island is shallow enough to be snorkeled. *Above:* Jim Stayer videotapes the remains of the *John Randall.* PHOTOS BY CRIS KOHL.

14. *ATLASCO*

LORAN: 15968.0/59996.9	LAT 43° 52.76′ LON 076° 58.90′
DEPTH: 43 feet	LEVEL: Intermediate

LOCATION: South of Ostrander Point, near Point Traverse, eastern Lake Ontario.

The wooden steamer, *Atlasco* (218′5″ x 32′8″ x 13′4″), launched as the *Russell Sage* on May 21, 1881, at Buffalo, New York, sank in a violent storm on August 7, 1921. No lives were lost, but her cohort, the schooner-barge, *Condor,* was also destroyed (her remains lie along the shoreline).

On a tip from commercial fisherman Doug Harrison in the summer of 1990, Doug Pettingill was the first diver to see the wreck of the *Atlasco,* initially called "the wire wreck" because of her cargo, until her identity was established. Items to see here include the "valley of wire," the huge coils that lay rusting in the forward half of the vessel, four (!) anchors, a winch, bollards, rudder and ship's wheel.

GREAT LAKES MARINE COLLECTION OF THE MILWAUKEE PUBLIC LIBRARY/WISCONSIN MARINE HISTORICAL SOCIETY.

Above: Doug Pettingill peers through the spokes of the *Atlasco's* wheel. *Left:* Commercial diver James Taylor glides through the "valley of wire." PHOTOS BY CRIS KOHL.

Site Drawing of the *Atlasco*

ship's wheel
rudder
salvage mooring block
chain
boards
hanging knees
small anchor
coils of wire (cargo)
hanging knees
rail
winch
chain
Depth: 43' (12.9 metres)
large anchor leaning on bollards
anchor with end up through wreck
davit
large anchor

Drawing by Cris Kohl, based on on-site observations and information from Doug Pettingill.

15. *R. H. RAE*

LORAN: 15932.2/60032.8	LAT 45° 53.136' LON 076° 50.340'
DEPTH: 105 feet	LEVEL: Advanced

LOCATION: South of Point Traverse, eastern Lake Ontario.

Marcy McElmon views the *R.H. Rae's* unusual bilge pump pipes. PHOTO BY CRIS KOHL.

The 137-foot-long, three-masted bark, *R.H. Rae*, built in St. Catharines, Ontario (then Canada West) in 1857, capsized and sank during a white squall on August 4, 1858, during her first full season afloat, with the crew barely escaping with their lives. Located by Barbara Carson in 1976, the *R.H. Rae* was offered for exploration to the 1980 Jacques Cousteau expedition, the only time they ever visited the Great Lakes. They recovered many artifacts, including the ship's wheel, all of which are presently held at the marine museum in Kingston. Unfortunately, the Cousteau expedition also lost a diver at this site. The wreck location returned to secrecy, known but to a few divers unwilling to "open" this site. The wreck was relocated by a group of Great Lakes divers (including the author) on July 25, 1996, and opened to the diving public.

The wreck's huge, wooden rudder rests on a twisted angle, and most of the ship's decking has collapsed, except at the bow. Interesting items include an ornately-carved bow stem, a large windlass, copper cappings on the bow, samson and windlass posts, a pump, a deck winch, blocks, deadeyes, and an 1857 toilet.

16. *OCEAN WAVE*

LORAN:	LAT 43° 50.753' LON 076° 54.139'
DEPTH: 153 feet	LEVEL: Technical

The paddlewheel steamer, *Ocean Wave* (174'2" x 26' x 11'6"), built in Montreal in 1852, burned and sank with great loss of life (28) on April 30, 1853. The wreck lies upside-down in deep, dark, usually silty water. Her engine stands upright almost half a mile from the hull. Barbara Carson and Doug Pettingill found this deep wreck in 1991.

7. Other Lake Ontario Sites

Hundreds of divers take part in the Treasure Hunt at Presqu'ile Provincial Park near Trenton, Ontario, every June. PHOTO BY CRIS KOHL.

1. *Belle Sheridan*
2. *Ida Walker*
3. *John A. MacDonald*
4. *Juno*
5. *Alexandria*
6. *Lyman M. Davis*
7. *Julia B. Merrill*
8. *Sligo*
9. *Hamilton* **and** *Scourge*
10. *Henry Clay (?)*
11. *St. Peter*
12. *Laura Grace*
13. *David W. Mills*
14. *Mary Kay*
15. *Cormorant*

1. BELLE SHERIDAN

LORAN:	LAT	LON
DEPTH: 12 feet	LEVEL: Novice	

LOCATION: Outside Weller's Bay, near Beecroft Point, south of Trenton, Ontario.

WHERE THE "BELLE SHERIDAN" POUNDED TO PIECES

The Toronto Telegram, November 7, 1928.

A captain and three of his four sons perished when the two-masted schooner, *Belle Sheridan* (123′ x 22′8″ x 10′2″), grounded during the Great Gale of November, 1880, while running a load of coal to Toronto. Captain McSherry and his sons, John (21), Thomas (17) and Edward (13), plus two other crewmembers, died 100 yards from shore while their ship was pounded to pieces. The sole survivor was the captain's 18-year-old son, James, who clung tightly to a timber, jumped into the raging waters, and swam madly, finally reaching shore more dead than alive. This schooner was built in Oswego, New York, in 1852. In 1933, portions of the *Belle Sheridan's* deck and ribbing were raised and returned to Toronto. This wreck lies badly broken up and scattered, with portions of it buried in the sandy bottom.

2. IDA WALKER

LORAN:	LAT 44° 00′ 57″ LON 077° 36′ 22″
DEPTH: 10 to 12 feet	LEVEL: Novice

LOCATION: At the mouth of Weller's Bay, near Presqu'ile Point, Ontario.

The two-masted schooner, *Ida Walker,* sought storm shelter on November 19, 1886, while loading at the nearby unprotected port of Wellington. The sweeping seas forced her, half-loaded with barley and dragging her anchor, onto the shoal at the mouth of Weller's Bay. The Wellington lifesaving station rescued the entire crew before the vessel broke up.

Today, the wreck lies broken and scattered and partially buried in the sandy bottom at a depth of about 12′ of water. Caution: boating traffic can be heavy here during summer.

3. JOHN A. MACDONALD

LORAN:	LAT 44° 00′ 36″ LON 077° 40′ 30″
DEPTH: 6 to 8 feet	LEVEL: Novice

LOCATION: Off the east shore, at the mouth of Presqu'ile Bay, Ontario.

Launched as the *John A. Torrance* in 1841 at Burlington, Ontario, the two-masted schooner, *John A. MacDonald* (112′ x 19′9″ x 9′), received her name change in 1860. On November 17, 1872, while enroute from Hamilton to Kingston with a coal cargo, she began to leak badly and was run ashore at the mouth of Presqu'ile Bay, where she broke up with no loss of life. While most of this wreck is broken up and buried in the sand, decking, with its planking and spikes, is visible. Use a dive flag; boating traffic can get heavy.

4. JUNO

LORAN:	LAT 43° 53′ 01″ LON 078° 80′ 02″
DEPTH: 6 to 12 feet	LEVEL: Novice

LOCATION: Just off shore, south of Bowmanville, Ontario.

Built in Wallaceburg, Ontario, in 1885, the oak-hulled propeller, *Juno* (139′7″ x 26′8″ x 8′8″) was stripped of her machinery in 1914 and used as a breakwall and loading pier for a shoreline quarry. A few years later, her commercial use ended when her hull broke up..

Lying about 200′ from shore, the wreck site is 42 miles east of Toronto, south of Highway 401, near Waverly Road. The site is usually marked with jugs early in the season. The badly broken up bow, with a half-buried windlass, rests in the shallows; the slightly deeper stern offers the 8′ upright propeller. The wreck sits on a hard sand bottom in a current-free location. Use a dive flag, as passing boaters can pose a problem.

5. ALEXANDRIA

LORAN:	LAT	LON
DEPTH: 5 to 10 feet	LEVEL: Intermediate	

LOCATION: Below the Scarborough Bluffs, off Markham Road, in suburban Toronto.

WARNING: Divers require permission from the Metropolitan Toronto Police Marine Unit to dive this area, and they must sign liability release forms.

The sidewheel steamer, *Alexandria* (161′7″ x 25′2″ x 8′1″), built in Montreal in 1866, stranded during severe weather on August 3, 1915 and broke up with no loss of life. Locals quickly picked this shallow shipwreck clean. The boiler remains visible

The wrecked *Alexandria*.
AUTHOR'S COLLECTION.

from the surface, and bits and pieces of wreckage lie scattered widely. The usually poor visibility and the busy boating traffic make this site unpopular among scuba divers.

6. *LYMAN M. DAVIS*

LORAN:	LAT 43° 36.165' LON 079° 24.973'
DEPTH: 148 feet	LEVEL: Technical

LOCATION: Off Toronto.

The ship, *Lyman M. Davis* (123' x 27'2" x 9'4"), built in Muskegon, Michigan in 1873, was one of the last working schooners on the Great Lakes. However, she was a remnant of a bygone era in an unappreciative time, so she was sacrificed for the mindless entertainment of the masses in a flaming spectacle off Toronto's Sunnyside Park on June 29, 1934. Her charred hull lies half buried in the lake's soft bottom in deep water notorious for poor visibility.

7. *JULIA B. MERRILL*

LORAN:	LAT 43° 37.054' LON 079° 26.801'
DEPTH: 60 feet	LEVEL: Intermediate-Advanced

LOCATION: Off Toronto, near the mouth of the Humber River.

A mob's fondness for Viking-funeral-style spectacle doomed the classic schooner, *Julia B. Merrill* (125'5" x 26'5" x 8'2"), to be purposely engulfed by flames at Sunnyside Park in Toronto in July, 1931. Built in 1872 at Wenona, Michigan, the ship had maintained her original purpose of working under sail right up to the time of her demise.

The superstructure of this wreck is totally burned away, but her keel, rudder and posts are intact. Again, this is a silty area of poor visibility. Metropolitan Toronto Police Marine Unit permission/signed waiver are required to dive this site.

The *Julia B. Merrill*.
AUTHOR'S COLLECTION

8. SLIGO

LORAN:	LAT 45° 45.454′ LON 075° 45.454′
DEPTH: 67 feet	LEVEL: Advanced

LOCATION: Off Toronto, near the mouth of the Humber River.

Launched as the three-masted bark, *Prince of Wales,* in 1860 at St. Catharines, Ontario, and rebuilt as a schooner renamed the *Sligo* (138′ x 23′ x 11′8″) in 1874, this ship worked on the Great Lakes for many years, mainly as a schooner-barge. But a fierce gale parted her towline on September 5, 1918, and she foundered with her 90 tons of limestone cargo. Located by Toronto diver Don MacIntyre in the early 1980's, this wreck features an anchor, a windlass, and her wheel. The site is usually buoyed. Unfortunately, this is an area of low visibility. Use caution when diving here. Metropolitan Toronto Police Marine Unit permission and waiver are needed to dive here.

The schooner-barge *Sligo,* made an impressive, elegant sight in Kincardine, Ontario, harbor in the late 1800's. AUTHOR'S COLLECTION.

Artwork ©Adam Henley

9. HAMILTON AND SCOURGE

LORAN:	LAT LON: On the Internet
DEPTH: 275 to 289 feet	LEVEL: Technical

LOCATION: Off St. Catharines, Ontario, in Canadian waters of Lake Ontario.

The two vintage schooners, *Hamilton* (built in Oswego, New York, in 1809 as the 112-ton *Diana*) and *Scourge* (built at Fort George, Ontario, in 1811 as the 110-ton *Lord Nelson*) are extremely historic, War of 1812, figureheaded shipwrecks laden with cannons, swords and human remains. Both ships were caught in a squall and sank on August 8, 1813, with 53 of their 72 sailors perishing. Well-known technical diver Gary Gentile is presently fighting a costly court battle against the province of Ontario for divers' rights to explore these wrecks (which, reportedly, half a dozen technical divers have done already illegally). Stay tuned!

10. HENRY CLAY (?)

LORAN:	LAT	LON
DEPTH: 118 feet	LEVEL: Advanced	

LOCATION: Off Port Dalhousie, Ontario.

Located by Canadian diver Jim Garrington and first explored by him in 1996, this small but significant, unidentified schooner appears to be of considerably early vintage. It could possibly be the (then) new Oswego schooner, *Henry Clay,* which sank after capsizing in a gale on July 19, 1831, during its first season.

11. ST. PETER

LORAN:	LAT 43° 18.321′ LON 077° 07.707′
DEPTH: 98 to 120 feet	LEVEL: Advanced

LOCATION: Five miles northwest of Sodus, New York.

This three-masted schooner (135′7″ x 26′ x 12′1″), launched in Toledo, Ohio, on Saturday, May 24, 1873, foundered on October 27, 1898, with a load of coal plus six of the seven people who were on board. The ship's master, Captain Griffin, clinging to a spar, was rescued by the tug, *Proctor.*

The wreck of the *St. Peter* was located in 1971 by Robert Bristol and his team of divers. Sitting upright and impressively intact, and rising a fair

MPL/WMHS

distance off the lake bottom, this schooner offers visiting divers views of a winch and pump sitting on the bow, both anchor catheads still in place, deadeyes lining the railings, and much more.

12. LAURA GRACE

LORAN:	LAT 43° 17.570′ LON 077° 40.200′
DEPTH: 15 feet	LEVEL: Novice

LOCATION: Just west of Oswego, New York.

The Laura Grace was a steam-powered, wooden tugboat which sank in Lake Ontario close to shore in 1920. The site is directly off Long Pond Road, but a boat is required because all of the shoreline is private residences. Sitting on a soft, sandy lake bottom are some of the site's highlights: the winch, anchor chain, boiler, rudder and propeller. Boaters use caution: the boiler sits within four feet of the surface.

13. DAVID W. MILLS

LORAN:	LAT 43° 26.360′ LON 076° 35.450′
DEPTH: 25 feet	LEVEL: Novice

LOCATION: On Ford Shoal about 3.5 miles west-southwest of Oswego, New York.

The wooden steamer, *David W. Mills* (220′ x 34′ x 15′), stranded on August 11, 1919, because of smoke from forest fires in Canada disorienting the navigator. The ship, built in Cleveland in 1874 as the *Sparta*, broke up in later storms. The wreck lies broken and scattered.

14. MARY KAY

LORAN: 16094.77/28669/81	LAT 43° 27.705′ LON 076° 33.198′
DEPTH: 42 feet	LEVEL: Novice-Intermediate

This 1957, 55-foot-long tug foundered on September 21, 1988, just west of Oswego, NY, with no loss of life. It is in excellent condition considering how shallow it sits.

15. CORMORANT

LORAN:	LAT LON
DEPTH: 135 feet	LEVEL: Advanced-Technical

This tug sank five miles north of Oswego, NY, on October 17, 1958, and remains very much intact, complete with a spotlight, a penetrable engine room, and the ship's wheel.

8. Sites near Lake Ontario

1. *Minnie*
2. *Otter*
3. The Mint site
4. *Ivy*
5. *Bruce*
6. *William King*
7. *Mansfield*
8. *Resolute*
9. *Quinte Queen*
10. Braeside: Sand Point lighthouse
11. Calabogie
12. *Mayflower*
13. Mazinaw Lake's highway signs
14. Bon Echo Provincial Park
15. Marmora's Crowe River
16. Kirkfield Quarry
17. Seneca Lake State Park
18. Coal Barge in Seneca Lake
19. Keuka Lake: Tanglewood barge

PHOTO AT LEFT: The long-running **Peterborough Ice Floe Race** each March in Peterborough, Ontario, grandstands imaginative, unique, colorful, absurd and eccentric participants and inventions, all used to propel a block of ice down a fast-moving river in the quickest time. This non-scuba-diving event for divers offers competition, camaraderie and individuality, as bag-piping Todd Shannon attests while he musically encourages his wild team to victory. PHOTO BY CRIS KOHL.

1. *MINNIE*

LOCATION: The Ottawa River, below Parliament Hill, just off the western end of Stirling's Wharf (also called the Ottawa Locks Wharfage). The 109-gross-ton rectangular barge, *Minnie* (95'5" long), constructed in 1873, sprang a leak and sank in 22' of water in 1930 next to the *Otter*. Beware of low visibility and boating traffic.

2. *OTTER*

LOCATION: The Ottawa River, below Parliament Hill, just off the western end of Stirling's Wharf (also called the Ottawa Locks Wharfage). On November 5, 1870, the 99-gross-ton tug, *Otter* (102'5" x 23'5"), built in 1840, burned to the waterline and sank in 22' of water while her captain socialized (i.e. drank) at the lockmaster's house. Beware of low visibility and boating traffic.

3. THE MINT SITE

LOCATION: The Ottawa River, in downtown Ottawa, just behind and a bit downstream from the Royal Canadian mint. Head out of Ottawa on Sussex Drive. Just past the mint, turn left at the first set of lights. This is Lady Grey Drive. From the parking lot just off Sussex, when you are facing the river, turn left down a short, rough road, or park in the lot and carry your gear down.

This intermediate-advanced shore dive will take the diver from 0' to 60' in the dark,

Divers return from a dusk dive at the Ottawa River's mint site. PHOTO BY CRIS KOHL.

tea-colored (take a dive light with you) waters along the river drop-off. Beware of some current and boating traffic. Use a divers down flag. In spite of this site's proximity to the place where Canada's money is made, it is not likely that you will find any here. Instead, you'll see old bottles, perhaps a clay pipe or two, lots of sunken logs and trees, and, if you're lucky, the 7-foot-long sturgeon which resembles a log -- until he swims away! His name is Oliver. Don't hurt him.

4. *Ivy*

LOCATION: The Ottawa River, at the southeastern end of Hull Wharf at Hull. This is an intermediate-advanced dive in 18′ to 22′ of water in usually poor visibility (1′ to 3′). The 100′-long sidewheeler, *Ivy*, built in 1871, exploded on September 21, 1890, while at dock.

5. *Bruce*

LOCATION: From the mint site, drive downstream along that road off Lady Grey Drive to the Rideau Rowing Club. The 87-ton, 100-long wooden paddlewheel steamer, *Bruce*, built at Goderich, Ontario, in 1862, mysteriously burned to the waterline in March of 1875 and sank in 20 to 30 of water at the foot of the Rideau Canal Locks close to shore. This is an intermediate-advanced dive. Sometimes a rope is tied between the dock and the wreck to help overcome the low visibility. Boating traffic can be heavy, beware of entanglement in old fishing line (carry a knife or two), and there is a bit of a current (about one-and-a-half knots) which is usually no problem.

6. *William King*

LOCATION: The Ottawa River, next to the site of the *Bruce*. This is an advanced dive to 45′ of water about 35′ from shore in usually zero visibility. Launched as the *William Annesty* in Montreal in 1826, this 95′-long sidewheeler was abandoned in 1841.

7. *Mansfield*

LOCATION: The Ottawa River, near the Prime Minister's wharf. This is an intermediate-advanced dive to 25′ of depth about 80′ from shore in usually poor visibility. The steam-powered ferry, *Mansfield*, operated between Ottawa and Gatineau Point from 1888 to 1896 when, on May 7, she caught fire and burned to a complete loss with no lives lost.

8. *Resolute*

LOCATION: Rockcliffe Point at the northeastern end of Governor's Bay. This is an intermediate-advanced dive to 35′ of water about 50′ from shore in very limited visibility. This small (54′ long) propeller-driven steam tug, built in 1875, caught fire on the evening of July 29, 1890 and was cast adrift to save the dock from damage. Beware of boating traffic.

9. *QUINTE QUEEN*

LOCATION: The Ottawa River, southwest end of Kettle Island. This is an intermediate-advanced dive in 20′ of poor visibility water about 260′ from shore. Built in 1902 and launched as the *Salaberry* in Valleyfield, Quebec, the *Quinte Queen* ran as a pleasure ferry carrying picnickers to and from Kettle Island. In about 1920, the ship struck a sandbar and sank at its present location.

10. BRAESIDE: SAND POINT LIGHTHOUSE

LOCATION: About 40 miles west of Ottawa along the Ottawa River. This is an intermediate level shore dive to 60 of dark water (take along a dive light). The old cross-river ferry ran from here, and the light-house's base is the old 1910 wharf. About 300′ downstream are the submerged remains of an older wharf which runs out from shore. Old bottles have been found here. Some current, plus boating and fishing traffic, exist.

11. CALABOGIE

LOCATION: The town of Calabogie is about 50 miles west of Ottawa. From town, follow signs to Black Donald Lake. This unusual divesite is the foundations of a small town (once the site of Ontario's richest graphite deposit) which was flooded by Ontario Hydro in 1967. This is an intermediate dive to 30′. An old Packard and plenty of snails can also be seen here, but stay out of the old mineshaft nearby. Respect the rights of adjacent homeowners. Nearby Green Lake offers intermediate rock wall dives to a depth of 50′ with plenty of smallmouth bass, perch, lake trout, sunfish and pike and usually good visibility.

12. *MAYFLOWER*

LOCATION: Lake Kamaniskeg, near Barry's Bay, Ontario. This wreck lies about 500′ off the eastern shore of the lake, with a public boat launch at Combermere. A compass bearing of 040 degrees magnetic to the southern end of Mayflower Island and a bearing of 135 degrees magnetic to Sand Beach will pinpoint the wreck site. The depth of this novice-intermediate dive is about 20′.

The wooden steamer, *Mayflower* (77′ x 18′ x 4′), sank in a storm on November 12, 1912, while underway from Barry's Bay to Combermere with 12 people and a corpse in a coffin . The floating coffin saved three people, but the other nine died. On the lake's sandy bottom, the *Mayflower's* hull, boiler, engine and paddlewheel, as well as resident bass and sunfish, may be seen. Save Ontario Shipwrecks has surveyed and placed a plaque on this wreck. Use a dive flag and respect the rights of cottage owners when diving here.

Artwork ©Adam Henley

The 59-ton sternwheeler, *Mayflower*, was built at Combermere in 1904. PUBLIC ARCHIVES OF CANADA.

13. MAZINAW LAKE'S HIGHWAY SIGNS

LOCATION: Exactly 2.2 miles north of the Bon Echo Provincial Park entrance, turn right (east) on the Mazinaw Heights North Road (just before Bon Echo Villa). Drive for 1.1 miles and park along the roadway just before the public boat ramp. This novice-intermediate shore dive will take you to 50′ and beyond in tea-colored water. Between 20′ and 40′, you will find dozens of old, dumped Ministry of Transportation "King's Highway" signs indicating the highway number, curves and speed limits (don't swim too fast!). The water is dark and beware of submerged trees.

14. BON ECHO PROVINCIAL PARK

LOCATION: About 70 miles northwest of Kingston and about 100 miles from Ottawa. This intermediate-advanced shore or boat (preferred) dive offers variable depth along the best wall dive in Ontario. In this park, drive to the large parking lot at the Visitor

Some of the old highway signs in Mazinaw Lake. PHOTO BY CRIS KOHL.

Centre. From here, it is a brief hike to "The Narrows," a popular area for diving. Sometimes the local pontoon boat ferry is hired to take scuba divers to the cliff face to the northwest of "The Narrows." Cascading rocks and jagged cliffs slope down the rock face to a depth of about 50′. Beyond that is a sheer, straight wall plunging into the black abyss (the lake is 473′ deep!). There is considerable fish life here. Above water, impressive cliffs rise 373′ above the lake. Bring your camera.

Mazinaw Lake cliffs, Bon Echo Provincial Park, at sunset. PHOTO BY CRIS KOHL.

15. MARMORA'S CROWE RIVER

LOCATION: At the town of Marmora, 28 miles north of Trenton, Ontario. Dive below the dam near the "Marmora Ironworks" historic marker to the west of town. Besides tea-colored water to a depth of 30′, the novice-intermediate diver can see bass, lots of crayfish, bottles, cans and submerged trees. Beware of these trees and seasonal strong currents.

16. KIRKFIELD QUARRY

LOCATION: Northeast of Toronto, just to the east of Lake Simcoe. The popular Kirkfield Quarry contains the usual quarry formations, rocks and sunfish. Depth is variable.

17. SENECA LAKE STATE PARK

LOCATION: About 42 miles east-southeast of Rochester, New York. Highlights include good bottle diving and easy entrance and exit shoreline for novice-intermediate scuba divers and a depth of 15′, but avoid the swim area.

18. COAL BARGE IN SENECA LAKE

LOCATION: Off the center west side of Seneca Lake, at Severn Point at the end of Severn Road. This large coal barge lies in 70′ of water, and a boat is necessary as it is illegal to dive from the New York state boat launch.

19. KEUKA LAKE: TANGLEWOOD BARGE

LOCATION: On the east side of southern Keuka Lake, 40 miles southwest of Rochester, NY. A boat is needed to reach the Tanglewood Barge in 20′ to 65′ off 431 East Lake Road.

9. Eastern Lake Erie

1. *Barge 43*
2. *Alabama*
3. *W. C. Richardson*
4. *Acme* (tug)
5. *Finch*
6. *Tonawanda*
7. *O. W. Cheney*
8. *Briton*
9. *Dacotah*
10. *Raleigh*
11. *Marengo*
12. *C. B. Benson*
13. *J. G. McGrath*
14. *Brunswick*
15. *Annabell Wilson*
16. Canadaway Creek
17. *Passaic*
18. *Washington Irving*
19. *Acme* (propeller)
20. *Carlingford*

1. BARGE 43

> **LORAN: 44933.28/59237.85**   **LAT 42° 52.435′ LON 078°54.098′**
> **DEPTH: 30 feet**   **LEVEL: Intermediate**

LOCATION: About one-quarter of a mile off Buffalo, New York, at the east harbor entrance just inside the western breakwater.

The old, beamy, steel *Barge 43* (150′ x 36′ x 12′1″), built at Manitowoc, Wisconsin, in 1911, sprang a leak 50 years later on May 24, 1961, while being used as a floating wood-burner when Buffalo's north harbor entrance was relocated and all the ancient wooden cribs were yanked up and had to be disposed of somehow. The sinking barge was moved from her workplace to her present location. She sits upright and shallow, with much boating traffic and fish life, as well as occasional current. For trained and experienced wreck penetration divers, there are several openings on the deck offering access below.

2. ALABAMA

> **LORAN:**   **LAT 42° 52.399′ LON 078° 54.720′**
> **DEPTH: 35 feet**   **LEVEL: Intermediate**

LOCATION: About 3/4 of a mile off Buffalo, New York, north harbor entrance.

The very old, 799-ton, wooden sidewheel steamer, *Alabama* (234′ x 29′ x 12′), was built, apparently poorly, at Detroit in 1848 and sank in a waterlogged condition only six years later on August 29, 1854. Realizing that the ship needed a major overhaul, and being told that the Buffalo drydock could not be tied up for that long, the *Alabama's* owners tried to take her to another drydock (at Huron, Ohio), but did not get very far. Arranging salvage took too long, and within a week, parts of the ship floated down the Niagara River. The engine was ultimately salvaged from the site in 1855.

The wreck is broken up and scattered in a busy boating area, with the identifiable portions including iron paddlewheel parts, the keel and a capstan.

3. W. C. RICHARDSON

> **LORAN: 44923.18/59228.87**   **LAT 45° 45.454′ LON 075° 45.454′**
> **DEPTH: 40 feet**   **LEVEL: Intermediate**

LOCATION: About 1.5 miles off Buffalo, New York, east harbor entrance.

Built at Cleveland, Ohio, in 1902, the flax-laden steel freighter, *W.C. Richardson* (374′ x 48′ x 28′), foundered off Waverly Shoal during the December 8, 1909, storm (which also sank the *Clarion* and the *Marquette & Bessemer #2* in Lake Erie) with the loss of five lives; the 14 other crewmembers were rescued by another ship. The dynamiting of this wreck four years

W.C. Richardson. AUTHOR'S COLLECTION

later left it leveled to a height of eight feet off the bottom, with considerable debris to the east of the main site in this area of heavy boating traffic.

4. ACME (TUG)

> **LORAN: 44922.12/59222.68**   **LAT 42° 50.698′ LON 078° 57.837′**
> **DEPTH: 36 feet**   **LEVEL: Intermediate**

LOCATION: Three and a half miles off Buffalo, New York, north harbor entrance.

The wooden tug, *Acme* (66′8″ x 17′ x 9′6″), built at Buffalo in 1893, sank on April 15, 1902, after a collision with the vessel she was towing through ice. The boiler, hull frames, rudder and steering mechanism remain identifiable at this busy boating traffic site.

5. FINCH

LORAN: 44940.85/59191.87	LAT 42° 50.944′ LON 078° 59.011′
DEPTH: 45 feet	LEVEL: Intermediate

LOCATION: This wreck lies about six miles west of Buffalo, New York, harbor.

The wooden barge, *Finch* (105′ x 22′6″ x 7′9″), began leaking in heavy seas and sank on August 2, 1883, with no loss of life. The relatively broken up site features chain, a capstan, the stove at the starboard quarter and the rudder about 100′ to the northwest.

6. TONAWANDA

LORAN: 44902.17/59191.68	LAT 42° 50.734′ LON 078° 58.998′
DEPTH: 47 feet	LEVEL: Intermediate

LOCATION: Almost five miles off Buffalo, New York, harbor.

The wooden package steamer, Tonawanda (202′3″ x 32′3″ x 13′3″), was lost on October 18, 1870, in a severe storm which sank three other ships with great loss of life. Heavily loaded with a huge cargo of corn, flour and lead, she foundered with no loss of life. The ship had been built in 1856 at Buffalo, New York. One boiler was removed in 1875, and salvage efforts to raise the hull succeeded only in damaging it. In this immense collection of timbers, one hogging arch lies broken at midship starboard, while the stern offers views of the propeller and engine. Beware of the boating traffic around this site.

Artwork ©Douglas King, Sr.
E-mail: D_KingSr@yahoo.com

7. O. W. CHENEY

LORAN:	LAT 42° 50.282′ LON 079° 00.457′
DEPTH: 47 feet	LEVEL: Novice-Intermediate

LOCATION: The wreck lies about six miles off Buffalo, New York, harbor.

Built in Buffalo, New York, in 1881, the wooden tug, *O.W. Cheney* (66′ x 16′ x 9′8″), sank on June 23, 1903, after having raced out to the steamer, *Chemung,* in hopes of contracting their business and towing their ship into Buffalo harbor. Instead, the *O.W. Cheney,* in its enthusiasm, accidentally crossed the path of the *Chemung* and was almost sliced in two in the subsequent collision. Two firemen below deck on the tug were killed.

Scuba divers found this shipwreck in 1991. The bow section of the hull has broken up completely, but the stern still holds the propeller and its shaft. The rudder lies about 100′ to the west, while her boiler lies about 100′ to the southwest. In between these recognizable parts is a large debris field of the tug's pieces and contents.

8. BRITON

LORAN:	LAT 42° 49.934′ LON 079° 06.014′
DEPTH: 21 feet	LEVEL: Novice-Intermediate

LOCATION: This site is about one-quarter mile southwest of the Point Abino Light.

A brand new captain, an aging ship which had twice been cut in two, some heavy seas with strong winds and a malfunctioning foghorn combined forces to create an embarrassing situation. The steel freighter, *Briton* (128′5″ x 24′5″ x 12′5″), ran ashore at Point Abino,

The steamer, *Briton.* GREAT LAKES HISTORICAL SOCIETY

Ontario, on November 13, 1929, only a dozen miles out of Buffalo where she had just taken on a full cargo of grain. This ship, which had survived very active saltwater duty during World War I, for which she needed to be cut in half to pass her through the short locks of the old Welland Canal and then welded back together again, twice over, was now pounded to a total loss within two days by the Great Lakes' notorious gales of November. Fortunately, her entire crew was rescued by the Buffalo Coast Guard.

The wreckage from the steamer, *Briton*, which had been built in Cleveland in 1891, is widely scattered, as she was flattened by dynamite in the early 1930's, and her steel pieces lie jumbled among the large boulders off this part of Point Abino.

9. DACOTAH

LORAN: 44813.22/59119.24	LAT	LON
DEPTH: 20 to 25 feet	LEVEL: Novice-Intermediate	

LOCATION: Off Sturgeon Point, New York.

The *Dacotah* (193′4″ x 30′3″ x 12′5″) was a 698-ton wooden steamer which survived on the Great Lakes for only three years after she was launched at Cleveland in 1857. On November 24, 1860, this vessel (as well as two others) was pounded to pieces in a fierce storm with the loss of all 24 people on board.

This pre-Civil War ship's pieces (like the capstan and rudder) and general cargo (which included everything from pottery to horseshoes) lie strewn across a broad debris field.

10. RALEIGH

LORAN: 44868.88/59104.18	LAT 42° 51.890' LON 079° 09.260'
DEPTH: 33 feet	LEVEL: Novice-Intermediate

LOCATION: The wreck lies about five miles off Port Colborne, Ontario.

On November 30 (yes, those nasty gales of November once again), 1911, the wooden freighter, *Raleigh* (235' x 34' x 23'9"), damaged her rudder in severe winds, ran aground and foundered in the heavy seas. Three people, the chief engineer, the male cook and the cook's wife, lost their lives. The *Raleigh* was an old vessel, having been built at Cleveland in 1871.

The ship's boiler, engine room machinery, propeller, rudder, bow winch and anchor chain with an anchor remain at this site.

The steamer, *Raleigh*. AUTHOR'S COLLECTION

11. MARENGO

LORAN:	LAT 42° 51.122' LON 079° 20.589'
DEPTH: 23 feet	LEVEL: Novice-Intermediate

LOCATION: The wreck lies near Morgan's Point, west of Port Colborne, Ontario.

Built in 1873 at Milwaukee, Wisconsin, the huge schooner-barge, *Marengo* (195'6" x 32' x 15'5"), was driven ashore at Morgan's Point in a severe Lake Erie storm on October 12, 1912, which also sank the wooden steamer, *S.K. Martin*, off Erie, Pennsylvania. The steamer, *Lloyd S. Porter,* was towing the *Marengo,* loaded with a cargo of coal, when the powerful winds forced both ships ashore. The steamer, however, had the propulsion to free herself, while the helpless *Marengo* was only impaled further on the rocks until she broke up.

At such a shallow depth, the *Marengo is* broken up badly, with the wood of her frames, planks and decking intermingling with the vast debris area of her coal cargo.

The schooner-barge, *Marengo*. MPL/WMHS

12. C. B. BENSON

LORAN:	LAT 42° 46.260′ LON 079° 14.612′
DEPTH: 87 feet	LEVEL: Advanced

LOCATION: The wreck lies approximately six miles south of Port Colborne, Ontario.

The *C.B. Benson*. MPL/WMHS

The sturdily-built three-masted barquentine, *C.B. Benson* (136′5″ x 26′ x 13′), constructed in 1873 at Port Clinton, Ohio, had wanderlust. A year after her launch, she crossed the Atlantic Ocean to Ireland with a heavy load of corn, and then spent seven years plying the trade routes between the British Isles and South America. She returned to the Great Lakes for a dozen years before being overpowered by the fury of a shallow freshwater sea named Erie. The same storm which sank the *Dean Richmond* also claimed the coal-laden *C.B. Benson*, with the loss of all seven people on board.

The wreck of the *C.B. Benson* sits upright and is very intact. Wonderful nautical sights assist visiting divers in overcoming the tragedy of this site: belaying pins in the fife rail, deadeyes, blocks, a bilge pump, an anchor, the lifeboat davits and the ship's wheel still in place. To assist divers/boaters and to help protect this fabulous wreck, the site has had mooring blocks installed at both bow and stern.

C.B. Benson

Artwork ©Douglas King, Sr.
E-mail: D_KingSr@yahoo.com

© Copyright 1999 Douglas King Sr.

13. J. G. MCGRATH

LORAN: 44739.69/58949.82	LAT 42° 40.080′ LON 079° 23.761′
DEPTH: 90 feet	LEVEL: Advanced

LOCATION: About 12 miles slightly west of due north of Dunkirk, New York.

Built in 1870 in St. Catharines, Ontario, by famed shipbuilder Louis Shickluna, the two-masted schooner, *J.G. McGrath* (104′ x 26′ x 12′), foundered in a severe storm on October 28, 1878, with her crew barely surviving by rowing 16 miles to the Canadian shore. The ship's heavy stone cargo caused great damage to the vessel when she hit the lake bottom, but her working gear and artifacts seem to be in place. Please help keep them that way.

14. BRUNSWICK

LORAN: 44706.72/58931.12	LAT 42° 35.431′ LON 079° 24.558′
DEPTH: 85 to 105 feet	LEVEL: Advanced

LOCATION: The wreck lies about 7.5 miles west-northwest of Dunkirk, New York.

The four-masted iron steamer, *Brunswick* (236′9″ x 36′4″ x 14′), sank during her first season afloat. On November 12, 1881, she collided with the smaller wooden schooner, *Carlingford* (see page 96), and both ships sank within the hour with loss of life. Three of the 15 people on board the *Brunswick* perished as the captain tried in vain to steam his ship to Dunkirk. The *Brunswick* had been launched on May 21, 1881, at Wyandotte, Michigan.

Although portions of the *Brunswick* have deteriorated (all four masts are down, for example), the engine and boiler are in place at the stern, as are two capstans and the windlass on deck, as well as both bow anchors. The hole from the collision is on her starboard side.

235 Feet

Collision Damage
at Mud Line on
Starboard Side Bow

Mud & Silt Bottom
at 99 Feet

Artwork ©Douglas King, Sr.
E-mail: D_KingSr@yahoo.com

The four-masted iron steamer, *Brunswick,* in 1881. MPL/WMHS

Left to right: A shovel from the *Brunswick* appears welded into a strange position. A wooden double block lies on the deck. A heavy, concrete mooring block was accidentally placed in the middle of the ship. *Above:* Joyce Hayward takes a closer look at a *Brunswick* pump. PHOTOS BY CRIS KOHL.

15. *ANNABELL WILSON*

LORAN: 44682.77/58945.33	LAT 42° 29.915′ LON 079° 21.120′
DEPTH: 52 feet	LEVEL: Intermediate-Advanced

The three-masted schooner, *Annabell Wilson.* GLHS

LOCATION: About half a mile northwest of Dunkirk, New York, harbor.

Built in 1887 at Mount Clemens, Michigan, the three-masted schooner, *Annabelle Wilson* (180′ x 32′2″ x 12′), foundered in heavy seas just as she and the tug that was towing her almost reached the safety of Dunkirk harbor on July 12, 1913. The schooner sank with her captain and his wife (the three crewmembers were rescued) and her cargo of coal. Beware of all the boating traffic so close to the harbor entrance.

16. CANADAWAY CREEK

LOCATION: About two miles west of Dunkirk, New York, harbor, following the shoreline past Point Gratiot Light. Avoid the shallow water across the bay at Van Buren Point. In depths of 20′ to 25′ can be found everything from tree stumps to a propeller, a couple of rudders and a water intake pipe.

17. PASSAIC

> **LORAN: 44648.45/58883.16**   **LAT 42° 28.733′ LON 079° 27.776′**
> **DEPTH: 74 to 84 feet**   **LEVEL: Advanced**

LOCATION: This wreck lies about six miles due west of Dunkirk, New York.

The wooden steamer, *Passaic* (198′3″ x 27′7″ x 11′4″), launched on May 24, 1862, at Buffalo, foundered on November 1, 1891, with a load of lumber. No lives were lost.

The remains of the *Passaic* were dynamited about 30 years ago by a "salvager" who thought he had the wreck of the *Dean Richmond*! The wreck's sides have collapsed outwardly, revealing the large boiler and the entire steam engine, including the crankcase and connecting rods, right to the keel. At the stern are the rudder, a four-bladed propeller and propeller shaft. The bow displays an anchor and an anchor windlass. The site is usually buoyed.

Artwork ©Douglas King, Sr.
E-mail: D_KingSr@yahoo.

The wooden steamer, *Passaic*. AUTHOR'S COLLECTION

18. WASHINGTON IRVING

> **LORAN:**   **LAT 42° 32.365′ LON 079° 27.641′**
> **DEPTH: 120 feet**   **LEVEL: Advanced**

LOCATION: This wreck lies almost seven miles west-northwest of Dunkirk, NY.

The small, two-masted schooner, *Washington Irving* (81′1″ x 20′1″ x 7′7″), disappeared mysteriously one weekend (July 7 or 8, 1860) with all six people who were on board. Built in 1845 at Cleveland, the *Washington Irving* carried a load of pig iron and coal on her final voyage. The weather was calm and there were no reports of fire or collision on the lake, so her complete disappearance is a mystery. Today, her upright masts and intact bowsprit make her look like she's ready to sail once more. A windlass and the starboard anchor and chain adorn the bow. The port quarter, however, is partially buried.

19. ACME (PROPELLER)

> **LORAN:**   **LAT 42° 36.598′ LON 079° 29.848′**
> **DEPTH: 130 feet**   **LEVEL: Advanced**

LOCATION: The wreck lies about 11 miles north-northwest of Dunkirk, New York.

A wooden steamer propeller-driven and hog-arched, the *Acme* (190'10" x 33'3" x 12'9"), carrying a cargo of general farm products (corn, flour, beef, cowhides), sprang a leak and sank with no lives lost on November 4, 1867. The ship had been built at Buffalo in 1856.

The *Acme's* steam engine sits exposed on the open hull, while her hogging arches rise about 12 feet off the floor of the lake. Her windlass and other items provide diver interest.

20. CARLINGFORD

LORAN:	LAT 42° 39.274' LON 079° 28.596'
DEPTH: 90 to 105 feet	LEVEL: Advanced

LOCATION: The *Carlingford* lies about 13 miles north-northwest of Dunkirk, NY.

The 12-year-old three-masted schooner, *Carlingford* (154'7" x 31'1" x 12'3"), loaded with wheat, sank in the middle of Lake Erie after a collision with the iron bulk freight steamer, *Brunswick* (see pages 93-94) on November 12, 1881. Built at Port Huron, Michigan, in 1869, the *Carlingford* lost one life from the seven on board in this tragic sinking, and the *Brunswick,* which also sank, lost several.

The *Carlingford*, one of many shipwrecks located by Gary Kozak in the early 1980's in his quest for the legendary *Dean Richmond,* sits upright in water slightly shallower than the *Brunswick*. The deepest point is found inside the hull at the bow, a location requiring special penetration diving training, experience, preparation and attitude. The hole in the schooner's side offers sufficient proof of the collision. The stern is somewhat broken up. Of diver interest are an anchor, rudder, masts and numerous blocks.

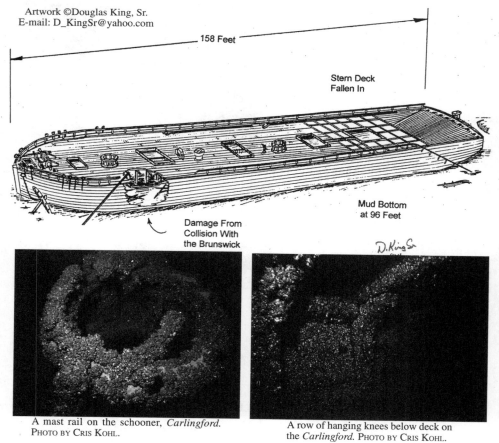

Artwork ©Douglas King, Sr.
E-mail: D_KingSr@yahoo.com

158 Feet

Stern Deck
Fallen In

Mud Bottom
at 96 Feet

Damage From
Collision With
the Brunswick

A mast rail on the schooner, *Carlingford.* PHOTO BY CRIS KOHL.

A row of hanging knees below deck on the *Carlingford.* PHOTO BY CRIS KOHL.

10. Lake Erie's Long Point

Long Point is a long, slender, sandy spit of land which juts halfway across Lake Erie from the north shore. Hundreds of ships met with calamity as a result of this obstacle to navigation and aberration of nature. This chapter covers many of those shipwrecks plus others in this general area.

1. *Cecil J.*	14. *Persian*	27. *S. K. Martin*
2. Tire reef	15. Cracker wreck	28. *Canobie*
3. *Ontario?*	16. *Oxford*	29. *Philip D. Armour*
4. Nanticoke Shoal	17. *Smith*	30. *Charles Foster*
5. *Wilma*	18. Arches/*Oneida?*	31. *Aycliffe Hall*
6. 17-Fathom wreck	19. Stern Castle	32. Drill rig
7. *Siberia*	20. *Atlantic*	33. *Majestic*
8. *Pascal P. Pratt*	21. *St. James*	34. *Barge #3* or *#4*
9. *Brown Brothers*	22. *Trade Wind*	35. *James H. Reed*
10. "T-8" schooner	23. *John J. Boland*	36. *John B. Lyon*
11. *Henry Clay*	24. *City of Rome*	37. Harbor wrecks
12. *C. W. Elphicke*	25. *Dean Richmond*	
13. *Swallow*	26. *Indiana*	

1. CECIL J.

> **LORAN: 44589.27/58529.88** **LAT 42° 45.777′ LON 080° 13.702′**
> **DEPTH: 17 feet** **LEVEL: Novice**

LOCATION: The wreck lies about two miles southwest of Port Dover, Ontario.

Built at Erie, Pennsylvania, in 1915, and launched as the steamboat, *Rambler,* the 14-gross-ton, (later) gasoline-powered fishing tug, *Cecil J.* (47′5″ x 12′5″ x 3′9″), was set ablaze and scuttled by her owner in 1943 after she had provided years of sinkings, a collision and other misfortunes. The scattered remains attract considerable fish life.

2. TIRE REEF

> **LORAN:** **LAT 42° 41.039′ LON 080° 08.496′**
> **DEPTH: 23 feet** **LEVEL: Novice**

LOCATION: About one mile off Turkey Point, Ontario.

An artificial reef of over 1,000 old, rubber tires was created in 1992 for the creation of a fish habitat, which has attracted large numbers of fish, mainly bass, since then.

3. ONTARIO?

> **LORAN: 44511.85/58436.63** **LAT 42° 38.107′ LON 080° 22.016′**
> **DEPTH: 9 feet** **LEVEL: Novice**

LOCATION: The wreck lies off Port Rown in Long Point's inner bay.

General opinion is that what little remains of this shipwreck (keel, framing, some planking, two centerboard boxes and mast steps) came from the three-masted schooner, *Ontario* (130′ x 23′), which sank in a storm on August 27, 1858, with the crew barely escaping with their lives. The ship had been built in Quebec City in 1851. Many artifacts, such as both centerboards, an anchor, and many smaller items, were removed from this site. Bass abound here, but beware of entanglement in weeds later in the dive season.

4. NANTICOKE (FIVE-MILE) SHOAL

> **LORAN:** **LAT 42° 44.238′ LON 080° 04.002′**
> **DEPTH: To 30 feet** **LEVEL: Novice**

LOCATION: This shoal is about six miles east-southeast from Port Dover, Ontario. The attraction of exploring this natural reef rests with the abundance of fish.

5. WILMA

> **LORAN:** **LAT 42° 42.151′ LON 080° 02.065′**
> **DEPTH: 74 feet** **LEVEL: Intermediate-Advanced**

LOCATION: The wreck lies ten miles off Port Dover, Ontario.

Built at Collingwood, Ontario, in 1911, the steam-powered fishing tug, *Wilma* (67′9″ x 16′ x 6′7″), was a bit early in trying to reach the fishing grounds. Ice punctured her hull on April 14, 1936, and she sank with no lives lost.

The main attractions at this popular site are the forward hatch and ladder, the boiler, the smokestack lying along the port side, portholes still in place at the bow, and the rudder and propeller at the stern. All in all, this is very much a fun dive, but beware of commercial fishing nets around this wreck; not all of the netting may be lying flat due to zebra mussel attachment, and it's no fun finding oneself entangled in it. Take along a dive knife or two just in case.

6. 17-FATHOM WRECK

LORAN: 44585.02/58602.77	**LAT 42° 39.101′ LON 080° 03.142′**
DEPTH: 106 feet	**LEVEL: Advanced**

LOCATION: The wreck is located almost 12 miles off Port Dover, Ontario.

This unidentified shipwreck was a small (about 75′ long) two-masted schooner. There is evidence of fire damage. Sitting upright on the silty lake bottom, with a slight starboard list, this wreck's main attractions are the windlass and chain locker at the bow, plus hatches near the stern. A mast lies across the starboard rail, close to the concrete mooring block.

7. *SIBERIA*

LORAN: 44538.57/58555.02	**LAT LON**
DEPTH: 19 feet	**LEVEL: Novice**

LOCATION: The wreck lies on Bluff Bar near the north side of Long Point, about 15 miles from Port Dover, Ontario.

The wooden bulk freight steamer, *Siberia* (272′ x 39′ x 18′), was built at West Bay City, Michigan, in 1882. More than two decades later, this ship was one of the victims (along with the schooner-barge, *Tasmania,* the schooner, *Mautenee*, and the steamer, *Sarah E. Sheldon*) of the massively violent storm of October 20, 1905. Heading for Buffalo with a cargo of barley, the *Siberia* stranded in the storm and broke apart after her crew had been rescued.

The steamer, *Siberia*. AUTHOR'S COLLECTION

For some strange reason, "salvagers" used dynamite to blow this wreck apart in the early 1960's. What remains today is scattered far and wide, with the boiler and keelson remaining the highlights of this site. Shifting sands cover and uncover parts of this wreck.

8. *PASCAL P. PRATT*

LORAN:	**LAT 42° 33.665′ LON 080° 05.558′**
DEPTH: 24 feet	**LEVEL: Novice**

LOCATION: This wreck lies about one mile off Gravelly Bay, three miles from the tip of Long Point.

The wooden bulk freighter, *Pascal P. Pratt* (272′4″ x 40′5″ x 21′5″), caught on fire while hauling a coal cargo from Buffalo to Milwaukee. Her captain grounded her on Long Point, where the ship burned to a total loss on November 16, 1908, with no lives lost. The vessel had been constructed in Cleveland in 1888.

The *Pascal P. Pratt* is fairly broken up due to the ravages of ice, wind and waves over the years. The wreck sits on a sand bottom, and the boiler is about 50′ away from the main wreckage, surrounded by coal. The boilers and the huge propeller are the site's highlights. Bass and perch abound at this site.

The *Pascal P. Pratt*. MPL/WMHS

9. BROWN BROTHERS

LORAN: 44583.77/58618.08	LAT 42° 37.644′ LON 080°005.905′
DEPTH: 120 feet	LEVEL: Advanced

LOCATION: This site is located almost six miles off Long Point Light.

The wooden fishing tug, *Brown Brothers* (75′2″ x 16′5″ x 7′7″), is a relatively modern shipwreck, having gone to the bottom of Lake Erie on October 28, 1959. This aging, low-freeboard ship foundered in a storm while being towed by another tug. No lives were lost. Built in 1915, her original steam propulsion system was replaced with diesel in the early 1950's. She sits upright, with her wheel lying flat near the bow. Fish life is abundant.

10. THE "T-8" SCHOONER (THE 22 1/2 FATHOM WRECK)

LORAN:	LAT 42° 35.222′ LON 080° 01.333′
DEPTH: 145 feet	LEVEL: Technical

LOCATION: Approximately three miles north-northeast of Long Point Light.

This unidentified two-masted schooner, discovered in the 1960's and nicknamed the 22 1/2 Fathom Wreck (renamed "T-8" when she was the eighth target in a 1995 sidescan survey) sank in a collision, as evidenced by hull damage. Her centerboard and surprisingly intact wooden railings offer interesting exploration for the specially trained and experienced.

11. HENRY CLAY (THE "LIGHTHOUSE WRECK")

LORAN: 44547.69/58589.12	LAT 42° 33.072′ LON 080° 02.717′
DEPTH: 15 feet	LEVEL: Novice

LOCATION: The wreck lies about a quarter of a mile off Long Point Light.

The wooden steamer, *Henry Clay* (134′4″ x 22′8″ x 11′), was named after a political figure and popular orator (Mansfield listed six Great Lakes vessels with that name!). But this vessel had a particularly tragic demise. During a violent gale on October 25, 1851, the steamer's cargo shifted and smashed the engine, putting the ship, crew and passengers at the mercy of the weather. Of the 17 people on board, only one sailor survived by clinging to an overturned yawl and reaching shore. The ship's cargo of baled wool washed ashore for weeks after the sinking. Keelson, framing timbers and fish remain at this site.

12. C. W. ELPHICKE

LORAN:	LAT LON
DEPTH: 22 feet	LEVEL: Novice

LOCATION: About one-and-a-quarter miles west from Long Point Light.

The wooden bulk freighter, *C.W. Elphicke* (273′ x 41′3″ x 23′), built at Trenton, Michigan, in 1889, sprang a leak on October 19, 1913, and was purposely run aground at Long Point to prevent her from sinking in deep water. The crew was rescued, but the ship broke in two and, along with her huge cargo of wheat, became a total loss. This broken up shipwreck "comes and goes" in Long Point's shifting sands; a south wind will uncover her.

The steamer, *C.W. Elphicke*. AUTHOR'S COLLECTION.

13. SWALLOW

> **LORAN: 44572.08/58645.31   LAT 42° 34.899′ LON 079° 56.451′**
> **DEPTH: 190 feet   LEVEL: Technical**

LOCATION: The wreck lies about five and a half miles east of Long Point Light.

The wooden steamer, Swallow (133′8″ x 25′8″ x 10′8″), built at Trenton, Michigan, in 1873, was caught in a severe storm which swamped and sank the ship on October 18, 1901, but not before she caught on fire. Fortunately, no lives were lost, as the crew transferred safely to the barge which they were towing. The wreck today displays fire damage. Her engine, boiler and bow anchor are still in place. Beware of commercial fishing nets here.

14. PERSIAN

> **LORAN: 44581.27/58661.33   LAT 42° 33.777′ LON 079° 54.703′**
> **DEPTH: 195 feet   LEVEL: Technical**

LOCATION: The wreck lies seven miles east of Long Point Light.

The wooden steamer, *Persian* (243′ x 40′ x 19′), sank on August 26, 1875, while enroute with a grain cargo from Chicago to Buffalo. A fire which started in the coalbunker spread quickly. The crew became so involved in fighting the flames that they failed to notice that their lifeboats were being destroyed. As a measure of desperation, floating hatch covers saved all 19 people on board, who were picked up by ships that were attracted by the smoke.

The *Persian* comes closest among known shipwreck sites to sitting in the deepest part of Lake Erie (215′). Her charred remains display an engine, boiler, and propeller.

15. CRACKER WRECK

> **LORAN: 44590.46/58687.11   LAT 42° 33.492′ LON 079° 51.652′**
> **DEPTH: 190 feet   LEVEL: Technical**

LOCATION: The wreck lies almost ten miles east of Long Point Light.

This unidentified, three-masted schooner, approximately 120 feet in length, appears to have been built in an early (pre-Civil War) style, and sank so slowly that the usual air pressure build-up from water entering the hull did not blow off the weaker superstructure items, such as the vessel's cabin. Attesting to the ship's intactness are her anchors, a bilge pump, and an ornately carved bow. A mast lies along the port side.

16. OXFORD

> **LORAN: 44558.67/58671.69   LAT 42° 28.852′ LON 079° 51.839′**
> **DEPTH: 164 feet   LEVEL: Technical**

LOCATION: The wreck lies about 25 miles north-northeast of Erie, Pennsylvania.

This early Great Lakes two-masted, 114-foot-long brig, built in 1842 at Three Mile Bay, New York, sank in a collision with the steamer, *Cataract,* on May 30, 1856, with five of the eight people on board the doomed vessel perishing, including Captain John Lee, his wife and his daughter. The *Cataract* continued her journey to Buffalo.

Also nicknamed the "Tiller Wreck" and the "Crowsnest Wreck" (because those items comprise very noticable parts of this shipwreck's

The *Oxford's* crowsnest. PHOTO BY CRIS KOHL.

101

Above and left: A unique feature of the *Oxford* shipwreck is its tiller in place of a wheel. *Below left:* A burbot's tail remains unhidden in the *Oxford's* winch. *Below:* the *Oxford's* unusual bilge pump. PHOTOS BY CRIS KOHL.

character), the *Oxford* makes a unique subject for study. Besides having a tiller (instead of a wheel) and a crowsnest, the vessel displays a windlass, a winch, a bilge pump, two bow anchors and an offset centerboard. Collision damage can be seen in the starboard bow area.

17. SMITH

LORAN: 44530.12/58607.09	LAT 42° 28.481′ LON 079° 59.064′
DEPTH: 165 feet	LEVEL: Technical

LOCATION: This wreck lies about six miles southeast of Long Point Light.

The aging tug, *Smith* (120′ x 22′ x 10′), built in 1881 at Buffalo, foundered while in tow on October 25, 1930. Her wheelhouse remains intact, with her wheel, a chadburn (telegraph), her whistle on top of the wheelhouse, and a mushroom anchor on the port bow.

18. ARCHES/*ONEIDA?*

> **LORAN: 44516.03/58586.86**   **LAT 42° 27.471' LON 080° 01.017'**
> **DEPTH: 129 to 160 feet**   **LEVEL: Technical**

LOCATION: This wreck lies about 6.5 mles south-southwest of Long Point Light, or about 21 miles north of Erie, Pennsylvania.

The length of this shipwreck, the upright hogging arches rising about 30' off the bottom and the fact that the wreck has many very visible barrels in its holds, all lead one to believe that it is indeed the package steamer, *Oneida* (138'3" x 24'1" x 11'). On November 11, 1852, the *Oneida,* loaded with 3,500 barrels of flour, left Cleveland for Buffalo, but fell victim to an extremely destructive storm. The ship was lost with all hands (about 20). Except for the decking being mostly missing, the shipwreck is intact, displaying rudder, propeller, boilers, engine, bow anchors, upright hogging arches and barrels viewable from her open hatches.

19. STERN CASTLE

> **LORAN: 44529.98/58583.37**   **LAT 42° 30.301' LON 080° 02.383'**
> **DEPTH: 185 feet**   **LEVEL: Technical**

LOCATION: About three miles west of Long Point Light, 24 miles north of Erie, PA.

The stern of this unidentified two-masted schooner rises sharply off the lake bottom (hence the nickname). Her bow also rises, with the vessel's midsection being mostly buried in the lake bottom. Her masts and ship's wheel are still in place.

20. *ATLANTIC*

> **LORAN: 44522.68/58561.09**   **LAT 42° 30.616' LON 080° 05.091'**
> **DEPTH: 135 to 160 feet**   **LEVEL: Technical**

LOCATION: The wreck lies about three miles south-southwest of Long Point Light.

The luxurious sidewheel steamer, *Atlantic* (265'7" x 33' x 14'6"), built at Newport (now Marine City), Michigan, in 1849, sank with enormous loss of life (about 150-200 people perished) after a night-time collision with the steamer, *Ogdensburg,* on August 20, 1852. Both vessels continued on their separate ways, but the *Ogdensburg* turned around when her captain heard the screams of the *Atlantic's* panicked passengers when they became aware that their ship was sinking. Subsequent salvage descriptions, such as the competition between hardhat divers Johnny Green and Elliot Harrington in the 1850's, and, much later, the *Atlantic's* 1984 discoverer, Mike Fletcher of Port Dover, Ontario, fighting California pirates in the 1990's who claimed that they had just discovered this "treasure wreck"

The luxurious paddlewheel steamer, *Atlantic*. MPL/WMHS

in Canadian waters and had the rights to salvage everything on it (eventually, the courts ruled against them), make for fascinating stories.

The famous/infamous *Atlantic's* giant paddlewheels rise dramatically from the lake bottom, where she sits upright but is slowly collapsing. The intact holds contain everything from farm implements to books. Penetration diving, particularly at this depth, is only for the highly trained, experienced and prepared. A double ship's wheel lies flat in the silty bottom.

21. St. James

LORAN: 44491.03/58530.38	LAT 42° 27.100′ LON 080° 07.328′
DEPTH: 164 feet	LEVEL: Technical

LOCATION: The wreck lies about 7.5 miles southwest of the Long Point Light.

For years, this incredibly preserved but unidentified shipwreck, first located in 1984, was referred to as "Schooner X" until Toronto marine historian, Art Amos, ascertained, from the tonnage numbers stamped into the main beam, that the vessel was the two-masted schooner, *St. James* (118′ x 25′), built in Milan, Ohio, in 1856, and lost mysteriously with all hands in late October, 1870. Both masts are upright and rise to a depth of 81′. The ship's anchors are in place, and this magnificent shipwreck is complete with bow chains, deadeyes, rigging, the ship's wheel, a wooden and an iron bilge pump, and a figurehead.

22. Trade Wind

LORAN: 44463.48/58483.81	LAT 42° 25.512′ LON 080° 12.061′
DEPTH: 120 feet	LEVEL: Advanced

LOCATION: The wreck lies about 11.5 miles southwest of the Long Point Light.

This 140-foot-long, three-masted bark, constructed at Buffalo in 1853, sank after a collision in a blinding blizzard with the bark, *Charles Napier,* on December 1, 1854. The *Trade Wind's* cargo was railroad iron, 1,000 stoves and two U.S. government lifeboats bound for Chicago. After the collision, the crew rescued themselves using the two government lifeboats. The wreck's masts lie on the mud bottom off the port side, while the site contains her capstan, ship's wheel, and many stove parts and railroad iron scattered around.

23. John J. Boland, Jr.

LORAN: 44545.48/58721.09	LAT 42° 22.794′ LON 079° 44.000′
DEPTH: 95 to 136 feet	LEVEL: Advanced-Technical

LOCATION: The wreck lies just over seven miles west-northwest of Barcelona, NY.

AUTHOR'S COLLECTION

Built as the *Tyneville* in England in 1928, the steel freighter, *John J. Boland, Jr.* (252′9″ x 43′4″ x 17′8″), foundered in a storm on October 5, 1932, because of a hatch left open to accommodate a pile of 400 excess tons of coal that would not fit below deck. Eventually the hold filled with enough water to capsize the ship, and she sank in four minutes, taking four lives with her.

The *John J. Boland, Jr.* lies on her starboard side, with her four-bladed propeller and rudder the highlights at the stern. One anchor is in the hull, while the other one lies on the lake bottom just off the wreck. railings, ladders, portholes and the huge cargo holds are still intact. Penetration at this silt-covered site should be done only by the best-trained, most-experienced and utterly-prepared divers.

The *Boland's* propeller and railing offer dramatic views. Photos by Cris Kohl.

24. CITY OF ROME

LORAN: 44507.82/58710.48	LAT 42° 17.167' LON 079° 43.075'
DEPTH: 15 feet	LEVEL: Novice

The steamer, *City of Rome*. AUTHOR'S COLLECTION

LOCATION: The wreck lies about one-half mile off Ripley, NY, west of Barcelona.

The wooden steamer, *City of Rome*, (268'2" x 40'2" x 20'3"), built at Cleveland in 1881, burned to a complete loss after being purposely grounded on May 7, 1914. No lives were lost. The wooden hull and some machinery remain at this site, with the propeller lying where "salvage divers" had abandoned it at the base of the cliff 750' from the main wreckage. This is a boat dive, since the property adjacent to the wreck is private.

25. DEAN RICHMOND

LORAN: 44471.03/58602.82	LAT 42° 18.436' LON 079° 55.857'
DEPTH: 100 to 120 feet	LEVEL: Advanced

LOCATION: This shipwreck lies about 11.5 miles northeast of Erie, Pennsylvania.

The wooden, arch-type, twin-propeller-driven freighter, *Dean Richmond* (238' x 35' x 13'5"), loaded with flour and zinc, disappeared with all hands (18 lives) in a severe storm on October 14, 1893. She was the largest package freighter on the Great Lakes when she was launched at Cleveland in 1864.

Located by Gary Kozak in 1983 after spending eight summers sidescanning various

The *Dean Richmond*. MPL/WMHS

The wreck of the *Dean Richmond*: dynamite damage, above, and the remaining propeller, right. PHOTOS BY CRIS KOHL.

parts of Lake Erie (and finding 31 shipwrecks before finally attaining his goal!), the *Dean Richmond* lies upside-down and, at one point, dynamited open. One of her twin propellers is still in place. Penetration is possible, but only by trained, experienced, prepared divers.

26. INDIANA

LORAN: 44451.66/58564.82	LAT 42° 17.762' LON 079° 59.902'
DEPTH: 90 feet	LEVEL: Advanced

LOCATION: The wreck lies a bit over ten miles north-northeast of Erie, Pennsylvania.

The barkentine, *Indiana* (136'9" x 25'2" x 11'), built at Oswego, New York, in 1852, sank shortly after she began to leak on September 24, 1870. Her cargo of stone was also lost, but her crew survived. This wreck is adorned with a windlass, capstan, winch, deadeyes, her collapsed bowsprit, two bow anchors, and a fallen rudder.

27. S. K. MARTIN

> **LORAN: 44441.76/58587.29**   **LAT 42° 14.551' LON 079° 56.001'**
> **DEPTH: 57 feet**   **LEVEL: Intermediate**

LOCATION: The wreck lies about nine miles northeast of Erie, Pennsylvania.

The wooden steamer, *S.K. Martin* (152'5" x 28' x 11'), built at Benton Harbor, Michigan, in 1883, began to leak during a storm on October 12, 1912. The crew escaped in the ship's yawl.

The wreck lies upright, with her large boilers and propeller in place. Other items lie just off the wreck site: a capstan, the smokestack, and two sets of bitts off the port stern side, and an anchor off the starboard bow. The rudder lies flat at the stern.

The steamer, *S.K. Martin.* MPL/WMHS

28. CANOBIE

> **LORAN: 44394.82/58533.88**   **LAT 42° 10.328' LON 080° 00.898'**
> **DEPTH: 15 feet**   **LEVEL: Novice**

LOCATION: The wreck lies three miles east-northeast of Erie, Pennsylvania.

The wooden steamer, *Canobie* (259'3" x 37'4" x 19'8"), launched as the *Iron King* at Detroit in 1887, sailed in a dilapidated condition into a violent storm on November 1, 1921. She barely survived to reach Erie harbor, where her owners knew they could no longer risk this ship on open water. So they towed her east of Erie, where they burned and scuttled her. Her hull timbers, huge propeller and boiler lie next to a buoy.

29. PHILIP D. ARMOUR

> **LORAN: 44339.22/58434.48**   **LAT 42° 07.680' LON 080° 10.701'**
> **DEPTH: 30 feet**   **LEVEL: Novice**

LOCATION: The wreck lies about five miles west-southwest of Erie, Pennsylvania.

The wooden barge, ex-steamer *Philip D. Armour* (280'6" x 40' x 23'), stranded in a storm on November 13, 1915, and was abandoned in place. A four-bladed propeller, rudder lying flat, two boilers, engine, piping and bitts adorn this large hull.

The *Philip D. Armour* as a steamer. IGLR

30. CHARLES FOSTER

LORAN: 44345.18/58406.16	LAT 42° 10.444' LON 080° 15.001'
DEPTH: 75 feet	LEVEL: Advanced

LOCATION: The wreck lies about nine miles west of Erie, Pennsylvania.

The oak-hulled, schooner-barge, *Charles Foster* (233'x 36' x 16'), built for the iron ore trade at Milan, Ohio, in 1877, became waterlogged and sank with all eight hands on December 9, 1900. Anchor and chain sit on the bow, along with a pump, a windlass and a metal tank. Two capstans stand in place on deck; the ship's wheel lies off the broken stern.

The *Charles Foster*. GLHS   The steel freighter, *Aycliffe Hall*. AUTHOR'S COLLECTION

31. AYCLIFFE HALL

LORAN: 44410.42/58393.17	LAT 42° 22.526' LON 080° 21.231'
DEPTH: 70 feet	LEVEL: Advanced

LOCATION: The wreck lies about 20 miles southwest of Long Point Light.

The steel freighter, *Aycliffe Hall* (253' x 43'6" x 20'6"), constructed in England in 1928, sank after being rammed on the port stern by the steel freighter, *Edward J. Berwind,* in the dense early morning fog of June 11, 1936. Fortunately, no lives were lost, and the *Berwind* proceeded to Buffalo with both crews.

The hull lies upside-down, with cracks and tears in the steel, likely caused by a failed salvage attempt. The large propeller and rudder remain impressive.

32. DRILL RIG

LORAN: 44396.98/58359.42	LAT 42° 22.467' LON 080° 25.111'
DEPTH: 80 feet	LEVEL: Advanced

LOCATION: This wreckage lies about 23 miles west of Long Point Light.

A storm destroyed this 40' by 40' oil drill rig on November 5, 1958, with the loss of all five men on it. Many scattered pipes form the highlight of this site.

33. MAJESTIC

LORAN: 44418.13/58325.82	LAT LON
DEPTH: 55 feet	LEVEL: Intermediate-Advanced

LOCATION: The wreck lies about 18.5 miles off Port Burwell, Ontario.

The wooden steamer, *Majestic* (291' x 40' x 21'1"), built at West Bay City, Michigan, in 1889, burned to the water's edge on September 10, 1907. The crew was rescued by a passing steamer. Highlights include the huge double boiler and propeller.

Left: The steamer, *Majestic,* as she appeared on a postcard postmarked July 13, 1908. AUTHOR'S COLLECTION. *Right: Barge #4.* MPL/ WMHS.

34. BARGE #3 OR #4

LORAN: 44388.39/58238.21	LAT	LON
DEPTH: 60 feet	LEVEL: Intermediate-Advanced	

LOCATION: The wreck lies about ten miles south-southeast of Port Burwell, Ontario. Identical *Barge #3* and *Barge #4* (335' x 44' x 11'),both built at Toledo, Ohio, in 1895, both sank carrying pulpwood on November 13, 1900, in a storm, with the towing tug rescuing both crews. This located wreck (is it #3 or #4?) sits upright; her sister may be 1/4 mile away.

35. JAMES H. REED

LORAN: 44277.78/58138.89	LAT 42° 16.172' LON 080° 47.777'
DEPTH: 76 feet	LEVEL: Advanced

LOCATION: The wreck lies about halfway between Ashtabula and Port Burwell.
The steel freighter, *James H. Reed* (128'5" x 24'5" x 12'5"), built in 1903 at Wyandotte, Michigan, sank after colliding with the steamer, *Ashcroft,* in dense fog on April 27, 1944. Twelve lives were lost in this mishap. The *Reed* was hauling iron ore for the war effort. The wreck was dynamited, so the twisted, broken steel remains are considerably scattered.

Left: The steel steamer, *James H. Reed.* AUTHOR'S COLLECTION. *Right:* The oak-hulled steamer, *John B. Lyon,* was built in 1881 at Cleveland. MPL/WMHS.

36. JOHN B. LYON

LORAN: 44222.42/58212.02	LAT 42° 02.369' LON 080° 33.757'
DEPTH: 52 feet	LEVEL: Intermediate-Advanced

LOCATION: This wreck lies about four miles north of Conneaut, Ohio.
The wooden steamer, *John B. Lyon* (255'9" x 38'8" x 20'), was caught in the tail end of the hurricane which destroyed Galveston, Texas, and sank with the loss of nine of the 15 crew. This shipwreck's highlights are two boilers, chain and a large four-bladed propeller.

37. HARBOR WRECKS: In 12' in Ashtabula harbor, lie the remains of three ships, the
schooner *James F. Joy,* the schooner *Gulnair,* and the wooden sandsucker, *Wonder.*

11. Middle Lake Erie

1. *Nimrod*
2. *Louis O'Neil*
3. *Dawn*
4. *Merida*
5. *H. A. Barr*
6. *Charles B. Hill*
7. *Queen of the West*
8. *North Carolina*
9. *Cleveco*
10. *James B. Colgate*
11. Sternless schooner
12. Morpeth schooner
13. *Lycoming*
14. Brians' wreck
15. *Robert*
16. *Colonial*
17. Light wreck
18. *Frank E. Vigor*
19. *Little Wissahickon*
20. *Valentine*
21. *F. A. Meyer*
22. *Steven F. Gale*
23. *Duke Luedtke*
24. *Dundee*
25. *Admiral*
26. *Algeria*
27. *Charles H. Davis*
28. *Fannie L. Jones*
29. *Mabel Wilson*
30. *117th St. wreck*
31. *H. G. Cleveland*
32. *John B. Griffin*
33. *Mecosta*
34. *Two Fannies*
35. Bay coal schooner
36. *Sand Merchant*
37. *John Pridgeon, Jr.*
38. *Craftsman*
39. *Ivanhoe*
40. *Hickory Stick*
41. *Sarah E. Sheldon*
42. *St. Lawrence & Quito*
43. *Morning Star*
44. *Marshall F. Butters*
45. Civil War wreck
46. Jackie's wreck
47. Net wreck
48. Bow cabin schooner
49. *Wend the Wave*
50. *Jorge B.*
51. *New Brunswick*

1. NIMROD

> **LORAN: 44279.7/58053.2**   **LAT 42° 22.649' LON 081° 00.309'**
> **DEPTH: 56 to 72 feet**   **LEVEL: Advanced**

LOCATION: The wreck lies about 22 miles southeast of Port Stanley, Ontario.

The three-masted schooner, *Nimrod* (184' x 31'7" x 13'4"), built in 1873 at Toledo, Ohio, sank with a cargo of corn after a collision with the schooner, *Michigan,* on November 8, 1874, in dense fog. No lives were lost, but the new ship was a total loss.

A windlass and much anchor chain adorn the bow, which faces southwest. An impressive

Artwork ©Adam Henley

bowsprit was in place until the weight of zebra mussels collapsed it in the late 1990's; now it lies next to the remaining large anchor (the first 3,000-pound bow anchor was raised in 1979 and is on exhibit next to the Port Burwell lighthouse). The stern offers the fallen rudder post, a davit, and bitts. Three dark holes indicate where the masts used to be. Much of the wooden railing remains intact.

Former U.S. Navy diver, Frank Troxell, studies a *Nimrod* double sheave block. PHOTO BY CRIS KOHL.

2. LOUIS O'NEIL

> **LORAN: 44269.2/57975.8**   **LAT 42° 25.444' LON 081° 10.312'**
> **DEPTH: 72 feet**   **LEVEL: Advanced**

LOCATION: The wreck lies 13.6 miles off Port Stanley, Ontario.

Nicknamed the "Coal Schooner Wreck" when local fishermen, who had snagged their nets on it, first told scuba charter boat operator Wayne Weingarden about it in 1987, this shipwreck was later identified as the schooner-barge, *Louis O'Neil* (196' x 31' x 13'). Launched in 1862 at Cleveland, the coal-laden *Louis O'Neil* was being towed along with four other schooner-barges by the tug, *Swain,* when they encountered severe gales on April 29, 1887. One tow, the *Thomas L. Parker,* collided

The *Louis O'Neil's* chain pile and blocks. PHOTOS BY CRIS KOHL.

Artwork ©Adam Henley

with the *Louis O'Neil,* sinking the latter. As the Port Huron newspaper succinctly put it on Monday, May 2, 1887: "...The crew went 70 miles in a rowboat but were saved...." when they landed near Conneaut, Ohio.

This shipwreck is loaded with sights: a huge pile of chain at the bow, a capstan, double blocks, hatches, pump, rudder, an enormous rudder post, the coal cargo, and an anchor partially buried at the bow. Beware of fishnets at various parts of this wreck.

3. DAWN

LORAN: 44233.4/57878.3	LAT 42° 25.251′ LON 081° 21.502′
DEPTH: 67 feet	LEVEL: Advanced

LOCATION: This wreck lies about 18 miles south-southwest of Port Stanley, Ontario.

This shipwreck sits upright with a slight starboard list. Its deck exhibits a windlass, two bilge pumps, a rudder post, two open hatches and parts of both masts, plus mid-hull collision damage. This is the schooner, *Dawn* (105′ x 20′4″ x 8′11″), which sank within ten minutes of being rammed by the steamer, *New York,* on October 21, 1859. Fortunately, no lives were lost. The *Dawn* had been built in 1847 at Milan, Ohio.

4. MERIDA

LORAN: 44160.0/57843.9	LAT 42° 13.951′ LON 081° 20.786′
DEPTH: 65 to 83 feet	LEVEL: Advanced

LOCATION: The wreck lies 24.6 miles east of Erieau, Ontario.

The steel freighter, *Merida* (360′ x 45′ x 25′8″), was one of four ships which sank on Lake Erie in the "Black Friday" Storm of October 20, 1916 (the others were the *D.L. Filer,*

Above: The steel steamer, *Merida.* GLHS. *Left:* A large school of burbots congregates on the *Merida. Right:* Roy Pickering studies a bow capstan on the *Merida.* PHOTOS BY CRIS KOHL.

the *James B. Colgate,* and the *Marshall F. Butters,* all in this book), but she was the only one lost with all hands (23 sailors). The *Merida* was the largest ship of her kind on the Great Lakes when she was launched at Bay City, Michigan, in 1892.

Local fishermen discovered the wreck in 1975. She sits upright and intact, but her back seems to be broken as her midsection virtually disappears into the lake bottom. The bow, rising from the lake bottom at a sharp angle, is adorned with a hinged fluke anchor lying flat on the deck, a capstan, a second anchor and chain in place, stanchions and railings. A few brass portholes still remain at the lower levels of the bow. The stern's engine room is penetrable, but silty; this is for very trained, experienced and prepared divers only.

The steamer, *Merida*

ARTWORK BY CRIS KOHL, © SEAWOLF COMMUNICATIONS, INC.

BILGE PUMP

HATCHWAY AND STEPS TO BELOW DECK

STEAM ENGINE

BOILERS

SMOKESTACK BASE

PROPELLER
(Depth: 83')

HATCHES
(Depth: 75-79')

SPARE PROPELLER BLADE

SPARE ANCHOR FLAT ON BOW DECK
(Depth: 57')

SILT LINE

CAPSTAN

WINCH

(Not to scale)

BOW ANCHOR IN PLACE

5. *H. A. Barr*

LORAN: 44118.3/57803.2	LAT 42° 09.112' LON 081° 23.412'
DEPTH: 84 feet	LEVEL: Advanced

LOCATION: The wreck lies about 22 miles east-southeast of Erieau, Ontario.

The schooner-barge, *H.A. Barr* (225' x 35' x 17'), built in 1893 at West Bay City, Michigan, foundered in a storm off Rondeau, Ontario, on August 24, 1902. No lives were lost.

The bow section of this large wreck sits upright, but the stern is completely broken up and encased by dangerous commercial fishnets which snagged onto the obstructions. A long line of deadeyes grace the port rail. A windlass has recently collapsed into the hold at the bow, but a capstan, fife rail, winch and belaying pins enhance the rest of the deck.

Left: Diver Joe Corsaro exchanges stares with a deadeye along the port rail of the schooner-barge, *H.A. Barr.* Deadeyes, so-named due to their resemblance to human skulls, were part of a ship's standing rigging. Rope passed through each hole ran to the top of a mast. PHOTO BY CRIS KOHL.

6. *Charles B. Hill*

LORAN:	LAT 41° 50.455' LON 081° 03.081'
DEPTH: 18 feet	LEVEL: Novice

LOCATION: This wreck lies about 1/2 mile off Madison, Ohio.

The wooden steamer, *Charles B. Hill* (261' x 36' x 23'), began to leak seriously during a storm and was driven ashore. All were rescued. The site is comprised of huge, wooden timbers, steam pipes and other metal pieces, including a large and a small boiler. Fish abound.

7. *Queen of the West*

LORAN: 43986.0/57735,1	LAT 41° 50.769' LON 082° 23.133'
DEPTH: 71 feet	LEVEL: Advanced

LOCATION: This shipwreck lies about eight miles north of Fairport, Ohio.

The wooden steamer, *Queen of the West* (215' x 32'6" x 16'4"), sprang a leak and foundered on August 20, 1903. The entire crew was rescued by a passing steamer.

The bow is the most intact area, with a windlass, some chain and a winch. The stern offers the engine and a huge boiler. The shipwreck's mid-section is mostly open hull.

8. NORTH CAROLINA

> **LORAN: 43934.28/57709.32**   **LAT 41° 43.810′ LON 081° 22.888′**
> **DEPTH: 40 feet**   **LEVEL: Novice-Intermediate**

LOCATION: This wrecked tug lies about 3/4 mile off Mentor-on-the-Lake, Ohio.

Built at Cleveland in 1908 as the *L.C. Sabin* and in 1941 renamed the *North Carolina* (74′8″ x 19′9″ x 11′6″), this is a modern wreck of an old ship. She foundered with no lives lost on December 9, 1968. The site, with the tug's hull facing south, includes the ship's rudder, propeller, smokestack and boiler.

9. CLEVECO

> **LORAN: 43926.18/57609.49**   **LAT 41° 47.468′ LON 081° 36.006′**
> **DEPTH: 63 to 78 feet**   **LEVEL: Advanced**

LOCATION: This wreck lies about 14 miles north of Euclid, Ohio.

The steel tanker barge, *Cleveco.* GLHS

Lost with all hands (18) when she foundered on December 3, 1942, the steel tanker barge, *Cleveco* (260′ x 43′ x 25′1″), was being towed by the tug, *Admiral,* which also sank with all hands (and is also in this book). Originally launched at Lorain, Ohio, in 1913 as the *S.O. Co. #85,* she was renamed three times before given her final name in 1940. Unfortunately, that was the name she held for the shortest period of time.

The wreck lies upside-down, rising about 14 feet off the lake bottom. Salvage in 1961 and 1995 removed most of her 1,000,000 gallons of fuel oil. Half a dozen sealed valves on the keel act as a reminder of the first salvage.

10. JAMES B. COLGATE

> **LORAN: 44032.52/57607.72**   **LAT 42° 05.378′ LON 081° 44.281′**
> **DEPTH: 85 feet**   **LEVEL: Advanced**

LOCATION: The wreck lies about twelve miles southeast of Erieau, Ontario.

The steel whaleback ship, *James B. Colgate* (308′ x 38′ x 24′), disappeared with almost all hands in the "Black Friday" Storm of October 20, 1916. Only her captain survived by

The unique whaleback steamer, *James B. Colgate.* GLHS

clinging to a raft for over 30 hours before being picked up by a passing railroad car ferry. Built in 1892 at West Superior, Wisconsin, the *Colgate* was one of only 43 whalebacks ever constructed.

Len Cabral, a commercial fisherman, located the *James B. Colgate* in the summer of 1991. The wreck lies upside-down, with the rudder and propeller being the site's highlights. Penetration is possible, but only for the trained, experienced and prepared. Silt thrives here. An interesting debris field, which includes the smokestack, lies off the stern.

11. STERNLESS SCHOONER

LORAN: 44071.09/57673.82   LAT 42° 08.380′ LON 081° 37.939′
DEPTH: 84 feet   LEVEL: Advanced

LOCATION: The wreck lies about 16 miles southeast of Erieau, Ontario.

This unidentified, three-masted schooner, measuring about 125 feet long with a 25 foot beam, has a stern so severely damaged and collapsed that the first divers at this site thought it was missing. This site, facing west, sports a port bow anchor, a windlass, chain on the deck, intact railing, part of a fife rail at the first mast hole, a capstan near midship, a pump near the stern, and the remnants of a rudder post. A capstan plate hints at 1850's construction.

12. MORPETH SCHOONER

LORAN: 44133.02/57629.09   LAT 42° 22.444′ LON 081° 49.278′
DEPTH: 15 feet   LEVEL: Novice

LOCATION: The wreck lies about 200′ off the concrete steps along the shoreline south of Morpeth. Ask permission first of the property owner if you plan to do this as a shore dive.

This unidentified schooner, measuring about 123 feet long and 24 feet wide, rises only about four feet off the lake bottom. For that reason, it gets covered and uncovered in sand at the whim of Lake Erie (in 2000 it was covered; in 2001, it was not). An unusual feature is her iron hanging knees, which supported the horizontal deck on the vertical hull; usually the hanging knees were made of wood. The hull, filled with wood and stone debris, also has trees snagged into it. The wreck is possibly that of the schooner, *Phalarope* (137′ x 26′3″ x 11′1″), built at Cleveland in 1854 and stranded near Rondeau on September 29, 1872.

13. *LYCOMING*

LORAN: 44073.0/57566.4   LAT 42° 15.080′ LON 081° 53.386′
DEPTH: 28 feet   LEVEL: Novice-Intermediate

LOCATION: This shipwreck lies about four miles east of Erieau, Ontario.

This wooden steamer, discovered by commercial gas divers in 1977, was called the "Erieau Wreck" until research on its engine by members of Kent Divers Association identified it as the *Lycoming* (251′ x 36′ x 15′3″), which burned to the waterline on October 21, 1910, while docked at Erieau. The floating inferno was cut loose to save the dock. The site today includes a large four-bladed propeller, a recently restored and returned capstan, a steam engine and a boiler. The *Lycoming's* sister ship, the *Conemaugh,* lies off Point Pelee.

The wooden steamer, *Lycoming.* IGLR

Left: The *Lycoming's* huge four-bladed propeller. *Right:* Roy Pickering and members of Kent Divers Association pose with the *Lycoming* capstan which they restored and returned to the site in 1996. PHOTOS BY CRIS KOHL.

14. BRIANS' WRECK

LORAN: 44072.59/57559.28	LAT 42° 15.415′ LON 081° 54.338′
DEPTH: 16 feet	LEVEL: Novice-Intermediate

LOCATION: This site lies just east of the East Erieau Channel breakwall.

Brian Jackson and Brian Roffel were diving with Roy Pickering (all Past Presidents of Kent Divers Association, like ye author) to explore this site. Brian R. came up and said he saw lots of quarry-cut stones. Brian J. came up and said that he saw a wooden shipwreck under the stones. Hence we have "Brians' (the apostrophe is in the right place because there was more than one Brian) Wreck" (it's a simple story, but one that had to be chronicled).

15. *ROBERT*

LORAN: 44044.0/57510.6	LAT 42° 13.100′ LON 081° 58.941′
DEPTH: 48 feet	LEVEL: Novice-Intermediate

The tug, *Robert*. AUTHOR'S COLLECTION.

LOCATION: The wreck lies about five miles southwest of Erieau, Ontario.

The commercial fishing tug, *Robert* (38′3″ x 13′1″ x 4′8″), built at Vermilion, Ohio, in 1948, sank in a collision with another fishing tug on September 26, 1982. Fortunately, the *Robert's* crew escaped uninjured, picked up by the other boat. When I first explored this new wreck in 1983, it still had everything from the ship's wheel and all the electronics to the fire extinguishers and propeller. Today, all that remains is some netting, a radar unit, the autopilot, and fish boxes.

16. COLONIAL

LORAN: 44042.5/57472.3	LAT 42° 15.065' LON 082° 04.292'
DEPTH: 13 to 22 feet	LEVEL: Advanced

LOCATION: The wreck lies about 1/4 mile off shore, seven miles west of Erieau.

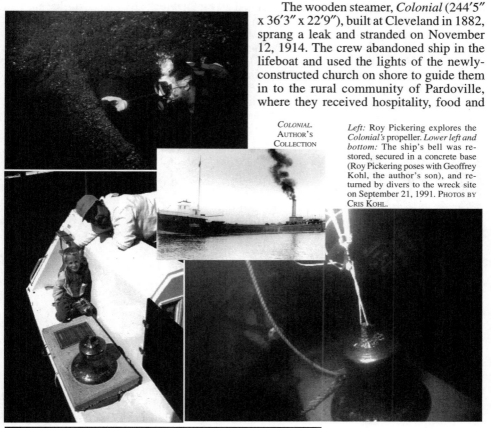

The wooden steamer, *Colonial* (244'5" x 36'3" x 22'9"), built at Cleveland in 1882, sprang a leak and stranded on November 12, 1914. The crew abandoned ship in the lifeboat and used the lights of the newly-constructed church on shore to guide them in to the rural community of Pardoville, where they received hospitality, food and

COLONIAL.
AUTHOR'S
COLLECTION

Left: Roy Pickering explores the *Colonial's* propeller. *Lower left and bottom:* The ship's bell was restored, secured in a concrete base (Roy Pickering poses with Geoffrey Kohl, the author's son), and returned by divers to the wreck site on September 21, 1991. PHOTOS BY CRIS KOHL.

shelter from the Pardo family. The ship broke up within two days.

Roy Pickering and Tim Roberts researched and located the remains of the *Colonial* in 1991. The wreck is broken up and scattered over a wide area in the shallows, with highlights including the ship's brass bell (newly anchored to a concrete base), the boiler, engine, anchor chain, winch, bilge pump, bollards, the rudder post and many smaller items such as blocks, sinks and tools.

The Steamer, *Colonial*

Built: Cleveland, Ohio, 1882
Dimensions: 253' 6" (76 metres) length
36' (10.8 metres) beam
20' 6" (6.2 metres) draft
Sank: Nov. 13, 1914, west of Erieau, Ontario (Lake Erie)
Located: May 16, 1991, by Roy Pickering and Tim Roberts.

Drawing by Cris Kohl, based on on-site observations and information from Roy Pickering.

17. LIGHT WRECK

LORAN: 43942.0/57414.4	LAT 42° 00.185' LON 082° 04.220'
DEPTH: 76 feet	LEVEL: Advanced

LOCATION: The wreck lies about 20 miles southwest of Erieau, Ontario.

This unidentified wooden steamer, named the "light wreck" by Canadians because the first divers on her lost a light (and referred to as the "brick wreck" by U.S. divers, in reference to the bricks in her firebox), was stripped and burned, as was the fate of many aging ships in the 1920's and 1930's. It has been conjectured that these remains are those of the steamer, *Fleetwood* (265'5" x 40'6" x 19'4"), and that the towing captain discreetly scuttled her rather than deliver her all the way to Buffalo (but how discreet can you be when you torch a 265-foot-long ship in the middle of Lake Erie? Dozens of vessels, upon seeing the smoke, would have steamed to the "rescue!") Her machinery is gone, but a large rudder post and steering quadrant remain at the stern. The vast planking of this wooden ship is impressive.

Fish nets are snagged on burned frames. Roy Pickering and Winston Smith study the steering post. Roy Pickering searches under charred planking for a diver's light while carefully holding on to his.   PHOTOS BY CRIS KOHL.

18. *FRANK E. VIGOR*

LORAN: 43941.9/57464.44	LAT 41° 57.549' LON 081° 57.238'
DEPTH: 92 feet	LEVEL: Advanced

Drawing by Cris Kohl, modified from a drawing by Keith Barnwell.

LOCATION: In the shipping lane in mid-lake.

Upside-down and facing north, the steel freighter, *Frank E. Vigor* (418'3" x 48'2" x 23'9"), sank in a collision with the steel steamer, *Philip Minch*, on April 27, 1944, the same night of dense fog that sank the *James H. Reed* (also in this book) in another collision just down the lake. Fortunately, the *Vigor's* crewmembers were all rescued by the *Minch*. The *Vigor* had been launched in 1896 at Cleveland as the *Sir William Siemens*, and, like the *Reed*, was carrying

REV. PETER VAN DER LINDEN COLLECTION

raw war materials (sulphur) at the time of loss.

The rudder and propeller are most interesting. In the late 1980's, Ohio divers dynamited a small opening in the stern area, but penetration diving, especially at that depth, is for those specially trained, experienced and prepared. The crane lies about 100' off the port bow.

Left: Diver Joe Corsaro poses with the lower gudgeon of the large, wooden, steel-encased rudder on the *Frank E. Vigor.* PHOTO BY CRIS KOHL.

19. LITTLE WISSAHICKON

LORAN: 43919.3/57454.8	LAT 41° 54.222' LON 081° 56.786'
DEPTH: 68 to 80 feet	LEVEL: Advanced

LOCATION: The wreck lies in the middle of Lake Erie between Erieau and Cleveland.

The three-masted schooner, *Little Wissahickon* (148' x 28'), launched in 1869 at Marine City, Michigan, sprang a leak as she was being towed across Lake Erie with a cargo of coal and foundered on July 10, 1896, with three lives lost.

The wreck sits upright and intact, with the ship's wheel at the stern and two anchors and a windlass at the bow. The ship's bell, originally removed by Ohio divers and exhibited in a dive shop there, was returned to the wreck bolted to a concrete block (Canadian authorities became upset at the removal of the bell from a shipwreck in Canadian waters, and encouraged its return).

Left: Examining the *Little Wissahickon's* wheel. PHOTO BY CRIS KOHL.

The schooner-barge, *Little Wissahickon*

ARTWORK BY CRIS KOHL, © SEAWOLF COMMUNICATIONS, INC.

STEERING POST

WHEEL   MIZZENMAST   VIEW OF CENTERBOARD BOX BELOW DECK

CLEAT   BLOCK BRACE

MAINMAST HOLE   DEADEYES   FALLEN CAPSTAN

CHAIN LOCKER

WINDLASS

RAILING IS INTACT ON BOTH SIDES

DAMAGED HATCHES

BOOM   FOREMAST HOLE   BELL   CHAIN   ANCHORS

BOW STEM

20. VALENTINE

LORAN: 43931.37/57476.32	LAT 41° 55.122' LON 081° 54.786'
DEPTH: 80 feet	LEVEL: Advanced

LOCATION: This schooner lies 23.6 miles off Erieau, Ontario.

Built in 1867 at Conneaut, Ohio, the three-masted schooner, *Valentine* (128' x 25'8" x 10'), foundered on October 10, 1877, with no lives lost. This silty site features a windlass with chain, two pumps, a winch, rudder post and a capstan. The coal cargo is visible in the open holds. The anchors and wheel are missing. Beware of snagged fishnets.

Left: Diver Sharon Troxell studies a broken mast and a fife rail, with belaying pins in it, on the wreck of the *Valentine.* PHOTO BY CRIS KOHL.

21. F. A. MEYER

LORAN:43912.03/57406.42	LAT 41° 55.441' LON 082° 02.952'
DEPTH: 68 to 78 feet	LEVEL: Advanced

LOCATION: This wreck lies in the middle of Lake Erie between Erieau, Ontario, and Avon Point, Ohio.

The steamer, *F.A. Meyer,* as the *J. Emory Owen.* AUTHOR'S COLLECTION.

Diver Roy Pickering cautiously approaches a snagged fishing net on the *F.A. Meyer.* PHOTO BY CRIS KOHL.

Punctured by ice on December 18, 1909, the wooden steamer, *F.A. Meyer* (256'4" x 38'5" x 19'8"), sank with a load of lumber and no lives lost; a passing steamer rescued the crew. The ship had been launched in 1888 at Detroit as the *J. Emory Owen*.

The site exhibits a huge triple expansion engine and two enormous boilers, as well as a capstan and a beautiful, rounded rail at the stern, where careful penetration is possible. The wreck is intact and upright, but the bow is in collapsed disarray. Beware of freighter traffic (you're in the shipping channel) and snagged fishnets at this site.

22. STEVEN F. GALE

LORAN: 43858.57/57449.42	LAT 41° 44.451' LON 081° 52.919'
DEPTH: 70 to 79 feet	LEVEL: Intermediate-Advanced

LOCATION: This wreck lies 17.8 miles northwest of Cleveland, Ohio.

The two-masted schooner, *Steven F. Gale* (122'6" x 24' x 9'9"), built at Chicago in 1847, foundered with a cargo of stone, all hands and a cat on November 28, 1876.

An old stove sits in the open (the cabin floated to Fairport) below-deck area near the stern, the forward mast lies atop the port bow area, the railings are lined with deadeyes, a pump rests on the deck near the stern, a winch sits midship, chain and windlass repose on the bow, and the forward hatch contains a ladder. This is a great Cleveland-area shipwreck!

The schooner, *Steven F. Gale*

ARTWORK BY CRIS KOHL, © SEAWOLF COMMUNICATIONS, INC.

23. DUKE LUEDTKE

LORAN: 43825.54/57396.29	LAT 41° 41.628′ LON 081° 57.651′
DEPTH: 65 to 71 feet	LEVEL: Intermediate-Advanced

LOCATION: The wreck lies 13 miles north of Avon Point, Ohio.

The tug, *Duke Luedtke* (68′7″ x 17′ x 11′), launched at Cleveland in 1917 as the *Alpena* and used in the attempted salvage of the *Prins Willem V* (also in this book) in Lake Michigan in the mid-1960's, sprang a leak and suddenly rolled and sank on September 21, 1993, with one life lost (a sailor trapped in the engine room). The wreck sits upright in mud listing to port, with rubber tires and hoses lying around the hull. Much silt sits inside.

24. DUNDEE

LORAN: 43841.0/57456.5	LAT 41° 41.333′ LON 081° 50.629′
DEPTH: 60 to 77 feet	LEVEL: Intermediate-Advanced

LOCATION: This wreck lies 13.8 miles north of Rocky River, Ohio.

Built in 1893 at West Bay City, Michigan, the large schooner-barge, *Dundee* (211′ x

35′ x 16′5″), lasted only seven years before foundering in a fierce storm with a load of iron ore on September 12, 1900, with the loss of one life (the female cook was washed overboard) from the seven on board. This storm, the tail end of the infamous "Galveston (Texas) Hurricane," also sank the *John B. Lyon* (which is also in this book).

Six holds make penetration possible into this wreck, but the silt inside makes this very dangerous. Outside, the stern has collapsed, and the bow is beginning to collapse from the weight of the donkey steam boiler, a windlass and chain. A *Dundee* anchor sits in Vermilion, Ohio, outside the Cargo Warehouse.

The classic schooner-barge, *Dundee*. MPL/WMHS

The schooner-barge, *Dundee*

ARTWORK BY CRIS KOHL, © SEAWOLF COMMUNICATIONS, INC.

WINCH

TURNBUCKLES CAPSTAN

MAST HOLE

DONKEY BOILER

HOLDS

WINDLASS

CHAIN

MAST HOLE

HOLDS

MAST HOLE

25. ADMIRAL

LORAN: 43808.88/57412.71	LAT 41° 38.243′ LON 081° 54.198′
DEPTH: 59 to 74 feet	LEVEL: Intermediate-Advanced

LOCATION: This wreck lies eight miles northwest of Cleveland, Ohio.

The tug, *Admiral* (93′3″ x 22′1″ x 11′7″), foundered with all hands (14) in severe weather while towing the tanker, *Cleveco* (which also sank and is described in this book), on December 2, 1942. The tug had been built at Manitowoc, Wisconsin, in 1922, and launched as the *W.H. Meyer* (she received the name, *Admiral,* for only the final 89 days of her life).

The *Admiral* was located by diver George Walton in October, 1969. The wreck's bow points towards Cleveland. The pilot house and the engine room may be entered only by divers specially trained, experienced and prepared for penetration diving. The smokestack lies along the port side.

The tragic tug, *Admiral*. MPL/WMHS

26. ALGERIA

LORAN: 43783.62/57482.18	LAT 41° 31.222′ LON 081° 42.940′
DEPTH: 40 feet	LEVEL: Novice-Intermediate

LOCATION: The wreck lies about one mile north of Cleveland harbor.

The schooner-barge, *Algeria* (288′7″ x 44′6″ x 19′1″), built at West Bay City, Michigan, in 1896, foundered in a storm on May 9, 1906, with one life lost. Lying east-to-west, this shallow site is broken up, with much wood and many cables. Beware of boating traffic!

27. CHARLES H. DAVIS

LORAN: 43778.57/57475.69   **LAT 41° 30.777' LON 081° 43.515'**
DEPTH: 38 to 42 feet   **LEVEL: Novice-Intermediate**

LOCATION: The wreck lies about a mile north of Cleveland, Ohio.

The small wooden steamer, *Charles H. Davis* (145' x 31' x 9'), foundered in a storm on June 13, 1903, with the loss of her captain (the six remaining crewmembers were rescued). The ship's boiler and pony boiler sit surrounded by wooden wreckage at this busy site.

28. FANNIE L. JONES

LORAN: 43777.03/57473.11   **LAT 41° 30.636' LON 081° 43.747'**
DEPTH: 37 feet   **LEVEL: Novice-Intermediate**

LOCATION: The wreck lies almost a mile northwest of Cleveland, Ohio.

The scow-schooner, *Fannie L. Jones* (92'8" x 22'6" x 7'4"), built in 1867 at Lorain, Ohio, foundered in a storm (the same one which claimed the schooner, *Two Fannies,* also in this book) on August 10, 1890. The captain went down with his ship, which carried a cargo of stone for the new Ashtabula breakwall. The wreck lies scattered in a busy boating area.

29. MABEL WILSON

LORAN: 43774.24/57470.48   **LAT 41° 30.333' LON 081° 43.913'**
DEPTH: 38 feet   **LEVEL: Novice-Intermediate**

LOCATION: The wreck lies about 1/2 mile west of the Cleveland lighthouse.

The huge, four-masted schooner, *Mabel Wilson* (242'9" x 39'2" x 16'2"), built in 1886 at West Bay City, Michigan, sprang a leak and foundered outside Cleveland on May 28, 1906, with the loss of one sailor and her iron ore cargo. The wreck was dynamited, leaving only the stern somewhat intact and the rest scattered in a busy boating area of low visibility.

30. 117TH STREET WRECK

LORAN: 43771.88/57452.58   **LAT 41° 30.780' LON 081° 46.151'**
DEPTH: 40 feet   **LEVEL: Novice-Intermediate**

LOCATION: This site is almost three miles west of Cleveland's main harbor entrance.

This unidentified tugboat is possibly one of the vessels scuttled due to their age by the Great Lakes Towing Company about 100 years ago. The bow is somewhat intact, but the rest is broken and scattered, with her boiler lying a fair distance from the main wreckage.

31. H. G. CLEVELAND

LORAN: 43775.55/57436.12   **LAT 41° 32.048' LON 081° 48.607'**
DEPTH: 55 feet   **LEVEL: Intermediate**

LOCATION: The wreck lies about four miles off Lakewood, Ohio.

The three-masted schooner, *H.G. Cleveland* (137'2" x 25'8" x 10'4"), built at Lorain, Ohio, in 1867, sprang a leak and foundered with a load of quarry stone from Kelley's Island on August 4, 1899, with no lives lost. At this site, the cargo is far more evident than the shipwreck; however, the centerboard box and a capstan are among the wreck sights..

32. JOHN B. GRIFFIN

LORAN: 43767.15/57427.39   **LAT 41° 31.100' LON 081° 49.172'**
DEPTH: 46 to 53 feet   **LEVEL: Novice-Intermediate**

LOCATION: The wreck lies about two miles off Lakewood, Ohio.

The tug, *John B. Griffin* (57'4" x 14'6" x 6'8"), burned to the waterline on July 12, 1892, with no loss of life. The ship had been built in 1874 at Buffalo, New York. Very evident at this east-facing site are the tug's rudder, smokestack and boiler.

33. MECOSTA

LORAN: 43763.32/57397.34	LAT 41° 31.854' LON 081° 52.997'
DEPTH: 50 feet	LEVEL: Novice-Intermediate

LOCATION: The wreck lies three miles north of Bay Village, Ohio.

The wooden steamer, *Mecosta* (281'7" x 40'6" x 20'), built at West Bay City, Michigan, in 1888, was stripped of her machinery and scuttled on October 29, 1922. An interesting aspect of this otherwise lackluster site is a Victorian bathtub. This is an area of heavy boating.

34. TWO FANNIES

LORAN: 43773.1/57385.2	LAT 41° 33.850' LON 081° 55.280'
DEPTH: 52 to 61 feet	LEVEL: Intermediate

LOCATION: This wreck lies 4.8 miles north of Bay Village, Ohio.

Built in 1862 at Peshtigo, Wisconsin, the three-masted bark, *Two Fannies* (152' x 33' x 12'), foundered with a load of iron ore and no lives lost on August 10, 1890. The wreck sits upright, with her rudder and rudder post dominating the stern, a capstan, windlass and chain at the bow, plus another capstan and a winch at midship; they make this a visually exciting dive.

Two Fannies. MPL/WMHS

35. BAY COAL SCHOONER

LORAN: 43764.47/57374.79	LAT 41° 33.007' LON 081° 56.080'
DEPTH: 55 feet	LEVEL: Intermediate

LOCATION: This unidentified wreck lies about four miles off Bay Village, Ohio.

Measuring about 75 feet in length and 20 in beam, this coal-carrying scow sits upright in mud with her bow facing north. Decking is absent, but there are support posts in the hull.

36. SAND MERCHANT

LORAN: 43771.77/57368.32	LAT 41° 34.431' LON 082° 57.520'
DEPTH: 65 feet	LEVEL: Advanced

LOCATION: The wreck lies four miles northeast of Avon Point, Ohio.

The steel sandsucker built at Collingwood, Ontario, in 1927, *Sand Merchant* (252' x 43'6" x 17'5"), tragically foundered on October 17, 1936, with the loss of 19 lives. She had just scooped up a load of sand from Point Pelee and was heading to Cleveland with it when the wind picked up heavily and the ship capsized. The wreck lies upside-down, bow southeast, with a crane lying off the starboard side and another one lying to the west in an interesting debris field which also contains a spotlight and a whistle. Do not penetrate this wreck at the mud banks.

Sand Merchant. AUTHOR'S COLLECTION.

37. JOHN PRIDGEON, JR.

> **LORAN: 43775.71/57362.29**   **LAT 41° 35.316' LON 081° 58.597'**
> **DEPTH: 55 to 62 feet**   **LEVEL: Intermediate-Advanced**

John Pridgeon, Jr. GLHS

LOCATION: The wreck lies five miles northeast of Avon Point, Ohio.

Constructed in 1875 at Detroit, the wooden steamer, *John Pridgeon, Jr.* (221'5" x 36'3" x 14'), sprang a leak and foundered on September 18, 1909. All 14 on board were rescued. The wreck lies on its port side, with the stern almost upside-down. Features include the huge propeller and engine, plus much of the ship's lumber cargo. Be careful in low visibility.

38. CRAFTSMAN

> **LORAN: 43745.64/57332.59**   **LAT 41° 31.938' LON 082° 00.370'**
> **DEPTH: 42 feet**   **LEVEL: Novice-Intermediate**

LOCATION: The wreck lies about one mile north of Avon Lake, Ohio.

The wooden derrick barge, *Craftsman* (90'1" x 28'1" x 8'3"), built in 1921 at Lorain, Ohio, foundered while in tow on June 3, 1958, with both crewmen surviving.

The wreck lies along an east-west line, with the crane lying about 100' to the southeast. The upright barge displays winches and hatches on its flat deck, but it's silt city down there, so penetration is not advised. Beware of fishermen trying to hook some of the resident fish.

39. IVANHOE

> **LORAN:**   **LAT 45° 45.454' LON 075° 45.454'**
> **DEPTH: 58 feet**   **LEVEL: Intermediate**

LOCATION: This wrecked schooner lies about three miles off Avon Lake, Ohio.

Built in 1849, the Buffalo schooner, *Ivanhoe* (110' x 25'9" x 9'3"), sank with her coal cargo after a collision with the schooner, *Arab,* on October 4, 1855. Called the "Jug Wreck" by early divers, the vessel sits upright with a slight port list. The windlass and starboard railing are intact, while the stern, with its rudder upright, is mostly collapsed.

40. HICKORY STICK

> **LORAN: 43733.88/57282.82**   **LAT 41° 32.299' LON 082° 06.241'**
> **DEPTH: 52 to 57 feet**   **LEVEL: Intermediate**

LOCATION: The wreck lies about three miles north of Sheffield Lake, Ohio.

The 1944 dredge barge, *Hickory Stick* (110' x 30' x 8'), sank with no lives lost during a storm on November 29, 1958, while being towed by the tug, *Black Marlin.* Both tug and tow sank after the towline parted; the tug has yet to be found. The dredge's crane, boiler and hull form the most conspicuous items at this scattered site.

41. SARAH E. SHELDON

> **LORAN: 43713.77/57268.59**   **LAT 41° 29.737' LON 082° 06.676'**
> **DEPTH: 20 feet**   **LEVEL: Novice**

LOCATION: The wreck lies about 1/2 mile off Sheffield Lake, Ohio.

The wooden steamer, *Sarah E. Sheldon* (184'1" x 32'4" x 13'8"), was one of several ships lost on Lake Erie in an extremely violent storm on October 20, 1905 (two others, the *Siberia* and the *Tasmania,* are also described in this book). The *Sheldon,* built at Lorain, Ohio, in 1872, ran aground in the storm and began to break up. Two crewmen were washed overboard, while the other five clung to the mast before being rescued by a tug. The wreck lies scattered, with the broken propeller and two capstans forming the highlights. The boiler lies on shore. Boat traffic is very heavy here; use boating and diving caution.

42. *St. Lawrence* and *Quito*

LORAN: 43696.9/57233.9	LAT	LON
DEPTH: 10 to 22 feet	LEVEL: Novice	

LOCATION: These two wrecks lie intermingled about 3/4 mile east of Lorain harbor.
The schooner, *St. Lawrence* (137'1" x 26' x 11'5"), built in 1863 at Cleveland, stranded on November 21, 1900, and broke up with no lives lost. The wooden steamer, *Quito* (204' x 36'2" x 21'7"), constructed at Bangor, Michigan, in 1873, grounded and broke up on November 25, 1902, also with no lives lost. The scattered wreckage from both vessels includes an anchor and a vast debris area of wood and metal.

43. *Morning Star*

LORAN: 43752.7/57246.5	LAT 41° 36.812' LON 082° 12.530'
DEPTH: 59 to 68 feet	LEVEL: Intermediate-Advanced

LOCATION: This tragic wreck lies about eight miles north of Lorain, Ohio.
The sidewheel steamer, *Morning Star* (248'2" x 34' x 14'7"), built at Trenton, Michigan, in 1862, sank in a collision with the bark, *Courtland*, on June 21, 1868, with the loss of 31 lives from the 90 that were on board. The *Courtland* also sank, but has not yet been located or positively identified. While much of the vessel has sunk into the soft lake bottom, the *Morning Star's* engine, boiler, walking beam and parts of a paddlewheel are intact. Fish abound at this site, so beware of anglers putting pointy things into the water from the surface.

44. *Marshall F. Butters*

LORAN: 43791.13/57233.05	LAT 41° 43.639' LON 082° 17.368'
DEPTH: 62 to 70 feet	LEVEL: Intermediate-Advanced

LOCATION: The wreck lies in Canadian waters about 15 miles north of Lorain, Ohio.
When the wooden lumber hooker, *Marshall F. Butters* (164' x 30'4" x 10'5"), succumbed to the "Black Friday" Storm of October 20, 1916, no lives were lost, unlike the tragic losses on the other three wrecks from the same storm: the *Merida*, the *James B. Colgate*, and the *D.L. Filer* (all are described in this book). The *Marshall F. Butters* had been built in 1882 at Milwaukee, Wisconsin. With her bow pointing north, she sits upright with a slight starboard list. Both bow and stern have collapsed, with a bow anchor off to starboard and the windlass in place. The midship section, the boiler and the engine remain intact.

The lumber hooker, *Marshall F. Butters.* MPL/WMHS.

45. CIVIL WAR WRECK

LORAN: 43817.48/57274.31	LAT 41° 46.070′ LON 082° 13.750′
DEPTH: 65 feet	LEVEL: Intermediate-Advanced

This two-masted sailing vessel, about 72′ long and 16′ wide, with a stone cargo, appears to be from the 1860's and is fire damaged. It lies about 20 miles north of Lorain, Ohio.

46. JACKIE'S WRECK

LORAN: 43839.42/57233.69	LAT 41° 51.710′ LON 082° 21.083′
DEPTH: 50 feet	LEVEL: Intermediate

Lying eight miles southeast of Point Pelee, the unidentified "Jackie's Wreck," a two-masted schooner about 120′ long, lies flat with her centerboard just off the wreck.

47. NET WRECK

LORAN: 43889.22/57307.59	LAT 41° 56.561′ LON 082° 14.869′
DEPTH: 70 feet	LEVEL: Intermediate-Advanced

This unidentified coal-laden schooner, about 90′ by 18′, lying 14 miles east of Point Pelee, features pumps, a windlass, an anchor, a winch, deadeyes, blocks and lots of fishnets.

48. BOW CABIN SCHOONER (*E. K. GILBERT?*)

LORAN: 43892.62/57315.02	LAT 41° 56.807′ LON 082° 14.110′
DEPTH: 70 feet	LEVEL: Intermediate-Advanced

With her bow facing west and lying 13 miles northeast of Point Pelee, this two-masted schooner (possibly the *E.K. Gilbert,* 92′6″ x 23′6″ x 8′4″, which leaked and sank on November 11, 1868) rises only 4′ off the bottom. Artifacts include a winch, a capstan, a bilge pump, a windlass, a stove, an anchor, some chain, plus blocks and deadeyes.

49. *WEND THE WAVE*

LORAN: 43829.21/57174.29	LAT 41° 52.915′ LON 082° 28.530′
DEPTH: 30 feet	LEVEL: Novice

The schooner-barge, *Wend the Wave* (128′ x 28′ x 10′) lay at anchor with a coal cargo during a storm on October 6, 1889, when she sank in a collision. One life was lost. This wreck is buried in the sand, with only some of the flattened hull and a windlass showing.

50. *JORGE B.*

LORAN: 43851.19/57184.02	LAT 41° 56.307′ LON 082° 29.058′
DEPTH: 38 feet	LEVEL: Advanced

This commercial fishing tug, about 50′ long, capsized and sank in a storm on September 16, 1983, taking all three crew to the bottom almost one mile east of Point Pelee. The many fishnets from the tug, plus usually poor visibility, make this a hazardous dive.

51. *NEW BRUNSWICK*

LORAN: 43950.88/57321.22	LAT 42° 06.777′ LON 082° 18.120′
DEPTH: 48 to 54 feet	LEVEL: Intermediate-Advanced

The three-masted bark, *New Brunswick* (128′8″ x 22′), built at St. Catharines, Ontario, in 1847, foundered 4 miles south of Port Alma, ON, with 5 lives lost on August 26, 1858. Located in 1980 by Mike Diltz and salvaged extensively, only bare hull and deadeyes remain.

12. *ErieQuest*
Western Lake Erie

ErieQuest is the name of the Marine Heritage Area, officially designated in the mid-1990's, off the shores of Point Pelee and the Town of Leamington. These shipwrecks are buoyed annually.

ONTARIO

Wheatley

Leamington

Kingsville

Colchester

POINT PELEE

PELEE PASSAGE

MIDDLE SISTER ISLAND

EAST SISTER ISLAND

HEN & CHICKS

PELEE ISLAND

NORTH BASS ISLAND

MIDDLE BASS ISLAND

SOUTH BASS ISLAND

MIDDLE ISLAND

-N-

Point Pelee aerial. PHOTO BY CRIS KOHL.

1. *George Stone*
2. *Specular*
3. *Northern Indiana*
4. *Tioga*
5. *Tasmania*
6. *Jay Gould*
7. *Dominion*
8. *Clarion*
9. *Willis*
10. *Conemaugh*
11. *M. I. Wilcox*
12. *Grand Traverse*
13. *George Worthington*
14. *Case*
15. *Capstan wreck
    (Charger?)*

1. GEORGE STONE

LORAN: 43820.3/57135.3	LAT 41° 53.247′ LON 082° 33.246′
DEPTH: 32 to 42 feet	LEVEL: Novice-Intermediate

LOCATION: The southern edge of Grubb's Reef, four miles southwest of Point Pelee.
The wooden steamer, *George Stone* (270′ x 40′ x 9′1″), built at West Bay City, Michigan, in 1893, stranded and caught on fire on Grubb's Reef while loaded with a coal cargo on

The steamer, *George Stone*. IGLR

Examining the *George Stone's* hull. PHOTO BY CRIS KOHL.

October 13, 1909. Six lives were lost during the rescue efforts in heavy weather conditions.
The site contains a huge, wooden hull, complete with a boiler, anchor, anchor chain, propeller, steam engine and boiler cradle. There is plenty of lumber and piles of burned wood. The rudder lies flat on the reef in shallower water. Other machinery (e.g. windlass, capstans) is missing because the wreck was partially salvaged. In 1999, a small, steel boat was scuttled next to the wreck.

2. SPECULAR

LORAN: 43795.3/57128.4	LAT 41° 49.371′ LON 082° 32.170′
DEPTH: 37 feet	LEVEL: Novice-Intermediate

LOCATION: Southwest of Point Pelee, 5 miles east of the northern tip of Pelee Island.
A collision with the steamer, *Denver,* sank the iron-ore-laden, wooden steamer, *Specular* (263′7″ x 38′4″ x 20′1″), on August 22, 1900, with no lives lost. Launched on September 7, 1882, at Cleveland as a schooner, the *Specular* (named after a high grade of iron ore) was converted to a steamer in 1888. The wreck was dynamited as a hazard to navigation on October 23, 1900. Although the site is scattered over a wide area, her engine, boilers, anchor and propeller form interesting highlights for the visiting diver.

Above: The steamer, *Specular,* under-way. IGLR. *Right:* Diver Jennifer Elcomb approaches the fluke of the *Specular's* anchor. PHOTO BY CRIS KOHL.

Sidescan sonar image of the steamer, *Specular*. Note the two boilers at the stern. © Aqua Vision Research

3. NORTHERN INDIANA

LORAN: 43830.6/57160.5	LAT 41° 53.879′ LON 082° 30.599′
DEPTH: 20 to 25 feet	LEVEL: Novice-Intermediate

LOCATION: This wreck lies just southwest of Point Pelee's very tip.

Built in 1852 at Buffalo, New York, the passenger paddlewheel steamer, *Northern Indiana* (300′6″ x 36′10″ x 13′8″), owned by the Michigan Southern and Northern Indiana Railroad, dramatically burned to a tragic loss with about 28 people perishing on July 17, 1856. The vessel is broken up and scattered, and the huge, shallow debris field includes a capstan, boiler, and much wood and piping. Beware of the Point's occasional strong currents.

The paddlewheel steamer, *Northern Indiana,* as she appeared in a contemporary drawing (*right*, AUTHOR'S COLLECTION) and Peter Rindlisbacher's modern watercolor (*below*, COURTESY OF THE ORIGINAL ART'S OWNER, ROY PICKERING). *Lower right:* A grill lies in the vast debris field where diver Brian Roffel located this railroad tag in 1996 which positively identified this shipwreck. PHOTOS BY CRIS KOHL.

4. TIOGA

LORAN: 43813.5/57115.9	LAT 41° 53.058′ LON 082° 35.339′
DEPTH: 40 feet	LEVEL: Novice-Intermediate

LOCATION: This wreck lies five miles west of Point Pelee and north of Pelee Island.

The wooden steamer, *Tioga* (177′4″ x 24′7″ x 11′2″), built at Cleveland in 1862, caught on fire and sank on October 5, 1877, with no loss of life. Sitting on the combination sand and mud bottom are the ship's capstan, windlass, rudder, four-bladed propeller and boiler.

5. TASMANIA

LORAN: 43786.8/57140.1	LAT 41° 47.302′ LON 082° 29.799′
DEPTH: 38 to 40 feet	LEVEL: Novice-Intermediate

LOCATION: Southwest of Point Pelee, about seven miles east of Pelee Island.

Launched on April 22, 1871, at Port Huron, Michigan as the *James Couch,* the large, wooden, four-masted schooner, *Tasmania* (221′ x 35′ x 16′), foundered in a severe storm with all hands (8) and an iron ore cargo on October 20, 1905 (the *Siberia* and the *Sarah E. Sheldon,* also in this book, sank in the same storm). Part of the *Tasmania* wreck was dynamited on July 13, 1906, to remove her as a hazard to navigation.

The large wreck site includes a capstan, a winch, a cargo donkey boiler, vast amounts of iron ore and two anchors, one of which was removed by Ohio divers in 1987. Crossing an international boundary line with stolen archival property caused problems galore for those divers (including confiscation of their boats!) Federal agents seized the anchor and it was returned to the wreck site by the Canadian Coast Guard ship, *Kenoki,* on June 3, 1989, due in large part to the efforts of the Windsor chapter of Save Ontario Shipwrecks, as well as other agencies and individuals. This enormous anchor is probably the highlight of this site.

The schooner, *Tasmania.* IGLR

The media were out in full force on June 3, 1989, when the *Tasmania's* stolen anchor was returned to the shipwreck. Minutes after its placement, diver Art Vermette read the historic plaque next to the anchor. PHOTOS BY CRIS KOHL.

Sidescan sonar image of the *Tasmania*. Note the anchor at the wreck's upper right. © AQUA VISION RESEARCH

6. *JAY GOULD*

LORAN: 43829.2/57202.6	LAT 41° 51.530′ LON 082° 24.608′
DEPTH: 36 to 44 feet	LEVEL: Novice-Intermediate

LOCATION: This wreck lies about five miles southeast of Point Pelee.

Constructed at Buffalo, New York, in 1869, the 840-gross-ton wooden steamer, *Jay Gould* (213′8″ x 33′9″ x 11′5″), foundered with a cargo of coal on June 17, 1918. The entire crew was rescued by a passing steamer. The highlight of this wreck site is the tall, early (which makes it a rare one) steeple compound steam engine, in which even the Smithsonian Institute has expressed an interest. Although dynamited as a threat to navigation, this wreck still displays her four-bladed propeller, stern capstan and many scattered artifacts.

The steamer, *Jay Gould*. IGLR

A diver examines the *Jay Gould's* large propeller; the steam engine towers high above the lake bottom. PHOTOS BY CRIS KOHL.

Sidescan sonar image of the *Jay Gould*. © AQUA VISION RESEARCH

7. DOMINION

> **LORAN: 43880.5/57218.3**   **LAT 41° 59.751′ LON 082° 26.719′**
> **DEPTH: 45 feet**   **LEVEL: Novice-Intermediate**

LOCATION: This site lies a bit over five miles south of Wheatley, Ontario, harbor.

The flat, steam-powered dredge barge, *Dominion,* about 75 feet long and 25 feet wide, capsized while under tow on October 28, 1892. Once hoped to be the long-lost steamer, *Kent,* these shipwreck remains do offer the visiting diver views of a huge boiler, a winch with chain, and a variety of tools and artifacts.

> *Right:* A scuba diver descends to the boiler of the barge, *Dominion.* PHOTO BY CRIS KOHL.

8. CLARION

> **LORAN: 43890.1/57298.2**   **LAT 41° 57.262′ LON 082° 16.308′**
> **DEPTH: 58 to 77 feet**   **LEVEL: Advanced**

LOCATION: This wreck lies about 13 miles northeast of Point Pelee.

The composite (iron and wood) package freight steamer, *Clarion* (240′9″ x 36′1″ x 15′5″), launched at Wyandotte, Michigan, on July 27, 1881, burned to a total loss during a storm on December 8, 1909, off Point Pelee. Tragically, 15 of the 21 men on board the *Clarion* perished. The rescue of the 6 survivors is a fascinating tale of heroism.

The *Clarion.* AUTHOR'S COLLECTION

The steamer, *L.C. Hanna,* taking off some crew from the burning steamer, *Clarion.* THE MARINE REVIEW, JAN., 1910.

This storm also sank the *W.C. Richardson* (also in this book) at the other end of Lake Erie, and the train car ferry, *Marquette & Bessemer #2,* a long-sought Great Lakes shipwreck.

This upright wreck offers a very intact stern section which is penetrable by trained, experienced and prepared divers (beware of much silt!) In contrast, most of the bow burned off or is buried. The first divers at this site called this the "Stern Wreck" because they could find no bow at all. Items of interest at this site include a mushroom anchor and windlass and chain at the bow, a propeller, rudder, steam engine and boiler at the stern, and, in between, a capstan, bollards and locomotive wheels in the holds.

9. *WILLIS*

LORAN: 43897.2/57349.5	LAT 41° 55.879' LON 082° 09.669'
DEPTH: 60 to 73 feet	LEVEL: Intermediate-Advanced

LOCATION: This wreck lies about 15 miles east-northeast of Point Pelee.

The three-masted schooner, *Willis* (131'7" x 27'9" x 9'), sank in her first year afloat on November 11, 1872, after a collision with the bark, *Elizabeth Jones.* Built at Manitowoc, Wisconsin, the short-lived *Willis* was downbound with grain from Escanaba, Michigan, at the time of loss. Although no lives were lost in the sinking, a long court case ensued.

Originally located by Canadian gas-well-working hardhat diver, Michael Schoger, in about 1960, and finally identified when Cleveland diver, James Paskert, found the tonnage numbers on the rear hatch combing in the late 1980's, the *Willis* is an impressive shipwreck. The steering gear is interesting, even though the wheel was removed. Several

The *Willis*: under sail and under water. Art by Peter Rindlisbacher, courtesy of Roy Pickering, art owner.

Above: Diver Sharon Troxell follows steel rigging to a cleat on the *Willis. Below:* A missing *Willis* stern porthole. PHOTOS BY CRIS KOHL.

Sidescan sonar image of the *Willis.* Note such details as the bowsprit, rails, posts and hatches. © AQUA VISION RESEARCH

deadeyes and blocks remain, as well as a capstan, a bilge pump and a long portion of the bowsprit.. The smallest of the spars straddling the starboard rail could be the bowsprit of the *Elizabeth Jones,* torn off in the impact of the collision.

10. CONEMAUGH

| LORAN: 43835.2/57162.8 | LAT 41° 54.568′ LON 082° 30.660′ |
| DEPTH: 16 to 20 feet | LEVEL: Novice-Intermediate |

LOCATION: This wreck lies about 400′ off shore on the west side of Point Pelee right where the forest ends at the point. But make it a boat dive; you can't drive up to it on shore.

The wooden freighter, *Conemaugh* (251′3″ x 36′ x 15′2″), sister ship to the *Lycoming* (which is also in this book), was built at Bay City, Michigan, in 1880. On November 24, 1906, a violent storm beached the *Conemaugh* just off Point Pelee with such smashing force that three of her four propeller blades broke off on the sandbar. Fortunately, the entire crew was rescued by the men at the nearby Lifesaving Station.

Above: The *Conemaugh.* IGLR. *Below:* Joyce Hayward inspects *Conemaugh* machinery. PHOTO BY CRIS KOHL.

The sand covers and uncovers the timbers, the boiler and the broken propeller that comprise the main items left of this ship. Years ago, a local scuba diver salvaged the capstan and donated it to Point Pelee National Park, which put it on outdoor display. Unfortunately, it was not properly conserved and it soon became a broken pile of rust, especially after vandals rolled it around the concession stand.

11. M. I. WILCOX

| LORAN: 43802.2/56959.8 | LAT 41° 58.832′ LON 082° 56.455′ |
| DEPTH: 20 to 26 feet | LEVEL: Novice-Intermediate |

Drawing by Cris Kohl, based on on-site observations and information from Ed Fabok.

LOCATION: About 1/3 mile south of the Colchester, Ontario, dock.

The three-masted schooner, *M.I. Wilcox* (137′ x 27′5″ x 12′7″), built at Toledo in 1868, sprang a leak and sank on May 8, 1906, with no lives lost. Site sights include a windlass, donkey boiler, capstan, anchor, wheel, deadeyes and sometimes low visibility. This wreck was found on July 2, 1990 by Ed Fabok, Joe Drummond, & Lloyd & Betty Kerr.

AUTHOR'S COLLECTION

12. GRAND TRAVERSE

> **LORAN: 43796.0/56975.1**   **LAT 41° 56.902′ LON 082° 53.688′**
> **DEPTH: 35 to 40 feet**   **LEVEL: Novice-Intermediate**

LOCATION: This wreck lies off Colchester Reef, three miles southeast of Colchester. Now broken and scattered on a silty bottom, the wooden steamer, *Grand Traverse* (181′ x 33′ x 14′1″), sank in a collision with the steamer, Livingstone, on October 19, 1896. Considerable machinery salvage took place after the sinking, but the hull remains.

13. GEORGE WORTHINGTON

> **LORAN: 43800.1/56994.4**   **LAT 41° 56.687′ LON 082° 51.319′**
> **DEPTH: 32 to 40 feet**   **LEVEL: Novice-Intermediate**

LOCATION: This wreck lies off Colchester Reef.

The twin-masted schooner, *George Worthington* (119′9″ x 25′2″ x 10′1″), built in 1852 at Euclid Creek, Ohio, sank after a collision with the schooner, *George W. Davis,* on July 12, 1887. No lives were lost. This intact, upright wreck sports twin bow anchors, windlass, deadeyes, centerboard, tools on deck and a coal cargo. The wreck was discovered on July 28, 1987, by Ed Fabok and Art Vermette.

14. CASE

> **LORAN: 43744.3/56956.9**   **LAT 41° 48.586′ LON 082° 51.660′**
> **DEPTH: 18 to 20 feet**   **LEVEL: Novice**

LOCATION: This wreck lies about 600′ off the southwest side of East Sister Island.

The large, wooden steamer, *Case* (286′ x 42′5″ x 22′), loaded with coal (which was later salvaged, along with some machinery), stranded, caught on fire and broke up in a storm on May 1, 1917. No lives were lost. Built at Cleveland in 1889, wood and metal parts of the *Case* lie scattered over a wide area on a rocky bottom.

15. CAPSTAN WRECK (CHARGER?)

> **LORAN: 43812.7/57141.2**   **LAT 41° 51.659′ LON 082° 31.769′**
> **DEPTH: 30 to 36 feet**   **LEVEL: Novice-Intermediate**

LOCATION: This wreck lies in the Pelee Passage, west of Point Pelee.

This unidentified sailing vessel may be the remains of the schooner, *Charger* (136′ x 25′ x 10′), which sank in a collision with the steambarge, *City of Cleveland,* on July 31, 1890. The *Charger* sank within ten minutes, the crew barely escaping with their lives.

As the nickname implies, this site on a silty bottom has a capstan, as well as a windlass, wheel and deadeyes.

13. Other Western Lake Erie Sites

They have long winters in Canada, so ice diving in places like Kingsville harbor is popular. PHOTO BY CRIS KOHL.

1. *David Stewart*	11. *F. H. Prince*
2. *Isaac W. Nicholas*	12. *Adventure*
3. *David Vance*	13. *Keepsake*
4. *America*	14. *Isabella J. Boyce*
5. *Armenia*	15. *Toledo*
6. *Charles B. Packard*	16. *Charles Spademan*
7. *Philip Minch*	17. *Success*
8. *George Dunbar*	18. *Wesee*
9. *City of Concord*	19. *Magnet*
10. *Exchange*	20. *D. L. Filer*

1. DAVID STEWART

LORAN: 43858.0/57160.2	LAT 41° 58.695' LON 082° 32.939'
DEPTH: 25 to 32 feet	LEVEL: Novice

LOCATION: 700' off the western shore of Point Pelee, two miles from Leamington.

The 545-ton merchant schooner, *David Stewart* (171' x 31' x 13'), launched at Cleveland in 1867, stranded and broke up in a storm on October 6, 1893. The six men and one woman on board were daringly rescued from the sunken ship's masts by the fishing tug, *Louise*. Weather conditions were so odd and powerful that the *Louise* could not make headway into Leamington harbor two miles away, and instead steamed all the way across the lake to Sandusky with the rescued crew. Ice, wind and waves have flattened this wreck, but the stern is upright and belaying pins and a hawse pipe are on the bow. Beware of silt and nets.

2. ISAAC W. NICHOLAS

LORAN: 43819.39/57138.69	LAT 41° 52.932' LON 082° 32.701'
DEPTH: 30 to 36 feet	LEVEL: Novice-Intermediate

LOCATION: This wreck lies at Grubb's Reef to the southwest of Point Pelee.

Built at Vermilion, Ohio, in 1862 by Isaac W. Nicholas and named after himself, this three-masted schooner (137'8" x 26'2" x 12'2"), attempting to ride out a tempestuous storm on October 20, 1873, dragged her anchor and stranded on what was later named Grubb's Reef (after the Point Pelee light keeper who reported the shoal to officials). The crew took to the rigging, from which they were rescued the next day by the schooner, *Denmark*.

This wreck, in surprisingly very good condition, features a rudder, steering gear, blocks, deadeyes, belaying pins, windlass, anchor and wheel! Beware of fishnets and boating traffic.

3. DAVID VANCE

LORAN: 43813.82/57144.29	LAT 41° 51.724' LON 082° 31.440'
DEPTH: 42 feet	LEVEL: Novice-Intermediate

LOCATION: This wreck lies to the south-southwest of Point Pelee.

The three-masted schooner, *David Vance* (206'6" x 33'7" x 14'4"), built at Manitowoc, Wisconsin, in 1874, sank in a collision on July 20, 1873, with the schooner-barge, *Lizzie A. Law*, which was, like the *David Vance,* being towed by a steamer at the time. Both the *David Vance* and the *Lizzie A. Law* sank, but the latter was salvaged and returned to service.

Flattened by nature, the wreck of the *David Vance*, with the bow facing south on a sand bottom, exhibits a rudder post, centerboard, wheel and deadeyes. It lies within a few hundred feet of the wreck of the *Charger* (which is also in this book).

4. AMERICA

LORAN: 43783.49/57078.39	LAT 41° 49.679' LON 082° 38.069'
DEPTH: 15 feet	LEVEL: Novice

The *America*, based on a drawing by Heyl.

LOCATION: This wreck lies 175' off the northeast tip of Pelee Island, 1/2 mile south of the abandoned lighthouse.

The sidewheel steamer, *America* (240'2" x 34'2" x 13'8"), ran aground on April 5, 1854, with no lives lost. Spring storms quickly broke up the ship. A tall boiler, planking, and other remains are scattered in a large debris field.

5. ARMENIA

> **LORAN: 43806.62/57091.06**   **LAT 41° 52.948′ LON 082° 38.503′**
> **DEPTH: 35 to 39 feet**   **LEVEL: Novice-Intermediate**

LOCATION: This wreck lies off Colchester Reef. Beware of fishnets.

The schooner-barge, *Armenia* (288′6″ x 44′6″ x 19′1″), with a cargo of iron ore, foundered in a storm on May 9, 1906, with no lives lost. Built at West Bay City, Michigan, in 1896 by James Davidson, the *Armenia* was eventually dynamited, but not before she caused another shipwreck, the *Charles B. Packard* (which is the next wreck in this book). The *Armenia's* wood, rudder and machinery lie scattered, and in a silt-heavy area where one good fin-kick an arm's length above the shipwreck will destroy the visibility in that area for the rest of the day.

Left, the schooner-barge, *Armenia* (IGLR), which caused the steamer, *Charles B. Packard* (MPL/WMHS), *above,* to sink.

6. CHARLES B. PACKARD

> **LORAN: 43808.49/57053.82**   **LAT 41° 55.222′ LON 082° 43.661′**
> **DEPTH: 37 to 40 feet**   **LEVEL: Novice-Intermediate**

LOCATION: This wreck lies near the *Armenia* off Colchester Reef.

Sunk after colliding with the wreck of the *Armenia* on September 16, 1906, with no lives lost, the wooden steamer, *Charles B. Packard* (180′5″ x 35′7″ x 13′3″), had been built in 1887, also at West Bay City, Michigan, but by James Davidson's competition, F.W. Wheeler & Company. How the jokes must have flown in Bay City about a wrecked Davidson boat sinking a Wheeler steamer! This site, in much silt, consists of a huge boiler sitting in a broken hull surrounded by a large debris field.

7. PHILIP MINCH

> **LORAN: 43741.93/57106.21**   **LAT 41° 41.301′ LON 082° 30.813′**
> **DEPTH: 42 to 48 feet**   **LEVEL: Intermediate**

LOCATION: This wreck lies about eight miles east of Middle Island.

Built at Cleveland in 1888, the wooden steamer, *Philip Minch* (275′ x 40′8″ x 22′), caught on fire and sank with no lives lost on November 20, 1904. Machinery and seemingly endless collapsed hull sections make up most of this site, with the huge (but recently toppled over) steeple compound steam engine at the stern. Beware of snagged nets.

Right: The steamer, *Philip Minch.* MPL/WMHS

At the *Philip Minch's* bow.
PHOTO BY CRIS KOHL.

Sidescan sonar image of the *Philip Minch*. The engine and boiler are evident at the left. © AQUA VISION RESEARCH

8. GEORGE DUNBAR

> **LORAN: 43729.63/57076.39   LAT 41° 40.627′ LON 082° 33.891′**
> **DEPTH: 42 to 45 feet   LEVEL: Intermediate**

LOCATION: This wreck lies about six miles southeast of Fish Point, Pelee Island.

The small steamer, *George Dunbar* (133′5″ x 25′3″ x 9′1″), sprang a leak and foundered on June 29, 1902, with a coal cargo and all seven crewmembers who did not survive their lifeboats capsizing. The captain, his wife and their daughter, the only ones wearing lifejackets, were rescued by islanders in a small boat. The wreck sits in mud, with a boiler, windlass and upright support posts the dominant features.

Sidescan sonar image of the *George Dunbar*. Note the central support post shadows. © AQUA VISION RESEARCH

9. CITY OF CONCORD

> **LORAN: 43675.02/57052.68   LAT 41° 32.730′ LON 082° 32.808′**
> **DEPTH: 45 feet   LEVEL: Intermediate**

LOCATION: This wreck lies about ten miles north of Huron, Ohio.

The wooden steamer, *City of Concord* (135′2″ x 25′8″ x 11′), constructed in 1868 at Cleveland, took on water during a storm and foundered on September 29, 1906, with the loss of two lives. One crewman was rescued by a passsing vessel, while the rest of the crew reached land near cedar Point in a yawlboat. Sitting upright in mud, this wreck site features a rudder, engine, boiler, windlass, chain, decking and the relatively intact hull.

10. EXCHANGE

LORAN: 43672.22/56974.02   LAT 41° 35.644' LON 082° 43.229'
DEPTH: 15 feet   LEVEL: Novice

LOCATION: 200' off the south side of Kelley's Island, east of the ferry dock.
The schooner, *Exchange* (138' x 26' x 11'8"), stranded with a load of stone on November 21, 1874, and was abandoned. Planking, ribs and chain remain at the site.

11. F. H. PRINCE

LORAN: 43683.02/57000.38   LAT 41° 36.242' LON 082° 40.518'
DEPTH: 18 feet   LEVEL: Novice

LOCATION: This wreck lies about 1/2 mile off the east side of Kelley's Island.
Launched at Detroit in 1890, the wooden steamer, *F.H. Prince* (240' x 42' x 23'4"),

MPL/WMHS

caught on fire in the lake on August 8, 1911, and was beached and extinguished. On Aug. 14th, the fire re-ignited, and she burned to a total loss. Large timbers and machinery rest on a rock bottom, but the engine/boiler were salvaged. Beware of heavy boating traffic!

Sonar image: *F.H. Prince*. © AQUA VISION RESEARCH

12. ADVENTURE

LORAN: 43688.09/57000.92   LAT 41° 37.088' LON 082° 40.871'
DEPTH: 10 feet   LEVEL: Novice

LOCATION: This wreck lies in North Bay, Kelley's Island. The steamer, *Adventure* (108' x 24' x 8'3"), burned on October 7, 1903. Hull timbers and machinery remain.

13. KEEPSAKE

LORAN: LAT 41° 40' 55" LON 082° 41' 16"
DEPTH: 10 feet   LEVEL: Novice

LOCATION: 125' off SW side of Middle Island. The small schooner, *Keepsake* (72'6" x 19'9" x 3'7"), stranded on August 11, 1911. Parts and artifacts lie scattered on rocks.

14. ISABELLA J. BOYCE

LORAN: 56972.21/43708.99	LAT 41° 41.831′ LON 082° 46.507′
DEPTH: 5 to 10 feet	LEVEL: Novice

LOCATION: East Point Reef off Middle Bass Island. The wooden sandsucker, *Isabella J. Boyce* (138′ x 29′6″ x 11′), stranded and burned on June 6, 1917. This wreck is very broken and widely scattered among rocks in VERY SHALLOW WATER!

15. TOLEDO

LORAN: 43690.68/56916.60	LAT 41° 41.141′ LON 082° 52.601′
DEPTH: 35 feet	LEVEL: Novice-Intermediate

LOCATION: One mile west of Rattlesnake Island. The barge, *Toledo*, foundered on November 19, 1924, with all 7 men surviving. She is broken and scattered on a rock bottom.

16. CHARLES SPADEMAN

LORAN: 28853.28/56920.12	LAT	LON
DEPTH: 32 feet	LEVEL: Novice-Intermediate	

LOCATION: About 2/3 mile 160° from South Bass Island Lighthouse. The schooner, *Charles Spademan* (134′2″ x 25′9″ x 10′8″), sank after her hull was punctured by ice on Dec. 10, 1909. Her coal cargo was salvaged and the wreck was dynamited, so little remains.

17. SUCCESS

LORAN: 43616.38/56855.91	LAT 41° 31.319′ LON 082° 54.703′
DEPTH: 15 feet	LEVEL: Novice

AUTHOR'S COLLECTION

LOCATION: 1/2 mile off Port Clinton. This historic teak barquentine (135′ x 30′ x 14′), built in India in 1840 but passed off as being older, toured the world as a "Prison Ship" which had conveyed convicts to Australia. *Success* left for America the same day *Titanic* did, only she made it. However, she burned in Lake Erie on July 4, 1946. Keel, ribs, planking, metal parts and fish are plentiful.

18. WESEE

LORAN: 43739.3/56895.1	LAT 41° 50.597′ LON 082° 59.565′
DEPTH: 22 feet	LEVEL: Novice

LOCATION: This wreck lies off Middle Sister Island. The wooden steamer, *Wesee* (265′5″ x 42′ x 22′7″), burned to a total loss on November 12, 1923. The crew, plus two starving fishermen who had been marooned on the island, were rescued. Although engine/boiler were salvaged, much remains scattered.

19. MAGNET

LORAN: 43757.82/56926.73	LAT 41° 52.866′ LON 082° 57.406′
DEPTH: 35 feet	LEVEL: Novice-Intermediate

LOCATION: The two-masted schooner, *Magnet* (141′8″ x 24′ x 7′4″), foundered in a storm east of Middle Sister Island. Her crew was rescued. This shipwreck lies scattered.

20. D. L. FILER

LORAN: 43787.81/56925.78	LAT	LON
DEPTH: 20 feet	LEVEL: Novice-Intermediate	

The schooner-barge, *D.L. Filer* (156′6″ x 30′ x 10′), sank (in the same storm as the *Merida, James B. Colgate* and *Marshall F. Butters*) with only the captain surviving. Silty !

146

The Zebra Mussel Invasion of the Great Lakes

My home town of Windsor, Ontario, is located about five miles from where the zebra mussel invasion was first noticed in shallow Lake St. Clair. I wrote my first article on the zebra mussel invasion of the Great Lakes in the spring of 1989, and it appeared in _Diving Times_ (Royal Oak, Michigan) that summer under the heading, "Shipwrecks Threatened by Freshwater Barnacles" (their identification as zebra mussels was made later that summer by two University of Windsor biology students).

I gave a presentation on this topic, focusing primarily on how these uninvited guests were affecting shipwrecks and, hence, scuba diving, at the annual meeting of the Ontario Archaeological Society in October, 1989 (held that year in London, Ontario), at the annual Save Ontario Shipwrecks Forum in November, 1989 (held that year in Windsor, Ontario), and at the annual Great Lakes Shipwreck Festival, Dearborn, Michigan, in February, 1990. Since then, I have kept updating that presentation, which I have given dozens of times to a wide variety of audiences mostly in the Great Lakes region but also as distant as New York City.

The next four pages provide the essence of that presentation.

♦   ♦   ♦   ♦   ♦   ♦   ♦   ♦   ♦

In the spring of 1988, I received a letter from Graeme Henderson, author of the book, _Maritime Archaeology in Australia_ and curator, Department of Maritime Archaeology, at the Western Australian Maritime Museum in Fremantle near Perth. He stated, among other things, that "I have of course read about your amazingly well-preserved Great Lakes shipwrecks...."

He was naturally comparing them to saltwater shipwrecks, with their fast-forming coral encrustations, such as the steel vessel, _Denton Holmes,_ off Rottnest Island near Perth in the Indian Ocean, or the purposely sunk World War II minesweeper, the _Mahi,_ off the coast of Oahu, Hawaii.

Left: Denton Holmes wreckage in the Indian Ocean. _Middle:_ The _Mahi_ off Oahu in 1988 after 6 years of submergence. _Right:_ Joan Forsberg examines coral encrustation on the _Mahi_ in 2001 when the ship had been submerged for 19 years. We expect saltwater shipwrecks to look like this, but our freshwater shipwrecks in the Great Lakes looked comparatively pristine! PHOTOS BY CRIS KOHL.

The shipwrecks in our own Great Lakes area are now being threatened by the saltwater invader known as the zebra mussel (or by its Latin name: dreissena polymorpha). Present in the ballast water of ocean-going freighters, these zebra mussels somehow adapted to freshwater conditions when this ballast water was dumped in Lake St. Clair in about 1986. The unknown ship(s) which did the dumping probably filled its ballast tanks in coastal Europe and, instead of dumping and replenishing in mid-Atlantic Ocean (where the saltwater is devoid of zebra mussel larvae) as was the custom, it waited until it was in the Great Lakes system before it dumped and replenished.

Recent laws have been enacted prohibiting the dumping of ballast water from ocean-going freighters in the Great Lakes, but that's like closing the gate after the horses have escaped.

The opening of the St. Lawrence Seaway system more than 40 years ago paved the way for greater wealth in the Great Lakes region, but now we who live, work and play there are paying a potentially severe price for that participation in world trade.

There are several biological hitchhikers now in our Great Lakes, including the River Ruffe fish and European water fleas, but the zebra mussel seems destined to be the most destructive in overall terms.

Physically, zebra mussels are small and unimposing. Averaging the size of a ten-cent coin, they individually look quite harmless and perhaps even "cute," as one of my scuba diving colleagues described them.

However, they attach themselves by the millions to anything that is solid in the lakes, and their reproduction abilities make rabbits seem celibate.

Originating in the saltwater Caspian Sea between Russia and Iran, the zebra mussels started spreading to western Europe's coasts in the mid-1800's, at about the same time that steam-powered ships developed Caspian Sea trade with the rest of Europe

Mature zebra mussels' size compared to a dime. PHOTO BY CRIS KOHL.

along the River Volga and the Baltic Sea and Black Sea routes.

By the late 1800's, coastal Europe, with its combination of salt and fresh water areas (from its freshwater rivers flowing into the saltwater ocean), was inundated by zebra mussels. To date, the Europeans have found no effective method of eliminating this problem.

In late 1988, these "vile crustaceans" (as one newspaper article at that time described them) were clogging water intake pipes along southeastern Lake St. Clair and the northwestern shore of Lake Erie. By February, 1989, the mussels had spread along Lake Erie's north shore as far east as Port Burwell. They reached Dunkirk, New York, by October 16, 1989, and by year's end, western Lake Ontario. Carried upstream by freighters to which they had attached themselves in Lake Erie, the first zebra mussels were identified in Green Bay harbor, Wisconsin, Lake Michigan, in late October, 1989. The harbors of Duluth, Minnesota, and Thunder Bay, Ontario, both on Lake Superior, were also soon colonized. Generally, the largest and coldest of our five Great Lakes contains too little calcium which zebra mussels need to form their shells, as well as the wrong amount of Ph (acidity) which zebra mussels in the southern, heavily-populated half of the Great Lakes find so nourishing.

Each zebra mussel female can produce 30,000 to 40,000 offspring in one season. Zebra mussel larvae resemble fine grains of sand as they drift along with the current encased in an

148

invisible jelly-like blob. As they grow larger, they seek anything solid to which they can attach themselves by means of a hair-like thread called a byssal thread. This makes them different from their bivalve relatives called clams. Mussels attach themselves to objects, while clams just sit freely on the bottom.

The first dramatic incident of scuba divers being awed and dazed by the surprising presence of zebra mussels occurred in late February, 1989, when Roy Pickering and Jeff Bliss, members of Kent Divers Association, Kent County, Ontario, were exploring the Erieau channel on Lake Erie. In about 18 feet of water, they unexpectedly came upon an automobile. However, it seemed to be almost totally encrusted with what the divers, not knowing what they were dealing with, termed "barnacles." One of the local media profiled the police retrieval of this vehicle, which had been stolen the previous August and likely had been submerged for those preceding six months. The zebra mussels had attached themselves to virtually every part of the vehicle, not just to the metal body, chrome bumpers and rubber tires, but also to the vinyl interior.

As more water intake pipes started clogging because of gradual zebra mussel build-up inside them, more media attention in that central Great Lakes area was paid to this new problem. At about this time (May, 1989), I began reshooting underwater photos of some of the shipwrecks in the western Lake Erie area. At that early stage, the shipwrecks lying in less than 40 feet of water were almost totally covered by zebra mussels. I noticed that portions where there were no mussels were parts of the shipwreck where the silt or sand covering was too thick for mussel attachment. They need something solid, such as steel, iron, or wood. We could no longer discern what we were looking at because a lump of coal or a chunk of limestone cargo from a shipwreck resembled exactly an indigenous lake-bottom rock or a ship's compass when it was covered in several layers of zebra mussels (they do attach themselves to each other and, like in a coral reef system, the lower layer dies once it

Diver Joyce Hayward with the propeller hub of the steamer, _Conemaugh,_ western Lake Erie, in June, 1988, just before the zebra mussel invasion. PHOTO BY CRIS KOHL.

That same propeller hub photographed from the same angle in July, 1989, a mere 13 months later. It is totally unrecognizable. PHOTO BY CRIS KOHL.

is covered by another layer). I have even seen clustered balls of zebra mussels attached to each other rolling around the sandy lake bottom off Rondeau Point in their desperation to attach themselves to anything solid. A biologist in Wheatley, Ontario, declared that the zebra mussels are mildly caustic, which means that they damage their roosts. At least one archaeologist has argued that the zebra mussels will help preserve our Great Lakes shipwrecks for future generations, but he is grasping at straws. The weight of thousands upon thousands of zebra mussels, for another thing, has not only caused Coast Guard buoys to sink, but also parts of shipwrecks to collapse, such as the once-impressive bowsprit of the schooner, _Nimrod._

One potential effect of dubious benefit in that illegal shipwreck-stripping will be made more difficult, since the identification of choice shipwreck souvenirs will be made more difficult. A chadburn, or telegraph, sitting on the lake floor coated with five layers of zebra mussels could well be shrugged off by the passing scuba diver as being merely a rock.

I photographed the Colchester Reef wreck of the schooner, *George Worthington,* in western Lake Erie, and it was totally covered in multi-layers of zebra mussels -- except for one unusual item. It was a light-colored pipe which we, at first, suspected was made of lead. It turned out to be copper. Initially, zebra mussels avoided attaching themselves to anything made of copper, brass or bronze, but within two years, they had acclimatized to those metals as well.The readily-adaptible zebra mussels rolled on like the plague.

By September, 1989, biologists were predicting the probable destruction of our large freshwater clams because the smaller zebra mussels are attaching themselves to them in such vast numbers until the native clams can no longer open their shells, and thus they

The *Merida's* bow anchor, August, 1987. PHOTO BY CRIS KOHL. | The same, August, 1992. PHOTO BY CRIS KOHL. | The *Merida's* starboard bow anchor chain, April, 1990. PHOTO BY CRIS KOHL. | The same, August, 1992. PHOTO BY CRIS KOHL.

starve to death. Zebra mussels even attached themselves to freshwater crayfish. Ropes left dangling in the water from docks soon became home to thick clusters of zebra mussels.

A questionable benefit of the zebra mussel invasion has been a cleansing of our Great Lakes waters. Zebra mussels are filter feeders, each tiny individual filtering about one liter of water each day. Since they remove the floating particles in the water, increased visibility has been a boon to scuba diving in Lakes Erie, Ontario and the St. Lawrence River in recent years. But at what a price! Besides the aesthetic destruction of our shipwrecks, the cleaner water is allowing more sunlight to reach greater depths -- forcing fish, such as pickerel, or walleye, which prefer darker, colder water, to seek deeper spawning grounds. In the shallows, the increased clarity and sunlight have caused incredible growth of aquatic plants, which, when they die, wash ashore. The shoreline of Lake St. Clair was inundated by foul-smelling, decaying seaweed, and the aerial photographs I took of Lake St. Clair in 1991 showed enormous beds of weeds in clear, shallow water, giving the lake different hues of green and blue. It almost looked like the Bahamas!

Of course, once the zebra mussels have depleted their food supply in that area, they die. Unfortunately, most of their shells remain attached to the object to which the animal attached itself when it was alive. When particle-rich waters (low visibility) return, zebra mussels will thrive again. Scientists in Europe have observed zebra mussels thriving in cycles which recur about every six or seven years. They have also found zebra mussels in Europe's cold inland lakes (carried there by waterfowl in all likelihood) at depths of 300 feet, so the hope that the cold will eliminate them from certain Great Lakes regions or depths was dashed. In March, 2000, Capt. Jerry Guyer showed videotape at Milwaukee's Ghost Ships Festival of zebra mussels attached to a new shipwreck discovery in 300 feet of Lake Michigan water.

As far as marine archaeology is concerned, Great Lakes interests may have to accept and learn saltwater methods of conducting their business. Many well-traveled scuba divers have observed that the Great Lakes possess, without question, the best preserved shipwrecks in the world. For now, we can only hope that these shipwrecks, Great Lakes scuba diving and freshwater marine archaeology will continue to have a future.

14. Sites near Lake Erie

Aerial view of Crystal Bay, with its many party boats, and Hidden Lake in the Detroit River. PHOTO BY CRIS KOHL.

1. Chippawa Creek
2. Sherkston Quarry
3. Elora Gorge Quarry
4. Trout Lake (Innerkip) Quarry
5. St. Marys Quarry
6. Nelson's Ledges Quarry
7. White Star Quarry
8. Portage Quarry
9. Gilboa Quarry
10. Baw Beese Lake
11. Crystal Bay/ Hidden Lake

1. Chippawa Creek

Near the town of Chippawa, Ontario, along the Niagara River, this site is a popular drift dive in swift water (so it's not for novices) for old bottles and other discarded items. There are many public exit and entry points along this short creek. The depth reaches 35 feet.

2. Sherkston Quarry

Located five miles east of Port Colborne, Ontario, this quarry, to a depth of 35 feet, still contains old locomotives and railway tracks from its active quarry days. There is also an underwater pumphouse and lots of fish life to enjoy. Fee. Camping is available.

3. Elora Gorge Quarry

Located between the towns of Elora and Fergus, Ontario, north of Kitchener, this popular quarry has very limited hours for scuba diving (10 AM to noon daily in season) and divers must sign a waiver at the gate. Fee. Sandy beach, camping and facilities are available.

4. Trout Lake (Innerkip) Quarry

Located at the town of Innerkip, Ontario, near the city of Woodstock, this quarry offers submerged airplanes, boats, a car, a schoolbus, and a mineshaft for the specially trained. Maximum depth is 28 feet, but the mineshaft goes down to 54 feet. Fee.

5. St. Marys Quarry

Located just south of the town of St. Marys, Ontario, this old limestone quarry reaches a depth of 60 feet and is a day-use only park. May to September. Fee.

6. Nelson's Ledges Quarry

Located halfway between Cleveland and Youngstown, Ohio, at the town of Nelson, this 30-acre park offers two sunken boats, several cars, large boilers, old machinery and fish (bluegill, catfish and bass) in a maximum depth of 40 feet. Fee. Camping is available.

7. White Star Quarry

The 15-acre White Star Quarry Park is located between the towns of Gibsonburg and Helena, Ohio, southeast of Toledo. It offers rocky drop-offs, an underwater forest, and a spiral staircase to a stone-crushing room. Depths reach 70 feet. Fee. Limited facilites.

8. Portage Quarry

Located one mile south of Bowling Green, OH, south of Toledo, this 22-acre quarry has an underwater silo, dynamite hut, school bus, cars, telephone booth and six boats. Fee.

9. Gilboa Quarry

This 14-acre quarry, 20 miles west of Findlay, Ohio, features a sunken forest, a van, bus and boat, and averages 40-foot depths, but gets deeper than 120 feet at one end. Fee.

10. Baw Beese Lake

Located one mile southeast of Hillsdale, which is about 25 miles south of Jackson, MI, this lake reaches 70-foot depths, with a cabin cruiser in 55 feet and two others shallower.

11. Crystal Bay/Hidden Lake

Just upstream from Amherstburg, ON, on the downstream side of a Detroit River island, the bay is a popular party place for Detroit area boaters who drop a lot of things overboard. Hidden Lake is a manmade cut 30 feet deep just off the bay. A boat is needed to get there.

15. St. Clair River

1. *Gladstone* and other wrecks
2. *Fontana*
3. *Charles H. Weeks*
4. *John B. Martin*
5. Dump scow ("The Barge")
6. *Monarch*
7. C. S. L. Docks
8. *Sidney E. Smith, Jr.* boom
9. *M. E. Tremble* & 2 salvage boats
10. Fishing boat
11. *A. R. Colborn* & crane
12. *Sidney E. Smith, Jr.* dock
13. *Saltillo*
14. Unknown wreckage
15. Ferry Dock Hill
16. *Erin*
17. *William Dickinson*
18. *William H. Wolf*
19. Highbanks Park
20. Snye Channel

1. GLADSTONE AND OTHER WRECKS

DEPTH: 10 to 15 feet   LEVEL: Novice-Intermediate

LOCATION: The wreck of the wooden steamer, *Gladstone* (282' x 40'3" x 23'), lies intermingled with the remains of the old schooners, *Arrow* and *A.W. Wright.* All three of them were used as the foundation for a dock in 1923; in 1936, the dock burned.

The *Gladstone,* built in 1888 at Cleveland, lies 200' offshore from the western end of Canatara Park. Leave your car in the lot north of the traffic circle at the park's western entrance. Enter Lake Huron about 200' east of the old boat ramp at the end of the parking lot. Look for pieces of the hull, piping and other metal items. Boating traffic is heavy, so use a divers down flag. Compensate for the mild current before it takes you into the swift mouth of the St. Clair River.

The steamer, *Gladstone.* AUTHOR'S COLLECTION   The dramatic shipwreck, *Fontana.* ONTARIO ARCHIVES

2. FONTANA

DEPTH: 65 feet   LEVEL: Advanced

LOCATION: This wreck lies a fair distance upstream of the Bluewater Bridge.

The *Fontana* (241'3" x 39'1" x 17') was a graceful, huge schooner built at St. Clair, Michigan, on the shores of the St. Clair River, in 1888. Originally sailing under four masts, she was cut down to two when she was demoted to a towbarge.On the hot night of August 3, 1900, the *Fontana,* with over 2,500 tons of iron ore, sank in a collision with the schooner-barge, *Santiago.* One life was lost, a sailor named John McGregor who was sleeping below deck on the *Fontana.* While Canada and the U.S. bickered over which country the wreck was in (and who was responsible for removing her), the dangerously positioned *Fontana* caused the *John B. Martin* (which is also in this book) to sink with 4 lives lost. The *Fontana* was later dynamited. This is a challenging shore or boat dive. The current is extremely fast and the river bottom zooms by quickly. Enter from shore upstream of the wreck, or pull yourself upstream in the shallows before descending. It is difficult to stop and study the wreck if you are lucky enough to be carried onto it. If you missed it, follow the bottom back to shore. Never surface anywhere but at the shore! The boating traffic is horrendous.

3. CHARLES H. WEEKS

DEPTH: 68 feet   LEVEL: Advanced

LOCATION: This wreck, just downstream from the *Fontana,* is often mistaken for her.

The schooner, *Charles H. Weeks* (134'2" x 26' x 11'), built at Marine City, Michigan, in 1873, was stranded at Point Edward, Ontario, in the very damaging gale of October 6, 1889, and slid off into deep water at the mouth of the St. Clair River. The mate of the *Charles H. Weeks* died the next day from injuries he had received at the ship's wheel when the vessel struck the beach. Both bow anchors were removed in the early 1960's, with one of them sold to a Wisconsin collector for $1,000. The capstan was also removed, restored and placed in front of a local restaurant, but it disappeared when the building burned down in 1986, This very challenging dive should be handled the same way as a dive to the *Fontana.*

154

4. JOHN B. MARTIN

DEPTH: 65 to 80 feet   LEVEL: Very Advanced

LOCATION: 500' off the Michigan shore, just upstream of the Bluewater Bridge.

The three-masted schooner, _John B. Martin_ (220'2" x 34'2" x 14'2"), was forced to pass in a narrow part of the St. Clair River on September 21, 1900, because of the wrecked _Fontana_ (also in this book), thereby, indirectly because of the wreck, becoming a wreck herself after she collided in such close quarters with the steel steambarge, _Yuma._ Four lives were lost from the _John B. Martin._ Government and shipping representatives hastily met and worked out plans for the removal of two wrecks as obstructions to navigation.

Longtime local divers describe the _John B. Martin_ as the most dangerous wreck in the entire St. Clair River to dive. She sits in one of the deepest depressions in the river bottom, adding depth challenges to those already evident in the extremely strong 5-10 knot current which reportedly plays direction games in that depression. The boating traffic here in the shipping channel is heavy. Diving from shore, locals enter at the foot of Riverview Street, where there is a small, public beach, and they exit on the large, flat rocks just beneath the Bluewater Bridge. In between, they hope to reach the wreck of the _John B. Martin_ and do some exploring. The wreck's anchor, on display in the park below the bridge, was raised by Bill Patterson, his sons and some friends in early 1981.

The _John B. Martin._ AUTHOR'S COLLECTION

5. DUMP SCOW ("THE BARGE")

DEPTH: 40 feet   LEVEL: Advanced

LOCATION: This wreck lies off the Canadian shore just south of the Bluewater Bridge.

This unnamed barge is the dump scow which sank on May 7, 1948, about 250' south of the bridge and 100' from shore. A tug was towing her, laden with mud, into the lake, when she suddenly nose-dived and sank. One man on the scow swam to shore. A cable from the north corner of the cement retaining wall runs to the wreck from shore. The scow's trap door, chains and three holds can be studied. Beware of strong current, boating traffic, and fishing lines here. Experienced divers with plenty of air can drift down to the _Monarch._

6. MONARCH

DEPTH: 58 feet   LEVEL: Advanced

LOCATION: This wreck lies 500' south of the Bluewater Bridge in Canadian waters.

This is one of the most popular St. Clair River shore dives for experienced divers. Entry point is a convenient set of steel stairs to the river in the cement wall, remnants of the Canada Steamship Line's glory days. Parking is a few feet away. The wreck of the tug, _Monarch_ (63'3" x 19'1" x 7'7"), lies about 200' off shore. Just follow the submerged cable

R. HARRISON

Tim Philp studies the *Monarch's* steering machinery. PHOTO BY CRIS KOHL.

Alan Armbruster pulls himself upstream on the port railing. PHOTO BY CRIS KOHL.

The *Monarch.* AUTHOR'S COLLECTION

that runs across the sand bottom to the site. The *Monarch*, built at Sheboygan, Wisconsin, in 1889 as the *W.H. Simpson,* swung out of control while towing the old steamer, *C.F Bielman* (also in this book) on July 6, 1934, and sank with the loss of four lives. The deck is missing, but penetration is possible at the bow. The strong 4-8 knot current makes this a challenging dive. If you get blown off the wreck, follow the bottom back to shore (the <u>Canadian</u> shore!). Also, beware of boating traffic and fishing lines.

7. C. S. L. DOCKS

DEPTH: 20 feet   **LEVEL: Novice-Intermediate**

LOCATION: This shore dive is just downstream of the *Monarch* shore entry.

Tour submerged posts (from the old Canada Steamship Lines docks) and find everything from bottles and cans to fishing rods, lures and bicycles. Good for current dive beginners. Don't go out too far, and exit at the same point where you entered.

8. SIDNEY E. SMITH, JR., BOOM

DEPTH: 50 to 55 feet   **LEVEL: Advanced**

Part of the *Sidney E. Smith, Jr.'s* boom remains in the river. PUBLIC ARCHIVES OF CANADA

LOCATION: About 100 feet off Whipple Street, Port Huron.

On June 6, 1972, the 66-year-old steel freighter, *Sidney E. Smith, Jr.* (489' x 52'2" x 26'5"), sank near the mouth of the St. Clair River after a collision with another steel freighter, the *Parker Evans* (which remained afloat, although damaged). Over the next 6 months, the *Smith* was salvaged (the bow

156

Left: Divers at the C.S.L. docks. *Above:* Fast water rushes past the wrecks in the mouth of the St. Clair River. PHOTOS BY CRIS KOHL.

was removed and the stern became a dock across the river in Canada). Part of the self-unloader boom broke off at the site. It helps to dive with someone who knows precisely where this boom is located. Launched as the *W.K. Bixby* in 1906 at Wyandotte, Michigan, this ship was renamed the *J.L. Reiss* in 1920, and finally the *Sidney E. Smith, Jr.* in the spring of 1972. Her new name's paint was barely dry when she sank. In 1997, I had the unique honor of doing a 25th anniversary presentation about this shipwreck in Port Huron with Mr. Sidney E. Smith, Jr., the one after whom this vessel was named, in the audience. Also present was Mr. Robert Campbell, who had rescued the crew in his boat that night.

9. *M. E. TREMBLE* AND TWO SALVAGE BOATS

DEPTH: 50 to 70 feet   LEVEL: Advanced

LOCATION: This wreck lies off the U.S. side just below the Bluewater Bridge.

The large, three-masted schooner, *M.E. Tremble* (198' x 34'5" x 13'4"), was under tow of the steamer, *B.W. Blanchard,* on the night of September 7, 1890, when the downbound steamer, *W.L. Wetmore* (which is also in this book) crashed into her port side. The crew hastily launched the yawl boat and left the sinking ship, realizing too late that one of their number had been left behind and was struggling for survival in the doomed ship's rigging. Unfortunately, he perished. Recovery of the coal cargo resulted in the accidental sinking of the salvage schooner, *Ben Hur,* along with a small lighter which tended its cables, on November 8, 1890. The *Ben Hur* today lies upside down, upstream of, but alongside the wreck of the *M.E. Tremble,* which lies across the current, while the lighter sits broken up just downstream from the *Tremble.* With the installation of a long, steel breakwall here in the late 1980's, it has become more challenging to reach this wreck and then exit the water. Divers often suit up and jump in right beneath the Bluewater Bridge and let the current swiftly take them to the wrecks. This could be tricky in low visibility and is not recommended, as the strong current could pin a diver against the wreck. Use of a dive flag is mandatory in Michigan waters, although some divers tie one off where they enter the water and have another one anchored where they intend to surface. You have to be good to do this, because the law states that you must surface within 50 feet of your flag.

10. FISHING BOAT

DEPTH: 22 feet   LEVEL: Novice

LOCATION: This unidentified fishing tug lies abandoned at the northwest end of the channel leading from the St. Clair River to Bridgeview Marina in Sarnia, Ontario.

11. *A.R. COLBORN* AND CRANE

DEPTH: 35 feet   LEVEL: Novice-Intermediate

LOCATION: This wreck lies just north of the YMCA Building in Port Huron, Michigan.

The wooden steamer, *A.R. Colborn* (129'9" x 27'7" x 9'5"), launched at Saugatuck, Michigan, on April 18, 1882, was, after a long career in the lumber industry, formally abandoned at this location on April 28, 1922, with her final enrollment surrendered and endorsed as "abandoned as unfit for service." The boiler, engine and hull remain at the site, while the propeller graces a college lawn in Port Huron. Miller's crane, which was lost here in about 1953, also lies at this site.

12. SIDNEY E. SMITH, JR. DOCK
DEPTH: 30 feet   LEVEL: Novice-Intermediate

LOCATION: The remains of half of the steel freighter, Sidney E. Smith, Jr., were raised from the bottom of the St. Clair River in late 1972 (see site # 10 in this chapter) and moved to the Canadian side for use as a dock. When you dive here, it may be hard to imagine that this was once a large vessel. Many fish congregate around the broken end. Take Exmouth Road in Sarnia towards the river, turn left (south) at Harbour Road, and swing west on that road to the government dock. The *Sidney E. Smith, Jr.* is part of that dock.

13. SALTILLO
DEPTH: 35 to 45 feet   LEVEL: Advanced

LOCATION: This wreck lies straight out into the river from the Canadian government dock in Sarnia. Diving from a boat is the best way. The schooner, *Saltillo,* is the oldest known shipwreck in the St. Clair River, having gone there after a collision with another schooner on November 25, 1853. She carried a cargo of coal and railroad iron. Her holds are mostly filled with sand and silt, but her hatches, blocks and deadeyes are intact. Her anchors were removed by early divers. Beware of the current and much boating traffic.

14. UNKNOWN WRECKAGE
DEPTH: To 15 feet   LEVEL: Novice-Intermediate

LOCATION: The remains of unidentified, abandoned shipwrecks lie scattered in the southern section of Sarnia Bay, just to the north and west of the entry channel. That's not surprising, since Sarnia Bay was the dumping ground for wrecked or abandoned vessels from both sides of the border around the turn of the last century. Vessels that were taken here to get them out of the way included the *City of Genoa, Yakima, Aztec, Province* and at least a dozen others, most of which were removed in the 1920's and 1930's by raising them or their pieces and scuttling them out in Lake Huron about 11 miles from Sarnia.

15. FERRY DOCK HILL
DEPTH: To 20 feet   LEVEL: Novice-Intermediate

LOCATION: Just off Front Street, along the southern portion of Sarnia Bay.
This site is the location of the Canadian side of the Sarnia-Port Huron ferry service which was put out of business in the late 1930's with the construction of the Bluewater Bridge. Beware of boating traffic and fishing lines from active anglers.

16. ERIN
DEPTH: 45 feet   LEVEL: Advanced

LOCATION: Opposite the Courtright (Ontario) Light.
The wooden, Canadian steamer, *Erin* (174' x 26' x 12'6"), sank after a collision with the huge, steel freighter, *John B. Cowle*, on May 31, 1906, taking to the bottom her cargo of coal and five of her crew sleeping below deck at the time. The *Cowle* continued on her downbound course. The remains of the *Erin* lie right across the middle of the river. Technically, her bow is in the USA, while her stern is in Canada (take your birth certificate with you on this dive!) The hull is badly twisted, and the middle part of the vessel was dynamited. Much of the wreck is buried in sand, but she rises about ten feet off the bottom. Her large four-bladed propeller, engine and boiler are the highlights. Beware of freighters!

17. WILLIAM DICKINSON

DEPTH: 18 to 25 feet   **LEVEL: Novice-Intermediate**

LOCATION: This wreck lies along the drop-off on the Michigan side of the river at the southern end of Marine City just off a trailer park.

The tug, *William Dickinson* (78'2" x 19'5" x 10'9"), built at Benton Harbor, Michigan, in 1893, burned to a complete loss on September 16, 1923. Her boiler rising high off the river floor is the most noticeable part of the wreck. Considerable machinery and parts lie scattered around the boiler. Beware of boating traffic.

The *William H. Wolf.* IGLR

A diver explores machinery from the tug, *William Dickinson*. PHOTO BY CRIS KOHL

A sense of humor, very evident in the smiling face of diver Greg Schieman, overcomes any difficulties at a depth of 55' at the propeller of the *William H. Wolf.* PHOTO BY CRIS KOHL

18. WILLIAM H. WOLF

DEPTH: 6 to 60 feet   **LEVEL: Advanced**

LOCATION: This wreck lies along the drop-off just north of Marshy Creek Park, which is to the south of Sombra, Ontario. You can suit up and wade upstream from that park.

The wooden steamer, *William H. Wolf* (285'5" x 42'5" x 18'5"), began life catastrophically when three people were killed at her launch in 1887 at Milwaukee. But she worked the waters of the Great Lakes successfully for several decades before succumbing to flames on October 20, 1921, with the loss of two lives. Tragedy marred her entry into, and her departure from, the world.

The wreck's superstructure completely burned off, and, once inside the large hull, the diver is protected from the three-knot current. The wreck lies with her broken bow in the shallows and her stern at the bottom of the drop-off. The large engine, boiler and four-bladed propeller are still in place. The rudder lies flat about 100' off the stern on this combination sand, clay and stone bottom. Beware of boating traffic and entanglement in fishing line.

19. HIGHBANKS PARK

DEPTH: To 35 feet   LEVEL: Novice-Intermediate

LOCATION: At the north tip of Walpole Island, where the Snye Channel branches off to the right (southeast) from the St. Clair River. This area can be done from shore or from a boat. Walpole Island is First Nation land. Please respect the rights of private property owners in the area of Highbanks Park, for both scuba entries and exits. This area has been used by picnickers for many years, and the natural split of the Snye and the St. Clair has also made this point a sort of catch-basin for old bottles washed down from upstream. There is a 2-to-3 knot current, with much boating traffic. Beware of fishing lines, snagged and active.

Bottle diving at Highbanks Park. PHOTOS BY CRIS KOHL.

20. SNYE CHANNEL

St. Clair River diving is good from any of the dozen public parks along the Canadian side. The Snye Channel, a branch of the St. Clair River, is also accessible from many spots along the shoreline/roadway, as well as by boat. Its depth reaches 38' and is a good place for learning swiftwater diving. Many old bottles have been found here and continue to be located. Boating traffic is heavy, especially on summer weekends. Use a dive flag. Entanglement in old, snagged fishing line is a possibility, so take along a good, accessible dive knife.

The author examines some old bottles and anchors which he found in the St. Clair River. An inflatable boat and outboard motor are ideal for exploring these waters. Two dives yielded five small anchors, each weighing from 10 to 20 pounds. Not bad for a day's fun! PHOTOS BY CRIS KOHL EXCEPT MIDDLE PHOTO, WHICH IS BY KEN SHAW.

16. Southeastern Lake Huron

The Great Storm of November, 1913

The worst storm in recorded Great Lakes history occurred in November, 1913, and claimed 8 freighters with all hands in lower Lake Huron. About 250 sailors lost their lives. Many of the bodies washed ashore in Canada; the funeral above took place in Goderich (ONTARIO ARCHIVES), and those five unidentified sailors rest in Maitland Cemetery there (PHOTO BY CRIS KOHL.) Their shipwrecks, the *Wexford, Regina, Charles S. Price, Argus, John McGean,* and *Isaac M. Scott* are explored by today's scuba divers. Of the 8 lost ships, the *Hydrus* and possibly the *James Carruthers* remain missing.

MICHIGAN **ONTARIO**

1. *Sweetheart*
2. *Wexford*
3. **Early Kincardine shipwrecks**
4. *John S. Miner*
5. *Adelaide Horton*
6. *Singapore*
7. *Ann Maria*
8. **The "Long Dock"**
9. *W. E. Gladstone*
10. *Erie Stewart*
11. *Islet Prince*
12. **Goderich wrecks**
13. *Azov*
14. *James Carruthers?*
15. **Fishing Islands wrecks**
16. *Sarah*
17. *Goudreau*
18. *Africa*
19. *Ripple*
20. *Explorer*

1. SWEETHEART

> **LORAN: 30834.0/49671.6** **LAT** **LON**
> **DEPTH: 30 feet** **LEVEL: Novice-Intermediate**

AUTHOR'S COLLECTION

LOCATION: This wreck lies about three miles north-northeast of Sarnia, Ontario.

The 176-foot-long schooner, *Sweetheart,* was scuttled due to her advanced age. Because of the shallow depth, the wreck is broken and scattered on the sand-and-rock bottom. The keelson, ribbing and planking attract many fish. Beware of disturbing the silt and getting snagged in any fishnets.

2. WEXFORD

> **LORAN:** **LAT 43° 24.080' LON 081° 53.322'**
> **DEPTH: 78 feet to the bottom** **LEVEL: Advanced**

LOCATION: About 7 miles off the Canadian shore northwest of Grand Bend, Ontario.

The steel steamer, *Wexford* (250' x 40'1" x 23'7"), was one of eight freighters which disappeared with all hands in lower Lake Huron during the Great Storm of November, 1913. This long-sought shipwreck, the subject of several false claims to discovery, was finally found -- accidentally, no less -- by Don Chalmers, a retiree who was out fishing in his sailboat when he passed over this wreck and picked up its presence on his depthsounder in August, 2000. Being a scuba diver, he and two friends were the first to see this ship in 87 years. The *Wexford,* built in Sunderland, England in 1883, was the oldest of the eight ships the storm sank in Lake Huron, and, so far, the only one found sitting upright on the bottom (the others were all flipped upside-down by the storm). The *Hydrus* and possibly the *Carruthers* remain to be located. The *Wexford,* contrary to rumors that she was stripped

The steamer, *Wexford*. AUTHOR'S COLLECTION

Above: A diver glides past the ghostly superstructure of the tragic *Wexford*. PHOTO COURTESY OF OUT OF THE BLUE PRODUCTIONS. *Left:* Michigan artist Robert McGreevy's rendition of the wreck of the *Wexford*. COURTESY OF ROBERT MCGREEVY/CTM ASSOCIATES.

long ago by divers who could keep a secret, features a chadburn, brass portholes, a brass identification plate on deck, and many fascinating artifacts below deck (penetration diving is only for those with training, experience, attitude and equipment). Respect this tragic site.

Below deck on the *Wexford,* brass portholes, their glass still intact, remain in place (please keep them that way for other divers to enjoy seeing; Ontario laws protect them, and punishments are severe). A coiled hose and a coffee mug are among the many artifacts found at this site. PHOTOS COURTESY OF OUT OF THE BLUE PRODUCTIONS.

3. EARLY KINCARDINE SHIPWRECKS

Broken up in 5'-15' with a sand, gravel and clay bottom just north of the harbor channel are the 374-ton schooner, *A.J. Rich,* storm-stranded with a wheat cargo on Nov. 10, 1864, and, a bit further out, the sidewheeler, *Bonnie Maggie,* stranded on Oct. 14, 1869.

4. JOHN S. MINER

In under 8' of water lie the broken remains of the 97-ton schooner, *John S. Miner,* grounded on Oct. 15, 1871. Only the bottom timbers remain at the foot of Harbour Street.

Kincardine, Ontario, harbor

5. ADELAIDE HORTON

This 91-ton newly-launched steamer (107' x 18' x 8') struck the pier and broke up on Oct. 19, 1871. She lies in 6' of water. Beware of boaters and fishing lines.

6. SINGAPORE

This schooner (110'9" x 25'4" x 9'9") stranded and broke up on Sept. 15, 1904. Much of this wreck lies under sand, with some timbers visible in 8' of water.

7. ANN MARIA

This schooner (131'2" x 26'3" x 11'3") stranded and broke up on Oct. 7, 1902, with 4 of her 6 sailors lost. The remains lie in 6' of water, much of it buried.

Two stranded schooners: *left,* the *Singapore* (AUTHOR'S COLLECTION); *right,* the *Ann Maria* (ONTARIO ARCHIVES).

8. THE "LONG DOCK"

This now-submerged breakwall (begun in 1871) with wooden cribs begins at Southampton and arches to Chantry Island, with a gap in the middle. Depth: to 25′.

9. *W. E. GLADSTONE*

This small schooner, built at Goderich in 1886, broke up in 15′ along the north wall of the eastern portion of the Long Dock on Nov. 23, 1908. Use a dive flag; boating gets heavy.

10. *ERIE STEWART*

This schooner (117′ x 23′ x 10′), built at Port Dover, Ontario, in 1874, missed the gap on Oct. 7, 1907, rammed the breakwall, and sank. No lives were lost. Her bow lies wedged against the island portion of the Long Dock in the gap. Depth is 18′. Beware of boaters!

11. *ISLET PRINCE*

On July 19, 1938, this passenger & freight steamer (118′ x 24′6″ x 8′), built at Saugatuck, MI, in 1894, burned and sank in 15′ at the Long Dock. The few remains are mostly buried.

The schooner, *Erie Stewart,* in Port Dover harbor, and the steamer, *Islet Prince.* AUTHOR'S COLLECTION

12. GODERICH WRECKS

< DEPTH: 20 feet   LEVEL: Novice-Intermediate >

LOCATION: These two wrecks lie off the arch over the roadway to Cove Beach,

Goderich harbor, Ontario. The wreck to the left (south) is a tugboat from the 1920's that had its machinery removed before it was purposely burned. There is a four-bladed propeller and shaft. The wreck to the right (north) might be two wrecks, but only wood planking and framing remain. Boating traffic is heavy here; use a dive flag. For the best visibility, dive in the spring after a couple days of calm.

13. *AZOV*

< DEPTH: 6 to 10 feet   LEVEL: Novice >

The wreck of the Canadian schooner, *Azov* (108′4″ x 23′7″ x 10′), lies close to shore inside the boundaries of McGregor Point Provincial Park, one concession south of Port Elgin, Ontario. These remains can be seen from the surface on a calm day. Take a boat, as car access to the shore is non-existent. Vis is usually poor, so this is not the most popular dive site. The *Azov,* built in 1866 at Hamilton, Ontario, capsized during a gale on Oct. 25, 1911, about 20 miles east by north of Point aux Barques, Michigan (off the thumb). The hull drifted about 60 miles all the way east across the lake before settling near Port Elgin. The ship's captain, his wife and son, plus the crew,

The *Azov.* ONTARIO ARCHIVES

jury-rigged their yawlboat and sailed to safety in Goderich, Ontario. The wreck was located by the captain's grandson in the 1950's, and an *Azov* anchor, recovered by scuba divers in August, 1956, is on display at the marine museum at Goderich.

14. *JAMES CARRUTHERS?* UNIDENTIFIED DREDGE?

< DEPTH: 120 feet   LEVEL: Advanced >

LOCATION: This huge wreck lies upside-down several miles off Port Elgin, Ontario.

A wreck which may be the immense steel freighter, *James Carruthers* (550′ x 58′2″ x 26′7″), is a recently publicized discovery. The *James Carruthers* was the newest and largest of the ships lost in the Great Storm of November, 1913. Launched less than six months earlier at Collingwood, Ontario, she foundered with a cargo of wheat and 22-24 lives. Definite identification has not yet been made of this hull, which may be that of a dredge.

The *James Carruthers.* AUTHOR'S COLLECTION

15. FISHING ISLANDS WRECKS

The Fishing Islands consist of a series of islands and shoals stretching from Chiefs Point about five miles north of Sauble Beach, Ontario, to Pike Bay just south of Stokes Bay and Lyal Island. The largest of the Fishing Islands is Cranberry Island, just off the mainland community of Oliphant. The incredible number of shoals makes this a navigator's nighmare!

The only access is by boat. Since this is an inaccessible area, comparatively little shipwreck search and exploration has been done; the area is ripe for diving.

Some of the known shipwrecks in this area include:

Blanche Shelby: This wooden tug hit a submerged rock on October 15, 1885 and sank almost immediately at the entrance to the channel between Main Station and Burke Island. All hands escaped in the yawl boat.

Phoenix: This 25-ton tug is mostly buried in the sand of the shallow channel between Indian Island and the east shore of Main Station Island. She stranded during a storm and was lost on November 30, 1901. Boiler and machinery were salvaged and only the ship's bottom remains now in about four feet of water. She measured 53'5" x 13'7".

Gold Hunter: Built in 1862 at Milford, Ontario, by John Tait, this schooner struck a shoal off Ghegheto (Round) Island in October, 1890, while attempting to pass the narrow channel to the open lake. She and her cargo of cedar logs went to pieces within days. The vessel's value in 1866 was $8,000, but that had dropped to $2,000 by the time of her loss in 1890. The wreck lies about 600' off the west shore of Ghegheto (Round) Island, near Howdenvale, in 6' to 18' of water. She is on the north side of the reef extending west of the island. The anchors and other items of interest are scattered over a wide area.

16. SARAH

DEPTH: 10 feet	LEVEL: Novice

LOCATION: This wreck lies off the east shore of Burke Island, Ontario.

The two-masted, 65-ton schooner, *Sarah* (73'3" x 19'4" x 6'6"), became trapped in an ice floe and was abandoned on November 28, 1906. The captain, his wife and two crewmen struggled for hours to get their yawl boat through the floe. Originally launched as the *Emma Laura*, she was rebuilt at Port Burwell, Ontario, in 1864 and again at Port Dover in 1871, and in 1881, she was renamed the *Sarah*.

The wreck of the *Sarah* lies broken up in shallow water about 900' off the east shore of Burke Island.

The *Sarah*. MPL/WMHS

17. GOUDREAU

LORAN:	LAT 46° 03' 45" LON 082° 12' 55"
DEPTH: 18 to 28 feet	LEVEL: Novice

LOCATION: This wreck lies 5 miles southwest of Lyal Island, near Stokes Bay, Ontario.

The 2,298-ton steel freighter, *Goudreau* (300' x 40' x 24'8"), built by the Cleveland Ship Building Company and launched as the *Pontiac* on July 3, 1889, set a record in her first year by hauling a payload of 2,849 tons of ore in a single trip. She sank in a collision with the *Athabasca* in the St. Mary's River on July 14, 1891, in 30 feet of water, but was salvaged and returned to service.

The steel steamer, *Goudreau*. IGLR

Renamed the *Goudreau* in 1916, she stranded with a load of pyrites on a shoal on November 23, 1917, after losing her rudder and trying to make the shelter of Stokes Bay. There were 24 people on board at the time, and fortunately no lives were lost. Much of this wreck's steel was salvaged for the war effort in 1942.

The wreck rests on a rocky shoal, and the visibility is almost always good. The boilers and the engine were salvaged, but two acres of steel hull plates, iron ore cargo, numerous large gears and winches with coiled cable, hatchway frames and steel portholes make this ideal for exploration and photography.

A *Goudreau* winch and cable. PHOTO BY CRIS KOHL.

18. AFRICA

DEPTH: 18 to 28 feet   **LEVEL: Novice**

The steamer, *Africa*. MPL/WMHS

LOCATION: Near Stokes Bay, Ontario, west of Lyal Island.

The wooden steamer, *Africa* (148′ x 26′ x 13′), loaded with 1,270 tons of coal, disappeared in a storm on October 7, 1895. The bodies of some of the crew were found along shorelines near Lyal Island. The wreck lies scattered along a wide swath of hazardous shoals just south of the wreck of the *Explorer* southwest of Greenough Point.

19. RIPPLE

This tug, built at Chatham, Ontario, in 1884, hit a reef on September 9, 1905 and quickly broke up. The remains of the hull lie upside-down and the rest of the wreck is scattered in less than 10′ of water along Ripple Reef off the west side of Lyal Island.

20. EXPLORER

On September 4, 1883, this small, 32.6-ton, two-masted schooner (48′ x 16′ x 5′6″) ran aground in a storm on the rocks at Greenough Bank, northwest of Lyal Island. With her crew of four clinging desperately to the rigging while sailors safe in Greenough Harbor observed them through a telescope, the ship slid into deep water. All four crew perished. This ship, built in Chatham, Ontario, in 1866, already had a tumultuous history. She disappeared in 1867 with her two crew, her captain surviving. The ship was found and raised in 1881, with the two crew discovered locked below deck and holes bored into the hull! She was returned to service with tragic results. The wreck lies in 35′ of water, considerably intact.

17. Tobermory

Tobermory's **Fathom Five National Marine Park,** established as a provincial park in 1972 and transferred to national park status in 1987, was the first underwater park/preserve created in the Great Lakes. Not all of the sites on this map are within this park's boundaries.

1. *Sweepstakes*	11. *Newaygo*	21. **Unidentified**
2. *City of Grand Rapids*	12. *Philo Scoville*	22. **Unidentified**
3. **Big Tub Lighthouse**	13. *Charles P. Minch*	23. **Unidentified**
4. **The Anchor**	14. *Arabia*	24. *Lady Dufferin*
5. **The Tugs**	15. *Marion L. Breck*	25. *Caroline Rose*
6. *Cascaden*	16. *Forest City*	26. *Niagara II*
7. *China*	17. **The Caves**	27. **Flowerpot I.**
8. *John Walters*	18. **Dave's Bay**	28. *Points West*
9. *W. L. Wetmore*	19. **Dunk's Point**	29. *San Jacinto*
10. *James C. King*	20. *Avalon Voyager II*	30. *Vita*

Ranked by diving experts as one of the top scuba diving destinations in Ontario, this mecca offers a variety of superb shipwrecks, excellent underwater visibility, geological formation dives, several scuba dive shops, a large concentration of scuba charter boats, beautiful wilderness scenery, a huge range of accommodations (from rudimentary camping to first-class resorts), restaurants (but no fast-food chains -- yet!) and interesting land sites for diver and non-diver alike.

I first visited Tobermory in the summer of 1966 after persuading my parents and sister that we absolutely had to satisfy our curiosities about what lay at the end of that long stretch of land called the Bruce Peninsula. I was not disappointed, and I shot 8mm movie film of the quiet harbor and the commercial fishing nets drying on the docks while stretched out on large, cylindrical racks. There were no scuba dive shops in town, and I wasn't a scuba diver yet.

Tobermory's scenic harbor and a reminder of its maritime past, an anchor from the nearby wreck of the *Charles P. Minch*. PHOTO BY CRIS KOHL.

In 1972, not long after the discovery of the wonderfully-intact schooner, *Arabia,* and the controversy over someone dynamiting the wreck of the *W.L. Wetmore* to salvage the goodies inside, the first designated underwater park/preserve in the Great Lakes was created there as a provincial park. I took up scuba diving not too long after that. By the time I first went scuba diving at Tobermory, there were dive shops in town and charter boats in the harbor, and the commercial fishing nets drying on the docks had disappeared.

With a quarter of a million tourists passing through Tobermory annually nowadays (many of them simply there to catch the ferry to Manitoulin Island), and several thousand scuba divers each year doing an average of four dives each, there is much action along the docks and in this town of 600 permanent residents, particularly on summer weekends.

Somehow, in spite of all the hubbub, Tobermory retains an old-fashioned quaintness.

There are 21 known shipwrecks (some unidentified) within five miles of Tobermory, Ontario, inside the boundaries of Fathom Five National Marine Park, plus another three just outside the park. Each scuba diver visiting here is required to register at the Diver Registration Center prior to diving (even shore diving) in the park; boaters must also register. There is a small registration fee for divers,

The park's Visitor Centre in the middle of town welcomes all. The scuba diver registration office is half a block away. PHOTO BY CRIS KOHL.

payable only once each calendar year. You must show a certification card when registering. Use of a dive flag while diving is mandatory. For now, until the cost of sinking her is paid off, there is also a fee for diving Tobermory's newest wreck, the steel freighter, *Niagara II.*

1. SWEEPSTAKES

| DEPTH: 8 to 20 feet | LEVEL: Novice |

LOCATION: This popular shipwreck lies at the head of Big Tub Harbour, Tobermory.

The 218-ton schooner, *Sweepstakes* (119' x 22'8" x 10'1"), built at Burlington, Ontario, in 1867, was driven ashore and seriously damaged at Cove Island in August, 1885, but was pulled off and towed by the tug, *Jessie,* to Big Tub Harbour, where she sank before repairs could be made. Her coal cargo was salvaged.

The *Sweepstake's* windlass attracts diver Joan Forsberg. PHOTO BY CRIS KOHL.

The *Sweepstakes* lies about 150' from the head of Big Tub. Because trapped divers' bubbles were damaging the wreck, wooden and wire grates have been installed to prohibit penetration diving. But her external hull and deck exhibit wonderful items, such as a large windlass, an intact starboard railing, the mast holes and Roman numeral bow markings. the Sweepstakes is one of the best preserved 1800's Great Lakes schooners to be found, in spite of Nature taking her toll every year. Diver/tourboat hours are limited and

Artwork ©Adam Henley

staggered during the summer so they don't clash; check the office for times. Please respect the rights of the private landowners around the site.

2. CITY OF GRAND RAPIDS

| DEPTH: 5 to 15 feet | LEVEL: Novice |

LOCATION: This wreck lies at the head of Big Tub Harbour, Tobermory.

The wooden steamer, *City of Grand Rapids* (123' x 25' x 9'3"), built in 1879 at Grand Haven, Michigan, burned to a total loss on October 29, 1907.This wreck is located about 100' off the starboard bow of the *Sweepstakes,* and is usually explored as part of the same dive. Portions of the engine, boiler and boiler cradles remain.

Above: The steamer, *City of Grand Rapids.* IGLR.
Right: Exploring her remains. PHOTO BY CRIS KOHL

3. BIG TUB LIGHTHOUSE

DEPTH: To 75 feet   LEVEL: Novice-Intermediate

LOCATION: Lighthouse Point, Big Tub Harbour, Tobermory.

This shore dive, frequently used for check-out dives by instructors, offers interesting geological features just below the historic (1885) lighthouse. Limited parking is available.

Artwork ©Adam Henley

Left: The author, with his second cousin, Christoff Kohl and son, Geoffrey Kohl, after snorkeling at Big Tub Lighthouse. PHOTO BY ERIKA KOHL. *Right:* Divers at the anchor. PHOTO BY CRIS KOHL.

4. THE ANCHOR

DEPTH: 70 feet   LEVEL: Intermediate-Advanced

LOCATION: Just off the shoreline almost halfway between Big Tub Harbour and Little Tub Harbour. This shore or boat dive is to a huge, wooden-stocked iron anchor and heavy-linked chain from an unknown vessel. The suit-up and entry area is at the "Gap" just to the east of the church at the end of Highway 6. Parking is limited. Please respect the rights of adjacent landowners. Be aware of depth, windy wave-producing weather, and boating hazards. Don't miss the anchor! Once you get to the huge underwater boulder, the anchor lies just beyond. Stay at about the 65' level and keep a sharp eye.

171

5. THE TUGS

DEPTH: To 40 feet   **LEVEL: Novice-Intermediate**

LOCATION: These four wrecked tugs lie at Little Tub Harbour, Ontario.

The *John & Alice*, a 59′ fishing tug built at Port Dover, Ontario, in 1924, burned here on December 6, 1947. The *Bob Foote* sank in 1905. The 68′ *Robert K.*, built at Port Dover, Ontario, in 1917, burned on June 23, 1935. The 67′ *Alice G.* went aground in gale force winds and sank in November, 1927.

Diver access is from the wooden deck just off the road. For the most part, the first three of these wrecks, all of which burned, are badly broken and scattered in the harbor. The *Alice G.*, however, is nearly intact; her steam engine, boiler, driveshaft and propeller are interesting and photogenic. The stern railing gracefully curving with the lines of the fantail attests to the beauty and workmanship of that era.

The Wreck of the tug, *Alice G.*

Artwork ©Adam Henley

Above: This diver platform offers suit-up/access to the 4 tugs. *Below:* The author's 13-year-old second cousin, Christoff Kohl, explores the stern of the tug, *Alice G.* PHOTOS BY CRIS KOHL.

6. CASCADEN

DEPTH: 20 feet   **LEVEL: Novice**

LOCATION: This wreck lies just northeast of Cape Hurd, Ontario.

The 138-ton wooden schooner, *Cascaden,* built at Southampton, Ontario, in 1866, was wrecked here on October 15, 1871. This site, although still within the park boundaries, is a fair distance southwest of Tobermory, and a boat is required. Wreckage lies scattered over a large, shallow area, and hence this is not a popular dive site. Don't let your boat hit any of the rocky shoals in this area!

Left: A diver closely examines some wooden wreckage from the schooner, *Cascaden.* PHOTO BY CRIS KOHL.

7. CHINA

DEPTH: 10 feet	LEVEL: Novice

LOCATION: This wreck lies southwest of Tobermory, close to shore, but a boat is necessary to reach the site. The wreckage, which can be seen from the surface, lies just on the inside of a small island a short distance southeast of Wreck Point.

The 314-ton schooner, *China* (137' x 23'2" x 11'2"), built at Port Robinson, ON, in 1863, was wrecked on Nov. 20, 1883 (in the same storm which claimed the *John Walters*), at the reef which was later named after her. The wreckage is badly broken up; the largest and most interesting pieces lie close to shore. Many rocks and ledges form boating hazards.

Left: Diver Tim Philp examines the bow end of the schooner *China's* keelson, and later, *right,* the centerboard box of the schooner, *John Walters.* PHOTOS BY CRIS KOHL.

8. JOHN WALTERS

DEPTH: To 15 feet	LEVEL: Novice

LOCATION: This wreck lies off the southwest tip of Russel Island. A boat is necessary to reach the island, and the dive can be done there from shore.

The 176-ton schooner, *John Walters* (108'5" x 23'5" x 8'3"), built at Kingston, Ontario, in 1852 by George Thurston (who also constructed the *Arabia* which lies here at Tobermory), and launched as the *Sarah Bond,* was owned by Henry Patterson of Chatham, Ontario, when she was stranded here on Nov. 20, 1883. The bow lies broken near the shore, while the stern and rudder are in deeper water. The thick keelson and centerboard box are interesting.

RUSSEL ISLAND

-N-

"Griffon" Cove, where the shipwreck (incorrectly) thought to be the famous 1679 *Griffon* was found.

9. W. L. WETMORE

LORAN:	LAT 45° 15.200′ LON 081° 42.612′
DEPTH: 28 feet	LEVEL: Novice-Intermediate

LOCATION: This wreck lies just under the northwest tip of Russel Island.

Considered one of the best shipwrecks in the Tobermory area, the wooden steamer, *W.L. Wetmore* (213′7″ x 33′4″ x 12′6″), while towing her usual barges, the *Brunette* and the

James C. King, was driven ashore on Russel Island in a storm on Nov. 29, 1901. No lives were lost, but only the *Brunette* was salvaged. The *W.L. Wetmore* was launched at Cleveland on May 17, 1871.

Highlights of this site include the massive rudder, the sheared-off propeller, the striking boilers, bow anchor chain, anchor, hawse pipes and much planking with hanging knees and other features. Warning: a west wind will whip up the waves!

Artwork ©Adam Henley

Left: Diver Roy Pickering approaches the sheared-off propeller of the *W.L. Wetmore. Right:* The rudder of the *James C. King,* examined by Roy Pickering, lies flat on hard limestone in the shallows. PHOTOS BY CRIS KOHL. *Top Middle:* The steamer, *W.L. Wetmore* (IGLR). *Bottom Middle:* The *James C. King's* aft section (MPL/WMHS).

10. JAMES C. KING

LORAN:	LAT 45° 16.069′ LON 081° 42.543′
DEPTH: 22 to 93 feet	LEVEL: Intermediate-Advanced

LOCATION: This wreck lies off the northwestern tip of Russel Island.

The schooner-barge, *James C. King* (181′6″ x 33′ x 13′), built at East Saginaw, Michigan, in 1867, was driven ashore with her towing steamer, the *W.L. Wetmore,* on November 29, 1901. No lives were lost, but, unlike the *Wetmore,* the *James C. King* slid into deep water. The wreck lies on a steep incline, with the rudder lying flat in the shallows close to the broken, split hull. At depth, a capstan and Roman numeral draught markings can be seen.

11. NEWAYGO

LORAN:	LAT 45° 16.238′ LON 081° 45.063′
DEPTH: To 25 feet	LEVEL: Novice

LOCATION: This wreck lies in the Northwest Bank, Devil Island Channel.

The wooden steamer, *Newaygo* (196′ x 37′2″ x 13′4″), launched at Marine City, Michigan, on July 18, 1890, stranded in a storm at this site on November 17, 1903, and broke up. No lives were lost. The *Newaygo,* owned by Port Huron businessman Henry McMorran and underway light from Cleveland for French River, Ontario, was towing the schooner-barge, *Checotah*, at the time of loss (the *Checotah* survived this time, but is elsewhere in this book). The highlights of this scattered wreckage are a boiler and the huge, heavily-built bottom of the hull, 160′ long. This open site is susceptible to bad weather and west winds.

The steamer, *Newaygo*. AUTHOR'S COLLECTION

12. PHILO SCOVILLE

LORAN:	LAT 45° 16.134′ LON 081° 41.832′
DEPTH: 35 to 95 feet	LEVEL: Intermediate-Advanced

LOCATION: This wreck lies along the north shore of Russel Island.

The 325-ton schooner, *Philo Scoville* (139′5″ x 30′4″ x 11′3″), constructed at Cleveland in 1863, drifted off course during a storm on October 6, 1889, while enroute light (that is, carrying no cargo) from Collingwood, Ontario, to Escanaba, Michigan. Dragging her anchors, she struck Russel Island, where her captain died when he fell between the ship and some rocks. A Tobermory tug rescued the other four crewmen. Lying on a steep incline, the broken stern lies scattered along the slope in the shallows, while the bowsprit lies in about 93′ near the mooring buoy anchor. A ship's anchor about 150′ to the east lies at the same depth, with a twin set of anchor chains running uphill along the rocks to about the 30′ depth. Part of the stern lies in 35′ about 100′ west of the main wreckage.

Diver Joe Drummond follows the *Philo Scoville's* twin set of anchor chains down the rocky drop-off. PHOTO BY CRIS KOHL

13. CHARLES P. MINCH

LORAN:	LAT 45° 17.670′ LON 081° 42.670′
DEPTH: 20 to 60 feet	LEVEL: Novice-Intermediate

LOCATION: This wreck lies just off the south shore of Tecumseh Cove at Cove Island. A boat is needed to reach Cove Island; this site can be done as a shore dive from there, or from a boat. The three-masted schooner, *Charles P. Minch* (154′7″ x 28′2″ x 11′8″), built

The *Charles P. Minch*. AUTHOR'S COLLECTION

Exploring the *Minch's* hull. PHOTO BY CRIS KOHL.

at Vermilion, Ohio, in 1867, was enroute to Chicago with a lumber cargo on October 26, 1898, when adverse weather forced her into the protected harbor of Tecumseh Cove. When the wind suddenly shifted, the harbor lost its "protected" status, the captain and crew just barely reached the island, and the Minch was destroyed within three hours.

Two mooring buoys usually mark the *Charles P. Minch* sites. The centerboard box, sides, bow and bottom of the hull lie on the incline east of the submerged cribs near the head of the cove (a good place to make an entry). The rudder situated west of this mooring buoy is likely from the schooner, *Tecumseh,* wrecked here in 1882. Between the second mooring buoy, about 600′ south of the cove, and the shore lie a keel and rudder portion, plus part of the deck. Numerous artifacts, including a .38 revolver, were recovered here years ago.

14. ARABIA

LORAN: 30202.9/48669.8	LAT 45° 18.713′ LON 081° 40.444′
DEPTH: 97 to 117 feet	LEVEL: Advanced

LOCATION: This wreck lies to the northeast of Echo Island.

This is the most intact shipwreck in the Tobermory area, as well as one of the deepest. The barque, *Arabia* (131′ x 26′ x 12′), bound from Chicago to Midland, Ontario, with a corn cargo, began taking on water during heavy seas on October 4, 1884. After hours of pumping,

Artwork ©Adam Henley

the weary crew took to the yawlboat while the *Arabia* sank. The three-masted ship had been built by George Thurston at Kingston, Ontario, in 1853. The mostly-intact hull, lying north to south, has two mooring buoys positioned just off the wreck, with a thin line guiding divers from the buoy anchor to the wreck. The bow is impressive with its bowsprit, anchors, catheads, windlass and bilge pump. Deadeyes and pulleys decorate the railings. The afterdeck, separated from the hull, rests against the starboard quarter. the ship's wheel and steering mechanism are located alongside the afterdeck. The three collapsed masts lie alongside the hull. This is a deep, cold, low-visibility (sometimes) site for very experienced divers only. Give this site all the experience and preparation it demands; at least 12 scuba divers have died here over the past 30 years since this shipwreck's 1971 discovery.

Right: Diver Roy Pickering explores the *Arabia's* port rail. PHOTO BY CRIS KOHL.

15. *MARION L. BRECK*

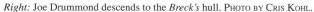

DEPTH: 10 to 100 feet	LEVEL: Variable re. depth

LOCATION: This wreckage lies off the pointy south end of remote Bear's Rump Island.

With much of her canvas lost to the fury of November gales, the schooner, *Marion L. Breck* (127' x 23'6" x 12'), stranded and broke up on October 16, 1900, her crew reaching the safety of Flowerpot Island. This ship, built in 1840 as the *William Penn* at Garden Island, Ontario, lies broken with her cargo of brick fragments scattered over a wide area. A large hull section lies in 75', a section of keel in 50', a capstan and anchor at 25', and the main wreckage at 90'. This is a remote site; use caution.

Right: Joe Drummond descends to the *Breck's* hull. PHOTO BY CRIS KOHL.

16. *FOREST CITY*

LORAN: 30158.0/48675.1	LAT 45° 18.909' LON 081° 33.422'
DEPTH: From 60 to 150 feet	LEVEL: Advanced to Technical

LOCATION: This wreck lies off the northeast side of remote Bear's Rump Island.

Launched at Cleveland on May 7, 1870, as a three-masted schooner, the *Forest City* (213'7" x 33'5" x 21'3") was converted to a steamer two years later. On June 4, 1904, in a dense fog, she struck the island at full steam. Equipment was salvaged before the ship slid into deep water. On shore, a rusty chunk of bow plating marks the ship's impact point. In the water, the broken bow is in 60', while the rest of the ship drops to 150', retaining intactness with depth. Deep coldwater diving is demanding; plan well. Careless and/or inexperienced dives have died here.

Far left, top: The steamer, *Forest City*. IGLR. *Far left, bottom:* A diver studies the *Forest City's* framing bolts at 120'. PHOTO BY CRIS KOHL.

Artwork ©Adam Henley

177

17. THE CAVES

DEPTH: 30 feet   **LEVEL: Novice-Intermediate**

LOCATION: These caverns (they are not really "caves" because you never lose sight of light from an opening) are about 10 miles east of Tobermory. Take a boat and forget about hiking in with all your scuba equipment from the parking lot at Cyprus Lake.

Two small, submerged caverns lead from the open bay waters to "The Grotto," a secluded, hushed pool protected by a massive limestone vault, where scuba divers and skinnydippers have been known to encounter each other unexpectedly. Interesting sights, in the shape of underwater rock formations, exist just outside "The Grotto" as well. Dive lights can be used to check out the nooks and crannies of this site, but they are not necessary. The water drops off deeply down the slope beyond these caverns.

Scuba charter boats from Tobermory are lined up at the popular caves divesite. Although technically "caverns," these "cave" dives thrill visitors, and are usually selected as a charterer's second dive. PHOTOS BY CRIS KOHL.

18. DAVE'S BAY (LITTLE COVE)

DEPTH: To 40 feet   **LEVEL: All levels**

LOCATION: Take Warner Bay Road near the Township Museum east to Little Cove. Besides being a picturesque bay, this site offers interesting geological formations such as glacial erratics, pitting and layered dolomite along the bay's south shore. Used sometimes for diver checkouts, this site offers limited parking at the access point. Please respect the rights of the private property owners here, which is outside the Fathom Five National Marine Park boundaries.

19. DUNK'S POINT

DEPTH: To 60 feet   **LEVEL: All levels**

LOCATION: One mile east of Tobermory. A boat (an inflatable is ideal) is necessary. Interesting underwater geological formations, such as glacial pitting, abound. There is an

anchor and long chain out here, but the circumstances of their loss is not known. To reach them, begin your swim underwater at Dunk's Point and descend at the gradual dropoff to a depth of 40'. Follow the contour of the point, swinging north gradually. Ideally, you will eventually encounter a big mound of anchor chain at a depth of about 43'. Follow the chain as it twists and winds and dips over rocks and drops into gulleys on its seemingly endless route to the anchor itself. The anchor, similar to the one at "The Gap," is a wooden stock, iron-fluked one, common on vessels in the late 1800's. Keep an open eye; it's easy to miss.

Diver Dan Perry reached the Dunk's Point anchor! PHOTO BY CRIS KOHL.

20. AVALON VOYAGER II

DEPTH: To 25 feet   **LEVEL: Novice**

LOCATION: This totally submerged wreck, which can be seen from the surface, lies just off the west end of Bonnet Island near Hay Bay. A boat (again, an inflatable is ideal) is necessary to reach this site (although the first time I filmed the *Avalon Voyager II* was from a sailboat on which I was living for six weeks, cruising by in the summer of 1981; the *Avalon Voyager II* was still intact

The toppled bollards make an interesting view of the sunken *Avalon Voyager II*. PHOTO BY CRIS KOHL.

Artwork ©Adam Henley

and mostly above water, although impaled upon the rocks. A year later, I explored her underwater for my first time). This 325-ton, 135-foot-long wooden propeller, built at Clarenville, Newfoundland in 1946 and launched as the *Twillingate*, with various other name changes (*Thomas V. Hollett* from 1951 to 1967, *Avalon Voyager* from 1967 to 1976, *Avalon Voyager II* from 1976 to 1981) struck rocks off Cape Hurd on October 31, 1980, while enroute from Kincardine to Owen Sound for use there as the floating restaurant she had become. Her anchor failed to hold and she dragged into Hay Bay. Her registration was closed on March 5, 1981. Harsh weather and firebug vandals took their toll on this vessel, but she is still interesting and photogenic.

21. UNIDENTIFIED

Nothing is known about the backgrounds of these three unidentified shipwrecks (sites #21, 22 and 23) off various parts of Cove Island north of Tobermory.

Site #21, called "Cassle's Cove Wreck," is a centerboard schooner located below Cove Island lighthouse off Boat Harbour. An 88-foot-long section lies in the sand at 70', while the vessel's sides rest at 60', with the rudder, complete with a decorative, scalloped design carved into the top of its blade, sits on pebbles at 50'.

22. UNIDENTIFIED

This 62-foot-long section, thought to be a forward hull portion, exists with framing, planking and miscellaneous debris covering a large area. It lies in the shallows (maximum 8' of water) protected by an islet just east of the largest island east of Gat Point.

Right: A diver explores the unidentified Gat Point wreck. PHOTO BY CRIS KOHL.

23. UNIDENTIFIED

This wreckage, mainly in three chunks of boards lying in 20' to 80', is located beneath a Parks Canada Service sign naming "Cove Island." It's on the east side of Cove Island, just to the southeast of "Cassle's Cove Wreck," site #21.

24. *LADY DUFFERIN*

DEPTH: From 40 to 200+ feet   LEVEL: All levels to Technical

LOCATION: This wreck lies very much broken up in huge, wooden sections about 1.5 miles east of Little Cove and just west of Driftwood Cove.

In October, 1886, the 135-foot-long schooner-barge, *Lady Dufferin,* built at Port Burwell, Ontario, was swept onto the rocks after the towline from the steamer that was towing her parted. The crew escaped with their lives, but the ship was a total loss. To locate this wreck, take a boat to Dufferin Point and look for two small circles painted on the rock wall in a niche. Dive there. The wreck is broken up in slabs on a steep, rocky incline, with a steam engine, probably used in lumber salvage, located at about 100'. Technical divers have found more wreckage down the drop-off past 200'. The *Lady Dufferin's* rudder lies at 60' a fair distance away from the main wreck site. Heading east by boat from the beach at Dave's Bay, hug the shoreline, which consists of high limestone cliffs and cedar forests. When you arrive at a small "flowerpot" formation in the limestone cliff about halfway up, dive there to see the rudder. This is about halfway to the *Lady Dufferin* wreckage area from the Dave's Bay parking lot.

Dan Perry studies wooden slabs from the *Lady Dufferin.* PHOTO BY CRIS KOHL.

25. *CAROLINE ROSE*

LORAN: LAT 45° 14.535' LON 081° 34.572'
DEPTH: 55 feet   LEVEL: Intermediate

LOCATION: This scuttled ship lies in Driftwood Cove, about 4 miles southeast of Tobermory and about half a mile outside the park boundary.

The 250-ton, 132-foot-long schooner, *Caroline Rose,* built in 1940 at Lunenburg, Nova Scotia, was one of the last Grand Banks schooners to be used for fishing (and she is reputed to be one of the three ships pictured on the back of a Canadian $100 bill). Abandoned after being used as a cruise ship and sinking at her dock at Owen Sound, Ontario, the *Caroline Rose* was raised amidst controversy, towed north, and purposely sunk

Sights galore on the scuttled schooner, *Caroline Rose,* include a spare propeller. PHOTOS BY CRIS KOHL.

(authorities reportedly would not allow her to be scuttled inside Fathom Five National Marine Park) in late August, 1990, as a new, intact dive site. Three weeks later, a severe storm moved the wreck 150' closer towards shore, extensively damaging her. She is no longer penetrable but yields an incredible variety of areas to explore and sights to see.

26. *NIAGARA II*

LORAN:	LAT 45° 15.039' LON 081° 36.179'
DEPTH: From 48 to 98 feet	LEVEL: Intermediate-Advanced

LOCATION: This wreck lies several miles to the east of Tobermory, close to the wreck of the *Caroline Rose*.

On May 15, 1999, the 700-ton, 180-foot-long former freighter and sand dredge, *Niagara II*, was scuttled for the express purpose of creating another exciting scuba dive site in the Tobermory area. Again, this vessel was sunk just outside the boundaries of Fathom Five National Marine Park because, reportedly, of official opposition to this plan. Several people formed the Tobermory Maritime Association in 1997, found and purchased this ship in 1998, and spent over 1,000 hours cleaning her up before the scuttling.

The *Niagara II* in drydock. AUTHOR'S COLLECTION

The *Niagara II's* name and final port of call appear on the bridge. PHOTO BY CRIS KOHL.

Divers now steer the *Niagara II* to their favorite destination. PHOTO BY CRIS KOHL.

The *Niagara II*, a steel ship launched in England in 1930, had five different names in the course of her 67-year career, receiving her last name in 1984. In 1990, her engine was removed and she was used as a barge. This is a magnificent site, with enough places to explore on this vessel to occupy a half dozen dives easily. The ship is intact and sits upright, and all doors and hatches have been removed for diver safety. There are railings and passageways galore to guide the diver along. A ship's wheel was added to the wheel-less bridge just prior to the sinking, in effect making this ship complete for the underwater explorer. Until the cost of scuttling this ship is recouped, there is a fee to dive her.

27. FLOWERPOT ISLAND

> **DEPTH: 30 to 150 feet**   **LEVEL: All levels**

Beautiful Flowerpot Island is a tourist attraction to the north-northeast of Tobermory, with several cruise boats taking sightseers there regularly during summer to explore the island on its several trails and to view the famous "flowerpot" rock formations. Once divers reach the island, they can shore dive in the area just off the "flowerpots", viewing submerged ledges, steep cliffs and underwater rock formations. Take the trail east of the small dock.

28. *POINTS WEST*

> **DEPTH: 50 feet**   **LEVEL: Intermediate**

LOCATION: Just east of Harbour Island, off the southwest side of Cove Island.

The Points West, a 32-foot-long wooden vessel, served the Tobermory area as a guide boat. Built in 1956 as the *Flowerpot,* she was scuttled in October, 1984, about 300′ east of Harbour Island. She sits intact on the sand in an area of usually poor visibility.

29. *SAN JACINTO*

> **LORAN: 30242.7/48619.1**   **LAT 45° 24.273′ LON 081° 47.722′**
> **DEPTH: 80 feet**   **LEVEL: Advanced**

LOCATION: This wreck lies off the northwest side of Yeo Island.

The 265-ton schooner, *San Jacinto,* launched in 1856 at Buffalo, New York, foundered in heavy weather off Yeo Island a fair distance north of Tobermory on June 20, 1881, with no

Divers hooked this two-sheave wooden block onto this metal bilge pump at the *San Jacinto* site. PHOTO BY CRIS KOHL.

lives lost. Found by Paul LaPointe in 1990, the *San Jacinto's* hull is split open, but she is quite intact; bilge pump, windlass, rigging, tools and many other items are found at the site.

Artwork ©Adam Henley

30. *VITA*

The opulent steam yacht, *Vita* (86′4″ x 18′4″ x 6′8″), built at Trenton, MI, in 1888, was wrecked on November 5, 1910, under unknown circumstances. Her broken remains lie in 2′ to 18′ of water between the daymark on Yeo Island and the rocks of Manitoba Ledge.

18. Eastern Bruce Peninsula

1. *Gargantua*
2. *Thomas R. Scott*
3. Dyer's Bay
4. Cape Chin wreck
5. Lion's Head wrecks
6. *Old Concord*
7. Wiarton wrecks
8. Underwater forest
9. *Mary Ward*

1. GARGANTUA

> **DEPTH: To 10 feet** **LEVEL: Novice**

LOCATION: The northwest corner of Wingfield Basin, a small, protected bay at Cabot Head. Shore access is possible; ask permission of the lighthouse keeper for access to Wingfield Basin. It's a bit of a swim; using a boat is better.

The large, wooden tug, *Gargantua* (130' x 32'1" x 15'4"), was built at McLouth Shipyard, Marine City, Michigan, as the *Seafarer* in 1919. On December 6, 1952, after her machinery had been removed, she was under tow in Georgian Bay when she took shelter from heavy seas in Wingfield Basin, where she sat until she sank. In 1971, a mysterious fire destroyed her super-

The *Gargantua.* AUTHOR'S COLLECTION

structure. Most of this shipwreck remains high and dry; snorkel/dive around her hull.

2. THOMAS R. SCOTT

> **DEPTH: 393 feet** **LEVEL: Technical**

LOCATION: This wreck lies off Dyer's Bay.

In July, 1994, the submersible from the Canadian Navy diving ship, HMCS *Cormorant,* doing a geological study, picked up a sonar image ahead of it that resembled a schooner. The searchers almost ran right into the shipwreck, since the visibility in that area is perpetually bad: about 6'. But they clearly read the name, *Thomas R. Scott,* on the port side. The wreck sits upright and is very intact.

The wooden steamer, *Thomas R. Scott* (129' x 28' x 7'6"), built at Grand Haven, Michigan, in 1887, became waterlogged and sank on September 2, 1914 (by coincidence, the real-life Thomas R. Scott, a lumber, shipping and ranching businessman after whom this vessel was named, died four days later at his ranch in Arizona.) Contact the Canadian Navy or their geologists for the co-ordinates to this deep shipwreck.

The *Thomas R. Scott.*
AUTHOR'S COLLECTION

3. DYER'S BAY

> **DEPTH: To 90 feet** **LEVEL: Variable**

There was a waterfront resort, consisting of several old, wooden buildings, which was used by scuba divers in the 1980's and 1990's, but has since been sold. Off this resort, which sits to the south of the dock, lies a large, wooden-stocked anchor, imported to this site by scuba instructors, with 12' of immense chain on it in 42' of water. About one mile south via boat from the town of Dyer's Bay is the impressive rock formation, both above and under water, called "The Devil's Face." Canyon-like passageways, cliffs and caverns abound.

4. CAPE CHIN WRECK

> **DEPTH: 20 and 70 feet** **LEVEL: Novice/Advanced**

Approach by boat, since this part of the Bruce Peninsula is lined with privately-owned cottages. Three chunks of unidentified schooner wreckage lie near Cape Chin just off the brown cottage with the gazebo near shore, south of three telephone poles. Just off the boulders used as a retaining wall, sitting on the sand, lie two of the pieces, 60' and 35' in length, in 20' of water. They can usually be seen from the surface. In 1992, we found an additional 35-foot piece in 70' just off the shallow portions. All the sections consist of a heavy, thick keelson, with many ribs emanating; it appears that they came from a large schooner.

5. LION'S HEAD WRECKS

DEPTH: To 15 feet   LEVEL: Novice

Sailing vessels in the lumber industry at the beginnng of the 20th century found themselves being abandoned to age in the many Georgian Bay harbors. Two of these unidentified wrecks lie in Lion's Head harbor. The more accessible of the two lies with the remains of its bow right against the shore of a small, rounded peninsula of land to the southeast of the public beach. These skeletal remains, probably of a sailing vessel, are about 140′ long. A bit further east and about 200′ off shore in 15′ of water are the remains of a tugboat. Beware of boating traffic here, especially in the summertime.

6. OLD CONCORD

DEPTH: 60 feet   LEVEL: Intermediate

LOCATION: This wreck lies off Gun Point, near Lion's Head, Ontario.

Located by Norm Black and Don Knowles in 1974, the 318-gross-ton schooner-barge, *Old Concord* (166′ x 27′8″ x 11′2″), launched in June, 1855, at Newport (present-day Marine City), Michigan, stranded and sank in July, 1888. The ship's wheel, steering gear, rudder, huge hull slabs and other items are on site.

7. WIARTON WRECKS

DEPTH: 12 to 15 feet   LEVEL: Novice

The identified remains of three wooden ships lie just off the shore of Colpoy's Bay north of the town of Wiarton, and can be done as shore dives or by boat. The flattened lower hull of the passenger ship, *City of Chatham* (136′3″ x 28′5″ x 9′), built in Toronto in 1888, lies just north of the Wiarton fish hatchery. The ship had been partially stripped in 1921 and removed to Wiarton for a rebuilding which never happened. Further north along the shore, just south of the pier at the community of Colpoy's Bay, lie the remains of the *Lothair,* a Scottish-built barge (and the closer wreck to shore, with its stern post reaching close to the surface) and the *Edward S. Pease,* a lumber barge with sails. They lie end-to-end, flat and broken up, purposely sunk in the early 1900's in front of Whicher's Mill to form a mill pond as protection for the log rafts. The mill company had paid $200 each for them.

8. UNDERWATER FOREST

DEPTH: To 34 feet   LEVEL: Novice

Diver and past mayor of Wiarton, Ontario, Alan Given, located this underwater forest in 1977 on the northwest side of Gundersen Shoal in Colpoy's Bay, but thought little of it until 1993, when he sawed off some samples underwater and sent them to botanists. They were excited. They were 4,500 to 7,600 years old. Underwater forests, which give us a date at which water levels rose from the retreat of the last Ice Age, can also be found adjacent to nearby Cyprus Lake and a bit south of it in 40′ to 60′, Johnson Harbour on the west side of the Bruce Peninsula, and just off Cape Croker, as well as off Chicago in Lake Michigan.

9. MARY WARD

DEPTH: To 15 feet   LEVEL: Novice

Lying between Craigleith, Ontario, and the Mary Ward Ledges in Georgian Bay are the engine, propeller and much broken wreckage from the wooden steamer, *Mary Ward* (139′ x 25′6″ x 11′6″), built in Montreal as the *North* in 1864, and stranded and sank on November 24, 1872, with the loss of 8 crewmembers who tried to reach shore in a lifeboat. A boat is necessary to reach this hard-to-find site.

Right: Drawing of the steamer, *Mary Ward.* PUBLIC ARCHIVES OF CANADA

19. Penetanguishene

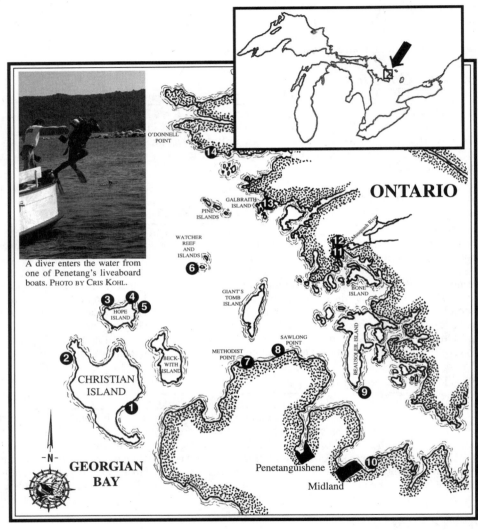

A diver enters the water from one of Penetang's liveaboard boats. PHOTO BY CRIS KOHL.

ONTARIO

O'DONNELL POINT

GALBRAITH ISLAND

PINE ISLANDS

WATCHER REEF AND ISLANDS

GIANT'S TOMB ISLAND

HOPE ISLAND

BECK-WITH ISLAND

METHODIST POINT

SAWLONG POINT

BONE ISLAND

BEAUSOLEIL ISLAND

CHRISTIAN ISLAND

Wmm River

-N-

GEORGIAN BAY

Penetanguishene

Midland

1. *Saucy Jim*	8. *Luckport*
2. *Mapledawn*	9. *Wawinet*
3. *Michigan*	10. *Midland City*
4. *Lottie Wolf*	11. *Chippewa*
5. *Marquette*	12. *Ontario*
6. *Thomas Cranage*	13. **Galbraith Island tug**
7. *Reliever*	14. *W. J. Martin*

1. SAUCY JIM

> **DEPTH: 5 feet**   **LEVEL: Novice**

LOCATION: This wreck lies off the sandy beach just east of the government dock at Christian Island. Built at Meaford, Ontario, in 1887, the small steam tug, *Saucy Jim*, burned to a total loss on November 18, 1910. Her boiler rises above the water's surface to act as a location marker for those wishing to snorkel/dive her broken, scattered remains.

2. MAPLEDAWN

> **LORAN: 29655.3/48931.5**   **LAT 44° 51' 52" LON 080° 14' 50"**
> **DEPTH: 10 to 30 feet**   **LEVEL: Novice-Intermediate**

LOCATION: This wreck lies off the northwest side of Christian Island.

The steel freighter, *Mapledawn* (349'1" x 40'2" x 21'3"), actually started life as the *Manola* (which is also in this book) when she was launched at Cleveland in 1890. As the *Manola*, her bow half sank in Lake Ontario. Later, a new bow half was constructed for the *Manola's* orphaned stern half, the resulting whole ship being named the *Mapledawn*. Although lives were lost when her original bow half sank in Lake Ontario, none was lost when the *Mapledawn*, loaded with barley, stranded in a blinding snowstorm on November 30, 1924. Some machinery was salvaged at that time, but more of this wreck was recovered for its metal during the time of need in World War II. The considerable remaining wreckage includes the winch, chains, engine, gigantic boilers and the propeller at the deepest part in 30' of water about 50' off the stern.

The *Mapledawn*. IGLR

Below and lower right: Divers explore the *Mapledawn*. PHOTOS BY CRIS KOHL.

Artwork
©Adam Henley

3. MICHIGAN

> **LORAN:** 29637.73/48912.73   **LAT** 44° 54′ 58″ **LON** 080° 12′ 15″
> **DEPTH:** To 15 feet   **LEVEL:** Novice

LOCATION: This wreck lies off the northwest corner of Hope Island, Georgian Bay.

The steel barge, *Michigan* (296′5″ x 41′3″ x 15′6″), launched at West Bay City, Michigan, on October 30, 1890, as a railroad carferry, was lightering the grain cargo from the stranded steamer, *Riverton,* at this site on November 24, 1943, when the gales of November blew the *Michigan* onto the rocks as well. Suddenly the salvage ship needed salvaging! Ironically, the *Riverton* was eventually recovered and returned to service, but the *Michigan* became a total loss. Giant gears, machinery and much metalwork offer intriguing sights here.

The steel barge, *Michigan,* sank in 1943. IGLR

The *Michigan* shipwreck covers a large area, with divers exploring the site as thoroughly as possible. PHOTOS BY CRIS KOHL.

4. LOTTIE WOLF

> **LORAN:** 29501.9/48914.3   **LAT**   **LON**
> **DEPTH:** 18 feet   **LEVEL:** Novice

LOCATION: This wreck lies about 450′ from the lighthouse dock, off the northeast corner of Hope Island, southern Georgian Bay.

The three-masted, 126′ schooner, *Lottie Wolf,* launched at Green Bay, Wisconsin, in 1866, sailed for Midland, Ontario, from Chicago with a cargo of corn when she struck a rock during severe weather on October 16, 1891. Purposely run aground to avoid sinking in deep water, the vessel broke up after the crew abandoned ship. The remains lie scattered on a sandy bottom, with the sides of the hull off the south and west of the main wreckage area.

5. MARQUETTE

> **LORAN:** 29620.0/48917.0   **LAT**   **LON**
> **DEPTH:** 29 to 45 feet   **LEVEL:** Novice-Intermediate

LOCATION: The wreck of the *Marquette* lies off the northeast corner of Hope Island.

The 139′3″ bark, *Marquette,* built at Newport (today's Marine City), Michigan, in 1856, foundered with a cargo of corn and no lives lost on November 28, 1867. Known as "the

Artwork ©Adam Henley

Exploring the windlass and chain at the *Marquette's* bow. PHOTO BY CRIS KOHL.

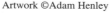

Hope Island Wreck" for about 10 years after divers located it in 1975, her identity was established in the mid-1980's. Although pilfered of many of its artifacts shortly after its discovery by divers who probably were unaware that they were helping destroy sport scuba diving in the Great Lakes, this wreck has quite a few interesting items left at the site: two wooden-stocked anchors (with chains still connecting them to the windlass), a samson post, a capstan lying on its side in the sand beside the hull, double framing on its hull, a centerboard box, a centerboard winch, the main mast step, hatch coaming, planksheers, transom wing, and a portion of the rudder.

6. THOMAS CRANAGE

LORAN: 29593.6/48906.0	LAT 44° 56′ 39″ LON 080° 05′ 27″
DEPTH: To 25 feet	LEVEL: Novice

LOCATION: This wreck lies off "The Watchers" Islands, southern Georgian Bay.

The *Thomas Cranage* (305′ x 43′ x 20′7″), was, for a short time after her launch on July 29, 1893, at West Bay City, Michigan, the Great Lakes' largest wooden steamer. On September 25, 1911, while on a voyage from Duluth, Minnesota, to Tiffin, Ontario, with a cargo of wheat, the *Thomas Cranage* struck Watcher Reef. Salvage efforts proved futile, and the ship broke to pieces in the early fall.

The steamer, *Thomas Cranage.* IGLR

The *Thomas Cranage's* triple expansion engine makes a unique photographic subject. PHOTO BY CRIS KOHL.

The broken remains of this vessel include the impressive triple expansion engine, the steel-reinforced rudder and much planking. The propeller and boilers were likely salvaged, as they are absent. This open site is susceptible to adverse westerly weather.

7. RELIEVER

Scattered along the bay bottom in about 12′ of water about 100′ off Way's Point, Ontario (near Methodist Point), lie the hull and other remains of the wooden steamer, *Reliever* (216′ x 36′ x 18′), launched at West Bay City, Michigan, on April 1, 1888, as the *Germanic*. The ship caught on fire while loading lumber on November 3, 1909. The flaming vessel, cut adrift to save the dock, grounded at Way's Point and burned to a total loss.

8. LUCKPORT

The 126′ wooden steamer, *Luckport,* built as the *St. Magnus* at Hamilton, Ontario, in 1880, burned to the waterline west of Sawlog Point in December, 1934. Only the charred hull remains about 200′ off shore. The privately-owned land here precludes shore access.

9. WAWINET

LORAN: 29501.9/48970.7	LAT 44° 49′ 30″ LON 079° 05′ 54″
DEPTH: 25 feet	LEVEL: Novice-Intermediate

The 87′ private yacht, *Wawinet,* built in 1904 and purchased by Bertrand Corbeau of Penetanguishene in 1938, became one of Georgian Bay's most tragic marine accidents. On September 21, 1942, returning from Honey Harbour to Penetanguishene with Corbeau and colleagues from the Midland Foundry & Machine Company, the vessel heeled over while making a sudden turn. Her lower windows were, unfortunately, open, and the ship filled and sank within two minutes, with 25 of the 42 people on board, including Corbeau, losing their lives. The survivors swam to nearby Beausoleil Island where they were soon rescued.

The *Wawinet,* upright and intact, faces bow southeast. The weakened hull of the wreck should be entered only with the greatest of care, training and preparation. Silt stirs up easily.

10. MIDLAND CITY

This site can be reached by shore or boat. Lying in 3 to 12 of water, only the bottom of the hull remains of the *Midland City* in Tiffin Basin, just east of the easternmost dock. This composite (built of both wood and steel or iron) passenger and freight steamer spent an incredible 84 years working on the Great Lakes! Built as the *Maud* at Kingston in 1871 by George Thurston, the *Midland City* (149′2″ x 33′2″ x 6′4″) was dismantled and deliberately burned on May 7, 1955 near the Wye River. Beware of busy boating traffic here.

11. CHIPPEWA

The 94′ wooden steamer, *Chippewa,* built in 1874, was abandoned in 1906, 3/4 mile up the Musquash River from the extreme southern end of Longuissa Point. She lies in 6′ to 20′.

12. ONTARIO

About 1.5 miles up the Musquash River from the extreme southern end of Longuissa Point, the abandoned wooden barge, *Ontario* (131′ x 24′), lies in 6′ to 12′ off the north bank.

13. GALBRAITH ISLAND WRECK

This unidentified, wooden tug lies in 2′ to 10′ of water in a quiet cove at the northeast corner of Galbraith Island. A 53-foot-long keel section and some framing remain.

14. W. J. MARTIN

The small, 75′ wooden steamer, *W.J. Martin,* burned to a complete loss in November, 1905, only two months after she was launched at Midland, Ontario. She lies at Middle Rock, between Ward Island and Fairlie Island, in 5′ to 20′ of water. Her boiler is the highlight.

20. Parry Sound

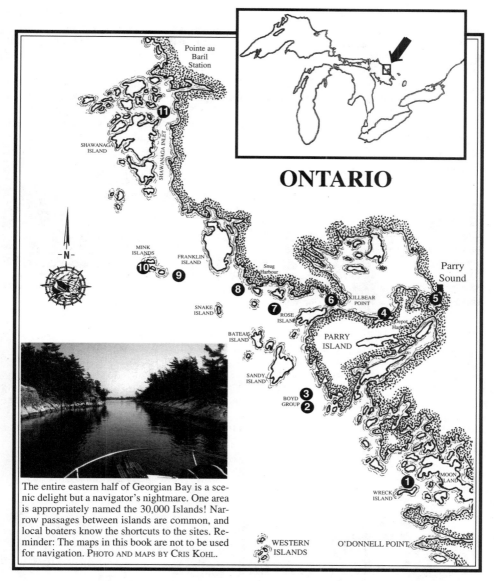

ONTARIO

Parry Sound

The entire eastern half of Georgian Bay is a scenic delight but a navigator's nightmare. One area is appropriately named the 30,000 Islands! Narrow passages between islands are common, and local boaters know the shortcuts to the sites. Reminder: The maps in this book are not to be used for navigation. PHOTO AND MAPS BY CRIS KOHL.

1. *Waubuno*
2. *Emma*
3. **Blackmore Island wreck**
4. **Depot Harbour**
5. *Ella Ross*
6. **Harold Point**
7. *Atlantic*
8. *Jane McLeod*
9. *Midland*
10. *Seattle*
11. *Metamora*

1. *WAUBUNO*

LORAN:	LAT 45° 07′ 15″ LON 080° 09′ 58″
DEPTH: To 15 feet	LEVEL: Novice

LOCATION: This wreck lies in an inlet on the southern tip of Bradden Island, just north of Wreck Island, halfway between the Musquash River and Parry Sound.

The wooden, widewheel steamer, *Waubuno* (135′ x 18′3″ x 7′), worked on Georgian Bay for 14 years before becoming a mystery vessel. On November 22, 1879, the *Waubuno* left Collingwood, Ontario, with passengers and freight bound for Parry Sound. Later, a logging crew on shore heard the heavily-laden vessel's distress whistles in a blinding snowstorm. Then she simply disappeared with all 30 people on board. The following spring, this washed-up hull was located, but no bodies were ever found. The ship had been built in 1865 at Port Robinson, Ontario. The hull provides a habitat for pike, perch and bass. The engine, boiler and other machinery are all absent. Keep off the adjoining private property.

Left: The tragic sidewheeler, *Waubuno.* AUTHOR'S COLLECTION. *Above:* Examining the *Waubuno's* hull. PHOTO BY CRIS KOHL.

2. *EMMA*

DEPTH: 4 to 20 feet	LEVEL: Novice

LOCATION: This wreck lies in a small cove formed by three islands in the Boyd Group of the 30,000 Islands, just to the northeast of Bald Island.

Launched at Collingwood, Ontario, on May 1, 1894, the 75-ton steam yacht, *Emma* (89′3″ x 18′ x 6′6″), on her way from Parry Sound to Owen Sound, Ontario, to take advantage of busy summer tourism, caught on fire and burned to a total loss on the Fourth of July, 1912. No lives were lost. Only the broken, bottom portion of the hull remains; her engine and boiler were salvaged shortly after her loss.

Left: The Canadian steam yacht, *Emma,* plied Parry Sound waters at the turn of the last century before burning in 1912. PUBLIC ARCHIVES OF CANADA. *Right:* Bolts, boards and nails are all that remain of the *Emma* in a secluded little cove. PHOTO BY CRIS KOHL.

3. BLACKMORE ISLAND WRECK

DEPTH: 10 to 20 feet   LEVEL: Novice

LOCATION: This wreck lies off the northwest side of Blackmore Island, between that island and tiny Bayview Island, and just to the south of Schade Island. It is believed that this solidly-built, unidentified vessel, which is about 85′ in length and 20′ in beam, was used as a scow in this area's lumber trade.

4. DEPOT HARBOUR

DEPTH: To 30 feet   LEVEL: Novice-Intermediate

Depot Harbour is the community just to the west of Parry Sound, Ontario. It sits about halfway between Parry Sound and Killbear Provincial Park. Access is by boat.

The old, submerged cribs at this formerly thriving community offer excellent exploration possibilities. The intricate pattern of logs attests to the construction skills of a much earlier generation. Don't get lost or tangled up inside any of the passageway structures between cribs. "Cribs" were wooden-framed, rock-filled, submerged bases used to support an above-water dock superstructure. Beware: A portion of these cribs is caving in. Do not penetrate!

5. *ELLA ROSS*

DEPTH: 20 feet   LEVEL: Novice

LOCATION: This wreck lies in Parry Sound harbor off the Coast Guard Station.

The iron steamer, *Ella Ross* (99′2″ x 27′8″ x 6′4″), launched as the *Gypsy* at Montreal in 1873, burned to a complete loss at her dock in Parry Sound on June 5, 1912. The superstructure burned off, and the hull lies mostly buried in the bottom of the harbor, but inside the hull are the boiler, engine and other mechanical components.

6. HAROLD POINT IN KILLBEAR PARK

DEPTH: 40 to 90 feet   LEVEL: Variable

Harold Point is an impressive rock formation in Killbear Provincial Par, and you can drive your vehicle into the park. However, it is a bit of a walk from the nearest parking lot to Harold Point. This natural, rocky setting provides views of underwater boulders and fish.

7. *ATLANTIC*

LORAN: 29661.88/48743.12   LAT 45° 20′ 02″ LON 080° 15′ 39″
DEPTH: 6 to 50 feet   LEVEL: Novice-Intermediate

LOCATION: This wreck lies several miles west of Parry Sound, along the northwestern edge of Spruce Rocks, to the north of Spruce Island.

The *Atlantic*. AUTHOR'S COLLECTION

Flames fanned by the fierce gales of November 10th, 1903, destroyed, for the second and last time, the combination passenger and package freight steamer, *Atlantic* (147′ x 30′ x 11′). No lives were lost, although in her first incineration on May 18, 1882, when she was named the *Manitoulin*, about 30 people perished. Her relatively new hull at that time was raised and the vessel was rebuilt and renamed. She had been constructed originally at Owen Sound, Ontario, in 1880.

Easily located are the propeller and the huge rudder which lie in less than 10′ of water. The superstructure totally burned off or caved

193

Above: The *Atlantic's* bow was often heavy with excursionists. ONTARIO ARCHIVES. *Right:* A diver glides over the *Atlantic's* vast array of machinery. PHOTO BY CRIS KOHL.

in on the hull, and, lying there with the stern in the shallows and the bow in the deeper water, the seascape of tangled debris, which includes chain, capstan, gears, boiler, engine and other machinery, proves irresistible to divers. A modern snowmobile sits at the bottom. Boating hazards are many, as this wreck lies in the shoal-strewn, island-dotted "30,000 Islands." A strong west wind can prove dangerous at this open site.

Artwork ©Adam Henley

8. *JANE MCLEOD*

DEPTH: 20 to 25 feet	LEVEL: Novice

Artwork ©Adam Henley

LOCATION: This wreck lies off the south part of McLeod Island, in the 30,000 Islands.

The 117' schooner, *Jane McLeod*, built at St. Catharines, Ontario, in 1868, stranded on November 4, 1890, when her anchor chain parted. Her captain and crew camped on the inhospitable, rocky island for five days before they were rescued. Autumn winds battered their schooner to pieces. Lying about 100' from the island, the stern is slightly deeper than the bow. Scattered portions of this vessel cover a wide area. This area is susceptible to sudden, adverse westerly wind conditions.

McLeod framing. PHOTO BY CRIS KOHL

9. *MIDLAND*

LORAN: 29708.4/48718.5	LAT	LON
DEPTH: 50 feet	LEVEL: Intermediate	

This wreck lies on the east side of the Mink Islands, southeast of the site of the *Seattle*.

Built at Midland, Ontario, in 1896 as the *D.L. White,* this 56-ton wooden tug (62' x 13' x 6'8"), foundered in 1923. Her name had been changed to *Midland* in 1908. Sitting on a clay bottom, the site features the steeple compound engine, bilge pump, and the rudder and propeller a bit off the wreck. This site's remoteness makes it potentially dangerous.

Artwork ©Adam Henley

The Midland

The *Midland,* as the *D.L. White,* took sportsmen to remote areas. IGLR

10. SEATTLE

LOCATION: This wreck lies in 15'-25' of water just west of Green Island, in the Mink Islands. LORAN 29735.6/48706.8.

The wooden steamer, *Seattle* (160'7" x 36'5" x 9'9"), built in Oscoda, Michigan, in 1892, stranded here after engine failure in heavy seas on November 11, 1903. No lives were lost. The boiler and other wreckage can be seen from the surface. Sights include the propeller, engine and steering quadrant.

Top: The *Seattle.* IGLR. *Top Right:* The *Seattle's* propulsion system. PHOTO BY CRIS KOHL. *Below:* The *Metamora.* PUBLIC ARCHIVES OF CANADA. *Right:* The *Metamora's* boiler. PHOTO BY CRIS KOHL.

11. METAMORA

Located at the east end of Nadeau Island in the Shawanaga Inlet, the wooden tug, *Metamora* (115' x 39'3" x 10'8"), built at Cleveland in 1864, burned to a total loss on September 29, 1907. This novice site has a maximum depth of 15'. The stern section is the most alluring, since it contains the rudder, steam engine and propeller. The boiler, which protrudes above the water, serves as the base for a navigational daymark. This site also offers crayfish galore!

21. Northern Georgian Bay

ONTARIO

GEORGIAN BAY

MANITOULIN ISLAND

Little Current

Killarney

COLLINS INLET

BYNG INLET

Point au Baril Station

FITZWILLIAM ISLAND

1. *Northern Belle*	6. *M. J. Low*
2. *James Reid*	7. *Dove* and *Branch II*
3. Collins Inlet	8. "Parking Lot"
4. Killarney Channel	9. "Silica Wall"
5. *Wilma Ann*	10. "Boat Rock Wall"

1. NORTHERN BELLE

DEPTH: 10 feet	LEVEL: Novice

LOCATION: This wreck rests along the south shore of Byng Inlet, west of Old Mill Island. It can usually be located visually from the surface.

The *Northern Belle*. AUTHOR'S COLLECTION

The wooden steamer, *Northern Belle* (129′ x 22′6″ x 9′5″), launched as the *Gladys* on May 21, 1875, at Marine City, Michigan, burned to a total loss in the narrows at Byng Inlet on November 6, 1898. For over 20 years, she had served the tiny lumbering communities between Sault Ste. Marie and Collingwood. Beware of the current and occasional boating traffic at this site.

2. JAMES REID

DEPTH: 70 feet	LEVEL: Advanced

LOCATION: This wreck lies off Byng Inlet. Draw a line from the Bell buoy at the western edge of Magnetewan Ledges to the red "AM2" buoy at Morden Rock. The wreck lies halfway between these two points and just a bit east of that line.

The powerful tug, *James Reid.* MPL/WMHS

The large, iron-hulled tugboat, *James Ried* (117' x 23' x 12'7"), built in 1875 at Wilmington, Delaware, as the *Protector,* was purchased by famous Great Lakes shipwreck salvager, Tom Reid, in 1893 and was later renamed after his father. The ship foundered in August, 1917. Located in the late 1970's, this wreck sits upright and offers much to see.

3. COLLINS INLET

DEPTH: To 30 feet	LEVEL: Novice-Intermediate

LOCATION: This site lies six miles east of Killarney, Ontario.

The town of Collins Inlet, created in the 1880's, soon boasted a sawmill, boarding house, private residences, a store and a school. The community, however, came to a grinding halt when the mill burned down in 1917 and lumber operations were moved to Midland. Every building save one is a ruin. Access is by car or boat. By car, go west on Highway 637 from highway 69 for 21 miles. Turn onto the old unsurfaced Pike Road down to the present-day fish camp at Collins Inlet. Boaters can launch at Killarney. Ruins of docks and pilings where the lumber-laden schooners and steamers once tied up, plus turn-of-the-century cast-offs or losses, can easily be seen. Beware of sunken logs, trees and branches.

4. KILLARNEY CHANNEL

This novice-intermediate dive to 30' will take the diver to parts of burned and abandoned vessels, as well as garbage and losses from over the years. Boating season traffic is heavy!

5. WILMA ANN

In 65' to 80' adjacent to the Kokanongwi Shingle, southwest of Killarney, the fishing tug, *Wilma Ann,* built in 1932, was scuttled in 1983 as a dive site. she sits upright in mud, intact, including open holds, the wheelhouse and the after structure.

6. M. J. LOW

In 65' northeast of Killarney, this intact wooden fishing vessel was scuttled in 1951.

7. DOVE AND BRANCH II

These two wooden cabin cruisers lie in 23' past Killarney east light at Red Rock Point.

8. "PARKING LOT"

Three cars, two half-tons, and a large truck cab lie near site#7 in 15' to 30' of water.

9. "SILICA WALL"

Off the Indusmin Silica Mine near Killarney, this advanced wall dive drops to 120'. The wall offers views of rocks covered with white silica, a hard, glassy mineral.

10. "BOAT ROCK WALL"

This steep wall dive to 110' for advanced divers is near Badgeley Island off Killarney.

22. Manitoulin Island

ONTARIO

Quiet and quaint, Meldrum Bay sees the occasional tall ship. PHOTO BY CRIS KOHL.

Blind River

Spanish

Espanola

NORTH CHANNEL

Meldrum Bay

COCK-BURN ISLAND

Missisaugi Strait

BARRIE ISLAND

Gore Bay   Kagawong

Little Current

MANITOULIN ISLAND

GREAT DUCK ISLAND

– N –

Providence Bay

CLUB ISLAND

LAKE HURON

South Baymouth

FITZWILLIAM ISLAND

Manitoulin Island, the largest freshwater island in the world, is an odd blend of wilderness forests and livestock pastures, comfortable communities proud of their heritage and rocky shorelines unforgiving to vessels in distress.

1. **Club Island wreck**
2. *Michigan*
3. *City of Cleveland*
4. *Clarence E.*
5. *India*
6. *Alexandria*
7. *Hiawatha*
8. *B. B. Buckhout*
9. *Edward Buckley*
10. *Jacqueline*
11. *North Wind*
12. *Iroquois*
13. *Emma E. Thompson*
14. *Thomas J. Cahoon*
15. *Chamberlain* and *Webb*
16. *Wanipitee*
17. *Winona*
18. *Michipicoten*
19. *Winslow*
20. *Burlington*
21. *Joyland*
22. *Bielman* and *Chattanooga*

1. CLUB ISLAND WRECK

> **DEPTH: 15 feet**   **LEVEL: Novice**

LOCATION: This unidentified wreck lies in Club Island Harbour, which is about 20 miles north of Tobermory and six miles east of Rattlesnake Harbour on Fitzwilliam Island. This popular (we shared the harbor with 14 other boats the one night we spent there) overnight spot for boaters cruising between the North Channel and Tobermory is on the island's east side. This 57' metal-sheathed shipwreck lies 150' from shore opposite the fishing shanties.

2. *MICHIGAN*

> **DEPTH: To 15 feet**   **LEVEL: Novice**

LOCATION: This wreck lies in the well-sheltered Rattlesnake Harbour on the northern portion of Fitzwilliam Island, about 20 miles north of Tobermory. The 180' schooner-barge, *Michigan,* in operation until the 1930's, lies along the shoreline near the abandoned fishing shanties. A steel rod marks the bow. The wreck of the *Wauseda II* lies at the very eastern end of the inlet. Reportedly a small wreck lies along the south shore of the bay, and another one just to the east of the *Michigan.* Submerged logs and tree branches clutter the clay bottom of this bay, so explore with caution. And yes, there are rattlesnakes on the island.

3. *CITY OF CLEVELAND*

> **LORAN: 30256.2/48587.4   LAT 45° 28.222' LON 081° 50.723'**
> **DEPTH: 10 to 30 feet   LEVEL: Novice**

LOCATION: North of Perseverence Island, off the outlying shoal of Little Perseverence Island, 9 miles from South Baymouth, Manitoulin Island, and 18 miles north of Tobermory.

The twin-decked, four-masted, wooden steamer, *City of Cleveland* (255'7" x 39'5" x 18'4"), launched at Cleveland on June 17, 1882, ran aground in a blinding snowstorm and southwest gales on September 15, 1901, with her 2,300 tons of iron ore and no lives lost. The crew rowed to Fitzwilliam Island, from where they were rescued. This immense vessel, with her bow in the shallows, is one of the most impressive shallow-water shipwrecks you will ever see. The tall steam engine, seemingly on stilts, the massive boilers, the rudder and a huge propeller are very interesting and photogenic.

The huge steamer, *City of Cleveland,* was wrecked dramatically in 1889 (above), but was salvaged and returned to service. Twelve years later, she stranded again, but became a total loss. AUTHOR'S COLLECTION

Tim Philp studies some machinery from the *City of Cleveland's* engine. PHOTO BY CRIS KOHL.

199

4. CLARENCE E.

The tug, *Clarence E.*, which sank in 1936, lies in 25' of water off the northwest tip of the wharf at Providence Bay, southern Manitoulin Island. This can be a shore or boat dive.

5. INDIA

LORAN:	LAT 45° 58' 15" LON 081° 45' 55"
DEPTH: 20 to 30 feet	LEVEL: Novice

LOCATION: This wreck, correctly marked on the chart of this area, lies off the northeast side of West Mary Island, 8 miles east of Little Current, Ontario.

The wooden steamer, *India* (216'9" x 36'4" x 15'), built at Garden Island near Kingston, Ontario, in 1899, burned to a total loss on September 4, 1928. The vessel's keel, mast, boiler and propeller are the highlights of a visit to this popular site. Schools of sunfish and bass swim between the machinery, while lazy ling lie between the beams.

Left: The wooden steamer, *India,* ablaze on Sept. 4, 1928. IGLR. *Right:* Although the fire and Mother Nature have taken their toll, the wreck of the India offers many sights and is fun to explore. PHOTO BY CRIS KOHL.

6. ALEXANDRIA

The small, wooden steamer, *Alexandria* (91' x 25'), launched at Chatham, Ontario, in 1902, burned at Little Current in 1927. Her remains, mainly a boiler and wood debris, rest on the rock bottom in 24' of water at the east end of the government dock at Little Current. Beware of heavy boating traffic in the summer months.

7. HIAWATHA

Hiawatha's prop. PHOTO BY CRIS KOHL

The 93-foot-long, 163-ton steamer, *Hiawatha,* built at Dresden, Ontario, in 1874, spent most of her life plying the waters of the St. Clair River before being moved and abandoned up here in 1930. Much wood, a propeller and some pulleys and bracing form the main part of this site in 5' to 30' of water. A small barge lies beside her. She is at the northeast edge of Low Island, which is, in fact, connected to Manitoulin Island. Divers can drive right up to the wreck site and suit up there. This wreck is also marked on the local nagivation chart.

8. B. B. BUCKHOUT

The schooner-barge, *B.B. Buckhout* (158'2" x 28'8" x 10'), built at East Saginaw, Michigan, in 1873, transferred to Canadian ownership in 1912 and seemingly disappeared into history at that point. The long-unidentified lumber-laden shipwreck just west of Narrow Island was identified as the *B.B. Buckhout* by researcher Richard Hammond of Little Current. She lies in 40' just south of green buoy "J63" on the east side of the limestone shoal. One story tells of the *Buckhout*, while being towed by the tug, *Maitland*, stranding on that reef in

November, 1912 and sinking before she could be salvaged. This wreck, with its vast amount of lumber (some divers have wondered if this isn't really TWO wrecks), is broken up and shows signs of having caught on fire as well.

The lumber-laden *B.B. Buckhout.*
AUTHOR'S COLLECTION

Diver Sean Moore swims along charred timbers from one end of the vast wreckage of the schooner-barge, *B.B. Buckhout.* PHOTO BY CRIS KOHL.

9. EDWARD BUCKLEY

Southwest off Mink Island, a few miles to the northwest of Little Current, in about 110' of low-visibility water, lie the remains of the wooden steamer, *Edward Buckley* (154'3" x 31' x 10'6"), burned to a complete loss on September 1, 1929. The *Buckley,* built at Manitowoc, Wisconsin, in 1891, was located and identified in 1993 by researcher/diver Richard Hammond of Little Current. The anchor chain begins in 70' of water and follows the slope down to the shipwreck. The ship's engine, propeller and hull await the experienced.

10. JACQUELINE

The *Jacqueline* is a double-ender railroad car ferry which was abandoned on the west side of the only bay on the north tip of Clapperton Island. She lies in the shallows (5' to 12' of water), with parts in 40', between the 1st and 2nd stone beaches, before the drop-off.

11. NORTH WIND

LORAN: 30343.3/48293.4	LAT 46° 03.45' LON 082° 12.56'
DEPTH: 80 to 110+ feet	LEVEL: Advanced

LOCATION: This wreck lies just east of Robertson Rock, off the north side of Clapperton Island. A plastic jug, which often disappears, sometimes marks the site.

The steel freighter, *North Wind* (299'5" x 40'8" x 21'6"), launched at Cleveland on July 31, 1888, stranded on Robertson Rock on July 1, 1926, and slid into deep water two hours later. No lives were lost. Aquatic visitors usually land on the bow, with its twin anchors and anchor winch.

Portholes can be seen between 80' and 100', and a four-bladed propeller rests on the deck at 110'. Unfortunately, parts of this steel wreck are caving in, so stay out!

Left: The *North Wind.* MPL/ WMHS. *Right:* A diver examines a section of piping on the *North Wind.* PHOTO BY DAVID OSTIFICHUK.

12. IROQUOIS

The remains of the wooden steamer, *Iroquois* (112' x 20' x 8'7"), lie in 25' to 30' of water at East Rock in McBean Channel. Built at Wiarton, Ontario, in 1902, the ship burned to a total loss on Oct. 24, 1908. The green channel marker is about 650' away from this hull.

13. EMMA E. THOMPSON

LORAN: 44927.9/57943.0	LAT LON
DEPTH: 30 feet	LEVEL: Novice

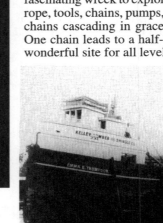

LOCATION: This wreck lies off the northeast side of Innes Island.

The wooden steamer, *Emma E. Thompson* (125'9" x 27'6" x 12'8"), built at Saginaw, Michigan, in 1875, sought shelter from a storm behind Innes Island, but caught on fire and burned to the water's edge on May 28, 1914. No lives were lost. The wreck sits upright and intact, and is sometimes marked with a plastic jug. This is a fascinating wreck to explore: rudder, engine, boiler, rope, tools, chains, pumps, and three sets of anchor chains cascading in graceful arcs down the bow. One chain leads to a half-buried anchor. This is a wonderful site for all levels of divers.

Above: Three anchor chains arch dramatically off the *Emma E. Thompson's* bow. PHOTO BY CRIS KOHL. *Right:* The *Emma E. Thompson,* afloat. MPL/WMHS

14. THOMAS J. CAHOON

Off the southwest side of Innes Island, at Kenny Point and inside Kenny Shoal, in a maximum of 20' of water, lie the remains of the 166' schooner-barge, *Thomas J. Cahoon,* launched in 1881 at Saginaw, Michigan, and, lumber-laden, stranded here in a storm on October 11, 1913. She can usually be seen from the surface. LORAN: 30398.1/48286.1

15. PORTER CHAMBERLAIN AND H. J. WEBB

These wrecks lie west of Darch Island, off Egg Island at Wallace Rock, north of Gore Bay (LORAN: 30437.9/48267.4), in 7' to 30' of water. The wooden steamer, *Porter Chamberlain* (134' x 26' x 10'3") was towing the schooner, *H.J. Webb* (167' x 28'4" x 11'5"), both ships loaded with lumber, when the *Chamberlain* caught on fire and ran aground. Her cohort also ended up stranding and burning. No lives were lost in that incident on November 11, 1901. The *Chamberlain's* boiler can be seen from the surface, and there is little evidence of burning on these wrecks. There are large areas of frames, but not much intact hull. There is a centerboard trunk, prop blade, and many other items at this big site.

16. WANIPITEE

The *Wanipitee,* a general purpose, mail/passenger/freight tug, sank in 20′ to 30′ next to Ethel Rock in the middle of boat-busy Little Detroit Passage near Spanish, Ontario.

17. WINONA

The passenger/freight steamer, *Winona* (110′ x 21′), built in 1902 at Port Stanley, burned and sank in 10′ on the south shore of the entrance to Spragge Harbour on Nov. 13, 1931.

The steamer, *Michipicoten,* a year before she burned. AUTHOR'S COLLECTION.

18. MICHIPICOTEN

Built in 1883 in Wyandotte, MI, as the *E.K. Roberts,* the wooden steamer, *Michipicoten,* caught fire and burned on Oct. 10, 1927, off Cook's Dock. The burned-out hull sits in 25′.

19. WINSLOW

Located in 20′ about 200′ offshore in the harbor opposite the Net Shed Museum in Meldrum Bay, the tug, *Winslow* (120′ x 19′), built in 1865, burned on Aug. 21, 1911.

20. BURLINGTON

DEPTH: 23 feet	LEVEL: Novice

LOCATION: In a bay on the north side of the Mississagi Straits Lighthouse. There are telephone poles in the camping area at the water's edge; where the wires enter the water on their way over to Cockburn Island is where the *Burlington* lies. Telephone pole number 721 is the closest one to the water. You can get a campsite right at the entry point!

The wooden steamer, *Burlington* (137′ x 25′3″ x 12′), launched in 1857 at Buffalo, New York, caught on fire while at anchor at the Mississagi Straits Lighthouse on August 24, 1895, and burned to a complete loss. She had been on her way from Detroit to Manitoulin Island to load up with lumber. The tug, *James Storey,* took her crew of 12 to Meldrum Bay, from where they found transportation home.

The electrical cable that was extended to Cockburn Island in the late 1980's runs right over the wreck of

Many interesting items remain at the *Burlington* site. PHOTOS BY CRIS KOHL.

the *Burlington!* Where were the heritage politicians when this was planned? The *Burlington's* salvagable items (prop, anchors, windlass, capstan, boiler, engine) were salvaged shortly after the fire, but visiting divers can still appreciate the rudder with chain, a pump, the engine mount and huge sections of framing and planking at this scattered site.

The *Burlington.* MPL/WMHS

21. *Joyland* (the "Honeymoon Wreck")

DEPTH: To 16 feet   LEVEL: Novice

LOCATION: This wreck lies just off the southeast shore of Burnt Island Harbour, in the southwest corner of Manitoulin Island.

Built in 1884 at Detroit as the wooden steamer, *William A. Haskell* (250'5" x 37' x 14'3"), this vessel carried package freight around the Great Lakes, later being converted to a sandsucker in 1924. The *Joyland* ran aground here in 1926 and was abandoned. Someone set her on fire in 1930, destroying all of her superstructure.

There is a virtually overgrown road/trail starting at the main road and running right to the water's edge. Search for it carefully on the right before you reach the commercial fishing community of Burnt Island.

Lying 100' offshore and perpendicular to it, with the bow facing the land, the *Joyland* is very shallow, but offers MANY worthwhile shipwreck

The *Joyland* in 1930, just before she burned. The ship had been abandoned here for four years already. Notice the sand scoops over the stern. MPL/WMHS

sights, such as a four-bladed propeller, boiler (the second boiler was recovered in 1934 and sits on shore, acting as a guide to this site), massive hull, spikes, bolts, sandsucker scoops, prop shaft and more. This site has, for years, been nicknamed the "honeymoon wreck" because my friend who told me about it came here on her honeymoon; she, a new diver, explored the *Joyland* with her husband. Actually, there *is* a certain romance to this place....

Huge *Joyland* gears and other machinery half-buried in the Lake Huron sands at Burnt Island offer underwater exploration galore for diver Sean Moore. PHOTO BY CRIS KOHL.

22. *C. F. Bielman* and *Chattanooga*

The old steamer, *C.F. Bielman* (291' x 41' x 19'8"), and the schooner-barge, *Chattanooga* (308' x 45' x 24'), both built in West Bay City, Michigan, in the late 1800's but by competitors, were derelicts by the 1930's. Both became breakwalls/docks at the fishing wharf on the southeast side of Great Duck Island, 13 miles south of Manitoulin Island. The reluctant *C.F. Bielman* swamped her towing tug, the *Monarch* (also in this book) in the St. Clair River on July 6, 1934, with the loss of four lives, when she was on her way to the island. The *Chattanooga's* hull is filled with stone, and both vessels lie at a maximum depth of 20'. The *Bielman's* rudder and propeller are in place, but her engine and boiler were removed. Part of her hull lies on the beach.

23. DeTour

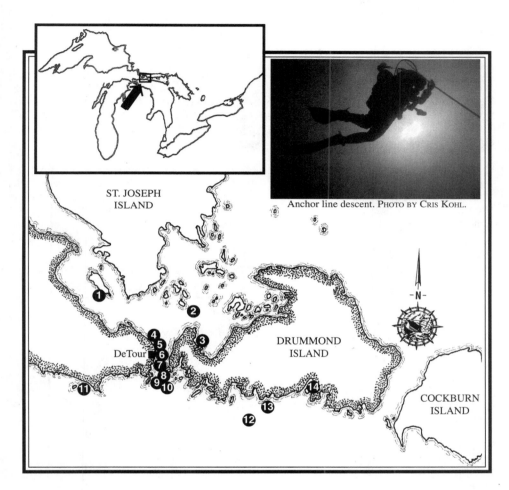

Anchor line descent. PHOTO BY CRIS KOHL.

ST. JOSEPH ISLAND

DRUMMOND ISLAND

DeTour

COCKBURN ISLAND

1. *Rome*
2. *J. C. Ford*
3. Pigeon Cove schooner
4. Kelly's dock
5. *Two Myrtles/Alice C.*
6. *Superior*
7. *John W. Cullen*
8. *Sainte Marie*
9. *General*
10. Frying Pan Island dock
11. Saddlebag Island wreck
12. *John B. Merrill*
13. *Agnes W.*
14. *Troy*

1. ROME

> **LORAN: 30946.31/48073.02**   **LAT 46° 05.212' LON 084° 00.763'**
> **DEPTH: 15 feet**   **LEVEL: Novice**

LOCATION: This wreck lies at the entrance to the harbor on the west side of Lime Island, Michigan.

The steamer, *Rome*. GLHS

The wooden steamer, *Rome* (265' x 36'10" x 16'3"), built at Cleveland in 1879 and launched as the *Chicago* (she was renamed *Rome* in 1901), burned to a total loss on November 17, 1909, off Lime Island in the St. Mary's River. This older style vessel, with the midship, external arched braces, was carrying a cargo of cement and hay when she burned. No lives were lost. The burned-out hull was put to use when it was filled with limestone blocks and sunk as a breakwall. Although her stern is considerably broken, the bow remains quite intact. With the many protruding planks and spikes at this site, beware of getting snagged on any of them. A general garbage dump site lies adjacent, but low visibility plagues this area.

2. J. C. FORD

> **LORAN: 30984.87/48116.97**   **LAT 46° 02.663' LON 083° 50.172'**
> **DEPTH: 5 to 15 feet**   **LEVEL: Novice**

LOCATION: This wreck lies just east of Little Trout Island.

The 432-ton wooden steamer, *J.C. Ford* (172' x 31'8" x 13'), burned to a complete loss with no lives lost on November 26, 1924. This vessel had been built 35 years earlier in 1889 at Grand Haven, Michigan, as a package freighter, but had been converted to a crane-equipped bulk carrier just the year before her demise.

This site, with its large debris field, usually has surprisingly good visibility, and the wreck can be seen from the surface. The large propeller remains connected to the shaft and engine, with the hull in several

The steamer, *J.C. Ford*, in her final year. MPL/WMHS

large sections surrounded by tools and other hardware. Burbots, bass, crayfish and freshwater sponges are often seen here.

3. PIGEON COVE SCHOONER

> **LORAN: 30888.20/48130.46**   **LAT 46° 01.453' LON 083° 48.422'**
> **DEPTH: 4 to 15 feet**   **LEVEL: Novice**

LOCATION: This wreck lies in the eastern bay of Pigeon Cove, just south of Nick's Marina and a bit north of a sandbar.

This unidentified vessel, definitely a schooner, lies shallow enough to be a hazard to local boaters, who sometimes mark the wreck with a plastic jug so they can steer clear of it. The hull is fairly intact and rises about ten feet off the bottom. The wreck, with damage at both ends, lies east-to-west. This ship was equipped with a steam cargo winch; a donkey boiler is present. Local anglers have left equipment here, including fishing line. Be careful!

4. KELLY'S DOCK

> **LORAN: 30922.91/48126.55**   **LAT 46° 00.36'   LON 083° 54.252'**
> **DEPTH: 4 to 18 feet**   **LEVEL: Novice**

LOCATION: This site lies north of DeTour village and about 300' off shore.

The entire shoreline is private property, so a boat is necessary to reach this site. Because the submerged dock comes close to the surface, a plastic jug is often used to indicate its presence to boaters. Several cribs can be found here, some filled with rocks and others hollow and penetrable (for the trained and experienced only). Beware of ships of all sizes.

5. *TWO MYRTLES/ALICE C.?*

> **LORAN: 30922.54/48131.61**   **LAT 45° 59.842' LON 083° 53.941'**
> **DEPTH: 10 to 15 feet**   **LEVEL: Novice**

LOCATION: This wreckage lies about 250' to 300' north of the east-west DeTour Harbor breakwall.

The 80' steamer, *Two Myrtles,* built at Manitowoc, Wisconsin, in 1889, was abandoned here in the 1930's. The remains of at least one other abandoned vessel, possibly the *Alice C.*, lie intermingled with the disturbed *Two Myrtles* (a 1970's construction crane raised the *Two Myrtles* from the water, at which point she broke into pieces and fell back in!) This scattered site can be shore-accessed from the marina or the breakwall.

6. *SUPERIOR*

> **LORAN:**   **LAT 45° 59.632' LON 083° 53.918'**
> **DEPTH: 10 to 15 feet**   **LEVEL: Novice-Intermediate**

LOCATION: This wreck lies near the entrance to the harbor at DeTour Village.

Launched as the sloop, *Mentor,* in 1881 at Manitowoc, Wisconsin, the wooden scow-steamer (she was converted to a bulk freighter in 1887 and to a self-unloading sandsucker in 1916 when her name was changed), *Superior* (142'3" x 30'5" x 9'2"), was moored for the night at DeTour when she caught fire and burned to a total loss on June 11, 1929. Visibility seldom exceeds 3' at this site, which consists mostly of large timbers, but it is accessible from shore.

The *Superior.* MPL/WMHS

7. *JOHN W. CULLEN*

> **LORAN: 30922.89/48133.32**   **LAT 45° 59.302' LON 083° 53.641'**
> **DEPTH: 5 to 40 feet**   **LEVEL: Novice**

LOCATION: This wreck lies between DeTour village and Frying Pan Island, and about 300' east of the boiler from the Sainte Marie.

The wooden steamer, *John W. Cullen* (141' x 29' x 10'8"), launched at Milwaukee in 1883 as the *George C. Markham,* received her name change in 1920. She was abandoned in 1933. Mainly large timbers comprise this site; beware of the spikes protruding from the wreckage and avoid getting any of your equipment caught on them.

The *John W. Cullen.* MPL/WMHS

8. SAINTE MARIE

> **LORAN: 30922.25/48136.69** **LAT 45° 59.303′ LON 083° 53.639′**
> **DEPTH: 0 to 40 feet** **LEVEL: Novice**

The carferry, *Sainte Marie*. AUTHOR'S COLLECTION

LOCATION: This wreck lies between DeTour Village and Frying Pan Island.

Launched as a railroad carferry in 1893 at Wyandotte, Michigan, the *Sainte Marie* (288′ x 53′ x 19′5″), carried 18 cars each trip across the Straits of Mackinac, which she did almost daily for 19 years. She became a barge in 1912 and was abandoned in 1927 at DeTour. This vessel can be done as a shore dive, as divers can wade a fair distance in the shallows to the wreck site. The boiler and large timbers form most of the visuals at this site. Avoid the spikes!

9. GENERAL

> **LORAN: 30923.52/48137.01** **LAT 45° 59.202′ LON 083° 53.829′**
> **DEPTH: 15 to 20 feet** **LEVEL: Novice**

LOCATION: This wreck lies off the northwest end of Frying Pan Island.

The tug, *General* (97′5″ x 24′ x 10′), launched at West Bay City, Michigan, in 1900, spent the years between 1910 and 1919 at the bottom of the St. Mary's River in 40′ of water off Lime Island. A collision with the huge steel ship, *Athabasca,* on November 30, 1910, took three lives and sank the 132-ton tug. After she was raised and returned to service, the *General* spent another 11 years working the northern waters, until she burned and sank at DeTour on April 7, 1930, and remained in place. Boaters can anchor near the large boulders at the site. Although the tug's large equipment, such as her boiler and engine, were removed after she sank, her hull offers much to see. Visibility in this area is generally good.

10. FRYING PAN ISLAND DOCK

These submerged docks, once the holding spot for vessels which were salvaged by the Durocher Company, are similar to Kelly's Dock, only deeper (they begin in 4′, but have ledges at the 45′ and 90′ levels.). Discards from the salvage company's raised ships also ended up on the bottom here. The island is privately-owned; stay on your boat. Debris fields lie along the island's north, east and south sides. Beware of large freighters passing nearby.

11. SADDLEBAG ISLAND WRECK

> **LORAN: 30973.3/48137.2** **LAT 45° 57.081′ LON 084° 01.498′**
> **DEPTH: 10 to 25 feet** **LEVEL: Novice**

LOCATION: This wreck lies off the southeastern end of Saddlebag Island.

It's a long swim from a park on shore; use a boat to take you to this small, unidentified freighter. Reportedly it sank with a cargo of farm equipment, most of which was salvaged. What little remains is the highlight of the dive, since not much of the ship is left.

12. JOHN B. MERRILL

> **LORAN: 30880.28/48191.97** **LAT 45° 54.981′ LON 083° 43.912′**
> **DEPTH: 30 to 80 feet** **LEVEL: Intermediate-Advanced**

LOCATION: This shipwreck lies on the west side of Holdridge Shoal.

Considered the best shipwreck dive in the DeTour area, the three-masted schooner, *John B. Merrill* (189' x 34' x 13'3"), foundered in a storm on October 14, 1893, with a cargo of coal and no lives lost. This ship, built at Milwaukee, Wisconsin, in 1873, was lost in the same storm which destroyed the *Dean Richmond* (which is also in this book) and several other vessels.

Located in 1992 by John Steele and Sam Mareci, the *John B. Merrill* shows evidence of having broken up on the rocks in the shallows, then slid into deeper water. Her anchor lies in 30', with chain cascading down to 65' where the forward keelson is located. The hull's starboard side lies with the outside facing up in about 70'; the port side lies with the inside facing up in 75'. Decking has been turned upside down near the bow area in 80'. Because the ship is broken

The *John B. Merrill*. AUTHOR'S COLLECTION

up like this, there are no actual penetration opportunities or danger. Beware of loose overhangs near the bow. The debris field is fairly extensive. Enjoy exploring it!

13. AGNES W.

LORAN: 30869.88/48191.39	LAT 45° 55.453' LON 083° 42.501'
DEPTH: 2 to 12 feet	LEVEL: Novice

LOCATION: This wreck lies off Traverse Point.

The large steamer, *Agnes W.* MPL/WMHS

Built at Milwaukee, Wisconsin, in 1887, and launched as the *Roswell P. Flower,* the huge, wooden bulk freight steamer, *Agnes W.* (264' x 38' x 17'6"), was renamed in honor of a new owner's wife in 1915. The vessel stranded on Drummond Island on July 12, 1918, and was pounded to pieces by the powerful storm. Machinery was recovered, but the bottom part of the hull lies in place, and the debris field is extensive. The wreck can be seen from the surface.

14. TROY

LOCATION: This wreck lies just off the eastern shoreline of Scammon Cove in about 8' to 12' of water, near the community of Johnswood on Drummond Island. The remains of this large, broken wreck can be seen from the surface.

The schooner-barge, *Troy,* (191'3" x 30' x 10'), built at Marine City, Michigan, in 1872, and used mainly in the lumber trade, was abandoned in this cove in 1921, almost half a century after she was launched. The remains of at least one other abandoned vessel, possibly the steamer, *Silver Spray,* lie north of the *Troy.*

The schooner-barge, *Troy.* AUTHOR'S COLLECTION

24. Sanilac Shores

LAKE
HURON

Sanilac Shores, designated in 1988, is one of Michigan's 10 underwater preserves. This designation serves only to let scuba divers know that there is a particularly high concentration of located shipwrecks within these preserve boundaries. Some shipwreck sites shown here lie outside the preserve boundaries. All shipwrecks and their artifacts in Michigan's Great Lakes waters are protected by state and federal laws.

KETTLE POINT

MICHIGAN

ONTARIO

-N-

PORT HURON   SARNIA

1. *Col. A. B. Williams*
2. *Checotah*
3. *New York*
4. *Charles A. Street*
5. *F. B. Gardner*
6. *City of Milwaukee*
7. *North Star*
8. *Mary Alice B.*
9. *Canisteo*
10. *Regina*

11. *Sport*
12. *Eliza H. Strong*
13. *John Breden*
14. *Queen City*
15. *City of Genoa*
16. *Charles S. Price*
17. *Yakima*
18. *Sachem*
19. *Aztec/Province*
20. *Clayton Belle*

1. COL. A. B. WILLIAMS

LORAN: 30779.1/49407.2	LAT 43° 36.234' LON 082° 30.804'
DEPTH: 73 to 84 feet	LEVEL: Advanced

LOCATION: This wreck lies 12.4 miles north-northeast of Port Sanilac.

The schooner, *Col. A.B. Williams* (sometimes listed as the *A.B. Williams;* 110' x 24' x 9'9") foundered with her coal cargo in an 1864 storm. she sits upright and quite intact, with her masts and

Artwork ©Pat Stayer

cabin missing, but this is the norm for Great Lakes shipwrecks. Her stern has collapsed, but the bow and midship area gives quite a profile, offering hatches, a huge windlass, two winches, a bilge pump and a stove. This wreck was discovered in 1957 by Garth Meyer. The bow anchors and wheel were removed in the 1960's; one anchor sits in front of the Sanilac Historical Museum in Port Sanilac.

2. CHECOTAH

LORAN: 30761.3/49413.5	LAT 43° 36.103' LON 082° 28.169'
DEPTH: 95 to 117 feet	LEVEL: Advanced

LOCATION: This wreck lies 12.3 miles north-northeast of Port Sanilac, Michigan.

The schooner-barge, *Checotah* (198'7" x 34'1" x 12'4"), built at Toledo, Ohio, in 1870, as the *George B. Russell,* foundered in a violent storm on October 30, 1906, with the crew

The schooner-barge, *Checotah.* MPL/WMHS

CHECOTAH
1870 - Oct. 30, 1906
Discovered June 28, 1988

Artwork ©Pat Stayer

safely taking to the yawl boat. Earlier, the ship had spent seven years (1882-1889) on the bottom of the St. Mary's River after sinking, with the loss of three lives, in a collision with the steamer, *Northerner.* In 1890, the restored ship was renamed *Checotah.* Discovered in the early summer of 1988 by Gary Biniecki, Tim Juhl and Jim and Pat Stayer (known collectively at that time as the Great Lakes Shipwrecks Exploration Group), the wreck sits upright, but with some damage to the stern deck and the starboard gunwhale. At the bow are the winch, windlass, capstan, port anchor and a donkey steam boiler, while the stern displays the rudder, steering gear and ship's wheel. Visibility is sometimes low in this part of Lake Huron.

3. NEW YORK

> **LORAN: 30761.0/49411.9**   **LAT 43° 36.230' LON 082° 28.267'**
> **DEPTH: 95 to 118 feet**   **LEVEL: Advanced**

LOCATION: This wreck lies 12.3 miles north-northeast of Port Sanilac, Michigan.

The wooden steambarge, *New York* (184'8" x 29'4" x 11'8"), foundered with the loss of one life on October 14, 1876, while she was towing three barges, also laden with lumber, from Cove Island. The *New York* had been built in 1856 at Buffalo, New York. This wreck

NEW YORK
1856 - Oct. 13, 1876
Found Aug. 12, 1988

Artwork ©Pat Stayer

was located in August, 1988, while the group that had found the nearby *Checotah* a month earlier (Gary Biniecki, Tim Juhl and Jim and Pat Stayer) were heading to that site. The two wrecks lie only a few hundred feet apart.

The *New York* sits upright, bow pointing south, with her twin oscillating steam engines, boiler and upright starboard bracing arch the site's highlights. Also of interest to divers are the smokestack hole, gauges and other machinery.

4. CHARLES A. STREET

> **LORAN: 30818.2/49413.1**   **LAT 43° 35.50'   LON 082° 27.50'**
> **DEPTH: 5 to 15 feet**   **LEVEL: Novice**

LOCATION: This wreck lies about 11.5 miles north of Port Sanilac, Michigan.

The wooden steamer, *Charles A. Street* (165'3" x 31'4" x 12'), caught on fire and was steered towards shore, where she stranded and burned to a complete loss. No lives were lost. The *Charles A. Street,* built at Grand Haven, Michigan, in 1888, usually carried coal or lumber. The top of the engine rises close to the surface, and the hull is broken and scattered.

The steamer, *Charles A. Street.* MPL/WMHS

The schooner-barge, *F.B. Gardner.* IGLR

5. F. B. GARDNER

> **LORAN: 30802.4/49446.8**   **LAT 43° 31.63'   LON 082° 31.77'**
> **DEPTH: 55 feet**   **LEVEL: Intermediate**

LOCATION: This wreck lies 6.5 miles north of Port Sanilac, Michigan.

The wooden schooner-barge, *F.B. Gardner* (177'2" x 31'3" x 10'), built in 1855 at Sheboygan, Wisconsin, plied and worked on Great Lakes waters for nearly five decades. On September 15, 1904, in tow of the steamer, *D. Leuty,* the *F.B. Gardner* suddenly caught on fire and burned to a total loss. Her sunken remains, a hazard to navigation, were dynamited. This wreck was located by Mike Kohut, using information from Chet Reddeman, in 1973. A huge windlass, complete with chain, is the main attraction amidst all the hanging knees and other ship's parts and equipment scattered at this site.

6. CITY OF MILWAUKEE

LORAN:	LAT	LON
DEPTH: 168 feet	LEVEL: Technical	

LOCATION: This wreck lies about 12 miles northeast of Port Sanilac, Michigan.
The schooner, *City of Milwaukee* (139' x 30' x 11'), is one of the few Great Lakes

CITY of MILWAUKEE

Artwork ©Robert McGreevy

vessels to have been built with a distinctive, elegant figurehead -- this one in the shape of a ferocious, open-mouthed dragon. Built in Cleveland in 1861, the *City of Milwaukee* sank in a storm on November 5, 1875, with no loss of life. The wreck was located by Dave Trotter (Undersea Research Associates) and his team on July 7, 1990. The vessel's stern has virtually disintegrated (probably crushed in the sinking), while her bow, with windlass and both anchors, is quite intact. At midship, masts, spars and booms crisscross the hull. Highlighted by the distinctive figurehead, this wreck is one of the prime examples of the preserving powers of our freshwater Great Lakes.

7. NORTH STAR

> **LORAN: 30787.3/49508.1**   **LAT 42° 23.959′ LON 082° 26.518′**
> **DEPTH: 85 to 99 feet**   **LEVEL: Advanced**

LOCATION: This wreck lies 5.3 miles east-southeast of Port Sanilac, Michigan.

The steel package freighter, *North Star* (299′5″ x 40′8″ x 21′6″), launched at Cleveland on February 12, 1889, sank in early morning fog after the steamer, *Northern Queen,* collided with her starboard side on November 25, 1908. No lives were lost, but the ship and her cargo of wheat and shingles were a total loss.

Located in the 1960's by John Steele, the Great Lakes' first modern wreck hunter, the *North Star* lies upright, broken into two main pieces due to the collision. The pilot house remains intact on the bow, while the enormous engine and boiler grace the stern. The cargo holds are also explorable in this very large shipwreck area.

The *North Star.* REV. PETER VAN DER LINDEN COLLECTION

North Star
Sank November 25, 1908

Artwork ©Pat Stayer

On the *North Star.*
PHOTO BY CRIS KOHL

8. MARY ALICE B.

> **LORAN: 30790.8/49521.0**   **LAT 43° 22.309′ LON 082° 26.301′**
> **DEPTH: 82 to 98 feet**   **LEVEL: Advanced**

LOCATION: This wreck lies 8.4 miles northeast of Lexington, Michigan.

Pat Stayer takes the helm of the *Mary Alice B.* PHOTO BY CRIS KOHL.

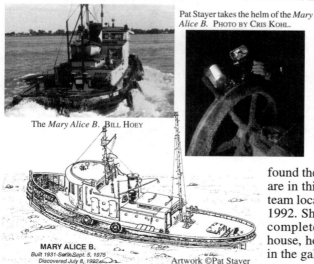

The tug, *Mary Alice B.* (62′1″ x 17′ x 6′3″), launched as the *Quintus* at Duluth, Minnesota, in 1931 and renamed the *Bonanka* in 1962 and *Lomax* in 1972, received her final name in her final year afloat (1975). On September 5th of that year, she became waterlogged and sank with no lives lost. About ten years later, Wayne Brusate began searching for her, but found the *Regina* and *Sport* instead (both are in this chapter). Jim and Pat Stayer's team located the *Mary Alice B.* on July 8, 1992. She sits upright and is very intact, complete with the ship's wheel, pilot house, horns, searchlight, stacked dishes in the galley, and engine compartment.

The *Mary Alice B.* BILL HOEY

MARY ALICE B.
Built 1931-Sank Sept. 5, 1975
Discovered July 8, 1992

Artwork ©Pat Stayer

9. CANISTEO

LORAN:	LAT 43° 14.142′ LON 082° 18.292′
DEPTH: 98 feet	LEVEL: Advanced

LOCATION: This wreck lies about 15 miles east-northeast of Lexington, Michigan.

The wooden steamer, *Canisteo* (191′ x 34′3″ x 12′2″), launched in 1886 at Mount Clemens, Michigan, was burned and scuttled on Oct. 25, 1920. The wreckage includes a large, four-bladed propeller, hull planking and framing, and small items like tools and a milk can.

Pat Stayer explores the propeller of the wooden steamer, *Canisteo* (inset; REV. PETER VAN DEN LINDEN COLLECTION),which was scuttled off Lexington, Michigan, in 1920. Located by the Stayers' team in 1997, these wreck remains were identified when Cris Kohl found archival material describing the scuttling and Pat located an engine cover with the ship's name on it (inset).   CRIS KOHL PHOTOS.

10. REGINA

LORAN: 30801.7/49534.9	LAT 43° 20.456′ LON 082° 26.888′
DEPTH: 60 to 83 feet	LEVEL: Advanced

LOCATION: This wreck lies about 6.5 miles northeast of Lexington, Michigan.

The steel freighter, *Regina* (249'7″ x 42'6″ x 20'5″), constructed in Scotland in 1907, capsized and sank with all hands during the Great Storm of November 10-13, 1913, which claimed seven other steel ships and their entire crews in lower Lake Huron (they were the *Charles S. Price, James Carruthers, Wexford, Argus, Isaac M. Scott, John McGean,* all in this book, and the yet-to-be-located *Hydrus*). The *Regina* was discovered on July 1, 1986, by Gary Biniecki, Wayne Brusate and John Severance, reportedly while they were searching for the tug, *Mary Alice B.* The *Regina,* at anchor when she met her end, lies upside-down, bow facing north, with much of her general cargo spilled onto the lake bottom. Her propeller and rudder are impressive. Penetration is possible only for those with proper training, experience, preparedness and attitude, but there is so much to see on the outside of the wreck that this site has become one of the prime destinations of divers in Lake Huron.

REGINA
Built 1907 - Sank Nov. 9, 1913
Discovered by Garry Biniecki
July 1, 1986

Artwork ©Pat Stayer

Upper left: The steamer, *Regina.* AUTHOR'S COLLECTION. *Above:* A diver studies the brass letters which make up the *Regina's* name on her overturned bow. PHOTO BY CRIS KOHL.

11. SPORT

LORAN: 30824.9/49569.2	LAT 43° 15.995′ LON 082° 27.925′
DEPTH: 35 to 50 feet	LEVEL: Novice-Intermediate

LOCATION: This wreck lies 3.0 miles east of Lexington, Michigan.

The tug, *Sport* (56'7″ x 14'7″ x 9'), constructed at Wyandotte, Michigan in 1873 and one of the first composite (both steel and wood) vessels built, sank with no lives lost in a storm on December 13, 1920. Found by diver Wayne Brusate in June, 1987, in his quest to locate the *Mary Alice B.*, the historic *Sport* lies upright with a starboard list, intact save for her missing cabin. Inside the hull and in plain view, since much of the decking is missing, are the engine and boiler. An anchor and winch sit on the bow, while the stern offers the propeller (broken off and lying flat), steering chain and ship's wheel. On August 4, 1992, the *Sport* became the recipient of the State of Michigan's first underwater historical marker, which stands mounted on a post next to the shipwreck. A $1,000.00 reward is being offered for information leading to the discovery of the diver who stole the *Sport's* bell recently.

Artwork ©Pat Stayer

Above left and above: The tug, *Sport,* at work and at dockside. MPL/WMHS. *Lower left:* The *Sport* marker on board the U.S. Coast Guard cutter, *Bramble,* just prior to being lowered to the site. *Below:* Joan Forsberg approaches the *Sport's* boiler. PHOTOS BY CRIS KOHL.

12. ELIZA H. STRONG

> **LORAN: 30847.0/49570.4**   **LAT 43° 15.77'   LON 082° 30.66'**
> **DEPTH: 24 to 28 feet**   **LEVEL: Novice**

LOCATION: This wreck lies 0.9 mile from Lexington, Michigan, harbor.

The *Eliza H. Strong*. AUTHOR'S COLLECTION

The wooden steamer, *Eliza H. Strong* (205' x 36'7" x 11'), built at Marine City, Michigan, in 1874, had a tumultuous history of sinkings and recoveries before succumbing once and for all on October 26, 1904, when she burned and sank with no loss of life. Her machinery was salvaged and the hull, a hazard to navigation, was dynamited. As can be imagined, this site is broken and widely scattered, with considerable decking, her keel and the propeller.

13. JOHN BREDEN

> **LORAN: 30823.4/49595.7**   **LAT 43° 12.638' LON 082° 26.248'**
> **DEPTH: 51 feet**   **LEVEL: Intermediate**

LOCATION: This wreck lies 5.4 miles southeast of Lexington, Michigan, harbor.

The three-masted schooner, *John Breden* (130' x 25'2" x 11'), built at Port Dalhousie, Ontario, in 1862, was, in her later years, reduced to a towbarge. On July 21, 1899, loaded with twice her rated carrying capacity of coal and towed by the tug, *Winslow* (which is also in this book), the *John Breden's* seams opened and she foundered with the loss of three lives. Located by Gary Biniecki and Nathan Butler on October 14, 1994, the wreck lies broken into huge pieces with an extensive debris field that contains the wooden-stocked anchors, the windlass and the ship's wheel, along with many other items.

14. QUEEN CITY

> **LORAN: 30831.2/49622.3**   **LAT 43° 09.125' LON 082° 25.712'**
> **DEPTH: 50 feet**   **LEVEL: Intermediate**

LOCATION: This wreck lies 9.3 miles southeast of Lexington, Michigan, harbor.

The sidewheel steamer, *Queen City* (292' x 30'7" x 12'7"), constructed at Buffalo, New York, in 1848, was, with the decline in passenger business after the railroads were built, converted into a lumber barge in 1862. On August 17, 1863, the *Queen City* struck rocks, broke up and sank, the crew safely abandoning ship. In late 1991, David Losinski and Paul Schmitt located this broken up wreck, with its round arches and brackets for paddlewheels.

15. CITY OF GENOA

> **LORAN: 30805.2/49625.0**   **LAT 43° 08.78'   LON 082° 22.31'**
> **DEPTH: 55 to 65 feet**   **LEVEL: Advanced**

LOCATION: This wreck lies 11.4 miles southeast of Lexington, Michigan, harbor.

The wooden steamer, *City of Genoa* (301' x 42'5" x 20'1"), built at West Bay City, Michigan, in 1892, sank in a collision in the St. Clair River on August 26, 1911. She was

The *City of Genoa*. AUTHOR'S COLLECTION

Right: Frank Troxell on the *City of Genoa*. PHOTO BY CRIS KOHL.

218

raised and towed into Sarnia Bay, where she sat for several years before having her large equipment removed and being set ablaze by vandals. In 1915, she was scuttled in Lake Huron several miles north of the river. Located by Detroit-area diver, Bud Uren, in 1983, the *City of Genoa* (once referred to as the "Wheelbarrow Wreck" because of the wheelbarrow which sat in her hull), bow pointing north, is an enormous hull with a boiler cradle, propeller shaft and valves. When I last saw her, only the wheel of that wheelbarrow was left.

16. CHARLES S. PRICE

LORAN: 30799.6/49622.5	LAT 43° 09.174′ LON 082° 21.771′
DEPTH: 47 to 72 feet	LEVEL: Intermediate-Advanced

LOCATION: This wreck lies 11.4 miles southeast of Lexington, Michigan.

The large, steel freighter, *Charles S. Price* (504′ x 54′ x 30′), built at Lorain, Ohio, in 1910, was one of the victims of the Great Storm of November 10-13, 1913. When the blizzard abated, an enormous, overturned hull was left floating offshore. Identification was not immediately possible, since several steel freighters went missing in this storm. After eight days, a hardhat diver identified the "Mystery Ship" as the *Charles S. Price*. Two days

later, she sank. There were no survivors to tell what had happened. *Price* bodies washed ashore, including one wearing a *Regina* lifebelt, hinting at a collision between the two ships. But that was not so. More than likely, human scavengers on shore returned the lifejacket to the wrong corpse when they noticed that the law was nearby.

This wreck lies upside-down and the steel hull is collapsing badly. She is in noticeably worse shape now than she was 20 years ago when I first visited her. Penetration dives are not recommended.

Above left: The *Charles S. Price.* GLHS. *Above right:* The "Mystery Ship." MPL/WMHS. *Right and left:* That same overturned hull and its upside-down rudder can be explored today. PHOTOS BY CRIS KOHL.

17. YAKIMA

> **LORAN: 30775.1/49612.6**   **LAT 43° 10.56' LON 082° 19.38'**
> **DEPTH: 78 feet**   **LEVEL: Advanced**

The wooden steamer, *Yakima* (279' x 40'5" x 20'6"), built at Cleveland in 1887, was the first commercial ship on the Great Lakes to be equipped with electric lights. She stranded and burned in the St. Clair River on June 10, 1905, after which she was towed into Sarnia Bay, abandoned and scuttled in Lake Huron in 1928. Located and identified in 1993 by the team of Jim and Pat Stayer, Tim Juhl, David Fritz and Cris Kohl, this wreck lies 12 miles southeast of Lexington, Michigan, harbor, and 11 miles north of Port Huron, Michigan.

Above: The historic steamer, *Yakima.* AUTHOR'S COLLECTION. *Right:* Jim Stayer videotapes the *Yakima's* huge hull. PHOTO BY CRIS KOHL.

18. SACHEM

> **LORAN: 30769.2/49617.6**   **LAT 43° 09.90' LON 082° 18.36'**
> **DEPTH: 68 feet**   **LEVEL: Advanced**

The wooden steamer, *Sachem* (187' x 33'5" x 14'8"), built at Grand Haven, Michigan, in 1889, burned and sank in the St. Clair River on Oct. 8, 1928. Raised and towed to Sarnia Bay, the ship was scuttled a few weeks later in lower Lake Huron, 13.1 miles southeast of Lexington, Michigan. Located by Bruce and Barbara Campbell of Grand Blanc, Michigan, in May, 1993, the wreck was identified by Jim Stayer and Cris Kohl later that summer. For a scuttled ship, this one has many items of interest on it.

The steamer, *Sachem,* burned in the St. Clair River on Oct. 8, 1928. REV. PETER VAN DER LINDEN COLLECTION

19. AZTEC/PROVINCE

The remains of the steamer, *Aztec* (180' x 33'3" x 13'9"; built at Marine City, Michigan, in 1889), and the barge, *Province* (162' x 40' x 10'; built at Fort William, Ontario, in 1911) lay rotting in Sarnia Bay until the 1936 clean-up, when the dynamited *Aztec* was placed aboard the refloated hull of the *Province* and both were scuttled in lower Lake Huron. The *Aztec* had burned at Marine City on Nov. 9, 1923, and the *Province* had capsized in the St. Clair River on Sept. 28, 1923, with 3 lives lost. Both wrecked ships were towed to Sarnia and abandoned.These wrecks, now in 68', were found and identified by Jim Stayer and Cris Kohl in 1993. **LORAN: 30770.5/49618.3, LAT 43° 09.83' LON 082° 18.49'**

20. CLAYTON BELLE

The schooner, *Clayton Belle,* collided with the *Thomas Parsons* and sank with 4 lives lost on April 10, 1882. The wreckage lies in 36' at **LAT 43° 07' 42" LON 082° 26' 06"**

25. Michigan's Thumb

The "Thumb" area of Michigan is the site of an underwater preserve, one of ten located throughout the state waters in areas with high concentrations of shipwrecks. Not all of the shipwrecks in this chapter are within the boundaries of the Thumb Area Underwater Preserve. Although never a maritime destination, this region was a busy thoroughfare where ships encountered severe storms, dense fogs and each other. Some of the deepest known shipwrecks in the Great Lakes lie in this area.

1. *Goshawk*
2. *City of Detroit*
3. *Troy*
4. Anchor: P. A. Reef
5. *Berlin*
6. *Jacob Bertschy*
7. Anchor: Kinch Rd.
8. *Philadelphia*
9. *Albany*
10. *Iron Chief*
11. Dump barge/scow
12. *Anna Dobbins*
13. *E. P. Dorr*
14. *Governor Smith*
15. *Emma L. Nielsen*
16. *Fred Lee*
17. *Detroit*
18. *Daniel J. Morrell* bow
19. *Daniel J. Morrell* stern
20. *Argus*
21. *Hunter Savidge*
22. Mystery schooner
23. *John McGean*
24. *Marquis*
25. *Chickamauga*
26. *Dunderberg*
27. *Waverly*
28. *Glenorchy*
29. *Goliath*
30. *Arctic*

1. GOSHAWK

> **LORAN: 31049.3/49055.5**   **LAT 44° 14.95' LON 083° 24.96'**
> **DEPTH: 40 to 50 feet**   **LEVEL: Intermediate**

LOCATION: This wreck lies 3 miles northeast of Tawas Point, Michigan.

The schooner-barge, *Goshawk* (180' x 32'4" x 11'5"), built at Cleveland in 1866, foundered with a cargo of salt on June 16, 1920, after having served on the Great Lakes, mostly in the lumber trade, for over half a century! No lives were lost in the sinking, the crew having taken to the lifeboats.

Left: The *Goshawk* under tow. MPL/WMHS.
Above: Diver Bill Atkins, a member of the 1992 survey team, approaches the *Goshawk's* wheel. PHOTO BY CRIS KOHL.

Vessel Type: Schooner
Survey Date: 8/14,15,16/92
Location: 3 Miles off Tawas Point
Depth: 50'
Loran C: 49055.5 31049.3
The Wreck of the GOSHAWK
Found by A&T Recovery
© Drawing by Valerie Olson
Artwork ©Valerie Olson-van Heest of theUnderwater Archaeological Society of Chicago

Located in 1990 by A&T Recovery of Chicago, IL, the *Goshawk* was the subject of an intense survey in August, 1992, by the Underwater Archaeological Society of Chicago, the author and others. At the wreck site, only the rudder post is taller than the average rise of 5'. The many artifacts include a windlass, capstan, bilge pump, donkey boiler, ship's wheel and four anchors! Much timber crisscrosses this busy site.

2. CITY OF DETROIT

> **LORAN: 30889.5/49101.2**   **LAT 44° 12.472' LON 083° 00.841'**
> **DEPTH: 176 feet**   **LEVEL: Technical**

LOCATION: This wreck lies due north of Port Austin, Michigan.

The wooden bulk freight steamer, *City of Detroit* (167' x 27'7" x 12'1"), built at Marine City, Michigan, in 1866, foundered in a storm on Dec. 4, 1873, with all 20 hands and a cargo of barrelled flour and wheat. The wreck lies upright and intact in deep water.

3. TROY

LORAN: 30909.0/49131.6	LAT 44° 08.655' LON 083° 01.939'
DEPTH: 97 feet	LEVEL: Advanced

LOCATION: This wreck lies about 7 miles north of Pointe aux Barques, Michigan.
The wooden steamer, *Troy* (182' x 27' x 11'), foundered in heavy seas with the loss of 23 lives on October 18, 1859. Discovered in 1999, the scattered wreck site includes the engine, boiler, propeller, four anchors and much wooden decking and planking.

4. ANCHOR: PORT AUSTIN REEF

LORAN: 30904.4/49172.2	LAT LON
DEPTH: 15 feet	LEVEL: Novice

This wooden-stocked anchor with approximately 200' of chain attached to it was lost at this location from an unidentified vessel in unknown circumstances.

5. BERLIN

LORAN: 30869.2/49170.7	LAT LON
DEPTH: 10 feet	LEVEL: Novice

LOCATION: This wreck lies about one mile northwest of Grindstone City, Michigan.
Four lives were lost when the schooner, *Berlin* (111'6" x 24' x 11'), built in 1854 at Milan, Ohio, stranded here in violent weather on November 8, 1877. Waves washed the captain, cook and a deckhand overboard, while the captain's son perished from exposure while lashed to the rigging. Two others survived. The lumber/limestone cargo lies scattered.

The *Wexford* painted by Robert McGreevy

Great Lakes art available from: Marine Art, CTM Associates,
Box 36441, Grosse Pointe, MI 48236
Tel: (313) 882-0827   Web Site: www.mcgreevy.com

6. JACOB BERTSCHY

LORAN: 30862.8/49181.4	LAT LON
DEPTH: 10 feet	LEVEL: Novice

LOCATION: This wreck lies 900′ southeast of Grindstone City pier, 1/4 mile off shore.
The 433-gross-ton, wooden bulk freight steamer, *Jacob Bertschy* (139′8″ x 27′4″ x 9′3″), built at Sheboygan, WI, in 1867, stranded on Sept. 3, 1879, with a cargo of shingles and wheat. She broke up shortly afterwards; no lives were lost. The wreckage lies scattered.

7. ANCHOR: KINCH ROAD

LORAN: 30834.8/49184.7	LAT 43° 03.388′ LON 082° 49.331′
DEPTH: 20 feet	LEVEL: Novice

This wooden-stocked anchor with approximately 300′ of chain attached to it was lost at this location from an unidentified vessel in unknown circumstances.

8. PHILADELPHIA

LORAN: 30786.44/49183.96	LAT 44° 04.120′ LON 082° 42.992′
DEPTH: 105 to 125 feet	LEVEL: Advanced

LOCATION: This wreck lies about 5.5 miles northeast of Pointe aux Barques, Michigan.
The iron-hulled propeller, *Philadelphia* (236′ x 34′3″ x 14′), built at Buffalo, New York, in 1868, collided with the steamer, *Albany* (see site #9) on November 7, 1893, with the loss of 16 lives and a cargo of coal and general merchandise.

Shipwreck hunter John Steele located the *Philadelphia* in the spring of 1973. The wreck's noteworthy sights include the engine, two boilers, rudder, propeller, stern capstan, and, on the port deck, a load of cast-iron stoves, some of which have spilled onto the lake floor or into the cargo holds. The bow damage from the collision is evident, and the port bow anchor on the lake floor leans against the hull. This wreck, and others in this underwater preserve, is usually buoyed in the springtime.

Two steamers, similar in size and appearance, sank after colliding with one another on September 5, 1893. *Left,* the *Philadelphia,* and *right,* the *Albany.* BOTH GLHS

9. ALBANY

LORAN: 30773.1/49166.8	LAT 44° 06.351′ LON 082° 42.016′
DEPTH: 132 to 149 feet	LEVEL: Technical

LOCATION: This wreck lies about 2.5 miles to the northeast of the *Philadelphia.*
Launched at Wyandotte, Michigan, in 1885, the steel bulk freight steamer, *Albany* (267′ x 38′5″ x 13′8″), sank first in the collision with the *Philadelphia* (site #8) on November 7, 1893, and lies in slightly deeper water. She went down with 8 crewmembers and her grain cargo. The wreck sits upright and intact.

10. IRON CHIEF

LORAN: 30779.0/49172.0	**LAT 44° 05.632′ LON 082° 42.588′**
DEPTH: 135 feet	**LEVEL: Technical**

LOCATION: This wreck lies about four miles northeast of Grindstone City, Michigan.

The steamer, *Iron Chief*. MPL/WMHS

The author and the *Iron Chief's* anchor at Grindstone City. PHOTO BY JOAN FORSBERG.

Launched as a schooner at Wyandotte, Michigan, on July 12, 1881, the *Iron Chief* (212′4″ x 35′ x 17′6″), converted to a bulk freight steamer, sprang a leak after breaking a stern pipe and foundered in heavy seas with her coal cargo on October 3, 1904. The crew was rescued by the steamer, *Andrew Carnegie*. Machinery is the site's highlight.

11. DUMP BARGE/SCOW

LORAN: 30836.6/49150.8	**LAT 44° 07.401′ LON 082° 51.276′**
DEPTH: 77 feet	**LEVEL: Advanced**

LOCATION: This unidentified wreck lies about six miles north-northeast of Grindstone City, Michigan, near the wreck of the *Anna Dobbins* (see site #12 in this chapter).

12. *Anna Dobbins*

LORAN:	LAT 44° 08.111′ LON 082° 51.277′
DEPTH: 90 feet	LEVEL: Advanced

LOCATION: This wreck lies about six miles north-northeast of Grindstone City.
The wooden tug, *Anna Dobbins* (101′8″ x 18′ x 10′), foundered on September 24, 1886, after a stern bearing gave way, breaking the stern pipe. No lives were lost. The upright wreck sits intact. The vessel had been built at Buffalo, New York, in 1862.

13. *E. P. Dorr*

LORAN: 30780.0/49145.5	LAT 44° 08.790′ LON 082° 43.960′
DEPTH: 175 feet	LEVEL: Technical

LOCATION: This wreck lies about seven miles north-northeast of Grindstone City.
The huge, 300-ton, wooden tug, *E.P. Dorr* (161′ x 25′), collided with the steamer, *Oliver Cromwell,* in June, 1856. The tug, built at Buffalo, New York, was only one year old at the time of loss. This is a deep site which requires special technical training and experience.

14. *Governor Smith*

LORAN: 30763.3/49141.3	LAT 44° 09.333′ LON 082° 42.001′
DEPTH: 178 to 197 feet	LEVEL: Technical

LOCATION: This wreck lies about eight miles north-northeast of Grindstone City, Michigan.
The wooden freighter, *Governor Smith* (240′ x 42′ x 23′4″), built in 1889 at Wyandotte, Michigan), sank in a collision in thick fog with the larger steel steamer, *Uranus,* on August 19, 1906. The *Uranus* rescued the *Smith's* crew, but the cargo of grain and package freight was lost. This deep, intact wreck is for only the specially trained.

The *Gov. Smith.* MPL/WMHS

15. *Emma L. Nielsen*

LORAN: 30763.9/49129.9	LAT 44° 10.878′ LON 082° 42.611′
DEPTH: 190 feet	LEVEL: Technical

LOCATION: This wreck lies about nine miles north-northeast of Grindstone City.
The three-masted schooner, *Emma L. Nielsen* (98′2″ x 20′6″ x 6′2″), launched at Manitowoc, Wisconsin, in 1883, sank in a collision in fog with the 346′ steel steamer, *Wyandotte*, on June 26, 1911, with no lives lost. This deep, but beautifully intact shipwreck was found by Dave Trotter in April, 1980.

Artwork ©Robert McGreevy

The *Emma L. Nielsen.* MPL/WMHS

16. *FRED LEE*

> **LORAN: 30780.83/49115.23** **LAT 44° 12.422' LON 082° 45.556'**
> **DEPTH: 200 feet** **LEVEL: Technical**

The tug, *Frederick A. Lee.* AUTHOR'S COLLECTION

LOCATION: The *Fred Lee* lies about ten miles north-northeast of Grindstone City.

Built at Port Huron, Michigan, in 1896, the tug, *Fred Lee* (70' x 16' x 9'), also known as the *Frederick A. Lee,* foundered with the entire crew of five on Friday the 13th of November, 1936. Dave Trotter and his team located this wreck in 1996. The hull is intact, with an anchor on the bow, chain out of a hawsepipe, a winch with braided steel cable and a steel ship's wheel.

17. *DETROIT*

> **LORAN: 30776.4/49105,4** **LAT 44° 13.611' LON 082° 45.436'**
> **DEPTH: 200 feet** **LEVEL: Technical**

This wreck, about ten miles north-northeast of Grindstone City, was located by Dave Trotter's team on June 5, 1994. Built at Newport (Marine City), Michigan, in 1846, the sidewheel steamer, *Detroit* (157' x 23'3" x 10'), sank in a collision in fog with the bark, *Nucleus,* on May 25, 1854, with no lives lost. The site's highlight is her bell.

Artwork ©Robert McGreevy

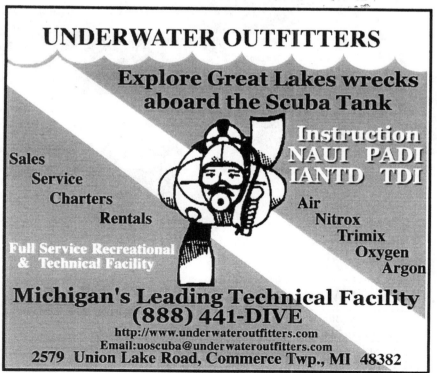

18. Daniel J. Morrell (bow)

LORAN: 30761.4/49068.4	LAT 44° 18.320′ LON 082° 45.161′
DEPTH: 205 feet	LEVEL: Technical

LOCATION: This wreck lies about 12 miles north of Grindstone City, Michigan.

The 60-year-old steel freighter, *Daniel J. Morrell* (586′5″ x 58′2″ x 27′9″), is another of the tragic yet legendary modern losses on the Great Lakes. She broke in half in a furious storm on November 29, 1966, and from her crew of 29 men, there was a single survivor, Dennis Hale, who spent 36 hours on a liferaft before the Coast Guard finally found him. The wreck's bow half begins at 100′, with the top of the mast; the pilot house is at 142′, and from there, it's another 70′ of massive shipwreck before one reaches the lake bottom. This site is definitely for trained, experienced, cautious deep divers only. Don't get careless here.

Clockwise, from upper left: The *Daniel J. Morrell* in the 1960's; Dennis Hale later identified himself as the sailor standing at the very bow. REV. PETER VAN DER LINDEN COLLECTION. An early photo of the *Daniel J. Morrell*. IGLR. Dennis Hale, 30 years after surviving the sinking, became reflective at the yard in West Bay City, Michigan, where the *Morrell* had been launched in 1906. PHOTO BY CRIS KOHL. The *Morrell's* halves, as they look today. Artwork ©Robert McGreevy. *Center:* The top of the *Morrell's* mast, the letter "C" for the Cambria Steamship Company, and Joan Forsberg emerging from the pilot house. PHOTOS BY CRIS KOHL.

19. Daniel J. Morrell (stern)

LORAN: 30803.7/49086.3	LAT 44° 15.478′ LON 082° 50.088′
DEPTH: 218 feet	LEVEL: Technical

LOCATION: The *Morrell's* stern half steamed off into the night for an incredible five miles after she broke in half! It lies slightly deeper than the bow, but not quite as interesting.

20. ARGUS

LORAN: 30790.6/49068.2	LAT	LON
DEPTH: 220 feet	LEVEL: Technical	

LOCATION: This wreck lies just to the northwest of the middle of a line drawn from the bow to the stern of the *Daniel J. Morrell.*

A victim of the Great Storm of November 9-11, 1913, the steel freighter, *Argus* (416' x 50' x 28'), disappeared with all 24 crew and her cargo of soft coal. The 10-year-old ship had been launched at Lorain, Ohio. Located in 1972, this wreck, like all the other victims of that storm in lower Lake Huron, except the *Wexford,* lies upside down.

The *Argus.* GLHS

21. HUNTER SAVIDGE

LORAN: 30742.3/49175.8	LAT	LON
DEPTH: 175 feet	LEVEL: Technical	

LOCATION: This wreck lies about 10 miles east-northeast of Grindstone City, Michigan.

Found by Dave Trotter's team on Aug. 13, 1988, the two-masted, 152-ton schooner, *Hunter Savidge* (117' x 26'6" x 8'2"), capsized on Aug. 20, 1899, after being hit by a sudden white squall. Five lives were lost. The vessel had been built at Grand Haven, Michigan, in 1879. The wreck hit the bottom hard bow-first and is fairly broken up; the masts all snapped and tumbled forward, but she is a prime example of a well-equipped Great Lakes schooner.

The schooner, *Hunter Savidge.* IGLR

22. MYSTERY SCHOONER

LORAN: 30746.4/49239.2	LAT 43° 57.851' LON 082° 35.018'
DEPTH: 145 feet	LEVEL: Technical

LOCATION: This wreck lies about 8 miles north-northeast of Harbor Beach, Michigan.

This unidentified schooner is called, by some divers, the "Challenge," but since no schooner of that name went down in this lake, that designation appears to have been given as a nickname referring to the daunting task of identifying her. The wreck has small ornamentation beneath her bowsprit, akin to a figurehead, indicative of an early design.

23. JOHN A. McGEAN

LORAN: 30723.8/49245.9	LAT 43° 57.198' LON 082° 31.718'
DEPTH: 198 feet	LEVEL: Technical

LOCATION: This wreck lies about 8 miles northeast of Harbor Beach, Michigan.

Built at Lorain, Ohio, in 1908, the large steel freighter, *John McGean* (432' x 52' x 28'), went missing with all hands (23) in the Great Storm of November 9-11, 1913, one of eight ships in lower Lake Huron to do so. The *McGean* was located by Dave Trotter and his team in 1986. She lies upside-down, like all the others except for one (the *Wexford*) and possibly the *Hydrus,* which remains the only ship from that tragic group not yet located. It's a deep dive to see lots of steel hull.

Artwork ©Robert McGreevy

Left: The steel freighter, *John McGean.* MPL/WMHS

24. MARQUIS

LORAN: 30795.0/49266.4	LAT LON
DEPTH: 15 feet	LEVEL: Novice

LOCATION: This wreck lies about three miles south of Port Hope, Michigan.

The three-masted schooner-barge, *Marquis* (148' x 29'), was caught in a blizzard on November 12, 1892, and stranded. The entire crew survived, thanks in part to the local lifesaving team. Because it is so shallow, the wreck is badly broken up and scattered.

25. CHICKAMAUGA

LORAN: 30787.9/49294.0	LAT 43° 50.952' LON 082° 37.425'
DEPTH: 32 feet	LEVEL: Novice

LOCATION: This wreck lies about half a mile east of Harbor Beach, Michigan.

The *Chickamauga.* GLHS

The schooner-barge, *Chickamauga* (322' x 45' x 21'5"), loaded with iron ore and towed by the steamer, *Centurion,* encountered immense seas on September 12, 1919, and stranded one mile north of Harbor Beach. Her crew was removed before the hull was twisted into an unsalvageable condition. She had been built at West Bay City, Michigan, in 1898. The wreck was moved to its present location the following year to clear the harbor entrance. The wreck lies broken and scattered over a wide area. This is too far offshore to be a shore dive; a boat is required.

26. DUNDERBERG

LORAN: 30740.7/49257.3   LAT 43° 55.640' LON 082° 33.390'
DEPTH: 143 to 157 feet   LEVEL: Technical

LOCATION: This wreck lies about five miles northeast of Harbor Beach, Michigan.

Located by Kent Bellrichard in 1971, the three-masted schooner, *Dunderberg* (186' x 33' x 13'), built at Detroit in 1867, worked in the grain trade. She was loaded with 40,000 bushels of corn and five passengers on August 13, 1868, in her second season afloat, when the steamer, *Empire State,* collided with her. One life, a female passenger, was lost.

The wreck is upright, intact and pristine. The bow displays a large windlass, both anchors and catheads. The thick railings are crowded with deadeyes and belaying pins. The open hatches invite exploration. Fair-sized sections of two masts remain in place and upright. Much running rigging lies on deck and off the wreck on the hard clay bottom. But the highlight of this site is the figurehead: a carved alligator, jaw dropped, tongue protruding, each eye still glinting with a dab of red paint, plus grapes, birds and curled vines, clustered leaves and arched branches carved into the trim boards curving back from the bowsprit.

The *Dunderberg*, with its superb craftsmanship, is deemed one of the finest, best-preserved and most intact shipwrecks in the Great Lakes.

The schooner, *Dunderberg,* proudly exhibits her unique and finely-crafted alligator figurehead and other ornate carvings just below the bowsprit. PHOTOS BY CRIS KOHL.

Dunderberg
length 187. beam 33.
built in Detroit in 1867, sank
by *Empire State* in 1868, Lake Huron.
figurehead detail

Artwork ©Robert McGreevy

©1982

27. WAVERLY

LORAN:	LAT	LON
DEPTH: 121 feet	LEVEL: Advanced	

The *Waverly.* MPL/WMHS

LOCATION: This wreck lies just north of the *Glenorchy* (site #28), about eight miles east of Harbor Beach, Michigan.

The wooden steamer, *Waverly* (191'2" x 33'7" x 13'4"), built at Buffalo, New York, and launched on May 28, 1874, sank in a collision with the steamer, *Turret Court,* on July 22, 1903. No lives were lost, but the ship, with her coal cargo, was a complete loss. This wreck, first located by John Steele, is relatively broken up.

28. GLENORCHY

LORAN: 30750.4/49314.2	LAT 43° 48.580' LON 082° 31.792'
DEPTH: 100 to 120 feet	LEVEL: Advanced

The *Glenorchy.* GLHS

LOCATION: This wreck lies about ten miles east-southeast of Harbor Beach, Michigan.

Built in 1902 at West Bay City, Michigan, and launched as the *A.E. Stewart,* the steel freighter, *Glenorchy* (356' x 50' x 28'), collided in dense fog with the steamer, *Leonard B. Miller,* and sank with no lives lost. The wreck sits upright and has penetration opportunities for properly trained and equipped divers.

29. GOLIATH

LORAN: 30761.8/49326.5	LAT 43° 47.007' LON 082° 32.720'
DEPTH: 104 feet	LEVEL: Advanced

LOCATION: This wreck lies about ten miles southeast of Harbor Beach, Michigan.

The package and bulk freight steamer, *Goliath* (131' x 25' x 9'), also referred to as *Goliah,* exploded on Lake Huron on September 13, 1848, taking 18 souls with her. The ship had caught on fire, and sparks reached her cargo of

bricks, general freight and 200 kegs of blasting powder. Discovered by Dave Trotter's team in 1984, the *Goliath's* main features are her tall, upright engine, boiler, stove, and unique, early propellers.

Artwork ©Robert McGreevy

Goliath's engine.
PHOTO BY CRIS KOHL.

30. ARCTIC

LORAN: 30748.4/49371.4	LAT 43° 41.460' LON 082° 28.710'
DEPTH: 136 feet	LEVEL: Technical

Located by Dave Trotter's team in 1987, the steamer, *Arctic* (193'7" x 28'1" x 10'8"), sprang a leak and foundered on Sept. 5, 1893, with no lives lost. The engine is distinctive.

26. Thunder Bay

This historically busy area of Lake Huron, as both a maritime center and as an intense thoroughfare for shipping, unfortunately also plagued with fogs and storms, prompted old mariners to call the region "Shipwreck Alley." The number and quality of shipwrecks will not disappoint the visiting diver. The Thunder Bay Underwater Preserve, established in 1981, became the Thunder Bay National Marine Sanctuary and Underwater Preserve, under N.O.A.A., in 2000. Most of these shipwrecks are buoyed annually with large, plastic barrels, white with a blue stripe.

1. *Shamrock*
2. **Unidentified schooner-barge**
3. *William P. Rend*
4. *Oscar T. Flint*
5. **Scanlon's barge**
6. *Barge No. 1*
7. **North Point wrecks**
8. *New Orleans* (1)
9. *Montana*
10. **Salvage barge**
11. *Grecian*
12. *Monohansett*
13. *E. B. Allen*
14. *Lucinda Van Valkenburg*
15. *Nordmeer*
16. **Limestone walls**
17. **Limestone formations**
18. *Nellie Gardner*
19. *Monrovia*
20. *W. P. Thew*
21. *D. R. Hanna*
22. *New Orleans* (2)
23. *Portsmouth*
24. **Rockport cribbing**
25. *Isaac M. Scott*
26. *Pewabic*
27. *Viator*
28. *W. H. Gilbert*
29. *New York*

1. SHAMROCK

LORAN: 30908.2/48651.4	LAT 45° 02.98' LON 083° 25.85'
DEPTH: 12 feet	LEVEL: Novice

LOCATION: This wreck lies south of the Alpena city marina, 2/3 mile off shore.

The wooden passenger and freight steamer, *Shamrock* (146' x 30' x 11'), built in 1875 at St. Clair, Michigan, as the schooner-barge, *John W. Hannaford,* foundered on June 26, 1905, off the mouth of the Thunder Bay River which flows through Alpena. The entire crew escaped unharmed. The vessel had just been converted to a steamer the year before her demise. This wreckage, for years thought to be that of the steamer, *P.H. Birckhead,* which was lost later that same year, 1905, contains boiler parts, propeller, shaft and hull portions.

2. UNIDENTIFIED SCHOONER-BARGE

LORAN: 30904.5/48649.7	LAT 45° 03.27' LON 083° 25.38'
DEPTH: 14 feet	LEVEL: Novice

LOCATION: This unidentified 148-foot-long wooden wreck lies 600' east of the marina and breakwall. The highlights of this site include the huge keelson and stern post.

3. WILLIAM P. REND

LORAN: 30981.0/48649.5	LAT 45° 03.69' LON 083° 23.49'
DEPTH: 15 to 22 feet	LEVEL: Novice

LOCATION: This wreck lies almost a mile east of the Huron Portland Cement Plant.

The *William P. Rend.* GLHS

The barge, *William P. Rend* (287'6" x 40' x 21'6"), a former steamer named the *George G. Hadley* launched in 1888 at West Bay City, Michigan, stranded on September 22, 1917, with no loss of life. She had been reduced to a barge just the year before her demise. As the *George G. Hadley,* this vessel collided with and sank the whaleback steamer, *Thomas Wilson* (which is also in this book) outside Duluth, Minnesota, harbor on Lake Superior in 1902. There is a partial cargo of limestone on board the wreck of the *William P. Rend,* with the rudder post, valves and boiler.

4. OSCAR T. FLINT

LORAN: 30879.8/48671.9	LAT 45° 01.48' LON 083° 20.69'
DEPTH: 28 to 36 feet	LEVEL: Novice

LOCATION: A mile off shore and four miles southeast of Thunder Bay River.

The *Oscar T. Flint.* MPL/WMHS

Exploring the *Oscar T. Flint.*
PHOTO BY CRIS KOHL.

The wooden steamer, *Oscar T. Flint* (218' x 37' x 15'7"), burned to a total loss during the night while at anchor on November 25, 1909, with no lives lost, the captain barely escaping from the forward part of the ship where the fire started. This vessel was built in 1889 at St. Clair, Michigan. Much of the hull remains intact, plus two wooden-stocked anchors, a windlass and much more remain at this interesting site.

5. SCANLON'S BARGE

LORAN: 30870.2/48669.1	**LAT 45° 02.02′ LON 083° 19.40′**
DEPTH: 5 to 15 feet	**LEVEL: Novice**

LOCATION: This wreck lies off the middle south shore of North Point.

This gravel dredging barge is broken into three pieces, and scattered among them are a crane boom, steam winches, boiler, two-cylinder steam engine and anchor.

6. *BARGE #1*

LORAN: 30865.0/48680.8	**LAT 45° 00.84′ LON 083° 18.08′**
DEPTH: 45 feet	**LEVEL: Intermediate**

LOCATION: This wreck lies about one mile off the tip of North Point.

The enormous wooden vessel named simply *"Barge #1"* (309′9″ x 44′2″ x 12′), was built at West Bay City, Michigan, in 1895 and launched as a railroad carferry before being converted to a bulk freight barge at Chicago in 1912. The ship stranded on the rocks of North Point in a storm on November 8, 1918, and wind and waves moved her into deeper water. The sidewalls of the hull are intact, as is the steering quadrant at the stern.

7. NORTH POINT WRECKS

LORAN: 30846.3/48688.4	**LAT 45° 00.46′ LON 083° 14.99′**
DEPTH: 15 feet	**LEVEL: Novice**

LOCATION: This site lies to the east off the tip of North Point.

Three as yet unidentified shipwrecks lie broken and scattered, with some interesting large pieces, such as a windlass and a large steel anchor, as well as other ship's parts.

8. *NEW ORLEANS* (1)

LORAN: 30836.2/48673.1	**LAT 45° 02.47′ LON 083° 14.24′**
DEPTH: 15 feet	**LEVEL: Novice**

LOCATION: This wreck lies between North Point and Sugar Island.

The 610-ton wooden, passenger and freight sidewheel steamer, *New Orleans,* ran aground in a dense fog on June 11, 1849, and became a total loss. All of the ship's crew and passengers, however, survived and used a small boat to reach Thunder Bay Island, where the hospitable lighthouse keeper took care of them until they could be transported to the mainland. The *New Orleans,* the oldest shipwreck in the area, was built in Detroit in 1844.

This wreck lies broken and scattered over a wide area.

9. MONTANA

LORAN: 30855.9/48699.9	LAT 44° 58.97' LON 083° 15.495'
DEPTH: 33 to 74 feet	LEVEL: Intermediate-Advanced

LOCATION: This wreck lies southwest of Thunder Bay Island.

The wooden steamer, *Montana* (236'3" x 36' x 14'), launched on June 18, 1872 at Port Huron, Michigan, burned to a total loss on September 7, 1914. No lives were lost.

This shipwreck is one of the most popular scuba dive sites in the Alpena area. The hull is intact and upright, with nautical items such as windlass, anchor chain, capstan, boiler, rudder and huge, four-bladed propeller. The highlight is the towering steam engine.

Above: The steamer, *Montana,* detail of a postcard postmarked June 22, 1907. AUTHOR'S COLLECTION. *Right:* Divers explore the *Montana's* tall engine. PHOTOS BY CRIS KOHL.

10. SALVAGE BARGE

LORAN: 30839.5/48707.5	LAT LON
DEPTH: 90 feet	LEVEL: Advanced

LOCATION: This wreck lies off North Point to the northwest of the *Grecian*.

This 68-foot-long salvage barge with a wheelhouse was used in the *Grecian* salvage.

11. GRECIAN

LORAN: 30832.7/48713.3	LAT 44° 57.98' LON 083° 11.93'
DEPTH: 70 to 105 feet	LEVEL: Advanced

LOCATION: About five miles southwest of the Thunder Bay Island Lighthouse.

The steel freighter, *Grecian* (296'2" x 40'4" x 21'1"), built at Cleveland in 1891, hit a rock and sank near DeTour, Michigan, on June 7, 1906. Refloated, she was being towed to Detroit for major repair work when the temporary patch gave way on June 15, 1906. The *Grecian* sank for the second time in eight days, only this time, it was permanent, as further

Above: The steel steamer, *Grecian.* MPL/WMHS. *Right:* A diver approaches the emergency steering at the stern of the *Grecian,* while another videotapes some machinery on this large shipwreck. PHOTOS BY CRIS KOHL.

salvage attempts failed.

This popular site, buoyed in season like most of the other shipwrecks in this designated area, offers much to see at the deck level of 70': tools, railing, bitts and machinery. The propeller rests in 105'. Penetration is possible into the holds for experienced, trained divers. The *Grecian* is broken in two, with the bow comparatively collapsed, so the stern is the more popular site.

12. *MONOHANSETT*

LORAN: 30822.6/48681.4	LAT 45° 01.89' LON 083° 11.90'
DEPTH: 14 to 20 feet	LEVEL: Novice

LOCATION: This wreck lies about 600' off the old dock at Thunder Bay Island.

The wooden steamer, *Monohansett* (164'8" x 31'9" x 9'4"), launched as the *Ira H. Owen* on June 26, 1872 at Gibraltar, Michigan, and renamed in 1882, burned to a total loss on November 23, 1907; 12 on board, no lives were lost. The site's highlights include an enormous boiler, a large propeller and considerable wooden hull (bottom portion only).

Left: The steamer, *Monohansett*. AUTHOR'S COLLECTION. *Right:* Diver Roy Pickering did a 70-minute dive exploring the *Monohansett's* main wreckage and debris field, over and over and over again. PHOTO BY CRIS KOHL.

13. *E. B. ALLEN*

LORAN: 30811.6/48693.1	LAT 45° 00.88' LON 083° 09.81'
DEPTH: 92 to 106 feet	LEVEL: Advanced

LOCATION: This wreck lies 2.5 miles southeast of Thunder Bay Island.

The 111'-long wooden schooner, *E.B. Allen,* sank after colliding with the bark, *Newsboy,* in thick fog common to the area. No lives were lost. Sailing from Chicago to Buffalo with a grain cargo at the time of loss, the 275-ton *E.B. Allen* was built in 1864 at Ogdensburg, NY.

This considerably intact shipwreck has her windlass, anchor chains and rudder in place.

14. LUCINDA VAN VALKENBURG

> **LORAN: 30807.3/48672.9** **LAT 45° 03.25' LON 083° 10.02'**
> **DEPTH: 65 to 72 feet** **LEVEL: Advanced**

LOCATION: This wreck lies located two miles northeast of Thunder Bay Island.
The schooner, *Lucinda Van Valkenburg* (137'8" x 26'2.5" x 12'8"), built at Tonawanda, New York, in 1862, was run down by the steamer, *Lehigh,* in the fog on June 1, 1887, with no lives lost. This popular wreck is upright and partially intact. The decks are collapsed, but the centerboard and its trunk remain upright. The coal cargo was partially salvaged.

15. NORDMEER

> **LORAN: 30790.7/48634.7** **LAT 45° 08.07' LON 083° 09.35'**
> **DEPTH: To 40 feet** **LEVEL: Novice**

LOCATION: This better-known wreck lies 7 miles northeast of Thunder Bay Island.
The steel ocean-going freighter, *Nordmeer* (470'8" x 60'9" x 28'2"), which means "North Sea" in German, stranded during a clear, calm night on Thunder Bay Island Shoals with a cargo of steel coils on November 19, 1966. Somebody wasn't paying attention. The crew of 43 was removed in two shifts several days apart once it became apparent that the Great Lakes' gales of November were going to claim this ship, which had been built at Flensburg, Germany, in 1954. Only a very small portion of this once mighty ship remains above water,

Above: The German freighter, *Nordmeer.* MPL/WMHS.
Right: Diver Joan Forsberg glides between broken sheets of steel hull at the *Nordmeer* site. PHOTO BY CRIS KOHL.

and the engine room and other below deck areas are now collapsed and impenetrable. But the fascination of exploring this site lies in the fact that around every corner there appears a new scene of immense wreckage to explore. This was a big ship, and it covers a lot of bottomlands. Fortunately, it's shallow. A wooden storm-sunk salvage barge lies on the *Nordmeer's* port side.

16. LIMESTONE WALLS

> **LORAN:** **LAT LON**
> **DEPTH: 20 to 70 feet** **LEVEL: Variable**

Off the southeast shore of Thunder Bay Island, a limestone wall drops to a depth of about 70', with a variety of shipwreck artifacts scattered around the bottom of the wall.

17. LIMESTONE FORMATIONS

> **LORAN:** **LAT LON**
> **DEPTH: 20 to 70 feet** **LEVEL: Variable**

A limestone wall and interesting formations, including room-like spaces created by springs, can be found off Middle Island.

18. NELLIE GARDNER

LORAN: 30893.7/48737.9	LAT 44° 53.55′ LON 083° 19.50′
DEPTH: 15 to 20 feet	LEVEL: Novice

LOCATION: Just north of South Point, between Scarecrow and Bird Islands.

The 178-foot-long, 567-gross-ton schooner-barge, *Nellie Gardner,* built in 1873 at Marine City, Michigan, stranded with a cargo of coal after breaking her towline in a storm on October 14, 1883. The crew reached shore in their yawl boat.

This wreck, once called the *Molly H.* or the *Molly T. Horner* by early divers, sits broken up and scattered on a mixed sand and stone bottom, with the ribs and sidewalls comprising most of this site.

19. MONROVIA

LORAN: 30724.1/48729.1	LAT 44° 58.93′ LON 082° 55.26′
DEPTH: 90 to 150 feet	LEVEL: Advanced-Technical

LOCATION: This wreck lies about 13 miles southeast of Thunder Bay Island.

The steel, ocean-going freighter, *Monrovia* (128′5″ x 24′5″ x 12′5″), built in Scotland in 1943, owned in Liverpool, England, sailing under Liberian registry and bound for Chicago with a Greek crew and a cargo of steel from Belgium (talk about a festival of nations!), sank in U.S. waters after a collision in thick fog with the Canadian freighter, *Royalton*, on June 25, 1959. It was the *Monrovia's* first (and last!) trip to the Great Lakes. As water gushed into her gashed port side, the 29 crew were rescued by the freighter, *Norman W. Foy* (thanks to

its radar); most of the steel cargo was subsequently salvaged using dynamite. The *Royalton's* captain testified that the *Monrovia* "struck us on the bow," but he forgot to mention *Monrovia* "struck" with her port side (kind of like getting punched in the fist by somebody's face). The inquiry found both captains responsible. This wreck, long popular among experienced divers, sits upright mostly intact, with her superstructure, hull and cargo holds. Considerable machinery remains on deck. Penetration is possible, but tricky, and has proven fatal here.

The *Monrovia.* AUTHOR'S COLLECTION

20. W. P. THEW

LORAN: 30802.7/48769.6	LAT 45° 02.66′ LON 083° 09.02′
DEPTH: 76 to 86 feet	LEVEL: Advanced

LOCATION: This wreck lies 1.8 miles east of the Thunder Bay Island Lighthouse.

The small, wooden steamer, *W. P. Thew* (132′5″ x 24′2″ x 8′3″), named after William Plymouth Thew by his son, Richard, who had the ship built at Lorain, Ohio, in 1884, sank after a collision (again in thick fog) with the steamer, *William*

Left: The *W.P. Thew.* AUTHOR'S COLLECTION. *Above and right:* Diver Roy Pickering interacts with the *Thew's* wreckage and fish life. PHOTOS BY CRIS KOHL

Livingston, on June 22, 1909. The *W.P. Thew* carried no cargo and lost no lives. The wreck's boilers and engine remain upright, with considerable hull still in place and an anchor with chain near the bow.

21. *D. R. HANNA*

LORAN: 30771.3/48666.4	LAT 45° 05.00' LON 083° 05.02'
DEPTH: 97 to 138 feet	LEVEL: Advanced-Technical

LOCATION: This site is about 6.5 miles northeast of Thunder Bay Island Lighthouse.

D.R. Hanna. REV. PETER VAN DER LINDEN COLLECTION

The steel freighter, *D.R. Hanna* (532' x 56' x 31'), launched in 1906 at Lorain, Ohio, sank with a wheat cargo in a dense fog after a collision with the steamer, *Quincy A. Shaw,* on May 16, 1919. All 32 on board survived. A hardhat diver located the wreck five months after she sank, but because she lies upside-down at that depth, salvage was not attempted. The wreck is penetrable, but only by well-trained divers who follow their training.

22. *NEW ORLEANS* (2)

LORAN: 30808.0/48613.7	LAT 45° 10.06' LON 083° 12.85'
DEPTH: 115 to 147 feet	LEVEL: Advanced-Technical

Left: The *New Orleans.* AUTHOR'S COLLECTION. *Right:* The forward-most mast and rail on the *New Orleans.* PHOTO BY CRIS KOHL.

LOCATION: This wreck lies about 4 miles east-southeast of Middle Island, and about 10 miles north of the Thunder Bay Island Lighthouse.

The wooden steamer, *New Orleans* (231'8" x 38' x 13'6"), built at Marine City, Michigan, in 1885, sank with a cargo of coal after a collision with the much larger steel freighter, *William R. Linn,* on June 30, 1906. No lives were lost. The middle part of this generally intact steamer is broken up and split at the coal bunker. The bow lies in the shallower part, with the stern deepest.

23. *PORTSMOUTH*

LORAN: 30847.6/48588.2	LAT 45° 45.454' LON 075° 45.454'
DEPTH: 15 feet	LEVEL: Novice

LOCATION: This wreck lies off the west side of Middle Island.

The wooden package freighter, *Portsmouth* (176' x 29' x 11'), built at Buffalo, New York, in 1853, tried to ride out a storm while at anchor on November 10, 1867, but the anchors dragged and the ship stranded on Middle Island, where she caught fire and burned before breaking up. Her cargo was pig iron. The scattered wreckage is home to many fish.

24. ROCKPORT CRIBBING

Cribbing, the base of old docks, supports much fish life at Rockport, north of Alpena.

25. ISAAC M. SCOTT

LORAN: 30758.3/48686.8	LAT 45° 02.98' LON 083° 02.20'
DEPTH: 180 feet	LEVEL: Technical

The steel freighter, *Isaac M. Scott* (504" x 54' x 30'), built at Lorain, Ohio, in 1909 and another of the victims lost with all hands (28) in the Great Storm of November 9-11, 1913, lies upside-down about 11 miles east of Thunder Bay Island Lighthouse. This wreck was located by Kent Bellrichard's team in September, 1975, while searching for the *Viator* (which is site #27 on this page).

The *Isaac M. Scott*. MPL/WMHS

26. PEWABIC

LORAN: 30795.6/48723.3	LAT 44° 57.82' LON 083° 05.96'
DEPTH: 148 to 168 feet	LEVEL: Technical

In one of the worst maritime accidents on the Great Lakes, the wooden passenger and freight steamer, *Pewabic* (200'3" x 31'1" x 12'5"), sank in a collision with her sister ship, the *Meteor,* on August 9, 1865, resulting in approximately 100 lives from the *Pewabic* being lost. The *Pewabic,* launched in September, 1863, at Cleveland, carried a valuable cargo of copper ingots, and several hardhat divers died during its recovery in subsequent years.

The only known photograph of the tragic steamer, *Pewabic*. Rev. PETER VAN DER LINDEN COLLECTION.

The wreck is deep and generally intact, although the upper works were removed long ago by a succession of salvagers. A *Pewabic* anchor sits outside a local museum in Alpena.

27. VIATOR

LORAN: 30766.4/48715.6	LAT 44° 59.43' LON 083° 02.07'
DEPTH: 150 feet	LEVEL: Technical

Built at Bodo, Norway in 1904, the 231'-long steel freighter, *Viator,* sank in the fog after a collision with the freighter, *Ormidale,* on October 31, 1935. No lives were lost, but her cargo of sardines went to the bottom. Kent Bellrichard found the wreck in late 1975.

28. W. H. GILBERT

LORAN: 30765.8/48795.0	LAT LON
DEPTH: 255 feet	LEVEL: Technical

Built at West Bay City, Michigan, in 1892, the steel steamer, *W.H. Gilbert* (328' x 42'5" x 20'5"), carrying a cargo of coal, sank after a collision with the *Caldera* on May 22, 1914; no lives were lost. She lies in very deep water 17.7 miles off Thunder Bay Island.

29. NEW YORK

LORAN:	LAT 43° 36.23' LON 082° 28.24'
DEPTH: 90 feet	LEVEL: Advanced

Built in 1879 at Buffalo, the wooden steamer, *New York* (281' x 37' x 28'), coal cargo, burned and sank about two miles off South Point on October 1, 1910. No lives were lost.

27. Northwestern Lake Huron

The intact and photogenic nature of the ship-wrecks in this access-challenged area is, for now, one of the best-kept secrets in the Great Lakes.

BOIS BLANC ISLAND

Cheboygan

LAKE HURON

HAMMOND BAY

FORTY MILE POINT

MICHIGAN

Rogers City

PRESQUE ISLE

-N-

Rockport

Alpena

The *John J. Audubon*
(see site #11 on p. 245). Artwork ©Tim Reed

Windlass — Holds — Dead eyes — Pin Rails — Ships Wheel — Cook Stove — Deck Cabin — Davits — Bilge Pump — Mast

1. *Newell A. Eddy*
2. *Kate Hayes*
3. *Perseverance*
4. *James R. Bentley*
5. *Persian*
6. *Henry J. Johnson*
7. *Joseph S. Fay*
8. *F. T. Barney*
9. *Duncan City*
10. **Unidentified barge**
11. *John J. Audubon*
12. *Cornelia B. Windiate*
13. *Typo*
14. *Norman*
15. *Florida*

1. NEWELL A. EDDY

LORAN: 31067.0/48194.8	LAT 45° 46.88′ LON 084° 13.75′
DEPTH: 145 to 168 feet	LEVEL: Technical

LOCATION: This wreck lies to the east of Bois Blanc Island.

The three-masted schooner-barge, *Newell A. Eddy* (242′ x 40′ x 16′), built at West Bay City, Michigan, in 1890, foundered in a storm with a cargo of grain and all nine hands near Spectacle Reef on April 20, 1893, while in tow of the steamer, *Charles A. Eddy*, bound from Chicago for Buffalo. Widely reported as "the great gale," this was the worst spring storm in recorded Great Lakes history, with at least 15 vessels wrecked or stranded. Three days later, the passing steamer, *G.W. Morley,* passed the *Eddy's* quarter deck and cabin. The relatively new *Newell A. Eddy* was valued at the time of loss at an immense $105,000, and carried insurance for $95,000. The *Newell A. Eddy* was accidentally located on July 25, 1992 by the University of Michigan scientific research vessel, *Laurentian,* while demonstrating sidescan sonar to students. The wreck's masts are still standing and rise to within 80′ of the surface (sometimes a line and buoy are tied to one of these masts). While the stern section is broken or absent, the bow is upright and virtually intact, with capstans, bow nameplates, an eagle figurehead and bow machinery in place.

2. KATE HAYES

LORAN: 31037.6/48211.3	LAT	LON
DEPTH: 45 to 70 feet	LEVEL: Intermediate-Advanced	

LOCATION: This wreck lies off Spectacle Reef.

The 130′, 349-ton schooner, *Kate Hayes,* built at Buffalo in 1856, punctured her hull on rocks when she stranded and sank on July 14, 1856, with no lives lost. She was carrying a cargo of wheat from Milwaukee to Oswego, New York. This shipping loss was cited for justifying the 1870 construction of the Spectacle Reef Lighthouse. This shipwreck was reportedly located by John Steele.

3. PERSEVERANCE

LORAN:	LAT 45° 42.08′ LON 084° 26.35′
DEPTH: 65 feet	LEVEL: Advanced

LOCATION: This wreck lies east-northeast of Cheboygan, Michigan.

Built at Buffalo in 1855, the 294-gross-ton, two-masted schooner, *Perseverance*, (121′2″ x 25′7″ x 10′4″) sank in a collision with the schooner, *Grey Eagle,* on November 24, 1864. The ship and her cargo of wheat, but no lives, went to the bottom. This is a photogenic shipwreck, even though she is a bit broken up. Much nautical equipment remains at the site.

4. JAMES R. BENTLEY

LORAN: 31057.7/48251.1	LAT 45° 41.44′ LON 084° 09.11′
DEPTH: 165 feet	LEVEL: Technical

LOCATION: This wreck lies east of Bois Blanc Island and north of Hammond Bay.

Discovered by John Steele in 1984, the three-masted schooner, *James R. Bentley* (178′5″ x 34′ x 13′4″), built at Fairport, Ohio, in 1867, foundered in a storm on Nov. 12, 1878, no lives lost. The mizzenmast is upright; the other masts have toppled. The stunningly unique dragon figurehead was safely on display in a Wisconsin museum until Michigan law enforcers confiscated it in their prosecution of the Illinois diver who originally recovered it, conserved it and gave it to the museum. In a unique but costly legal turnaround based on the interpretation of the law's wording, this diver reportedly ended up being granted ownership of this shipwreck by the court! Divers visiting this low-vis, high-profile site may actually be trespassing!

5. PERSIAN

LORAN: 31055.0/48246.0	**LAT**	**LON**
DEPTH: 159 to 172 feet	**LEVEL: Technical**	

LOCATION: This wreck lies north of Hammond Bay.

All ten men on board the wheat-laden, 128′ schooner, *Persian*, lost their lives when the ship sank after a collision with the schooner, *E.B. Allen* (which is also in this book) on September 16, 1868. The *Persian* (also sometimes referred to as the *Persia*) was built in 1855 at Oswego, New York. The wreck sits upright and is very intact.

6 HENRY J. JOHNSON

LORAN: 31050.0/48285.3	**LAT**	**LON**
DEPTH: 160 feet	**LEVEL: Tecnhical**	

LOCATION: This wreck lies north of Hammond Bay.

The wooden steamer, *Henry J. Johnson* (260′ x 40′2″ x 19′6″), built at Cleveland in 1888, collided in dense fog with the steamer, *Fred Pabst,* on July 24, 1902. The *Henry J. Johnson* was downbound from Escanaba, Michigan, with a cargo of iron ore. No lives were lost. The wreck sits upright and intact in deep water.

Portraits of two wooden steamers: the *Henry J. Johnson* (left) and the *Joseph S. Fay.* BOTH GLHS.

7. JOSEPH S. FAY

LORAN: 31007.3/48381.6	**LAT**	**LON**
DEPTH: 15 feet	**LEVEL: Novice**	

LOCATION: Off Forty Mile Point Lighthouse, six miles north of Rogers City.

Launched at Cleveland in 1871, the wooden bulk freight steamer, *Joseph S. Fay* (215′6″ x 33′6″ x 14′8″), foundered in the infamous October 20, 1905 storm which also sank the *Tasmania*, the *Siberia* and the *Sarah E. Sheldon* (which are all in this book). The *Joseph S. Fay* was transporting a cargo of iron ore towards Ashtabula, Ohio, when she began to leak and was beached to avoid sinking in deep water. But instead of being recoverable later, the ship was destroyed by the pounding waves. These shipwreck remains lie about 800′ off shore. It's a long swim with occasional current. Use a boat. The broken up wreck, which is visible from the surface, is home to a wide variety of freshwater fish: perch, suckers, burbots....

8. F. T. BARNEY

LORAN: 30984.1/48390.7	**LAT 45° 29.26′**	**LON 083° 50.50′**
DEPTH: 160 feet	**LEVEL: Technical**	

LOCATION: This wreck lies north of Rogers City, Michigan.

The two-masted, coal-carrying schooner, *F.T. Barney* (130'6" x 25' x 11'), sank in a collision with the schooner, *Tracy J. Bronson,* on Oct. 23, 1868. Built in Vermilion, Ohio, in 1856, this vessel, identified by Stan Stock in 1989, displays a mast with a crowsnest!

9. DUNCAN CITY

Built in 1883 at Manitowoc, Wisconsin, the tug, *Duncan City* (77'5" x 19'8" x 9'2"), abandoned since 1926, lies in 40' two miles west of Adams Pt. **LORAN: 30968.2/48436.5**

10. UNIDENTIFIED BARGE

This unidentified wooden barge lies off Rogers City in 65'. **LORAN: 30965.6/48436.5**

11. JOHN J. AUDUBON   (See shipwreck layout drawing on page 242.)

LOCATION: This technical dive site lies in deep (178') water north of Presque Ile.

Built in 1854 at Cleveland, the 370-ton, two-masted brig, *John J. Audubon,* sank later that same year. On the night of October 20, 1854, the schooner, *Defiance,* struck her amidship, and both vessels sank. Found by Stan Stock, the *Audubon* lies masts up and stern broken.

12. CORNELIA B. WINDIATE

Found by Paul Ehorn the same morning in May, 1986, that his colleague, John Steele, found the *Norman* nearby, the three-masted schooner, *Cornelia B. Windiate* (138'6" x 26'2" x 11'6"), built at Manitowoc, Wisconsin, in 1874, disappeared with all hands after leaving Milwaukee for Buffalo with a cargo of wheat on November 28, 1875. Assumed to have sunk in Lake Michigan, the wreck was found in Lake Huron. She sits upright and intact in 180' of water, making this a technical dive. **LORAN: 30824.6/48525.3**

Artwork ©Tim Reed

13. TYPO

The three-masted schooner, *Typo* (137'8" x 26'2" x 11'3"), built at Milwaukee in 1873, sank six miles east-southeast of Presque Isle Light after a collision with the steamer, *W.P. Ketcham,* on October 14, 1899. Four lives were lost. The wreck sits upright and intact. in 155' of water, making this a technical dive site. **LORAN: 30825.7/48543.4**

Artwork ©Tim Reed

14. NORMAN

Found by John Steele the same morning in May, 1986, that his colleague, Paul Ehorn, found the *Cornelia B. Windiate* nearby, the steel steamer, *Norman* (296'5" x 40'4" x 24'), sank in thick fog after a collision with the Canadian steamer, *Jack,* on May 30, 1895, with the loss of three lives. She was built at Cleveland in 1890, and sits intact on a 45-degree list in 210' of water, making this a technical dive site . **LORAN: 30809.2/48537.3**

15. FLORIDA

The wooden steamer, *Florida* (271' x 40' x 15'), built at Buffalo in 1889, sank in 235' after she was struck by the steamer, *George W. Roby,* on May 20, 1897; upright and intact.

28. Sites near Lake Huron

1. Higgins Lake
2. Brockway Lake
3. *John Fraser*
4. Kawigamog Lake
5. Bala Falls/Moon River
6. *Nipissing*
7. *Waome*
8. Lake Simcoe sites

1. HIGGINS LAKE

LOCATION: Ten miles south of Grayling, MI, just east of the I 75/US 27 intersection.

This enormous lake, comprising almost 10,000 acres of surface space, reaches depths up to 135' in the lake's northwest corner, but most of the many scuba divers that enjoy this lake stay considerably shallower. At the lake's southern end is a "sunken island" where vast numbers of fish congregate. Two state parks with boat launching ramps, as well as one independent launching facility, line the lake. There are several picnic/public access areas from where divers can do shore dives to explore the lake. The lake's visibility is exceptional, upwards of 50' on occasion. Sunken logs, boats and ice fishing shelters lie on the bottom.

2. BROCKWAY LAKE

LOCATION: Take US 131 to the Jefferson Road (Morley) exit, go east about 10 miles to 100th Avenue, and turn left (north). At the first road, which is Three Mile Road, turn right (west). Signs indicate the way to public access. A boat is not necessary.

Brockway Lake is a 14-acre body of water with a maximum depth of 30'. It is wonderful for either scuba diving or snorkeling. The "marl" was excavated from the sides of the lake, so there are walls up to 25' tall at the water's edge. Considerable aquatic life, such as bass, northern pike, perch, bluegills and sunfish, can be found around the many sunken logs. A shallow underwater island rises in the middle of the lake.

3. *JOHN FRASER*

LOCATION: This wreck lies at a depth of 50' just east of Goose Island in the center of Lake Nipissing in the northern Georgian Bay area of Ontario.

The oak-hulled steamer, *John Fraser,* built in 1888 at Sturgeon Falls on Lake Nipissing, was making its final run of the year across the lake on November 7, 1893. Seven crewmembers and 17 lumberjacks were aboard. In the middle of the lake, fire broke out near the boiler. Some people sought refuge in a scow which the *John Fraser* was towing, while others took to a lifeboat which overturned, drowning its occupants. Tragically, there were only 7 survivors from the 24 people on board. In 1972, the burned out hull was located, along with the steam engine, boiler and piping, by members of the North Bay Scuba Club. Often buoyed at the beginning of the year, this site suffers from poor visibility, and divers must use caution not to become entangled in the twisted pipes and rails.

4. KAWIGAMOG LAKE (LOST CHANNEL)

LOCATION: This lake lies east of Highway 69 and just off road 522 down Lost Channel Road, halfway between Parry Sound and Sudbury, Ontario.

This is a shore dive for novice to intermediate divers, with a maximum depth of 16'. At the edge of this lake lie the remains of the steamer, *Douglas L.,* and two barges. Hundreds of people lived and worked in this thriving community called the Lost Channel in the early 1900's, but they, their descendants and most signs of their habitation are now gone. The *Douglas L.* was a small steamer, about 70' in length, which carried goods and settlers to the more remote parts of Kawigamog Lake until approximately 1930 when the vessel was abandoned at this site. The barges were simple carriers towed behind a steamer. You can drive right up to this site, although the road is primitive. The low visibility in tea-colored water could be a problem for the inexperienced, but exploring the hull and boiler of the *Douglas L.,* with the many diver-friendly bass, is interesting.

5. BALA FALLS/MOON RIVER

A site for every level of diver experience is at Bala Falls on the Moon River, at the western side of Lake Muskoka, Ontario. With a depth from 22' to 100', and several levels of underwater cliffs, one can go deep or stay shallow. This site is adjacent to the Foodland grocery store in Bala. There is, of course, a current; stay within your level of experience.

6. NIPISSING

LOCATION: The wreck of the steamer, *Nipissing,* lies off Blueberry Island in the northern part of Lake Joseph, Ontario. Access is from a gravel road connected to Highway 69 just past Hamer Bay. A boat is needed to reach this novice site in 10′ to 23′ of water. The broken up steamer, *Nipissing,* which can be seen from the surface, abounds with fish life and is excellent for underwater photography. Beware of occasional boating traffic.

7. WAOME

LOCATION: This shipwreck lies off the west side of Keewaydin Island in the northern part of Lake Muskoka near Milford Bay, Ontario.

The steamer, *Waome* (78′ x 14′), launched as the *Mink* at Gravenhurst, Ontario, in 1912, received her name change on May 28, 1929. *Waome* (pronounced "Way-OH-mee") is an Ojibwa word meaning "water lily." On October 6, 1934, on her final run of the season (hasn't that so often been the case?), and carrying the captain, 5 crew, and a passenger (an old-fashioned minister who preferred to travel by ship rather than on the new busline), the *Waome* headed towards Beaumaris. A sudden, powerful gust knocked the ship onto her port side and water gushed into her holds. Within a minute, the ship sank, taking with her a crewmember and the minister. The elderly captain died of a heart attack as he swam for his life on the surface, but the other four reached the island.

This very popular wreck sits upright and intact in 50′ to 74′ of dark, tea-colored water. Penetration diving is possible, but should be done only by trained, experienced divers.

The steamer, *Waome.* AUTHOR'S COLLECTION

8. LAKE SIMCOE SITES

This is a large, inland lake north of Toronto. It has much boating traffic (use a diver down flag and caution), variable visibility from 3′ to 20′, and many dive sites, including:

Cook's Bay, depth from 10′ to 40′, with old bottles commonly found here.

"Four Friends Reef", north of the town of Keswick, in 30′, a manmade reef of rocks in 10′ by 10′ wooden crates, commemorating four fishermen who died in a boating accident.

Roches Point dock, to 30′, a lightly-grassed area rich with fish life (bass and pike).

Willow Beach, a shore dive to 25′, with ice-fishing remnants littering the bottom.

Jackson's Point, with the remains of the original wooden dock in 8′ to 20′.

Pefferlaw dock, a scrounge dive to a maximum of 30′, but low vis in river run-off.

Beaverton dock to 30′, again a good place to scrounge for things accidentally dropped.

Orillia and Barrie docks, to 28′, with a wide range of underwater debris.

Big Bay Point dock at Kempenfelt Bay, to a depth over 100′ close to shore. Use caution!

The wreck of the sidewheel steamer, *J.C. Morrison,* in Kempenfelt Bay at Barrie, ON. This ship, launched in 1854 and used as an excursion steamer on Lake Simcoe, caught fire on Aug. 4, 1857 while docked. Cut loose, the vessel drifted to the opposite shore, burned to the waterline and sank. Barrie diver Ron Marshall found the wreck in 1975. Remains include parts of the large paddlewheels and axles, bow, anchor, smokestack, boiler, plus small artifacts. The wreck lies 420′ from shore in 40′ between the fountain and the mini-golf course.

29. Straits of Mackinac

MICHIGAN:
Upper
Peninsula

The Straits of Mackinac, a very historic area popular with tourists, boaters and scuba divers alike, is one of Michigan's 10 underwater preserves. The region's symbol is the ubiquitous "Big Mac" bridge. PHOTO BY CRIS KOHL.

ST. HELENA ISLAND

St. Ignace

MACKINAC ISLAND

BOIS BLANC ISLAND

Mackinaw City

MICHIGAN:
Lower Peninsula

Cross Village

Cheboygan

1. *Milwaukee*	10. *Northwest*	19. **Rock maze**
2. *J. H. Tiffany*	11. **Sandusky**	20. *M. Stalker*
3. *Cayuga*	12. *Eber Ward*	21. *Cedarville*
4. *Canisteo*	13. **Chuck's barge**	22. *Wm. H. Barnum*
5. *Richard Winslow*	14. **C. H. Johnson**	23. *Albemarle*
6. *Uganda*	15. *Minneapolis*	24. *J. H. Outhwaite*
7. *Colonel Ellsworth*	16. **St. Ignace harbor**	25. *St. Andrew*
8. *Fred McBrier*	17. **Clam bucket barge**	26. *Leviathan*
9. *Maitland*	18. **M. I. harbor wreck**	

1. MILWAUKEE

> **LORAN: 31407.2/48077.8**   **LAT 45° 43.50′   LON 085° 14.85′**
> **DEPTH: 97 feet**   **LEVEL: Advanced**

LOCATION: This pre-Civil War wreck lies 5.2 miles southwest of Grays Reef Light.

Built in 1853 at Cleveland, the 185′ wooden, wheat-laden steamer, *Milwaukee*, bound from Milwaukee to Buffalo, sank in a collision with the schooner, *J.H. Tiffany,* which also sank and lies nearby (see Site #2), on Nov. 29, 1859. No lives were lost from the *Milwaukee*.

This shipwreck sits upright but is not intact; only the starboard quarter portion of the hull still stands upright. The remainder of the wreck has collapsed outward, or, in the case of the decking, to the bottom of the hull. Salvage in the 1870's removed much equipment, but the propeller, windlass and fallen wheel are still there.The *J.H. Tiffany* is very close, with the *Cayuga* (Site #3) 2.8 miles from the *Milwaukee*.

2. J. H. TIFFANY

> **LORAN: 31402.0/48081.7**   **LAT 45° 43.37′   LON 085° 13.76′**
> **DEPTH:103 feet**   **LEVEL: Advanced**

LOCATION: This pre-Civil War wreck lies 4.8 miles southwest of Grays Reef Light.

The 137′ schooner, *J.H. Tiffany,* built in 1856 at Cleveland, sank with the loss of five lives and a cargo of railroad iron after her collision with the steamer, *Milwaukee* (see Site #1) on November 29, 1859. Time and the 1870's salvage of her valuable cargo broke up and flattened the wreck of the *J.H. Tiffany*. The remains are basic and minimal.

Both collision shipwrecks (Sites #1 and #2) were located in modern times (1985) by scuba divers from Muskegon, Michigan, namely Brian Scott, Craig Scott, Dave Scott, George Manning and Bill Salsbury, and John Makuch from Detroit.

3. CAYUGA

> **LORAN: 31390.4/48089.8**   **LAT 45° 43.19′   LON 085° 11.36′**
> **DEPTH: 75 to 102 feet**   **LEVEL: Advanced**

LOCATION: This wreck lies 3.6 miles southwest of Grays Reef Light.

The steel freighter, *Cayuga,* (290′ x 40′8″ x 13′6″), launched on April 2, 1889 at Cleveland, sank in a collision with the steamer, *Joseph L. Hurd* on May 10,1895. One life was lost from the *Hurd,* which did not sink. Lengthy, costly salvage

Left: The steel steamer, *Cayuga*. AUTHOR'S COLLECTION. *Below:* Diver Sharon Troxell explores a long anchor chain running over a *Cayuga* hatch. PHOTO BY CRIS KOHL.

Artwork © Chuck & Jeri Feltner (Drawing by Chuck Feltner & Dave Donovan)

failed to raise the *Cayuga,* and instead cost one hardhat diver his life (Great Lakes lore has that diver still trapped beneath the small salvage barge next to the wreck). John Steele and Gene Turner of Illinois located the *Cayuga* in the spring of 1969. The wreck today is upright and quite intact, lying on an angle to portside, with salvage pontoons still strapped onto her sides and vast opportunities for trained and experienced divers to penetrate below deck.

4. CANISTEO

LORAN: 31341.9/48070.8	LAT 45° 47.32′ LON 085° 04.75′
DEPTH: 15 feet	LEVEL: Novice

LOCATION: This wreck lies 0.6 mile east of Waugoshance Light.

The 196′ wooden steamer, *Canisteo,* not to be confused with the other wooden steamer, *Canisteo,* which lies in Lake Huron, was launched in 1862 at Buffalo and sank in a collision with the schooner, *George Murray,* on Oct. 14, 1880, with a cargo of corn and lard, but no lives lost. This wreck, located from the air in 1988 by Chuck and Jeri Feltner and Mike Kohut, was moved by the ice and wind over the years about half a mile east of the place where she originally sank. The machinery was salvaged, so only broken wood remains.

5. RICHARD WINSLOW

LORAN: 31356.4/48026.4	LAT 45° 50.45′ LON 085° 09.48′
DEPTH: 32 feet	LEVEL: Novice

LOCATION: This wreck lies 1.4 miles west of White Shoals Light.

The 216′ schooner, *Richard Winslow*, built in 1871 at Detroit, foundered with an iron ore cargo and no lives lost on September 5, 1898. The wreck was dynamited to remove her as a hazard to navigation, so the wreckage lies scattered over a wide area.

6. UGANDA

LORAN: 31321.7/48047.2	LAT 45° 50.30′ LON 085° 03.49′
DEPTH: 185 to 207 feet	LEVEL: Technical

LOCATION: This wreck lies 4.3 miles due east of White Shoals Light.

Launched at West Bay City, Michigan, in 1892, the wooden steamer, *Uganda* (291′ x 41′ x 19′8″), was cut by ice on April 19, 1913, while carrying a cargo of corn from Milwaukee to Buffalo. No lives were lost in this sinking. Located by Chuck and Jeri Feltner and Stan Stock in 1983, the *Uganda's* depth and the strong current make her a difficult dive. She sits upright and intact,

The *Uganda.* MPL/WMHS

with her midship cabin the only one still in place. Engine, boiler, anchors and much more mechanical equipment remain at this site.

7. COLONEL ELLSWORTH

LORAN: 31317.2/48067.7	LAT 45° 48.26′ LON 085° 01.00′
DEPTH: 70 to 84 feet	LEVEL: Advanced

LOCATION: This wreck lies 6.2 miles east-southeast of White Shoals Light.

The schooner, *Colonel Ellsworth* (137′8″ x 26′ x 11′8″), built in 1861 at Euclid, Ohio, sank in a collision with the schooner, *Emily B. Maxwell,* on September 2, 1896. She carried no cargo and lost no lives. The *Maxwell* stayed afloat and in service for another 13 years before sinking in Lake Erie. The *Colonel Ellsworth,* located by Dick Race of Chicago in 1968, is upright, intact and penetrable, with much to see (windlass, mast, etc.) in spite of some salvage (e.g. her anchors) done shortly after she sank.

8. FRED MCBRIER

LORAN: 31287.8/48085.3	LAT 45° 48.11′ LON 084° 55.09′
DEPTH: 96 to 104 feet	LEVEL: Advanced

LOCATION: This wreck lies 9.3 miles west of Old Mackinac Point.

Launched at West Bay City, Michigan, in 1881, the comparatively small wooden steamer, *Fred McBrier* (161′ x 31′ x 12′), laden with iron ore, sank in a collision with the steamer, *Progress,* on Oct. 3, 1890, with no lives lost. Located in 1967 by Jim Ryerse from nearby St. Ignace, the wreck displays considerable machinery, such as her engine, boiler, and windlass, but lies in an area plagued with frequently silty water, reducing visibility considerably.

Joan Forsberg approaches engine machinery on the *Fred McBrier.* PHOTO BY CRIS KOHL.

9. MAITLAND

LORAN: 31273.1/48092.7	LAT 45° 48.20′ LON 084° 52.29′
DEPTH: 84 feet	LEVEL: Advanced

LOCATION: This wreck lies 7.1 miles west of Old Mackinac Point.

The bark, *Maitland* (133′7″ x 25′9″ x 11′6″), built at Goderich, ON, along the Maitland River, in 1861, sank with a corn cargo after colliding with both the steamer, *Golden Harvest,* and her tow, the schooner, *Mears,* on June 11, 1871. No lives were lost. The *Maitland* sits upright, intact and penetrable, with much equipment (e.g. windlass, bilge pump) on deck.

ANCHOR CHAIN CHOCK · BOWSPRIT STUB · SAMSON POST · COLLISION GASH · GUNWALE (depth 69') · MAINMAST HOLE · CENTERBOARD LIFTING WINCH · MIZZENMAST HOLE · Artwork © Chuck & Jeri Feltner (Drawing by Chuck Feltner & Larry Baron) · BILGE PUMP · FOREMAST HOLE · FORWARD HATCH · ACCESS HATCH · BOOM RIG HARDWARE · OUTLINE OF CABIN · RUDDER · RAILING · HATCH · RUDDER POST · SAMSON POST · CENTERBOARD BOX · MAITLAND · GUNWALE (depth 75') · DECK OPENING · WINDLASS · RAISED FOREDECK · 0' 5' 10'

10. NORTHWEST

LORAN: 31270.2/48102.2	LAT 45° 47.32′ LON 084° 51.30′
DEPTH: 73 feet	LEVEL: Advanced

LOCATION: This wreck lies 6.2 miles west of Old Mackinac Point.

Ice punctured the hull (a common malady among ships in the Straits) of the 233′ schooner, *Northwest,* on April 6, 1898, and she sank with her cargo of corn but no lives lost.

Built in 1873 at Bangor, Michigan, the *Northwest* was located in 1978 by Chuck and Jeri Feltner. This wreck, although broken up and in disarray, is very interesting and, as long as you can maintain bow and stern bearings, easy to navigate. The rudder lies flat off the stern.

Left: The schooner, *Northwest.* M P L / W M H S. *Right:* Joan Forsberg and *Northwest* machinery. PHOTO BY CRIS KOHL.

253

11. SANDUSKY

LORAN: 31262.0/48100.9   LAT 45° 48.09'   LON 084° 50.08'
DEPTH: 70 to 84 feet   LEVEL: Advanced

LOCATION: This wreck lies 5.2 miles west of Old Mackinac Point.

The brig, *Sandusky* (110' x 25'1"), built in 1848 at her namesake, Sandusky, Ohio, foundered with all seven hands and a grain cargo in a storm on September 20, 1856. The wreck, located by Chuck and Jeri Feltner's team on May 2, 1981, sits upright and intact, with magnificent sights such as the scroll figurehead, pictured on this book's cover (even though this one, compliments of several Detroit area divers, is a precise replica of the original, which was damaged in a bungled theft attempt in 1988 and is now in a museum), completely intact bowsprit with chains, bow anchors, and windlass. The *Sandusky,* excellently preserved, is the oldest located and most visited shipwreck in the Straits of Mackinac.

The *Sandusky's* bowsprit, chains and scrolled figurehead. PHOTO BY CRIS KOHL.

The huge starboard bow fluked anchor is one of the many items to appreciate at this site. PHOTO BY CRIS KOHL.

Artwork © Chuck & Jeri Feltner (Drawing by Chuck Feltner & Dave Donovan)

An unidentified *Sandusky* lookalike. AUTHOR'S COLLECTION

12. EBER WARD

LORAN: 31253.7/48096.9   LAT 45° 48.83'   LON 084° 49.04'
DEPTH: 111 to 142 feet   LEVEL: Advanced-Technical

LOCATION: This wreck lies 4.6 miles west-northwest from Old Mackinac Point.

Built in 1888 at West Bay City, Michigan, the wooden steamer, *Eber Ward* (213'2" x 37' x 22'2"), lost five lives and her cargo of corn on April 9, 1909, after she sank when ice holed her hull. Found by Chuck and Jeri Feltner in 1980, this double-decked wreck sits facing south, upright, intact and penetrable (by trained and experienced divers only, please). Three anchors, as well as two holes from the ice, grace her bow area. Her machinery includes a large steam engine, a scotch boiler and a four-bladed propeller. Quite a few shipwreck items lie on the lake bottom just off the wreck, particularly at the stern.

EBER WARD

Artwork © Chuck & Jeri Feltner (Drawing by Chuck Feltner & Dave Donovan)

Photos, clockwise from above right: The steamer, *Eber Ward*. MPL/WMHS. Shipwreck sights include an *Eber Ward* bathtub below deck, a burbot who becomes a very willing model at the *Eber Ward's* bow post, and the mushroom anchor on the port bow. PHOTOS BY CRIS KOHL.

13. CHUCK'S BARGE

LORAN: 31255.8/48074.3	LAT	LON
DEPTH: 33 to 43 feet	LEVEL: Novice-Intermediate	

LOCATION: This wreck lies about one mile east-southeast of St. Helena Island.

This upside-down barge, about 60′ long, was located by Chuck and Jeri Feltner in 1982. It is a dump scow used to dispose of dredge material, as the bottom consists of two hinged doors covering large openings. It is believed to have been lost in the 1940's.

14. C. H. Johnson

LORAN: 31247.0/48061.7	LAT 45° 52.20' LON 084° 50.08'
DEPTH: 13 feet	LEVEL: Novice

LOCATION: This wreck lies on the north shore of Gros Cap, Upper Peninsula, 9 miles northwest of Old Mackinac Point.

Constructed in 1870 at Marine City, Michigan, the 137' schooner, *C.H. Johnson,* stranded with a small cargo of large stone blocks while attempting to ride out a storm on September 23, 1895. No lives were lost when the ship sank. Lying at such a shallow depth, the wreck is broken up, but the keelson and many of the ribs are still in place. The cargo of about 20 large (8' x 4' x 2') stone blocks remain. This dive site can be done by boat or from shore.

15. Minneapolis

LORAN: 31226.2/48111.2	LAT 45° 48.32' LON 084° 43.54'
DEPTH: 124 feet	LEVEL: Very Advanced

LOCATION: This wreck lies 1.5 miles north-northwest from Old Mackinac Point.

Carrying a cargo of wheat from Chicago to Buffalo as early in the shipping season as possible, the wooden steamer, *Minneapolis* (226'3" x 34' x 11'2"), was (you guessed it!) holed by ice and sunk with no lives lost on April 4, 1894. Other ships which jumped the gun and sank in the Straits due to ice include the *Eber Ward, Uganda, Northwest* and (the day before the *Minneapolis* sank) the *William H. Barnum.* All are described in this chapter.

The steamer, *Minneapolis*. MPL/WMHS

Mackinac divers Fred Leete and Dick Charboneau located this wreck in 1963. The *Minneapolis* sits upright, largely intact, with her bow broken off. The most interesting items on site are the steam engine, boiler, four-bladed propeller, and her smoke stack which is still upright and rises to a depth of 75'. The usually poor visibility and strong currents make this a site for very experienced divers only. It is 500' southwest of the Mackinac Bridge's main south tower.

16. St. Ignace harbor

DEPTH: 90 feet	LEVEL: Advanced

St. Ignace, Michigan, is one of the oldest city in the United State, and, for most of its history, it relied heavily upon water transportation for people and goods. As a result, its harbor is strewn with an immense variety of artifacts, such as discarded or lost tools, machinery, anchors, pottery, household items, or pieces of wreckage from ships. There are two popular places for divers to enter the harbor: at the northernmost point of the bay at the end of Hazelton Street, and near the south end of the harbor off State Street, right from the city park. Stay out of the busy ferry lanes and display a dive flag.

17. Clam bucket barge

LORAN:	LAT 45° 51.273' LON 084° 41.061'
DEPTH: 115 feet	LEVEL: Advanced

LOCATION: This unidentified shipwreck lies between St. Ignace and Mackinac Island. The clam bucket barge, nicknamed after its metal scoop, was located in Sept., 2000.

18. MACKINAC ISLAND HARBOR WRECK

LORAN: 31180.1/48110.1	LAT	LON
DEPTH: 52 feet	LEVEL: Intermediate	

LOCATION: This wreck lies 150′ inside the east breakwall, Mackinac Island harbor.
Lying upside-down, this unidentified wooden wreck, about 100′ long and 22′ wide, is mounted with a centerboard in her hull. So much of this wreck lies buried in the muddy bottom that penetration is impossible. Beware of heavy boating traffic.

19. ROCK MAZE

LORAN: 31155.3/48080.0	LAT 45° 54.862′ LON 084° 36.402′
DEPTH: To 35 feet	LEVEL: Novice

LOCATION: This site lies about 900′ east of Mackinac Island's Arch Rock.
Caverns, walls and rock pillars with interesting patterns rise 30′ from the bottom.

20. M. STALKER

LORAN: 31213.6/48125.9	LAT 45° 47.38′ LON 084° 41.04′
DEPTH: 85 feet	LEVEL: Advanced

LOCATION: This wreck lies 2.3 miles east of Old Mackinac Point.
The schooner, *M. Stalker* (135′2″ x 25′ x 10′6″), built in 1863 at Milan, Ohio, sank on November 5, 1886, in a collision with the barge, *Muskoka,* which was one of three vessels in tow of the Canadian steamer, *Isaac May.* The *M. Stalker,* loaded with iron ore and riding out a storm at anchor, sank with no lives lost.

This shipwreck was located in July, 1967, by Dick Campbell, Fred Leete, Dick Race and John Steele. With her bow pointing north-northwest, the *M. Stalker* sits upright and intact, except for the stern, which is broken up. Items of interest include her windlass, bilge pump, wire rigging, centerboard and winch, and mast portions. Beware of current and visibility-reducing silt, as well as the Mackinac Island ferry boats, in whose path this wreck lies.

Painting of the *M. Stalker.* GLHS

21. CEDARVILLE

> **LORAN: 31210.7/48130.6**   **LAT 45° 47.13′   LON 084° 40.13′**
> **DEPTH: 40 to 106 feet**   **LEVEL: Intermediate-Advanced**

LOCATION: This wreck lies 2.8 miles east of Old Mackinac Point.

Launched as the *A.F. Harvey* on April 9, 1927, at River Rouge, Michigan, the steel freighter, *Cedarville* (588′3″ x 60′2″ x 30′8″), received her name change in 1957. She sank with the tragic loss of ten lives on May 7, 1965, after a collision in dense fog with the Norwegian freighter, *Topdalsfjord.* All but one of the bodies were recovered.

One of the best known and most frequently visited shipwrecks in the Straits, the immense *Cedarville* lies on her starboard side and remains quite intact, but don't rush inside this

Left: The freighter, *Cedarville.* AUTHOR'S COLLECTION. *Right:* Diver Sharon Troxell peers out of the heavily tilted pilot house. PHOTO BY CRIS KOHL.

Artwork ©Robert McGreevy

wreck. The daring rescue of a desperate diver lost inside the engine room in July, 2000, where an extra tank of air with a regulator had to be passed to him through a porthole before trained cave divers went in and got him out, made it clear that penetration diving is only for the trained, experienced, and totally prepared. Don't even think about doing this large wreck in a single dive; buoy markers are placed at the bow and at the stern. Take your pick.

22. *WILLIAM H. BARNUM*

LORAN: 31205.5/48153.3	LAT 45° 44.42' LON 084° 37.53'
DEPTH: 58 to 75 feet	LEVEL: Intermediate-Advanced

LOCATION: This wreck lies 5.6 miles east-southeast of Old Mackinac Point.

Built in 1873 at Detroit, Michigan, the wooden steamer, *William H. Barnum* (218'6" x 34'8" x 21'4"), foundered with a cargo of corn half a mile off shore on April 3, 1894, with no lives lost after ice opened the seams of her hull.

Located in 1963 by a team lead by Norm McCready of Indianapolis, the *William T. Barnum,* one of the most popular dive sites in the Straits, is upright and largely intact. Fascinating visuals include the boiler, steam engine, windlass and other machinery. The stern was destroyed when she was dynamited for the removal of her rudder. There are numerous opportunities for wreck penetration, particularly at the bow, for those trained and experienced in that type of diving.

Left: The steamer, *William H. Barnum,* at Buffalo, from a contemporary postcard. AUTHOR'S COLLECTION. *Below:* The large boiler is only one of the many machinery items at the *Barnum* site. Diver Joan Forsberg prepares to enter the *Barnum's* hull. PHOTOS BY CRIS KOHL.

23. ALBEMARLE

> **LORAN: 31188.7/48183.1**   **LAT 45° 42.57' LON 084° 33.50'**
> **DEPTH: 12 feet**   **LEVEL: Novice**

LOCATION: This wreck lies 9.4 miles east-southeast from Old Mackinac Point.

The 154' schooner, *Albemarle*, built in 1867 at Buffalo, New York, stranded with an iron ore cargo on November 6, 1867, and broke up. No lives were lost. The wreck lies scattered. Primarily ribs, a centerboard box, and hull planking make up this site.

24. *J. H. OUTHWAITE*

> **LORAN: 31187.3/48184.3**   **LAT 45° 42.28' LON 084° 33.18'**
> **DEPTH: 30 feet**   **LEVEL: Novice**

LOCATION: This wreck lies 9.7 miles southeast of Old Mackinac Point.

Built in 1886 at Cleveland, the 224' wooden steamer, *J.H. Outhwaite,* with a cargo of iron ore, stranded and burned to a complete loss with no lives lost on November 28, 1905, a victim of one of the worst storms in recorded Great Lakes history. Forty ships and almost the same number of lives were lost in this late autumn blizzard. The anchors, engine and boiler were salvaged. What remains today is mostly the hull, much of which is unfortunately covered in a sand bank. The wreck lies north to south, with her smokestack and other pieces of wreckage off the midship port side.

Left: J.H. Outhwaite. AUTHOR'S COLLECTION

25. ST. ANDREW

> **LORAN: 31180.2/48195.1**   **LAT 45° 42.07' LON 084° 31.46'**
> **DEPTH: 62 feet**   **LEVEL: Intermediate-Advanced**

LOCATION: This wreck lies 11.4 miles southeast of Old Mackinac Point.

The 135' schooner, *St. Andrew,* built in 1857 at Milan, Ohio, sank at night with a cargo of corn in a collision with the schooner, *Peshtigo,* on June 26, 1878. No lives were lost from the *St. Andrew,* but the *Peshtigo* also sank, taking two of her crew to the bottom. The *Peshtigo* remains to be found.

The *St. Andrew* sits upright and, for the most part, intact, with the stern broken up but the bow virtually untouched. Her interesting windlass is of an old-fashioned design, and her centerboard box remains intact. There is usually good visibility here with no current.

26. LEVIATHAN

> **LORAN: 31156.5/48228.0**   **LAT 45° 39.65' LON 084° 25.95'**
> **DEPTH: 12 feet**   **LEVEL: Novice**

LOCATION: This wreck lies at the mouth of Duncan Bay, 1.5 miles east-northeast of the mouth of the Cheboygan River.

Built at Buffalo in 1857, the wooden steamer, *Leviathan* (125'2" x 26' x 10'6"), worked as a wrecking tug her entire career, saving ships from destruction. She, however, could not save herself when she caught fire at the Cheboygan, Michigan, dock on November 12, 1891, and burned to a complete loss. She was raised, stripped of any useful gear, and scuttled nearby, out of the way. This broken wreck sits upright, consisting only of large timbers. The site, at least, is weather-protected, and the visibility is usually good.

30. Manitou Passage

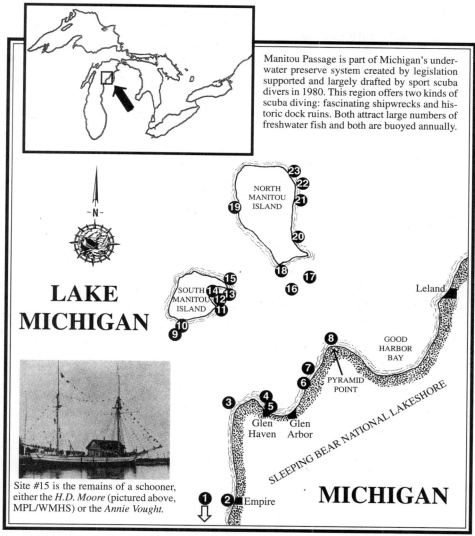

Manitou Passage is part of Michigan's underwater preserve system created by legislation supported and largely drafted by sport scuba divers in 1980. This region offers two kinds of scuba diving: fascinating shipwrecks and historic dock ruins. Both attract large numbers of freshwater fish and both are buoyed annually.

NORTH MANITOU ISLAND

LAKE MICHIGAN

SOUTH MANITOU ISLAND

Leland

GOOD HARBOR BAY

PYRAMID POINT

Glen Haven   Glen Arbor

SLEEPING BEAR NATIONAL LAKESHORE

MICHIGAN

Empire

Site #15 is the remains of a schooner, either the *H.D. Moore* (pictured above, MPL/WMHS) or the *Annie Vought*.

1. Aral dock	9. *Walter L. Frost*	17. *Alva Bradley*
2. Empire dock	10. *Francisco Morazan*	18. Unidentified wreck
3. *James McBride*	11. *Three Brothers*	19. Crescent dock
4. *J. S. Crouse*	12. *P. J. Ralph*	20. Stormer dock
5. Glen Haven dock	13. *Congress*	21. Pickard's wharf
6. Port Oneida dock	14. Burton's wharf	22. *Supply*
7. *Flying Cloud*	15. *Moore/Vought?*	23. *Montauk*
8. *Rising Sun*	16. *William T. Graves*	

1. ARAL DOCK

LORAN: 31899.9/48488.8	LAT 44° 45.49′ LON 086° 03.34′
DEPTH: To 15 feet	LEVEL: Novice

LOCATION: At the end of County Road 610 (Esch Road).

Aral, once a bustling lumber town with a large mill, saw considerable shipping traffic stop at its dock until the timber was depleted and business moved further north in the early 1900's. This site, just off a popular swimming beach with ample parking, boasts underwater pilings that run offshore for about 600′, and sights include anchor chain and a propeller. The National Park Service forbids removal of any items from these waters.

2. EMPIRE DOCK

LORAN: 31895.5/48482.0	LAT 44° 46.24′ LON 086° 04.01′
DEPTH: To 20 feet	LEVEL: Novice

LOCATION: At the municipal park at the western end of the village of Empire.

Also a popular swimming beach with much convenient parking, this site, submerged pilings of a dock which catered to lumber trade ships, lies just off the concrete structures visible on shore. As with every site in this area, shifting sands alternately cover and uncover submerged items. North of this dock, in 12′, lie tree stumps believed to be 3,000 years old.

3. *JAMES McBRIDE*

LORAN: 31864.9/48408.7	LAT 44° 53.69′ LON 086° 04.55′
DEPTH: 5 to 15 feet	LEVEL: Novice

LOCATION: Off Sleeping Bear Point. Use a boat; it's a long shore walk to this site.

The oldest known shipwreck site in this area, the brig, *James McBride* (121′ x 25′), launched on April 1, 1848 at Irving, New York, was perhaps best known in its time as the first vessel to deliver a cargo to Chicago from saltwater (it was salt from the British West Indies in 1848). A powerful autumn gale forced the *James McBride* ashore on October 19, 1857. No lives were lost, but the ship was pounded to pieces. Today, these large pieces prove to be quite interesting (when they are not covered by the constantly shifting sands). The sternpost rises to within 5′ of the surface. This wreck, lying stern to shore, plus the remains of others, can be seen from the top of the dunes at Sleeping Bear Point.

4. *J. S. CROUSE*

LORAN: 31840.7/48401.7	LAT 44° 55.28′ LON 086° 01.30′
DEPTH: 10 to 20 feet	LEVEL: Novice

LOCATION: This wreck lies at Glen Haven dock off County Road 209.

The small wooden steamer, *J.S. Crouse* (89′7″ x 16′8″ x 7′5″), built at Saugatuck,

Michigan, in 1898, burned with a cargo of potatoes and lumber and sank on November 15, 1919, with no casualties. This type of freight vessel, popularly called a "rabbit boat," had its pilot house at the stern (unusual for a Great Lakes ship), and was often seen with its midship area loaded tall with cargo, e.g. lumber or coal.

With roadside parking available, this site is popular as a shore dive. Charred timbers indicate parts of this shipwreck.

The *J.S. Crouse*. MPL/WMHS

5. GLEN HAVEN DOCK

LORAN: 31840.7/48401.7	LAT 44° 55.31′ LON 086° 01.31′
DEPTH: 12 to 25 feet	LEVEL: Novice

LOCATION: Off County Road 209, east of the U.S. Life Saving Service Station in Leeleanau County, and just offshore from the old fruit storage building.

Sites at this submerged lumber dock, marked by several groups of pilings, include a horse-drawn cart which ran on rails and the remains of two broken and scattered shipwrecks.

6. PORT ONEIDA DOCK

LORAN: 31807.4/48397.1	LAT 44° 57.09′ LON 085° 56.44′
DEPTH: 7 to 20 feet	LEVEL: Novice

LOCATION: North of Glen Arbor at the end of Kilderhouse Road.

The usual shifting sands cover and uncover items from this dock's past, as well as the remains of a small schooner which stranded here and lie in about 14′ of water.

7. FLYING CLOUD

LORAN:	LAT 44° 56.19′ LON 085° 57.39′
DEPTH: 4 to 14 feet	LEVEL: Novice

LOCATION: Off the southwest side of Pyramid Point.

Built in 1852 at French Creek, New York, the two-masted schooner, _Flying Cloud_ (124′ x 25′6″), stranded with a cargo of oats on October 29, 1892, after her anchors lost their grip while she tried to ride out the powerful gale which also sank the schooner _Ostrich_ and the steel steamer, _W.H. Gilcher._ No lives were lost from the _Flying Cloud._ Three sections of wooden wreckage lie in the sand and rocks, one in about 5′ and the others in about 14′.

8. RISING SUN

LORAN: 31799.5/48386.8	LAT 44° 58.23′ LON 085° 55.97′
DEPTH: 7 to 12 feet	LEVEL: Novice

LOCATION: About 300′ north of Pyramid Point.

Launched as the _Minnie M._ in 1884 at Detroit, the wooden steamer, _Rising Sun_ (133′3″ x 26′ x 10′8″), received her new name in 1915, just in time for her loss on October 29, 1917. She stranded with a cargo of cedar posts; no lives were lost. The steam engine and prop shaft, plus wooden framing, remain at the site; sometimes the boiler is uncovered.

The _Rising Sun._ MPL/WMHS

9. WALTER L. FROST

LORAN: 31859.0/48339.4	LAT 44° 59.66' LON 086° 08.69'
DEPTH: 10 to 14 feet	LEVEL: Novice

The *Walter L. Frost*. MPL/WMHS

LOCATION: This wreck lies about 600' due south of the very visible wreck of the steel freighter, *Francisco Morazan.*

The wooden steamer, *Walter L. Frost* (235'7" x 36'9" x 12'9"), built in 1883 at Detroit and carrying corn and general merchandise from Chicago to Ogdensburg, NY, stranded during a thick fog on Nov. 4, 1903, and was abandoned 10 days later. After much salvaging over the years, and some unintentional crushing from the *Morazan* in 1960, only the hull's bottom remains. A buoy usually marks her stern.

10. FRANCISCO MORAZAN

LORAN: 31858.5/48339.3	LAT 44° 59.07' LON 086° 08.09'
DEPTH: To 20 feet	LEVEL: Novice

LOCATION: This large wreck, partially above water, lies about 900' off the island.

The *Francisco Morazan*. MPL/WMHS

The most visited shipwreck in the Manitous, the ocean-going steel freighter, *Francisco Morazan* (246'9" x 36'10" x 16'8"), stranded in bad weather on November 29, 1960. No lives were lost and the cargo of lard and hides was salvaged, but the entire ship, launched as the *Arcadia* in Hamburg, Germany, in 1922, remains here. Visiting boaters usually tie off the wreck. The bow is sand-filled, but the machinery in the stern is of interest. Caution: seagull droppings make exploring the rusting, steel superstructure slippery and dangerous.

11. THREE BROTHERS

LORAN: 31839.2/48339.3	LAT 45° 00.54' LON 086° 05.58'
DEPTH: 5 to 45 feet	LEVEL: Novice-Intermediate

LOCATION: This wreck lies a few feet from shore off Sandy Point, S. Manitou Island. The wooden steamer, *Three Brothers* (162' x 31'4" x 11'8"), launched in 1888 at Milwaukee as the *May Durr,* leaking and beached on South Manitou Island on September 27, 1911, was broken by autumn weather with no lives lost. The wreck was covered deeply with sand until early 1996. The sudden appearance of a nearly perfectly intact shipwreck prompted a whirling dervish of scuba activity. The bow is broken, but the stern is intact, although filled with much sand, the weight of which is threatening to destroy its intact nature. Take part in the free diver registration program at the ranger station before diving and obtain an update on the wreck's condition.

The *Three Brothers*. MPL/WMHS

12. *P. J. RALPH*

LORAN: 31839.5/48333.5	LAT 45° 01.11' LON 086° 06.01'
DEPTH: 10 to 45 feet	LEVEL: Novice-Intermediate

LOCATION: This wreck lies at the south end of South Manitou Island harbor.
  The seams opened in heavy weather on the wooden steamer, *P.J. Ralph* (211'4" x 37' x 14'), on September 8, 1924, and she was beached just off this island. Salvage never came for this ship. Built at Marine City, Michigan, in 1889, the *P.J. Ralph's* pulpwood cargo was all that was salvaged. A large part of the hull and all of the steam engine remain at this site.

Left: The *P.J. Ralph* MPL/WMHS *Above:* The steamer, *Congress.* AUTHOR'S COLLECTION.

13. *CONGRESS*

LORAN: 31834.3/48330.4	LAT 45° 01.49' LON 086° 05.45'
DEPTH: 165 feet	LEVEL: Technical

LOCATION: This very deep wreck lies in South Manitou Island harbor.
  The large wooden steamer, *Congress* (267'4" x 35'5" x 14'2"), launched at Cleveland

in 1867 as the *Nebraska*, was waiting out a storm safely tied to the dock in the shelter of South Manitou Island on October 4, 1904, when she caught on fire. The storm suddenly became the lesser of two evils, but the *Congress* burned to a total loss, fortunately with no lives lost. This very deep shipwreck, seemingly out of place in a region where no shipwreck or dock site is deeper than 45′, sits in an area of extreme silt and usually very bad visibility (from 3′ to 8′). Due to its depth, this wreck site is not buoyed.

14. Burton's wharf

LORAN: 31833.4/48334.1	LAT 45° 01.31′ LON 086° 05.01′
DEPTH: 5 to 65 feet	LEVEL: Novice to Advanced

LOCATION: In the center of the crescent which forms South Manitou Island harbor.

At the end of an old roadway that runs through the Bay Campground, you will find the remnants of the old, busy Burton's wharf, the main dock on this island. Because of the high volume of shipping traffic in the old days, and due to the fast-sloping shoreline here, this dock runs as deep as 45′. A bit beyond, in 65′, sits a jeep. If only it could talk...

15. *H. D. Moore/Annie Vought?*

LORAN:	LAT 45° 02.02′ LON 086° 04.44′
DEPTH: 10 to 12 feet	LEVEL: Novice

LOCATION: This wreck lies about 300′ off shore on the north side of Gull Point.

The identity of this broken up schooner is in question. It is either the *H.C. Moore* (103′3″ x 23′5″ x 7′7″), built at Saugatuck, MI, in 1874 and stranded on Sept. 10, 1867, while seeking shelter, no lives lost, or the 199′ *Annie Vought* , built at Fairport, OH, in 1867, and stranded on November 21, 1892, again with no lives lost. Only the hull's bottom remains.

16. *Alva Bradley*

LORAN: 31798.5/48339.2	LAT 45° 02.27′ LON 085° 59.26′
DEPTH: 20 to 27 feet	LEVEL: Novice

LOCATION: This wreck lies on the shoal at the south end of North Manitou Island.

The three-masted schooner, *Alva Bradley* (192′2″ x 32′ x 20′2″), built in 1870 at Cleveland, foundered during a gale with a cargo of steel billets on October 13, 1894, with no lives lost. The site, located by Dave Trotter in 1990, displays the ship's wheel, blocks, chains, deadeyes, belaying pins, keelson, many tools, some machinery and much of the cargo of steel billets.

17. *William T. Graves*

DEPTH: 10′ to 20′ LEVEL: Novice
LORAN: 31802.8/48330.7
LAT 45° 02.95′ LON 086° 00.45′

LOCATION: North Manitou Shoal, far off shore.

The huge, three-masted barkentine, *William T. Graves* (207′ x 35′5″ x 14′2″), launched at Cleveland in 1867, stranded on North Manitou Island during a blinding snowstorm on October 31, 1855. The ship had been heading to Buffalo from Chicago with a corn

The *Alva Bradley.* MPL/WMHS

cargo. A large piece of the stern section lies flat on the sandy bottom. This shallow site is a fair distance off shore; a boat is necessary to reach it.

18. UNIDENTIFIED WRECK (EX-*J. B. NEWLAND*)

> **LORAN: 31803.3/48338.1**   **LAT 45° 02.29'   LON 086° 00.01'**
> **DEPTH: 4 to 10 feet**   **LEVEL: Novice**

LOCATION: This wreck lies off the southern end of North Manitou Island.

The broken up deck and hull of a wooden sailing vessel, with the rudder about 100' to the southwest, comprise this site. Although this is approximately where the schooner, *J.B. Newland,* stranded on September 8, 1910, and for years, divers have been calling this shipwreck the *J.B. Newland,* that vessel was recovered and returned to service under Canadian registry for several more years before finally being scuttled in Lake Ontario in 1929. The identity of these shipwreck pieces remain a mystery.

19. CRESCENT DOCK

> **LORAN: 31802.2/48288.4**   **LAT 45° 06.58'   LON 086° 03.34'**
> **DEPTH: 5 to 25 feet**   **LEVEL: Novice**

LOCATION: On the west side of North Manitou Island, off the big barn.

Many boulders lie interspersed at this site, which is marked by the tops of pilings.

20. STORMER DOCK

> **LORAN: 31784.4/48316.2**   **LAT 45° 05.02'   LON 085° 48.60'**
> **DEPTH: 5 to 20 feet**   **LEVEL: Novice**

LOCATION: Across from the old cemetery on North Manitou Island.

Pilings and some small machinery can be viewed on the gravel bottom.

21. PICKARD'S WHARF

> **LORAN: 31773.7/48296.5**   **LAT 45° 07.16'   LON 085° 58.29'**
> **DEPTH: 5 to 25 feet**   **LEVEL: Novice**

LOCATION: This site lies on the east side of North Manitou Island, about 600 north of the National Park Service dock. Items from bygone eras can be viewed on the sand bottom.

22. SUPPLY

> **LORAN: 31769.8/48285.0**   **LAT 44° 58.22'   LON 085° 58.48'**
> **DEPTH: 8 to 10 feet**   **LEVEL: Novice**

LOCATION: This wreck lies about 200' from shore off Vessel Point.

The brig, *Supply* (132' x 29'3" x 10'5"), built in 1855 at Buffalo, New York, stranded here with a cargo of 300,000 bricks in Nov., 1869. Piles of bricks still lie amidst the wreckage.

23. MONTAUK

> **LORAN: 31759.6/48270.6**   **LAT 45° 09.54'   LON 085° 59.51'**
> **DEPTH: 35 feet**   **LEVEL: Novice**

LOCATION: This wreck lies about 1000' off shore and is usually not buoyed.

The two-masted schooner, *Montauk* (137'5" x 25'9" x 12'6"), built at Oswego, NY, in 1863, stranded in a gale on November 23, 1882. The wreck lies in two sections on rocks.

31. Northeastern Lake Michigan

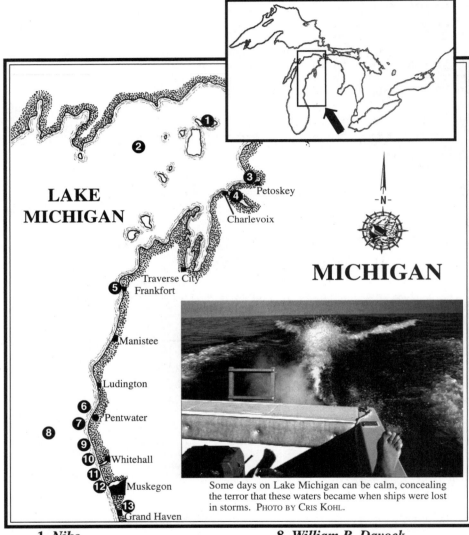

Some days on Lake Michigan can be calm, concealing the terror that these waters became when ships were lost in storms. PHOTO BY CRIS KOHL.

1. *Niko*
2. *Carl D. Bradley*
3. **Petoskey Diver Memorial**
4. *Keuka*
5. *Ida*
6. *Anna C. Minch*
7. *Novadoc*
8. *William B. Davock*
9. *Brightie*
10. *State of Michigan*
11. *Salvor*
12. *Henry Cort*
13. *Manistee*

1. NIKO

LORAN: 31451.0/48006.8	LAT	LON
DEPTH: 35 feet	LEVEL: Novice	

LOCATION: This wreck lies between Garden Island and Hog Island.

The wooden steamer, *Niko* (189' x 35' x 13'), built at Trenton, Michigan, in 1889, sprang a leak and sank on November 2, 1924, with no lives lost. This wreck lies broken up over a wide area.

The *Niko*. MPL/WMHS

2. CARL D. BRADLEY

LORAN: 32427.2/49190.4	LAT 43° 29.84' LON 086° 29.93'
DEPTH: 300 to 365 feet	LEVEL: Technical

LOCATION: This wreck lies almost six miles west-northwest of Boulder Reef Light.

Launched on April 9, 1927, at Lorain, Ohio, the steel freighter, *Carl D. Bradley* (623'2" x 65'2" x 30'2"), is one of a handful of modern, but very tragic, shipwrecks in the Great Lakes. The ship broke in two in a violent storm on November 18, 1958, with the loss of 33 of her 35 crew, most of whom came from Rogers City, Michigan. This is the second-largest shipwreck in the lakes, the *Edmund Fitzgerald* being longer (729' in length). The wreck lies deep in an area of predominantly low visibility, with the pilot house being the shallowest point at 300'. Cameras on remote-operated vehicles (ROV's) have taken underwater

The sunken *Carl D. Bradley*. Artwork ©Robert McGreevy

images of this wreck, but the first diver to reach the *Carl D. Bradley* was Detroit-area technical diver, Mirek Standowicz, on July 6, 2001, using tri-mix gases.

3. PETOSKEY DIVER MEMORIAL

DEPTH: About 30 feet	LEVEL: Novice

LOCATION: This site sits about 1,000' off shore east of the Petoskey municipal marina.

This unusual site consists of several plaques honoring scuba divers who have contributed to the sport (e.g. Dr. William Kenner, who was the driving force behind the legislation to protect Michigan shipwrecks). The centerpiece is a marble crucifix, intended for a church but arriving from Italy slightly damaged. The company allowed divers to place it underwater as a memorial. Park your car at a waterfront park along Lake St. Beware of boating traffic.

4. KEUKA

LORAN: 31495.5/48304.4	LAT 45° 18.40' LON 085° 14.34'
DEPTH: 35 to 50 feet	LEVEL: Novice-Intermediate

LOCATION: This wreck lies in Lake Charlevoix, half a mile from shore and about 2.5 miles from the point where this lake meets Lake Michigan.

Launched at Mount Clemens, Michigan, on June 19, 1889, as the *A. Stewart,* the lumber schooner-barge, *Keuka* (172' x 32'4" x 12'), given her last name in 1925, reportedly spent her final years afloat as an offshore speakeasy in the Charlevoix area. Scuttled in the early

1930's because she had become an eyesore, the *Keuka* sits upright and her bow cabins can

be penetrated by trained and experienced divers. Penetration to the cargo holds is possible from a forward hatch only, as all the other hatches were covered with a hardwood dance floor. Summer offers the poorest visibility due to algae growth; spring and autumn are the best diving time, although ice diving at this site is also popular.

The schooner-barge, *Keuka.* MPL/WMHS

5. IDA

DEPTH: 10 to 15 feet	LEVEL: Novice

LOCATION: About 200' off shore from the Congregational Church Assembly beach access (ask permission if you plan to dive from there) two miles north of Frankfort, MI.

The three-masted schooner, *Ida* (120'4" x 27' x 8'3"), built at Milwaukee in 1867, was abandoned by her crew in a raging storm when she began to founder on Sept. 29, 1908. She drifted to shore and broke up with a lumber cargo. Much wood and anchor chain remain.

6. ANNA C. MINCH

Bow: LORAN: 32326.3/49029.9	LAT 43° 45.68' LON 086° 27.79'
Stern: LORAN: 32327.1/49030.7	LAT 43° 45.60' LON 086° 27.87'
DEPTH: 36 to 45 feet	LEVEL: Intermediate

LOCATION: This wreck lies about 1.5 miles south of Pentwater, Michigan.

The steel freighter, *Anna C. Minch* (380' x 50' x 28'), built at Cleveland in 1903, foundered with everyone on board (24 people) and a cargo of coal in the notoriously severe Armistice Day Storm of November 11, 1940 (which also sank the freighters, *Novadoc,* see site #7, and *William B. Davock,* see site #8). This is a huge site of steel wreckage.

Above: The *Anna C. Minch.* REV. PETER VAN DER LINDEN COLLECTION. *Right:* The wrecked *Novadoc.* AUTHOR'S COLLECTION.

7. NOVADOC

LORAN: 32366.2/49064.4	LAT 43° 41.61' LON 086° 31.08'
DEPTH: 12 to 15 feet	LEVEL: Novice

LOCATION: This wreck lies about halfway between Ludington and Whitehall, off Juniper Beach near the town of Pentwater, Michigan.

Another of the three ships which fell victim to the severe and tragic Armistice Day Storm of November 11, 1940, the steel freighter, *Novadoc* (252'8" x 43'3" x 17'8"), stranded and broke in half with the loss of two lives and her coal cargo. A few men on board the small fish tug, *Three Brothers,* overcame great difficulties posed by the violent, towering seas and, with a superb display of seamanship, manoeuvered close enough to the shipwreck to rescue the remaining 17 crewmembers. The *Novadoc* had been built at Wallsend-on-Tyne, England in 1928. Today, this steel shipwreck lies broken up in shallow water.

8. WILLIAM B. DAVOCK

> **LORAN:** Bow: 32402.2/49065.9 Stern: 32402.6/49066.1
> **DEPTH: 215 to 240 feet**   **LEVEL: Technical**

LOCATION: This wreck lies 2.9 miles off Little Sable Light.

The third steel freighter lost in the Armistice Day Storm of November 11, 1941, the *William B. Davock* (420′ x 52′ x 23′), catastrophically foundered with all 32 hands and her coal cargo. This ship, built in 1907 at St. Clair, Michigan, and located in deep water in 1982, may have collided with the *Anna C. Minch,* which also sank with all hands (see site #6), but evidence is lacking.

The *William P. Davock*. REV. PETER VAN DER LINDEN COLLECTION

9. BRIGHTIE

> **LORAN: 32427.4/49190.4**   **LAT 43° 29.75′ LON 086° 29.99′**
> **DEPTH: 70 feet**   **LEVEL: Advanced**

LOCATION: This wreck lies about 8 miles north of Whitehall, Michigan.

The schooner-barge, *Brightie* (182′ x 33′2″ x 13′), launched at Cleveland in 1868, foundered with a cargo of pulpwood on August 23, 1928. No lives were lost. The *Brightie,* located by Gene Turner, sits 1.5 miles off shore, intact and penetrable.

10. STATE OF MICHIGAN

> **LORAN: 32453.7/49263.5** **LAT 43° 23.21′ LON 086° 27.91′**
> **DEPTH: 75 feet** **LEVEL: Advanced**

LOCATION: This wreck lies about two miles northwest of Whitehall, Michigan.

A connecting rod from her steam engine accidentally piercing her hull, the wooden steamer, *State of Michigan* (165′ x 29′ x 10′), sank with no lives lost on October 18, 1901. The vessel was launched as the *Depere* in 1873 at Manitowoc, WI. She sits on a sandy bottom, upright and intact except for her stern, which hit the lake bottom first and hard.

11. SALVOR

> **LORAN: 32467.1/49355.9** **LAT 43° 15.49′ LON 086° 22.19′**
> **DEPTH: 25 to 30 feet** **LEVEL: Novice**

LOCATION: This wreck lies almost three miles north of the Muskegon Lighthouse.

The pseudo-whaleback steamer, *Turret Chief* (253′ x 44′ x 22′), built in England in 1896, was reduced to a barge in 1927 and renamed *Salvor*. She foundered in a storm on Sept. 26, 1930, with 5 lives lost. The wreck sits upright, partially buried in sand.

The *State of Michigan.* MPL/WMHS

The *Salvor.* MPL/WMHS

The *Manistee.* AUTHOR'S COLLECTION

The wrecked *Henry Cort.* MPL/WMHS

12. HENRY CORT

> **DEPTH: 48 to 55 feet** **LEVEL: Intermediate**

LOCATION: This wreck lies alongside the north Muskegon, Michigan, breakwall.

The whaleback steamer, *Henry Cort* (320′ x 42′ x 25′), built at Superior, WI, in 1892 as the *Pillsbury,* stranded here on Nov. 30, 1934, with one life lost. She lies broken and scattered.

13. MANISTEE

> **LORAN: 32472.9/49487.1** **LAT 43° 04.75′ LON 086° 12.17′**
> **DEPTH: 25 feet** **LEVEL: Novice-Intermediate**

LOCATION: In Spring Lake (which flows into Lake Michigan), at Ferrysburg, MI. The steamer, *Manistee* (161′ x 32′ x 17′7″), burned at her dock on June 28, 1914.

32. Southeastern Lake Michigan

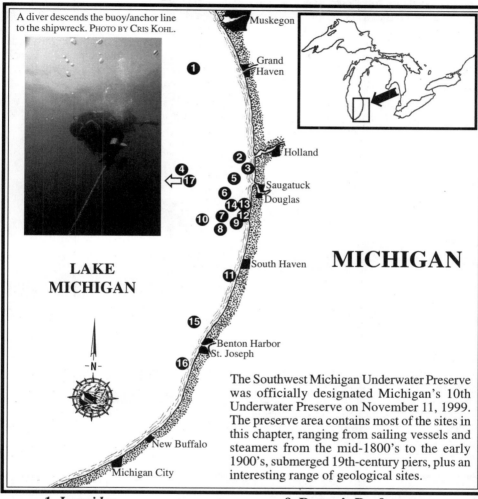

A diver descends the buoy/anchor line to the shipwreck. PHOTO BY CRIS KOHL.

Muskegon

Grand Haven

Holland

Saugatuck

Douglas

South Haven

MICHIGAN

LAKE MICHIGAN

- N -

Benton Harbor
St. Joseph

New Buffalo

Michigan City

The Southwest Michigan Underwater Preserve was officially designated Michigan's 10th Underwater Preserve on November 11, 1999. The preserve area contains most of the sites in this chapter, ranging from sailing vessels and steamers from the mid-1800's to the early 1900's, submerged 19th-century piers, plus an interesting range of geological sites.

1. *Ironsides*
2. **27-foot sailboat**
3. **Crane and barge**
4. **North shore tug**
5. *Francie*
6. **Hatch cover**
7. **South Haven clay bank**
8. *Verano*
9. **Donny's Reef**
10. *Rockaway*
11. *City of Green Bay*
12. **Pier Cove**
13. **Glenn Pier**
14. **John Butler II clay banks**
15. *Havana*
16. **Grand Mere Rocks**
17. *Chicora*

1. IRONSIDES

LORAN: 32525.20/49494.50	LAT 43° 02.903′ LON 086° 19.138′
DEPTH: 109 to 122 feet	LEVEL: Advanced

LOCATION: This wreck lies about four miles west of Grand Haven, Michigan.

The wooden, twin-propellered steamer, *Ironsides* (218′8″ x 31′7″ x 12′9″), built in 1864 at Cleveland, foundered in heavy seas on September 15, 1873, with a cargo of grain, pork, flour and passengers; 21 of the 50 people on board perished.

This shipwreck's stern, with its twin propellers and rudder, sits at the shallower end, in 109′ of water, while the broken up bow rests in 122′. The twin hogging arches sag towards the center of the hull in midship, and rise above the boilers, piping and engine. This wreck is just outside the Southwest Michigan Underwater Preserve. However, the removal of anything from this site is a violation of state and/or federal laws.

The steamer, *Ironsides,* from *American Steam Vessels,* 1895. Drawing by Samuel Ward Stanton. AUTHOR'S COLLECTION.

2. 27-FOOT SAILBOAT

LORAN: 32604.5/49681.9	LAT 42° 45.73′ LON 086° 14.84′
DEPTH: 22 feet	LEVEL: Novice

LOCATION: This small, modern wreck lies off Holland, Michigan.

This 27-foot sailboat is usually marked with a small, plastic buoy, and is a popular site among local divers.

3. CRANE AND BARGE

LORAN: 32616.3/49713.1	LAT 42° 42.71' LON 086° 13.92'
DEPTH: 45 to 55 feet	LEVEL: Intermediate

LOCATION: This site is about one mile off shore between Holland and Saugatuck.
This unidentified barge and crane were apparently lost in a storm while under tow. The wooden barge sits somewhat settled in the sand bottom, while **the crane (LORAN: 32616.4/ 49713.2   GPS: LAT 42° 42.75' LON 086° 13.85')** lies nearby.

4. NORTH SHORE TUG

LORAN: 32666.87/49732.95	LAT 42° 40.165' LON 086° 19.441'
DEPTH: 150 feet	LEVEL: Technical

LOCATION: This wreck lies about 8 miles off Saugatuck, Michigan.
This old tugboat was towed out of Saugatuck harbor and scuttled. It lies in deep water pointing east. Penetration is possible at this site for trained and experienced divers. Beware of snagged fishing lines and loose railing and other items at the site which could cause entanglement. The wheel house sits upside-down about 30' to the southwest of the hull.

5. *FRANCIE*

LORAN: 32644.7/49724.1	LAT 42° 41.350' LON 086° 16.932'
DEPTH: 92 to 102 feet	LEVEL: Advanced

LOCATION: This wreck lies about two miles west of Saugatuck harbor.
The sailing vessel, *Francie,* was a Chesapeake Bay oyster dredge working in the

commercial fishing industry before being converted to a passenger/pleasure boat. The vessel sank at her dock in the 1980's, when local divers reportedly raised the hulk and scuttled her.

6. HATCH COVER

LORAN:	LAT 42° 38.920′ LON 086° 14.517′
DEPTH: 50 feet	LEVEL: Intermediate

This lone piece of wreckage (a search for its ship/wreck has been made in close proximity to the hatch, but with no luck) is home to a fair number of fish.

7. SOUTH HAVEN CLAY BANK

LORAN: 32706.1/49840.4	LAT 42° 30.454′ LON 086° 15.737′
DEPTH: 50 to 60 feet	LEVEL: Intermediate

Small grottos, trenches and projections rising to 15′ in height are part of this multi-acre ancient beach zone, formed thousands of years ago as the last Ice Age glaciers melted.

8. VERANO

LORAN: 32707.72/49843.95	LAT 42° 30.21′ LON 086° 15.96′
DEPTH: 50 feet	LEVEL: Inermediate

LOCATION: This wreck lies near the Clay Banks about 7 miles north of South Haven.

The pleasure yacht, *Verano* (88′3″ x 16′ x 8′), constructed at Morris Heights, New York, at the height of the "Roaring '20's" (1925), foundered with all three

Artwork ©Valerie Olson-van Heest/Southwest Michigan Underwater Preserve

Southwest Michigan Underwater Preserve Committee

The *Verano*. MPL/WMHS

people on board on August 28, 1946. Located in September, 1994, by scuba divers Tom Tanczos and Robert Trowbridge, the *Verano's* site highlights include the ship's wheel, windlass, compass, pottery, twin engines, propeller and the ignition key still in place. The bow and the stern sections lie 185' apart.

9. DONNY'S REEF

> **LORAN: 32745.51/49890.85** **LAT 42° 25.484' LON 086° 16.999'**
> **DEPTH: 25 to 40 feet** **LEVEL: Novice-Intermediate**

LOCATION: This site lies several miles north of South Haven and 1/2 mile off shore.
Concrete stuctures and other manmade items were dumped among the natural glacial formations here, and as a result, the reef hosts a variety of fish life.

10. *ROCKAWAY*

> **LORAN: 32747.0/49878.1** **LAT 42° 25.63' LON 086° 17.65'**
> **DEPTH: 70 feet** **LEVEL: Advanced**

LOCATION: This wreck lies 2 miles off shore and 2.5 miles northwest of South Haven.
Launched in October, 1866, at Oswego, New York, the schooner scow, *Rockaway* (106' x 24' x 7'), foundered in a late season storm on November 18, 1891, with a load of lumber. No lives were lost.

This wreck, located accidentally by a fisherman in Sept., 1983, was almost completely excavated by marine archaeologists in 1984; most of her artifacts, such as the ship's wheel, were recovered and conserved for museum exhibition. The wreck itself, in three main sections, still exhibits her upright centerboard box, anchor chain and a windlass about 35' forward of the bow.

SOUTH HAVEN UNDERWATER ARCHAEOLOGICAL RESEARCH PROJECT
Lake Michigan Maritime Museum

11. CITY OF GREEN BAY

LORAN: 32773.4/49926.6	LAT 42° 22.01' LON 086° 17.97'
DEPTH: 6 to 15 feet	LEVEL: Novice

LOCATION: This wreck lies close to shore off South Haven, Michigan.

The three-masted schooner, *Green Bay* (128'5" x 24'5" x 12'5"), was prone to wanderlust and collisions. She carried cargoes to the British Isles and South America, and worked for a while in the Caribbean before returning to the Great Lakes. Meanwhile, she collided with another vessel on two separate occasions, plus she struck an unidentified obstruction which caused her damage, and later stranded near Alpena, Michigan, but was pulled off and repaired. On October 3, 1887, her time ran out when she stranded two miles south of South Haven in a fierce storm (which also claimed the nearby schooner, *Havana,* both ships coincidentally loaded with iron ore for St. Joseph, Michigan). The U.S. Life Saving Service crew's out-of-character bungled rescue efforts (only one crewmember from the seven was recovered alive), caused head-rolling controversy. This wreck has

Artwork ©Valerie Olson-van Heest/South-west Michigan Underwater Preserve

Vessel Type: Schooner
Location: S. of South Haven
Depth: 5-10 feet
Loran C: N/A - Shore Dive
Date Surveyed: July 1996
© Drawing by Valerie Olson

washed so close to shore over the years that it is now a shore dive. The keelson, centerboard box and frames remain. From South Haven, take Business I-96 south to Blue Star Hwy. Go northwest to 76th to the stop sign. Go west on 13th, cross the bridge and park at the dead end. Walk to the beach, cross the breakwall and walk another 150 paces north. From here, swim straight out into the water. Or get a boat and use GPS.

12. PIER COVE

LORAN: 32667.1/49793.5	LAT 42° 35.16' LON 086° 14.29'
DEPTH: 5 to 20 feet	LEVEL: Novice

LOCATION: This pier lies about about 14 miles north of South Haven, Michigan.

The mid-1800's community of Pier Cove was one of the busiest ports on Lake Michigan, with steamers bringing lumber, fruit and passengers. But commercial routes changed over the years, and, by 1917, the piers were no longer used because commercial activity had ceased. Today, they make an interesting shore dive, revealing numerous small artifacts from the boom years.

Take US 31 to Hwy 89, go west to 70th Street, go south to the historic marker for Pier Cove. Park in the public parking area and head north on the beach, keeping an eye out for a piling visible from shore. That's the dive site; go from there.

13. GLENN PIER

LORAN: 32697.5/49833.5	LAT 42° 31.22' LON 086° 15.20'
DEPTH: 5 to 20 feet	LEVEL: Novice

LOCATION: This pier lies about 10 miles north of South Haven, Michigan.

This once-busy community pier was about 650' long in its heyday when local farmers could get their produce, mostly fruit, to the large Chicago market within one day. The lumber trade and, later, the resort industry, also accounted for considerable maritime traffic to this pier. Today, pilings poking their heads out of the water are the only above-water reminders of those old days. The site includes underwater views of old tools, bottles and machinery.

To reach this shore dive site, take 96 to exit 30, go south to the community of Glenn, go west on 114th to a two-track road which will take you to the shoreline. Do not dive here in heavy seas, as entries and exits become dangerous, and the visibility will be reduced to very low levels.

Parking is a problem on summer weekends because this site is popular with swimmers.

14. JOHN BUTLER II CLAY BANKS

LORAN:	LAT 42° 34.964' LON 086° 15.358'
DEPTH: 50 to 55 feet	LEVEL: Intermediate

LOCATION: This site lies off Pier Cove, Michigan.

Originally mistaken for shipwreck debris in 1998 during a sidescan sonar survey, these irregular, underwater peaks and valleys offer an interesting close-up view of the remnants of glacial movement.

15. HAVANA

LORAN: 32888.1/50024.9	LAT 42° 11.690′ LON 086° 25.631′
DEPTH: 52 feet	LEVEL: Intermediate

LOCATION: This wreck lies about one mile off shore and six miles north of St. Joseph. The two-masted schooner, *Havana* (135′ x 25′ x 10′), built at Oswego, New York, in 1871, foundered with her iron ore cargo during the same storm that claimed the nearby *City of Green Bay* (see site #11) on October 3, 1887, with the loss of three of the seven lives on board. Their ship sinking fast, the men had all clambered into the rigging, but when the main-mast toppled over, three of them drowned. The bold crew of the tug, *Hannah Sullivan,* rescued the remaining four, heroically triumphing over the heavy seas and howling winds.

Vessel Type: Schooner
Location: 6 Miles N of St. Joseph
Depth: 52 feet
Loran C: 32888.1 50024.9
Date Surveyed: July 1995

Artwork ©Valerie Olson-van Heest/Southwest Michigan Underwater Preserve

Southwest Michigan Underwater Preserve Committee

Located by Gene Turner, the wreck of the *Havana,* although broken up, features the keelson, hull framing, centerboard box and hanging knees.

16. GRAND MERE ROCKS

LORAN: 33013.58/50135.37	LAT 42° 00.328′ LON 086° 33.753′
DEPTH: 15 to 23 feet	LEVEL: Novice

LOCATION: This site lies about 3/4 of a mile off shore from St. Joseph, Michigan.

This unique geological formation runs parallel to the shoreline for a length of about one mile. As usual, fly a dive flag. Boating traffic is heavier here than elsewhere in the area.

17. CHICORA

The *Chicora.* MPL/WMHS

LOCATION: In about 300′ of water off Holland, MI.

Launched at Detroit in 1892, the wooden steamer, *Chicora* (198′5″ x 35′ x 13′6″), disappeared completely with all 23 crew and 1 passenger on Jan. 21, 1895. The long-sought *Chicora,* sitting upright, was finally found between Holland and Saugatuck by Dave Trotter under contract to the Southwest Michigan Underwater Preserve in May, 2001. Video images show cargo hatches, capstans, a smokestack and a whistle.

33. Sites off Indiana

The five-masted schooner, *David Dows,* was wrecked in Lake Michigan in 1889. She was the largest sailing ship ever constructed on the Great Lakes, but her career record was disappointing. Read about her in this chapter. AUTHOR'S COLLECTION

- N -

LAKE MICHIGAN

Chicago

6 **5**

New Buffalo

3 **2** **1**

Michigan City

4

Gary

INDIANA

ILLINOIS

MICHIGAN

1. *Frank W. Wheeler*
2. *Eureka*
3. *Muskegon*

4. *J. D. Marshall*
5. *Louisville*
6. *David Dows*

1. FRANK W. WHEELER

LORAN: 33228.7/50278.9   LAT 41° 44.64' LON 086° 51.98'
DEPTH: 30 to 40 feet   LEVEL: Novice

LOCATION: About 1,200' off shore, 2.5 miles east of Michigan City, Indiana.

The wooden steamer, *F.W. Wheeler* (265'5" x 40'5" x 19'4"), built at West Bay City, Michigan, in 1887, stranded about a quarter of a mile off shore with a cargo of 2,100 tons of coal from Buffalo to Chicago during a blizzard on December 3, 1893, and became a total loss. The local lifesaving crew rescued all 16 sailors on the *F.W. Wheeler* in two trips. When asked how he ran ashore at Michigan City when he was heading for Chicago, Captain George Trotter stated, "I can only account for it by the fact that my compass was out of order, and led me to this side of the lake. Early the previous evening, I shut down the speed and did not know how many miles I had gone. Consequently I lost reckoning...."

Broken into three main sections, this wreck is covered/uncovered by shifting sands and offers newly-exposed portions each spring. A huge winch sits on a large portion of decking.

2. EUREKA

LORAN: 33237.4/50281.2   LAT 41° 44.28' LON 086° 53.06'
DEPTH: 30 feet   LEVEL: Novice

LOCATION: This wreck lies just to the north-northeast of Michigan City, Indiana.

The 240' sidewheeler, *Eureka,* built at Newport (now Marine City), Michigan, in 1864, stranded and was a total loss on October 12, 1873. The wreck lies broken up and scattered.

3. MUSKEGON

LORAN: 33266.0/50293.5   LAT 41° 42.71' LON 086° 56.15'
DEPTH: 25 feet   LEVEL: Novice

LOCATION: About 1/2 mile off shore, two miles west of Michigan City, Indiana, harbor.

Launched as the attractive passenger steamer, *Peerless,* in 1872 at Cleveland, and running mostly between Chicago and Duluth, in 1907, this now-aging, wooden vessel was renamed *Muskegon* (211' x 39'9" x 12'5") and converted first to a bulk freighter and later to a sandsucker. It was a sad swan song to a long career. The ship burned to a total loss at

Left: The *Muskegon* as the passenger ship, *Peerless. Above:* The charred remains of the *Muskegon.* BOTH REV. PETER VAN DER LINDEN COLLECTION

Michigan City on October 6, 1910. No lives were lost. The burned out hulk was towed beyond the harbor and abandoned.

4. J. D. MARSHALL

LORAN: 33329.3/50309.3   LAT 41° 40.04' LON 087° 04.20'
DEPTH: 32 feet   LEVEL: Novice

LOCATION: This wreck lies about 1/3 mile north of the water tower near the western boundary of the Indiana Dunes National Park, halfway between Gary and Michigan City.

The wooden steamer, *J.D. Marshall* (154'5" x 33'5" x 12'), built in 1891 at South Haven, Michigan, capsized with the loss of four lives on June 10, 1911, and floated close to shore several days later. Ironically, the company which lost the *Muskegon* (see site #3) used the insurance money which they received from that loss to buy the *J.C. Marshall*. Tools and machinery lie on the lake bottom near the wreck, the huge propeller and boiler being the main components here.

The steamer, *J.D. Marshall*. MPL/WMHS

5. *LOUISVILLE*

LORAN: 33366.0/50205.6	LAT 41° 46.16' LON 087° 20.39'
DEPTH: 60 feet	LEVEL: Intermediate-Advanced

LOCATION: 7 miles off shore; 3 miles east-southeast of the *David Dows* (site #6).

The wooden steamer, *Louisville* (137'5" x 25'6" x 11'2"), launched at Buffalo, New York, in 1853, sank following a fire on board on September 29, 1857. One life was lost, that of the *Louisville's* fireman, who drowned when his lifeboat capsized in the turbulence created by the still-revolving propeller as his ship was sinking. The *Louisville,* one of the first propeller-driven vessels on the Great Lakes, lies just west of the Indiana-Illinois state line. The site includes the upright engine, boiler, part of the smokestack, propeller, anchor chain and much piping and wooden hull and decking. The Underwater Archaeological Society of Chicago buoys this site annually.

Artwork © Underwater Archaeological Society of Chicago. Site drawing by Sam Frank.

A diver explores the upright, 8-legged steam engine of the historic ship, *Louisville*. PHOTO BY JIM JARECKI.

6. DAVID DOWS

LORAN: 33383.6/50201.7	LAT 41° 45.95′ LON 087° 23.58′
DEPTH: 40 to 45 feet	LEVEL: Intermediate

LOCATION: This wreck lies north of Indiana Shoals, five miles off the nearest shore.

Launched amidst great fanfare at Toledo, Ohio, on April 21, 1881, the 1,347-net-ton schooner, *David Dows* (265′4″ x 37′6″ x 18′), it was hoped, would revive the use of sailing ships over steamships for commercial purposes on the Great Lakes. She was, after all, the largest schooner in the world. The solid logs which comprised the masts, from bow to stern, reached a height, respectively, of 93′, 97′, 97′, 93′, and 88′. Add to that the topmasts, at 65′ in height each, and which were attached as extensions to the tops of the masts, and the *David Dows'* mainmast towered an incredible 162′ above the ship's deck! The mighty vessel was designed to carry an impressive 140,000 bushels of grain, and she had two, not just one, centerboards. The ship was designed to be handled by a relatively small crew of only 12 sailors, about twice the number that Great Lakes schooners typically carried.

But the largest (and the only five-masted) schooner on the inland seas proved too difficult to maneuver in the confined waters of the Great Lakes, even with her competent crew and a steam donkey engine to raise and lower her gigantic, heavy sails. After two collisions, the second one involving the loss of four lives, this maritime white elephant was demoted to a towbarge. As such, the *David Dows,* carrying a cargo of coal, foundered in a storm while at anchor on November 30, 1889, with no lives lost.

Located in 1964, much of her hull remains intact, especially the vast centerboad box, rudder, and rudder post. But at that shallow a depth, the mightiest of the Great Lakes sailing ships ever constructed on these fresh waters was soon, for the most part, flattened by time and nature. In spite of that, many items of interest remain at this relatively shallow site. Coal, likely from her last cargo, lies scattered near the centerboard box. The double-planked hull construction is quite visible as the diver swims around the perimeter of the hull. The starboard side has broken away and lies flat on the lake floor. At this depth, the visiting diver has time to explore all around the actual hull itself, just off the main wreck site.

The *David Dows* is a prime case where "big" was not necessarily "better."

The immense schooner, *David Dows,* the largest sailing vessel ever built on the Great Lakes. MPL/WMHS

34. Chicago

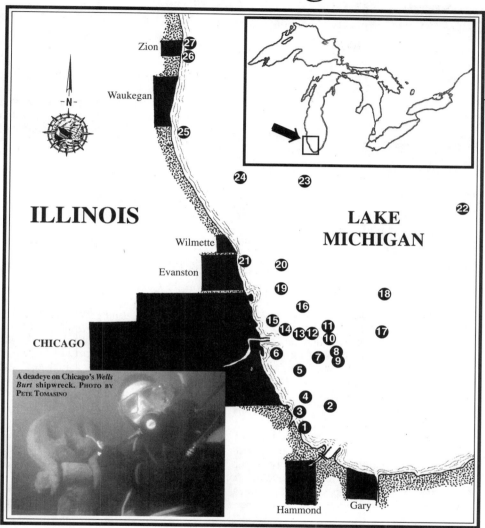

A deadeye on Chicago's *Wells Burt* shipwreck. PHOTO BY PETE TOMASINO

1. *George F. Williams*
2. *Barge #2*
3. *Material Service*
4. *Tacoma*
5. *Illinois* and *Holly*
6. *Rainbow*
7. Four-Mile Crib
8. Caissons
9. East tug
10. South tug/Tym barge
11. North tug
12. *Iowa*
13. Mike's wreck
14. *Flora M. Hill*
15. North Ave. schooner
16. *Wings of the Wind*
17. Box barge
18. *Rotarian*
19. *Lucille*
20. *Wells Burt*
21. *George Morley*
22. *UC-97*
23. *St. Mary*
24. *Lady Elgin*
25. *Seabird*
26. Zion schooners
27. Zion minesweeper

1. GEORGE F. WILLIAMS

LORAN: 33446.7/50230.6	LAT 41° 41.82' LON 087° 30.67'
DEPTH: 15 feet	LEVEL: Novice

LOCATION: This wreck lies about one mile west of the Hammond Water Intake plant.

Launched on July 24, 1889, at West Bay City, Michigan, the wooden steamer, *George F. Williams* (280' x 41'4" x 20'3"), was abandoned in 1913 and reportedly towed to her final resting place about 400' off shore and sunk on April 21, 1915. It took until 1988 for divers to locate this wreck; she was found by Tim Early. Besides her long, flattened hull, the site exhibits her scotch boiler and propeller. The Underwater Archaeological Society of Chicago did an extensive survey of this site in 2001. Beware of boating traffic, particularly annoying little "water fleas."

The *George F. Williams.* GLHS

2. BARGE #2 (CAR FERRY #2)

LORAN: 33407.62/50205.75	LAT 41° 44.82' LON 087° 26.99'
DEPTH: 42 feet	LEVEL: Intermediate

LOCATION: This wreck lies about three miles off the Calumet breakwall.

Barge #2 (324'6" x 44' x 11') was part of the Lake Michigan (Railroad) Car Ferry Transportation Company fleet which included identical *Barge #3* and *Barge #4*, both of which sank in Lake Erie (and are in this book), and *Barge #1*, converted to a freight barge after the car ferry business failed, and which sank off Alpena, MI (and is also in this book).

Built at West Bay City, Michigan, in 1895, *Barge #2* struggled in a Lake Michigan storm on September 29, 1906. She was carrying 30 railroad cars, about half filled with lumber and the rest with iron ore. Her seams opened and she capsized with her heavy cargo just inside the breakwall at Chicago, with the loss of three lives. In the spring of 1907, the U.S. Army Corps of Engineers towed the hulk out into the lake and sank her at her present location. Then realizing that she lay in the shipping lane and was a danger to navigation, they dynamited her in August, 1907. The wreck lies in many pieces, scattered over a wide area.

Barge #2, with railroad cars. AUTHOR'S COLLECTION

3. MATERIAL SERVICE

LORAN: 33426.3/50201.4	LAT 41° 44.50' LON 087° 30.50'
DEPTH: 22 to 38 feet	LEVEL: Novice-Intermediate

LOCATION: This wreck lies about 2000' northeast of Calumet Harbor Light, Illinois.

The barge, *Material Service* (239'7" x 40'1" x 13'9"), built in 1929 at Sturgeon Bay, Wisconsin, foundered with terrible loss of life (15 died from the 22 who were on board) with a cargo of sand and gravel on July 29, 1936.

The wreck is marked by buoy "WR10." Anchor

Material Service. AUTHOR'S COLLECTION

next to the wreck, since it is illegal to tie a boat to a government buoy. Visibility is usually low (about 7), but can improve considerably after several calm days in early spring. The ship's large holds are open and invite exploration by trained and experienced penetration divers. Warning: the silt stirs up easily and reduces visibility to zero! The stern shows scattered steel and pipes (signs of dynamiting), and the propellers are still in place, although half buried in the lake bottom.

4. TACOMA

> **LORAN: 33417.7/50178.9**   **LAT 41° 46.22′   LON 087° 31.37′**
> **DEPTH: 27 to 35 feet**   **LEVEL: Novice-Intermediate**

LOCATION: This wreck lies near Chicago's Clark Point Shoal, 2.5 miles north-northwest of the Calumet Harbor Light.

The tug, *Tacoma*. MPL/WMHS   The *Tacoma's* steam engine. PHOTO BY JIM JARECKI.

The wooden, steam-powered tug, *Tacoma* (73'4" x 18' x 9'), foundered with no lives lost on November 4, 1929. Built in 1894 at Benton Harbor, Michigan, the little tug had simply grown too old to handle Lake Michigan. The wreck sits on a sand bottom with the propeller and steam engine the highlights of this site, which is buoyed annually by the Underwater Archaeological Society of Chicago with help from dive shops and sponsors.

Tacoma's rudder and propeller. Photo by Jim Jarecki.

Artwork © Underwater Archaeological Society of Chicago. Site drawing by Valerie Olson-van Heest.

5. *Illinois* Dredge and *Holly* barge

LORAN: 33403.1/50128.4	LAT 41° 49.99' LON 087° 34.26'
DEPTH: 24 to 33 feet	LEVEL: Novice

Artwork © Underwater Archaeological Society of Chicago. Site drawing by Sam Frank.

LOCATION: About two miles east of 33rd Street, Chicago.

The hydraulic sand dredge, *Illinois,* reputedly the largest on the Great Lakes at the time, sank some time in the 1920's or 1930's. Much of the sand along Chicago's shoreline was carried by this dredge. Notable features of this site include a large pump, boom supports and an auger.

On May 6, 2000, a 120' long barge which had been used by the Holly Towing Company (hence the name, *Holly* barge) was scuttled next to the *Illinois* to give this shallow area some added pizzazz. Penetration into the barge's holds is possible for trained, experienced divers.

This site is buoyed annually by the Underwater Archaeological Society of Chicago, with help from dive shops and sponsors.

Left: The *Holly* barge sinking on May 6, 2000. Photo by Cris Kohl.

6. RAINBOW

LORAN: 33397.5/50098.5	LAT 41° 52.10′ LON 087° 36.46′
DEPTH: 20 feet	LEVEL: Novice

LOCATION: About a mile south-southeast of the Chicago harbor entrance.

The 3-masted schooner, *Rainbow* (125′ x 27′ x 10′), built in 1855 at Buffalo, New York, sank with her lumber cargo on May 18, 1894. She lies broken up and scattered.

7. FOUR-MILE CRIB

LORAN: 33379.9/50106.3	LAT 41° 52.400′ LON 087° 32.700′
DEPTH: 30 feet	LEVEL: Novice-Intermediate

LOCATION: This site lies four miles straight out of Chicago harbor.

For a change from shipwrecks, dive around the base of this historic site. Keep your eyes open for old tools and machinery discarded by crib workers years ago.

8. CAISSONS

LORAN: 33365.71/50092.0	LAT 41° 53.69′ LON 087° 32.01′
DEPTH: 45 to 50 feet	LEVEL: Intermediate

LOCATION: This unusual site lies about a mile east beyond the Four-Mile Crib.

The infamous Chicago Fire of 1871 killed about 300 people and destroyed much of the city. The survivors were determined to rebuild their homes and businesses as fast and as best as possible. First, however, was the question of what to do with all the rubble. The simple solution in those pre-environmental-concerns times was to load it onto dredges and dump it into the lake. The caissons is the location where the 1871 fire rubble was dumped. It covers quite a large area underwater, and many interesting items, such as watches and jugs, have been found over the years by divers. There is some unclarity as to why this site is called the "caissons," since a caisson is, among other things unrelated to water, a watertight chamber used in construction work under water (which this site is not), or a float for raising a sunken vessel (which this site is also not). Scuba divers should remember that another name for the "bends" is "caisson disease." Don't dive this site too long!

9. EAST TUG

LORAN: 33365.8/50099.0	LAT 41° 53.30′ LON 087° 31.25′
DEPTH: 45 feet	LEVEL: Intermediate

This unidentified tug sits about a mile east of the Four-Mile Crib.

10. SOUTH TUG AND TYM BARGE

> **LORAN: 33360.9/50087.6**   **LAT 41° 54.345′ LON 087° 31.680′**
> **DEPTH: 42 feet**   **LEVEL: Intermediate**

LOCATION: This two-sites-in-one is about 900′ southwest of the North tug.

This unidentified steam-powered tug, approximately 60′ long, features its engine, boiler and propeller, along with scattered pottery pieces. Next to it is the Tym barge, which was a relatively small (30′ in length by 15′ in beam) wooden, barrel/submarine-shaped experimental fuel-oil tank barge. Michael Tym of Chicago constructed this prototype for the Navy in 1942. No additional barges were manufactured, and this one was left to deteriorate in the harbor; divers moved it into the lake in 1999. Both wrecks can be visited on a single dive. This site is buoyed by the Underwater Archaeological Society of Chicago and its sponsors.

11. NORTH TUG

> **LORAN: 33359.8/50084.0**   **LAT 41° 54.50′ LON 087° 31.82′**
> **DEPTH: 45 feet**   **LEVEL: Intermediate**

LOCATION: This wreck lies just north of the South tug and Tym barge.

This unidentified tug, about 70′ long, displays its engine, boiler and propeller.

12. *IOWA*

> **LORAN: 33373.7/50087.1**   **LAT 41° 53.76′ LON 087° 33.76′**
> **DEPTH: 35 to 40 feet**   **LEVEL: Novice-Intermediate**

LOCATION: This wreck lies about 4 miles east of Navy Pier, between two cribs.

Launched as the *Menominee* in 1872 at Manitowoc, Wisconsin, this wooden steamer was constructed to replace the steamer, *Navarino,* which had been destroyed in the big Chicago fire of October 9, 1871. In fact, the steam engine from the *Navarino,* only a year old at the time of the burning, was placed into the *Menominee.* On the verge of being abandoned due to age, the ship was completely rebuilt in 1896 and renamed *Iowa* (202′5″ x 36′4″ x 12′). As such, this vessel experienced a string of at least six strandings and collisions which earned her the reputation of being a jinxed ship. Finally, the *Iowa,* with a cargo of general merchandise on her 13th trip of the year, was crushed by the ice off Chicago harbor and sank on February 4, 1915. The crew and the single passenger simply stepped onto the ice and walked

The steamer, *Iowa.* MPL/WMHS

to shore. The hull was partially removed, some cargo and machinery (engine and boilers) were salvaged and the rest was dynamited as a navigation hazard.

Re-located in the late 1950's and in 1976, the _Iowa_ lies scattered over a broad area. The remains of an old truck lie there, amidst kitchen items such as plates. Enough machinery remains at this site (even after the salvage and dynamiting) to make it interesting.

13. MIKE'S WRECK

LORAN: 33376.5/50087.4	LAT 41° 53.73' LON 087° 34.16'
DEPTH: 40 feet	LEVEL: Intermediate

This unidentified schooner, about 140' long, named after a charter boat captain who reportedly passed away while attempting to rescue a diver in trouble, is moderately intact.

14. _FLORA M. HILL_

LORAN: 33375.4/50077.0	LAT 41° 54.34' LON 087° 35.08'
DEPTH: 37 feet	LEVEL: Novice-Intermediate

LOCATION: About 1.2 miles north-northeast of the Chicago Harbor Light.

Constructed in 1874 at Philadelphia, Pennsylvania, as the lighthouse tender, _Dahlia_ and given her final name on May 12, 1910, the iron-hulled steamer, _Flora M. Hill_ (130'9" x 25' x 10'5"), on a run from Kenosha to Chicago, was crushed by ice and sank about 600' southeast of the Two-Mile Crib on March 11, 1912. The 32 crew and passengers, one of them the female cook, walked on the dangerous ice to the safety of the crib and were later picked up by a tugboat. Ironically, the _Flora M. Hill_ had been taken to Ferrysburg, Michigan, in 1909-1910 to install heavy plating which would give her year-round working capability by enabling her to go through the ice. The wreck was later dynamited as a navigation hazard.

With her stern aimed at the Two Mile Crib and her bow pointing southwest, the _Flora_

Left: The steamer, _Flora M. Hill._ _Right:_ Exploring the _Hill's_ iron hull. PHOTO BY JIM JARECKI.

M. Hill features iron hull plates, a boiler, propeller and rudder as its highlights. Remnants of her cargo of brass beds and automobile running lamps are still evident.

15. NORTH AVENUE SCHOONER

LORAN: 33375.9/50070.4   LAT 41° 54.73' LON 087° 35.85'
DEPTH: 30 feet   LEVEL: Novice

LOCATION: This wreck lies about 1.5 miles out in the lake east of North Avenue. This unidentified schooner has a fairly substantial debris field scattered to its south.

16. *WINGS OF THE WIND*

LORAN: 33357.5/50064.1   LAT 41° 55.86' LON 087° 33.50'
DEPTH: 40 to 45 feet   LEVEL: Intermediate

The WINGS OF THE WIND Wreck
Found by A&T Recovery

Vessel Type: Schooner
Survey Date: June 1, 1991
Location: 4 Miles off Chicago
Depth: 40
Loran C: 33357.5 50064.1

Artwork © Underwater Archaeological Society of Chicago. Site drawing by Valerie Olson and Jim Hansen.

The Underwater Archaeological Society of Chicago

LOCATION: This wreck lies about 3.5 miles north-northeast of the Chicago harbor entrance.

The two-masted schooner, *Wings of the Wind* (142' x 26' x 10'), built in 1855 at Buffalo, NY, sank with her coal cargo after a collision with the large bark, *H.P. Baldwin,* on May 12, 1866. The brand new *H.P. Baldwin,* basically undamaged, rescued the *Wings of the Wind's* crew. The coal cargo salvage later in 1866 destroyed the schooner's stern.

Located in 1987 by professional divers who revealed its location to sport divers, this shipwreck was reportedly soon stripped of most of its small artifacts. Only the forward half of this schooner remains intact, with her bowsprit, chains, windlass and centerboard trunk photogenically in place. A fallen mast lies off her port bow. A mooring buoy is attached annually to this site by the Underwater Archaeological Society of Chicago and its sponsors.

17. BOX BARGE

LORAN: 33339.0/50104.7   LAT 41° 54.079' LON 087° 26.267'
DEPTH: 60 feet   LEVEL: Advanced

LOCATION: This small, metal box-shaped wreck lies about 7.7 miles east of Chicago. This wreck, upright with an open hold, has a deck equipped with tow blocks and cleats.

18. *Rotarian*

LORAN: 33317.0/50072.0	**LAT 41° 57.016' LON 087° 26.066'**
DEPTH: 80 to 84 feet	**LEVEL: Advanced**

LOCATION: About 8.2 miles east-northeast of the Chicago harbor entrance.

Launched as the *A. Wehrle, Jr.* on July 17, 1889, at Sandusky, Ohio, this wooden steamer received the name *Rotarian* (146'8" x 41'9" x 9') in 1919. In 1928, the ship was dropped from documentation as "abandoned," but she was docked at Clark Street, Chicago, and used successively as a dance hall, as the home for the Cook County Democrats and as a restaurant. She sank at her slip on Oct. 10, 1930 "of old age" and was scuttled in Lake Michigan on September 28, 1931.

The remains of the *Rotarian* lie a considerable distance offshore, but there is much to see: boiler, hull and much wood debris scattered from this scuttled wreck.

The *Rotarian* underway. MPL/WMHS

The *Rotarian* underwater. The site offers much to see of this ship with the colorful history. At right is the boiler. PHOTOS BY JIM JARECKI.

19. LUCILLE

> **LORAN: 33355.1/50033.9** **LAT 41° 57.87′ LON 087° 36.23′**
> **DEPTH: 30 feet** **LEVEL: Novice**

LOCATION: This wreck lies 2 miles off shore from south Evanston, Illinois.
The schooner, *Lucille,* built at Chicago in 1884, sank off that city on February 2, 1893.
Although broken up, her hull and deck equipment are easily recognizable.

20. WELLS BURT

> **LORAN: 33325.5/49977.6** **LAT 42° 02.762′ LON 087° 37.104′**
> **DEPTH: 38-45 feet** **LEVEL: Intermediate**

LOCATION: This wreck lies about 3 miles east of Evanston, Illinois.
The huge, three-masted schooner, *Wells Burt* (201′ x 33′5″ x 14′2″), launched on July 12, 1873 at Detroit, Michigan, foundered in a storm on May 20, 1883, with the loss of all 11 people on board and her cargo of coal. Hardhat divers soon recovered the two anchors and her masts, while the rest of the ship was already settling into the soft lake bottom.

The schooner, *Wells Burt*

Vessel Type: 3-Masted Schooner
Survey Date: May 1989-October 1989
Location: 3 Miles off Evanston
Depth: 40′
Loran C: 33325.4 49977.7

Artwork © Underwater Archaeological Society of Chicago. Site
drawing by Valerie Olson.

Located in 1988 by professional divers from A & T Recovery of Chicago, the wreck of the *Wells Burt* was found to be in excellent condition in spite of its shallow site. She lies facing northwest with a slight port list. She sits embedded in about 8′ of clay, but her hold is open and accessible through the hatches. A capstan and a windlass remain on deck. The wreck was surveyed and photographed extensively by the Underwater Archaeological Society of Chicago. Maintaining the integrity of the shipwreck succeeded for a while, but in late 1990 or early 1991, a diver stole 10 of the large deadeyes from the site; there is a reward of $2,000.00 offered for information leading to the arrest and conviction of the thief. Contact the Illinois Historic Preservation Agency or the State Police if you know the whereabouts of these irreplacable items. Hopefully the *Wells Burt* and our other uniquely preserved freshwater shipwrecks will not be stripped to the bone as have a few other well-documented cases. This site is buoyed annually by the Underwater Archaeological Society of Chicago and its sponsors.

21. GEORGE W. MORLEY

LORAN: 33338.8/49970.2	LAT 42° 02.67' LON 087° 40.14'
DEPTH: 20 feet	LEVEL: Novice

LOCATION: This wreck lies about 300' off Greenwood Avenue, Evanston, Illinois.

Launched in April, 1888, at West Bay City, Michigan, the wooden steamer, *George W. Morley* (192'9" x 34' x 21'), caught fire and stranded on December 5, 1897, with no lives lost. the ship was travelling light betwen Milwaukee and Chicago. Her engine was salvaged in October, 1898. The bottom part of the hull lies broken, with other pieces scattered.

22. *UC-97*

LORAN:	LAT 42° 10' LON 087° 20'
DEPTH: About 250 feet	LEVEL: Technical

LOCATION: This wreck lies about 19 miles off Wilmette, Illinois.

A German U-boat, spotted by a sailor from a Great Lakes freighter in the middle of Lake Michigan on August 16, 1919, scared the daylights out of him. But the ship was only a harmless war prize, brought to the United States and towed to Chicago after Germany's defeat in World War I (1914-1918). The German mine-laying submarine, *UC-97* (185' x 18' x 12'), launched at Hamburg, Germany, on March 17, 1918 and technically renamed the *"USS Ex-UC97"* when the US Navy took over her command, was towed around Great Lakes ports to stimulate the sale of post-war Victory Bonds by giving buyers a close-up view of an enemy submarine.

The Treaty of Versailles, which ended World War I, called for the destruction of all German weapons of war within three years of confiscation. Accordingly, on June 7, 1921, the *USS Hawk* towed the German sub out into the middle of Lake Michigan and the Navy training ship, the *USS Wilmette* (formerly the disastrous passenger steamer, *Eastland,* which had capsized at dock in Chicago on July 24, 1915, taking over 800 people to a watery grave) used her as target practice. Eighteen rounds of 4-inch shells put the submarine on the bottom.

On board the confiscated German *UC-97,* memorial services were held on May 8, 1919, marking the 4th anniversary of the loss of the *Lusitania.* The submarine was later sunk in Lake Michigan after her Victory Bonds tour. US NAVY PHOTO.

The approximate location, given above, is from the log of the *USS Hawk.* Reportedly the Navy located the submarine in 1977, with verification given by the Combined Great Lakes Naval Association from their vessel, *Neptune,* and in 1992, A & T Recovery, a commercial salvage company, also located the shipwreck. In spite of its bombardment, the *UC-97* appears to be upright and quite intact, with a slight starboard list, according to remote-operated video shown recently to the public. Her number, *UC-97,* is clearly visible.

Since 1993, plans have been in the works to raise and restore the *UC-97,* and to place her next to the World War II German submarine on exhibit at the Museum of Science and Industry in Chicago. The author was told by Taras Lyssenko of A & T Recovery that, because of these plans, "it is illegal to try to dive on the *UC-97.*"

23. ST. MARY

LORAN: 33259.3/49882.5	LAT 42° 11.482′ LON 087° 35.927′
DEPTH: 110 feet	LEVEL: Advanced

LOCATION: This wreck lies 8 miles northeast of Wilmette, Illinois, harbor.

The two-masted schooner, *St. Mary* (114′ x 25′), received very little press coverage at the time of her tragic loss because she sank on the exact date that the *Lady Elgin* went down (see site #24), and the latter totally eclipsed the former in the media. Built in 1848 at Perrysburg, Ohio, the *St. Mary* sank with the loss of all 7 hands on September 8, 1860. This west-facing, collapsed but intact shipwreck, located by A & T Recovery in 1989, offers exquisite views of a large wooden stock anchor with its stem through a hawsepipe, a folding bow anchor, a windlass and anchor chain, a rudder with draft marks and the ship's wheel in place. Identification is not 100% yet (some argue that this could be the wreck of the schooner, *F.J. King,* which foundered on September 15, 1886). Regardless, it's a unique site!

24. LADY ELGIN

LORAN:	LAT LON
DEPTH: 55 feet	LEVEL: Intermediate

LOCATION: This wreck lies 4.3 miles due east of the harbor at Fort Sheridan, IL.

The elegant sidewheel passenger steamer, *Lady Elgin* (251′ x 31′8″ x 11′1″), built at Buffalo, New York, in 1851, sank after a collision off Winnetka, Illinois, with the small, lumber-laden schooner, *Augusta,* on the stormy night of September 8, 1860. The damaged *Augusta* limped into Chicago, but the mortally stricken *Lady Elgin,* with a gaping hole in her port side, ran desperately for shore in heavy weather but broke into pieces and sank within 30 minutes. She was bound from Chicago to Milwaukee with a large passenger list

The sidewheel steamer, *Lady Elgin,* at Northport, Michigan. REV. PETER VAN DER LINDEN COLLECTION

which included several civic officials, and enormous loss of life ensued, with estimates ranging from 282 to 373 people perishing, most of Irish descent from Milwaukee. Some history analysts have argued that the loss of the *Lady Elgin* transferred political control of Milwaukee from the Irish to the Germans.

The *Lady Elgin* had had her share of misfortunes, among them striking a rock off Manitowoc on August 30, 1854, and sinking right when she reached dock, with no lives lost, and catching on fire from sparks blown from another steamer on October. 17, 1857, damaging only the deck and one stateroom before the flames were extinguished.

This shipwreck, located by Harry Zych in 1989 (and he had reportedly been searching for her and the *Seabird* --see site #25-- since 1973), is badly broken up and widely scattered, with the bow and the boiler lying about a mile apart, connected by a vast debris field. Essentially the wreckage is divided among four main fields. A long, multi-year court case over this shipwreck's ownership ensued, with Harry Zych fighting the state of Illinois. His plans are reportedly to find a permanent display for the artifacts he will salvage and to have a traveling exhibit go to Great Lakes communities. At last count, the court had given ownership to Harry Zych, or perhaps more correctly, to his non-profit organization, the Lady Elgin Foundation. It is illegal for anyone else to visit the site, and there is a reason for that. During the court procedings, unknown (as yet) scuba divers stole a number of articles from the bow section, items which will, in all likelihood, never be seen again. With the establishment of private ownership, it is also illegal to photograph or to videotape the wreck of the *Lady Elgin.* Prior to the court's decision, parts of the various *Lady Elgin* wreck debris sites were catalogued in a study done by the Underwater Archaeological Society of Chicago.

In our efforts to be completely above board about this shipwreck, we sought permission to publish the *Lady Elgin's* coordinates plus two underwater photos of her. Our contact was with Harry Zych, who stated that it would have to be a decision rendered by the Lady Elgin Foundation. Permission had not been granted by press time several weeks later.

25. SEABIRD

LORAN: 33264.1/49759.9	LAT 42° 18.892' LON 087° 49.262'
DEPTH: 30 feet	LEVEL: Novice-Intermediate

LOCATION: About 1/2 mile northeast of the Great Lakes Naval Training Center Harbor.

Another one of the dozen worst Great Lakes maritime disasters, the sidewheel passenger and freight steamer, *Seabird* (190'8" x 27'5" --excludes paddlewheels-- x 10'9"), was built at Newport (today's Marine City), Michigan, in 1859. She also carried double 26' diameter paddlewheels. On April 9, 1868, running between Milwaukee and Chicago on this, her third

Drawing of the *Seabird*. MPL/WMHS

The Wreck of the SEABIRD
Found by Harry Zych

Artwork © Underwater Archaeological Society
of Chicago. Site drawing by Valerie Olson.
The Underwater Archaeological Society of Chicago

Vessel Type: Sidewheel Steamer
Survey Date: 7-25,8-7 & 8-22-93
Location: NE Great Lakes Harbor
Depth: 25'
Loran C: 33264.1 x 49759.9
© Drawing by Valerie Olson

run of the season, she caught on fire off Waukegan, Illinois. An unwitting porter had carelessly thrown hot ashes from the heater stove over the side -- lamentably the windward side! A thousand sparks flew like moths back on board ship onto the lower deck, right into the cargo of newly varnished buckets and straw. Approximately 72 lives (the estimates ran from 50 to 100) were lost. Only three people survived this horrible catastrophe: C.A. Chamberlain, Edwin Hanneberry and James H. Leonard. The blazing ship burned to the waterline before drifting close to shore and sinking.

The *Seabird* was located by Harry Zych in 1989, the same year he found the *Lady Elgin* (see site #24), and he immediately initiated court proceedings for ownership of both shipwrecks. At last count, the State of Illinois owns the *Seabird*. The highlights of this site include the large boiler and a rarity: a large, intact paddlewheel. Because the paddlewheel is deteriorating, please use the utmost caution when you are near it and make sure you practice buoyancy skills. Don't wreck the wreck with carelessness or clumsiness. Many small artifacts have been laid out to make it easier for divers to see and appreciate them. Please do not remove anything from this site. It is illegal and unethical. The wreck of the *Seabird* is buoyed annually by the Underwater Archaeological Society of Chicago and its sponsors.

Seabird sights: a paddlewheel, a kettle on timbers, and Joan Forsberg with ship's tools. PHOTOS BY CRIS KOHL.

26. ZION SCHOONERS

> **LORAN: 33202.1/49672.0**   **LAT 42° 27.158′ LON 087° 47.786′**
> **DEPTH: 20 feet**   **LEVEL: Novice**

LOCATION: These wrecks lie just off the Zion (Illinois) Power Plant.

These two unidentified schooners, each about 100′ long, were probably aging vessels abandoned at this site. They are broken up and lying in such a way that at least part of one appears to be lying on top of the other. A donkey boiler, often used on schooners and barges to provide steam-powered assistance with the loading and uploading of cargo, rests on one wreck. Construction debris, likely from the power plant on shore, is strewn about the site.

27. ZION MINESWEEPER

> **LORAN: 33199.0/49668.0**   **LAT 42° 27.535′ LON 087° 47.814′**
> **DEPTH: 12 feet**   **LEVEL: Novice**

LOCATION: This wreck lies 400′ off shore from Illinois Beach State Park, about 1 mile north of the Zion Power Plant.

Long referred to as the "Zion Mystery Ship" and the "old minesweeper", this 110′-long wooden vessel is actually a decommissioned Navy subchaser. Intense research done by members of the Underwater Archaeological Society of Chicago, spearheaded by Tony Kiefer, has concluded that this shipwreck is likely that of the *SC 419* (although the *SC 418* and *SC 416* are also contenders), part of the Navy's 440-strong "Splinter Fleet" of subchasers built during World War I. Many were sold to France, while some, after the war, converted to civilian use. This one was scuttled for the creation of a breakwall in front of a private residence, likely in the mid-1930's. If it is the *SC 419*, she was built at Milwaukee by the Great Lakes Boat Building Corporation. Research is ongoing.

The wreck lies on its port side, exposing its copper-clad, steel-reinforced wooden hull. The engine and the propeller are missing, but the propeller shaft remains intact. Several steel tanks, used either for extra fuel or water storage, are on board.

Miscellaneous Unidentified Chicago-Area Wreck Sites

These sites and co-ordinates have not been verified:

1. Wrecked airplane: **LORAN: 33428.8/50205.5   LAT 41° 44.03′ LON 087° 30.853**
2. World War I airplane in 35′: **LORAN: 33408.4/50161.8 LAT 41° 47.560′ LON 087° 31.76′**
3. T.B.F. airplane: **LAT 41° 51.09′ LON 087° 15.71′**
4. Schooner in 30′: **LORAN: 33355.0/50033.9   LAT 41° 57.98′ LON 087° 36.21′**
5. Unidentified wreckage: **LORAN: 33360.3/50036.9   LAT 41° 57.47′ LON 087° 36.77′**
6. Schooner-barge, about 200′ long, 1.5 miles north of Four-Mile Crib, in 45′: **LORAN: 33372.0/50091.2   LAT 41° 53.57′ LON 087° 33.06′**
7. Schooner: **LORAN: 33380.0/50175.8   LAT 41° 47.78′ LON 087° 25.65′**
8. Schooner in 65′: **LORAN: 33331.4/50083.2   LAT 41° 55.55′ LON 087° 27.38′**
9. Schooner: **LORAN: 33360.2/50036.9   LAT 41° 57.58′ LON 087° 36.75′**
10. Schooner: **LORAN: 33375.8/50070.4   LAT 41° 47.41′ LON 087° 36.90′**
11. Steamer in 40′: **LORAN: 33263.8/49759.3   LAT 42° 18.92′ LON 087° 49.30′**
12. Tug in 30′: **LORAN: 33359.8/50084.1   LAT 41° 54.44′ LON 087° 31.97′**
13. Tug: **LORAN: 33446.7/50230.1   LAT 41° 41.79′ LON 087° 30.82′**
14. Tug: **LORAN: 33325.5/49977.7   LAT 42° 02.71′ LON 087° 37.12′**

Shipwreck Conservation: Changing Ethics and Laws

Since the year 1679, the Great Lakes have seen more than 15,000 different commercial ships ply their waters. These were sailing vessels until the year 1816, when the first steamer on the Great Lakes was launched in the Kingston, Ontario, area at the eastern end of Lake Ontario. As the invention of steam-powered watercraft perfected itself, the predominance of sail toppled in 1874 when, for the first time, steamships outnumbered sailing craft on the inland seas. The mass production of steel ships began in the 1890's, with 600-footers becoming the norm by the year 1906. The last wooden-hulled steamer slid down the launch-ramp in the Great Lakes in 1902, and by the 1930's, most wooden ships had been abandoned or scuttled in ships' graveyards which dotted the region. In 1958, the largest ship on the freshwater seas, the *Edmund Fitzgerald,* was built, only to become, in 1975, the lakes' last major shipwreck tragedy. In 1972, the first of the "thousand-footers," of which there are now a dozen laboring with massive bulk cargoes on the upper Great Lakes, was launched.

When ships sank, people did everything possible to recover them, or to salvage the cargo and as many parts of the ship as possible. On the Great Lakes, professional hardhat divers performed salvage jobs by the early 1850's and reached the height of their profession during the four-decade span, from 1880 to 1920, when most of the shipwrecks occurred, a dark era for the shipping industry, but 40 golden years for a number of famous commercial salvagers headquartered around the Great Lakes. Salvage regulations were written into the shipping acts of both Canada and the United States, and "wreckers" were members of a dangerous but noble and elite profession. Even in the 1930's, recovery was the norm, with shipwreck conservation little more than a twinkle in an archaeologist's eye.

By the time World War II ended in 1945, the world, including the Great Lakes, was a very different place. Electronic devices provided greater safety for ships, with shipwreck frequency being reduced from a few a week in 1900 to a handful a year by 1950.

There was also a new invention capturing the imaginations of adventurers in 1950, something called a self-contained underwater breathing apparatus, or s.c.u.b.a. for short. Gradually this new breed of modern-day explorer using this scuba invention went in quest of shipwrecks, not only to explore but also to salvage, not on a commercial scale but for personal "tokens of accomplishment" which proclaimed their elite membership status. In the 1950's and '60's, thousands of ships' parts, from the smallest deadeyes to the largest anchors, were removed from Great Lakes waters by people feeling empowered by their new ability to breathe underwater without the constraint of massively heavy equipment, and free from hoses and lines connecting them to the surface. What was shrugged off as being merely a Jules Verne type of science fiction dream in the late 1800's had become a reality by the mid-1900's.

By 1970, the results were noticeable. Parallel to the California experience, where spearfishermen and women had switched from free-breathing to scuba equipment, making the taking of fish as easy as shooting them in a barrel, Great Lakes divers noticed something amiss in their waters as well. Off California, the once-plentiful supply of fish to spear had become heavily depleted. In the Great Lakes, new scuba divers would visit a shipwreck once, then never again, because there was nothing left to see but a bare hull. In California, divers put a moratorium on spearing fish so that the reefs could replenish themselves, but in the Great Lakes, it was heartbreaking to see what had become of many nonrenewable shipwrecks. A scuba diver who was dynamiting the wreck of the *W.L. Wetmore* at Tobermory in the early 1970's prompted the creation of the Great Lakes' first underwater park or preserve,

Members of shipwreck conservation groups learn about marine archaeology in pool sessions first.
PHOTO BY CRIS KOHL

Fathom Five Provincial Park, in 1972. In 1976, Ontario produced its Heritage Act, and in 1981, Michigan passed its Great Lakes Bottomlands Act, both serving to protect our submerged cultural resources. Also in Ontario in 1981, scuba divers who were genuinely concerned about the pillaging of our underwater history formed marine conservation groups called Preserve Our Wrecks (P.O.W.) in the Kingston area and Save Ontario Shipwrecks (S.O.S.) with chapters all across the province (and even one in Ohio today). These groups also took the initiative to create settings where scuba divers could learn about ship construction, shipwreck research, and marine archaeology techniques, even working hand-in-hand with professional marine archaeologists in surveying shipwreck sites. In the late 1980's, the Underwater Archaeological Society of Chicago was formed after divers splintered off from the Chicago Maritime Society. Since then, more groups, such as the Great Lakes Shipwreck Preservation Society in Minnesota, continue to organize in order to educate people about our maritime history and to save our Great Lakes wrecks, undoubtedly the world's best preserved shipwrecks, from those few who still feel that "wrecking" is a noble calling but are increasingly viewed as self-centered looters.

◆　　◆　　◆　　◆　　◆　　◆　　◆　　◆　　◆

Trying to sink legal teeth into shipwreck looters has been a problem, in spite of some highly publicized cases such as the theft of one of the enormous anchors from the *Tasmania*, a shipwreck in Canadian waters off Lake Erie's Point Pelee by two boatloads of Ohio divers in 1987. A small army of investigators, including Save Ontario Shipwrecks (particularly the Windsor chapter), a Toledo journalist and several government agencies, flew into action, with the results being the return of the anchor to the *Tasmania* site and the prosecution of those responsible for its theft. It took the perpetrators years and heavy legal fees to even get their boats back. But their big mistake had been in clandestinely transporting heritage material across an international border, an action which prompted the U.S. Customs Service to join the investigation. What can be done about divers who remove things from shipwrecks, but don't leave the country? A few minor cases of theft from shipwrecks have recently been taken to court with successful results, e.g. the divers who removed blocks from the Lake Huron wreck of the *New York*. However, the anticipated high-profile case which would set a lasting precedent among scuba divers remained elusive, in spite of the fact that shipwreck looting was still going on. There remains a $1,000 reward for the conviction of the party responsible for the theft of the tugboat *Sport's* bell, and P.O.W. has offered a similar reward over the theft of a metal plate from the historic dredge, *Munson*, off Kingston.

Then something very strange happened. A well-known shipwreck locator from Illinois, Paul Ehorn, had, many years ago, removed the truly unique dragon-shaped figurehead from the site of the schooner, *James R. Bentley,* in Michigan waters, taken the time to conserve that unusual and "at risk" wooden artifact, and donated it to the Manitowoc Maritime Museum, which put it on display under glass in an elaborate housing. In 1998, the Michigan Department of Natural Resources had Paul Ehorn charged with the theft of that artifact, which they ultimately removed from the museum as evidence. In a daring challenge to the wording of the laws, hinging mainly upon the word "embedded," Paul Ehorn was not only exonerated of the crime by a judge, but ended up taking legal ownership of the *James R. Bentley.* In the spring of 2001, he legally removed one of the *Bentley's* huge anchors as a DNR boat watched him wave his court-issued ownership papers. He plans to sell that anchor to recoup some of his legal expenses, which almost reached the six figures. He is presently fighting a similar battle in Wisconsin, charges that he illegally removed a porthole from the *Rosinco*. Will the outcome of the first case influence the outcome of the second? We can only wait and see how recent legal matters will ultimately affect our Great Lakes shipwrecks.

35. Milwaukee

LAKE MICHIGAN

MILWAUKEE

WISCONSIN

Racine

Kenosha

Zion

ILLINOIS

Waukegan

-N-

Milwaukee's most frequently visited shipwreck is the steel freighter, *Prins Willem V* (site #14 -- see pages 309-310), a Dutch vessel which sank in a collision just outside Milwaukee harbor in 1954. PHOTO BY JON ZEAMAN.

1. *Wisconsin*
2. *Rosinco*
3. *Evra Fuller*
4. *Kate Kelly*
5. *Lumberman*
6. *Grace A. Channon*
7. *Dredge 906*
8. *Norlond*
9. *Volunteer*
10. *Sebastopol*
11. **Jerry's wreck**
12. *Sumatra*
13. **"The Wall"--Rlrd. bridge**
14. *Prins Willem V*
15. *Edward E. Gillen*
16. *EMBA*
17. *St. Albans*
18. *Appomattox*
19. *Josephine*
20. *Milwaukee*
21. *Island City*

1. WISCONSIN

LORAN: 33147.41/49634.04	LAT 42° 31.961′ LON 087° 42.524′
DEPTH: 90 to 130 feet	LEVEL: Advanced

LOCATION: This wreck lies 6.5 miles east-southeast of Kenosha, Wisconsin.

Nine lives were lost from the 68 on board when the iron steamer, *Wisconsin* (209′ x 40′ x 20′9″), foundered in a storm on October 29, 1929. Built at Wyandotte, Michigan, in 1881, the ship was carrying a cargo of iron castings, automobile parts and oil at the time of loss.

Dick Race of Chicago located the *Wisconsin* in 1961. The port anchor chain winds around the bow and trails off to where her anchor lies firmly embedded in the sandy lake bottom. The superstructure is broken and/or missing. The smokestack lies lengthwise on the deck, its red paint still showing. The windlass sits below the capstan on deck. Three vintage 1920's automobiles grace the rear cargo hold. Beware of strong currents and darkness.

The *Wisconsin*. AUTHOR'S COLLECTION

Numerous sinks lie along the deck of the *Wisconsin*, evidence of her 100 staterooms. PHOTO BY JON ZEAMAN

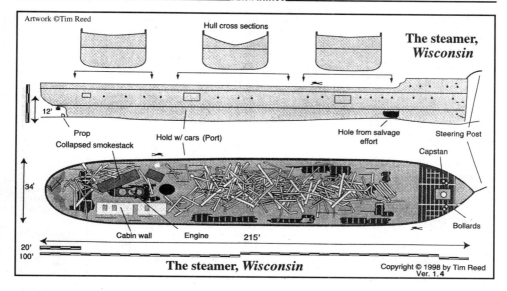

Artwork ©Tim Reed

Hull cross sections

The steamer,
Wisconsin

12'

Prop
Collapsed smokestack
Hold w/ cars (Port)

Hole from salvage
effort
Steering Post

Capstan

34'

Cabin wall   Engine   215'

Bollards

20'
100'

The steamer, *Wisconsin*

Copyright © 1998 by Tim Reed
Ver. 1.4

2. ROSINCO

LORAN: 33089.6/49586.8	LAT 42° 37.515′ LON 087° 37.650′
DEPTH: 195 feet	LEVEL: Technical

LOCATION: This wreck lies about 10 miles off Kenosha, Wisconsin.

The steel-hulled diesel-powered luxury yacht, *Rosinco* (88′ x 15′ x 7′8″), struck some floating timber in the middle of the night and surprisingly sank within 10 minutes on April 18, 1928, while enroute from Milwaukee to Chicago. The seven men on board took to the motorized tender and another boat in tow. Built as the *Georgiana III* at Wilmington, Delaware, in 1916, the *Rosinco* (renamed in 1925 from the name *Whitemarsh* given her in 1919) is upright, intact and in excellent condition, with penetration possible for trained/experienced divers in her main cabin and outer rooms along the main deck. Commercial fishermen found this wreck in 1961 when they snagged it in their nets. The State of Wisconsin is presently litigating against a diver who allegedly removed a porthole from this wreck in 1998.

3. EVRA FULLER

LOCATION: In 35′ of water about 400′-500′ east of the Racine Harbor entrance.

The 217-net-ton schooner, *Evra Fuller* (132′9″ x 26′3″ x 9′9″), constructed as the *Lena Johnson* at Fort Howard, Wisconsin, in 1873, stranded on Racine Reef with a load of lumber

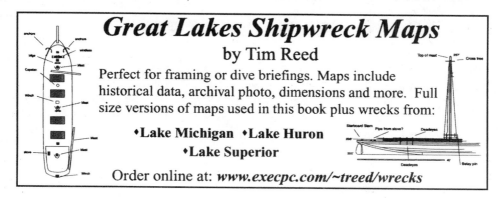

on October 8, 1893, and broke up, but the majority of the vessel washed in close to shore. The wreck, broken and scattered, lies in muddy water busy with boating traffic. Caution!

4. KATE KELLY

LORAN: 33053.5/49467.7	LAT 42° 46.676′ LON 087° 43.410′
DEPTH: 40 to 50 feet	LEVEL: Intermediate

LOCATION: This wreck lies almost two miles east of the Wind Point Lighthouse.

Built in 1867 at Tonawanda, New York, the twin-masted schooner, *Kate Kelly* (126′ x 26′ x 10′), stranded in a severe gale on May 13, 1895. With the crew of seven in the rigging, the storm broke the doomed vessel free from her perch, spiriting her towards shore. Unfortunately, the entire crew was lost, along with 6,000 hemlock railroad ties she carried. The wreck lies quite intact, with a windlass in place and pulleys and deadeyes in the sand.

5. LUMBERMAN

LORAN: 33026.4/49400.0	LAT 42° 52.172′ LON 087° 45.420′
DEPTH: 53 to 70 feet	LEVEL: Advanced

LOCATION: This wreck lies about 10 miles north of Wind Point, Wisconsin.

The *Lumberman's* deck.
PHOTO BY JON ZEAMAN

The three-masted, twin-centerboarded schooner, *Lumberman* (126′5″ x 23′5″ x 7′1″), built at Blendon's Landing (Grand Haven), Michigan, in the spring and summer of 1862, capsized on April 7, 1893, on her first trip of the season. This low-draft ship, traveling light (i.e. with no cargo) was easy prey for a strong western squall. As she sank, the vessel righted herself, and the five crew clung to her above-water masts until the steamer, *Menominee*, rescued them. The wreck's masts were later removed by a salvage company.

The *Lumberman*, located on July 16, 1983, by Dan Johnson, Eric Smith and Patricia Insko (who reportedly initially had plans to raise the ship in her entirety), sits upright and intact, with her empty cargo holds open to divers who want to swim from one end of the wreck to the other without impediment. Many items that were on her in 1983 (such as nameboards on her sides and moonshine bottles in the cabin) have now been lost, but this wreck still has enough artifacts to make her wonderful to explore. The *Lumberman* was the subject of survey and shore-up work in the summer of 2001.

6. GRACE A. CHANNON

LORAN: 32963.2/49388.1	LAT 42° 55.76′ LON 087° 36.12′
DEPTH: 185 to 198 feet	LEVEL: Technical

Artwork ©Tim Reed
Mast · Winch · Mast · Mast · Winch · Anchors · Bilge · Windlass · Capstan · Pin Rails · Bilge · Partial Deck House Structure · Stove · Dead Eyes

LOCATION: This wreck lies 6.8 miles southeast of Oak Creek, Wisconsin.

The schooner, *Grace Channon* (169′ x 29′), built in 1873 at East Saginaw, Michigan, sank after a collision with the steam barge, *Favorite,* broke a large hole in her port side on August 2, 1877. The seven-year-old son of a co-owner, sleeping below deck, died in this sinking, while the *Favorite* rescued the others. This wreck, located in April, 1985, by Kent Bellrichard and his team, sits upright, intact and in remarkably good shape, with an intact cabin. Rigging lies on the deck.

7. DREDGE 906

LORAN: 32996.0/49329.1	LAT 42° 57.92' LON 087° 47.24'
DEPTH: 50 to 75 feet	LEVEL: Intermediate-Advanced

LOCATION: This wreck lies four miles southeast of Milwaukee, Wisconsin.
Dredge 906 (110' x 40' x 11'5") was a 685-gross-ton, steel-hulled, box-type, nonself-

Dredge 906. AUTHOR'S COLLECTION

propelled, uninspected, unregistered "vessel" which took the lives of 9 men when it foundered while under tow in a storm on May 23, 1956. *Dredge 906* was built in 1912.

This wreck, one of Milwaukee's most popular scuba dive sites, lies upside-down, resting on two retracted spuds (steel arms sunk into the lake bottom to hold the dredge in place during work).Truly interesting sights include the massive crane, boiler and dredging machinery. Be totally in charge of your buoyancy so as not to stir up the considerable silt at this site; cave diving techniques are handy here. Penetrate the wreck only if you are trained and experienced.

Dredge 906's bitts hang upside-down just above the lake floor; a diver examines the boiler. PHOTOS BY JON ZEAMAN

8. NORLOND

LORAN: 32999.9/49320.5	LAT 42° 58.434′ LON 087° 48.671′
DEPTH: 65 feet	LEVEL: Advanced

LOCATION: Three miles southeast of Milwaukee.

The wooden steamer, *Norlond* (152′5″ x 25′ x 9′4″), built as the *Eugene C. Hart* in 1890 at Manitowoc, WI, foundered in heavy weather on Nov. 13, 1922, with no lives lost. The wreck lies broken and scattered, with her boiler just to the west of the main wreckage.

The *Norlond.* MPL/WMHS

9. VOLUNTEER

LORAN: 33008.5/49304.5	LAT 42° 58.88′ LON 087° 51.72′
DEPTH: 15 feet	LEVEL: Novice

LOCATION: This wreck lies just outside the breakwall south of Milwaukee. Beware of boating traffic!

The wooden steamer, *Volunteer* (270′8″ x 41′6″ x 20′4″), built in 1888 at Trenton, Michigan, was deemed too costly to rebuild when she aged, so she was dismantled, burned and abandoned at this location in 1914. Wreckage includes wooden planking and piping.

The *Volunteer.* MPL/WMHS

10. SEBASTOPOL

LORAN: 33009.1/49301.3	LAT 42° 59.03′ LON 087° 52.14′
DEPTH: 10 to 12 feet	LEVEL: Novice

LOCATION: Inside the outer breakwall off Milwaukee's South Shore Beach, straight out from Oklahoma Avenue.

Built at Cleveland in 1855, the wooden sidewheel steamer, *Sebastopol* (230′ x 26′ x 14′), didn't last her first season on the Great Lakes. With confusing shore lights misleading the ship's navigation during heavy weather, the *Sebastopol* stranded on September 18, 1855. Four crewmembers died during the safe evacuation of the 60 passengers, and the ship broke up. Ship's framing and planking remain, with occasional bits of cargo or baggage in between.

Frames from the *Sebastopol.* PHOTO BY JON ZEAMAN

11. JERRY'S WRECK

LORAN: 33000.4/49280.9	LAT 43° 00.87' LON 087° 52.53'
DEPTH: 41 feet	LEVEL: Intermediate

LOCATION: This wreck lies less than a mile north of Milwaukee harbor.
This unidentified wooden shipwreck, apparently a steam-powered sandsucker about 112' long, lies broken and scattered.

12. SUMATRA

LORAN: 32997.4/49272.4	LAT 43° 01.42' LON 087° 53.01'
DEPTH: 35 feet	LEVEL: Novice

The 204' schooner-barge, *Sumatra,* built in 1874 at Black River, Ohio, foundered in a gale on September 30, 1896, with the loss of four lives and her cargo of railroad iron.

13. "THE WALL" -- RAILROAD BRIDGE

LORAN: 32955.4/49273.4	LAT 43° 03.26' LON 087° 45.58'
DEPTH: 150 feet	LEVEL: Technical

LOCATION: South-southwest of the *St. Alban* wreck, and also located by Kent Bellrichard's team in Dec., 1975, this steel railroad bridge (190' x 58') was city scuttled.

14. PRINS WILLEM V

LORAN: 32979.6/49286.9	LAT 43° 01.35' LON 087° 48.59'
DEPTH: 48 to 90 feet	LEVEL: Advanced

LOCATION: This wreck lies three miles east of Milwaukee, Wisconsin.
Another "saltie" (ocean-going freighter) that never made it out of the Great Lakes (just like the *Nordmeer, Monrovia* and *Francisco Morazan,* which are all in this book), the steel freighter, *Prins Willem V* (250'5" x 42'1" x 14'7"), built in the Netherlands in 1948, sank in a freak collision with the tug, *Sinclair's* tow on October 14, 1954. No lives were lost, and the *Prins Willem V* sank with the loss of her cargo of automotive parts, animal hides and jukeboxes.

The *"Willy"* is the most popular dive site in the Milwaukee area, and perhaps in all of Lake Michigan. Memorable explorations can be made by remaining

The *Prins Willem V.* MPL/WMHS

outside the hull; the *Prins Willem V* is a huge, multi-leveled shipwreck which has been unforgiving towards scuba divers who overestimate their abilities or foresake their precautions. Once again, penetration diving is only for the trained, experienced and prepared.

Artwork ©Tim Reed

Artwork ©Tim Reed

Various scenes of the wreck of the *Prins Willem V:* photos reflect the fact that this shipwreck lies practically on its side, but superstructure railing is in ample evidence, and a swim through the pilot house is the highlight of any dive here; the ship's name is still visible on her stern (3 PHOTOS AT LEFT BY PETE TOMASINO); the galley offers much to see (e.g. stove in background), and steel steps lead ever deeper inside the shipwreck (2 PHOTOS BELOW AND RIGHT BY JON ZEAMAN)

15. *EDWARD E. GILLEN*

LORAN: 32981.5/49284.0	LAT 43° 01.44' LON 087° 49.18'
DEPTH: 62 to 74 feet	LEVEL: Advanced

LOCATION: This wreck lies 2.5 miles east of Hoan Bridge, Milwaukee, Wisconsin.

Above: The tug, *Edward E. Gillen*. MPL/WMHS. *Right:* A folding bunk inside the wreck. PHOTO BY JON ZEAMAN.

310

The old, wooden tugboat, *Edward E. Gillen* (56'5" x 15'3" x 7'9"), began her long life as the *Erastus C. Knight* at Buffalo, New York, in 1908. Just before noon on June 3, 1981, the *Edward E. Gillen* rolled over and sank after a wire parted suddenly while helping the Coast Guard test the towing winch on one of their vessels. No lives were lost.

The *Edward E. Gillen* sits upright, intact and penetrable by the trained and experienced.

16. EMBA

LORAN: 32949.6/49271.6	LAT 43° 03.72' LON 087° 45.05'
DEPTH: 170 feet	LEVEL: Technical

The *EMBA*, ex-*A.C. Tuxbury*. MPL/WMHS

LOCATION: This wreck lies off Milwaukee's North Point.

Built in 1890 at West Bay City, Michigan, the three- (later two) -masted schooner, *EMBA* (ex-*A.C. Tuxbury*) (128'5" x 24'5" x 12'5"), was converted to a twin-masted schooner-barge, a towed ship often carrying lumber or coal. This vessel was scuttled in 1932. This site was one of three located in a single day of scanning by Kent Bellrichard, Richard Zaleski and their group in late December, 1975 (the other

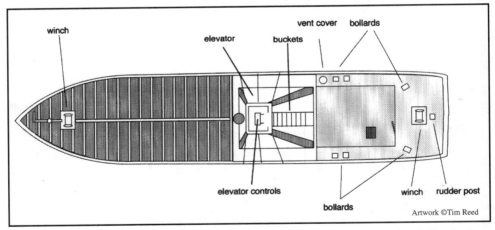

winch
elevator
buckets
vent cover   bollards

elevator controls
bollards
winch   rudder post

Artwork ©Tim Reed

two were the *St. Alban's* and the scuttled railroad bridge). Because the wreck lies broken from the impact with the lake bottom, there are few penetration possibilties here.

17. St. Albans

LORAN: 32951.8/49269.1	LAT 43° 03.79' LON 087° 45.65'
DEPTH: 160 to 178 feet	LEVEL: Technical

LOCATION: This wreck lies about seven miles off Milwaukee, Wisconsin.

The wooden steamer, *St. Alban's* (135'6" x 25'8" x 11'), launched at Cleveland on July 18, 1868, was sunk by ice northeast of Milwaukee on January 30, 1881, with no loss of life. Her crew of 21 and 6 passengers (2 men and 4 women) took to the four lifeboats and, with great difficulty, reached shore, but the cargo of flour (1,000 barrels and 1,800 sacks) and four head of livestock was lost.

This wreck was located by Kent Bellrichard, Richard Zaleski and their team on the day in late December, 1975, when they found the *EMBA* and the scuttled railroad bridge as well. The ship's double wheel was removed by divers in January, 1976, but there remains a lot for the visiting diver still to see of this mostly intact, upright steamer in deep water.

Artwork ©Tim Reed

Above: The *St. Alban* at Cleveland. GLHS.
Below: A burbot and netting adorn the *St. Alban's* deck. PHOTO BY JON ZEAMAN.

The wooden steamer, *Appomattox* (site #18). MPL/WMHS

18. APPOMATTOX

LORAN: 32969.4/49231.1	**LAT 43° 05.35' LON 087° 52.24'**
DEPTH: 15 to 23 feet	**LEVEL: Novice**

LOCATION: This wreck lies just south of the first north pier off Atwater Beach, Whitefish Bay, Wisconsin, about 450' off shore.

The large wooden steamer, *Appomattox* (319'8" x 42' x 23'), launched on July 25, 1896 at West Bay City, Michigan, stranded on November 2, 1905, with a coal cargo. Broken and scattered, the wreck lies on a sand and gravel bottom, with the boiler just to the east.

19. JOSEPHINE

LORAN:	**LAT 45° 45.454' LON 075° 45.454'**
DEPTH: 10 feet	**LEVEL: Novice**

LOCATION: About 70' off shore north of Atwater Beach, 3 piers down the beach.

The wooden steam barge, *Josephine* (99' x 25' x 6'), built at Milwaukee in 1874, sank with a sand cargo after hitting a rock on April 15, 1888. She is broken and scattered in sand.

20. MILWAUKEE

LORAN: 32943.2/49208.7	LAT 43° 08.178′ LON 087° 49.925′
DEPTH: 90 to 125 feet	LEVEL: Advanced

LOCATION: This wreck lies 3.5 miles northeast of North Point, Milwaukee

The steel railroad car steamer, *Milwaukee* (338′ x 56′ x 19′5″), tragically foundered in an autumn storm on October 22, 1929, while bound from Milwaukee for Muskegon, Michigan, with a load of railroad cars. All 52 people who were on board perished. Launched on December 6, 1902, at Cleveland with the long name *Manistique-Marquette & Northern No. 1,* she was given a more managable name, *Milwaukee,* in 1908.

This is a challenging dive, as the visibility is frequently low (15′ or less) and the maze of wires and twisted cables invite entanglement. Some of the railroad cars can be explored, since this part of the wreck is relatively open. One car contains a cargo of bathtubs and toilet seats, while another holds three automobiles. The wreck is split in some places, with thick silt filling the crevices. Do not disturb the silt, as it will destroy your visibility and possibly your orientation. Very experienced divers with proper training, conditions and equipment can enter the shipwreck.

The carferry, *Milwaukee.* AUTHOR'S COLLECTION

Views of the *Milwaukee* shipwreck: A porthole still in place, and the ship's name painted (and still readable) above a door. PHOTOS BY JON ZEAMAN.

21. ISLAND CITY

LORAN: 32908.5/49138.1	LAT 43° 14.30′ LON 087° 50.71′
DEPTH: 135 to 140 feet	LEVEL: Technical

LOCATION: This wreck lies southeast of Port Washington, Wisconsin.

Captain William R. Wood, who drifted ashore unconscious at the bottom of the 9′ yawl boat and was found by a farmer, was this shipwreck's sole survivor (the other two crewmen drowned). The small, 52-net-ton, two-masted, lumber-laden schooner, *Island City* (81′ x 17′ x 6′), built in 1859 at St. Clair, Michigan, sank on April 8, 1894, while enroute from Ludington, Michigan, to Milwaukee. The 26-year-old captain had every dollar he owned invested in his little schooner. Sailors who knew him at Milwaukee collected donations so he could purchase some necessities and pay for passage back home across the lake.

This little shipwreck is badly broken up with commercial fishing nets snagged on her pieces. It is surprising that the site is in such bad shape, considering how deep it lies (depth usually ensures greater intactness and preservation). Apparently she sank so fast that her deck was blown off the hull from the great pressure of the air trying to escape from below.

36. Wisconsin's East Coast

WISCONSIN

– N –

Algoma

Kewaunee

Two Rivers

Manitowoc

Sheboygan

LAKE MICHIGAN

Port Washington

MILWAUKEE

Divers Joan Forsberg and Cris Kohl hang off the anchor line making a safety stop. PHOTO BY PETE TOMASINO.

1. *Northerner*	9. *Helvetia*	17. *S. C. Baldwin*
2. *Toledo*	10. *Selah Chamberlain*	18. *Vernon*
3. *Niagara*	11. *Silver Lake*	19. *Rouse Simmons*
4. *Byron*	12. *Walter B. Allen*	20. *Pathfinder*
5. *Atlanta*	13. *McMullen & Pitz drg.*	21. *Continental*
6. *Advance*	14. *Floretta*	22. *Francis Hinton*
7. *Hetty Taylor*	15. *Home*	23. *America*
8. *Phoenix*	16. *Henry Gust*	24. *Daniel Lyons*

1. NORTHERNER

> **LORAN: 32874.7/49091.8**   **LAT 43° 18.89′   LON 087° 49.45′**
> **DEPTH: 122 to 138 feet**   **LEVEL: Technical**

LOCATION: This wreck lies southeast of Port Washington, Wisconsin.

The twin-masted, 77-gross-ton "pocket schooner," *Northerner* (78′ x 18′ x 7′), constructed in 1859 at Wells Island, Michigan, foundered in severe weather on November 29, 1868, with a cargo of cord wood below deck. No lives were lost. This almost totally intact, upright site includes the railing, windlass, masthead, a mainmast which rises 75′ above her deck, centerboard winch, bowsprit, anchor chain and, the most unique feature of

this site, her figurehead, still with signs of white paint on it and which closely resembles the figurehead on the *Sandusky* in the Straits of Mackinac.

The *Northerner's* figurehead.
PHOTO BY JON ZEAMAN.

Artwork ©Tim Reed

2. TOLEDO

> **LORAN:**   **LAT**   **LON**
> **DEPTH: 20 feet**   **LEVEL: Novice**

LOCATION: This wreck lies about 300′ off the northern Port Washington breakwall out from the water pumping station.

Launched at Buffalo in 1854, the 179′ wooden passenger and freight steamer, *Toledo*, was carrying a total of about 50 passengers and crew, plus a cargo of general merchandise, when she encountered extremely harsh weather on October 24, 1856 (this was only about one month after the tragic loss of the *Niagara*; see site #3). Initially attempting to ride out the storm at anchor, Captain John Densham sensed disaster unless he beached his ship. He gave the orders to raise the anchors, and, in doing so, one of the chains fouled and an enormous wave crashed a heavy anchor against the ship's hull, splitting her bow. The mortally wounded *Toledo* was swept towards land by the wind and waves, but soon went to the bottom, taking with her all but three members of the hardy crew who managed to reach shore alive. The victims were buried alongside those from the *Niagara* in the Port Washington Union Cemetery; a *Toledo* anchor recovered in 1900 is on display at this cemetery. Salvagers recovered the *Toledo's* boiler and engine in 1857.

The wreck lies broken and scattered on the sand bottom, much of it (e.g. smokestack) being alternately covered and uncovered at the whim of nature.

3. NIAGARA

> **LORAN: 32800.0/48988.5**   **LAT 43° 29.31′   LON 087° 46.49′**
> **DEPTH: 55 feet**   **LEVEL: Intermediate**

LOCATION: This wreck lies about seven miles northeast of Port Washington and about two miles off Harrington Beach in the town of Belgium, Wisconsin.

The wooden sidewheel passenger and freight steamer, *Niagara* (245′ x 33′6″ x 14′), one of the numerous (about 25 in all) fast and opulent "palace steamers" which carried thousands of immigrants from the East to the Midwest in the years 1844 to 1857 just prior to the construction of railroad connections, caught on fire in the middle of the afternoon on September 23, 1856 off Port Washington. Captain Miller immediately ordered the ship steered towards shore, about five miles away, but within five minutes, the steam engine quit, and the blazing ship drifted helplessly. The flames, the smoke and the language barrier combined to create panic among the primarily Scandinavian passengers. In the ensuing chaos, about 60 people perished from the approximately 180 who were on board. The *Niagara* is one of the worst (in terms of loss of life) disasters to happen on the Great Lakes. Many of the deceased lie in Port Washington Union Cemetery.

The sidewheel steamer, *Niagara*. ERIC HEYL.

Built at Buffalo, New York, in 1845, the *Niagara* spent most of her life transporting people between the eastern and western ends of Lake Erie. She was, however, traveling between Collingwood, Ontario, and Chicago, Ilinois, when the disaster occurred.

The wreck and cargo lie broken up and scattered, with the bow facing shore. Much of the keel, ribs and machinery remains, with the hull broken in two with the sides fallen outward. The walking beam and engine rise 15′ off the bottom. One paddlewheel is nearly intact, the other, quite damaged. The three huge (8′ x 18′) and impressive boilers lie 278′ to the north-northeast of the main wreckage. This site is buoyed annually by the State Historical Society of Wisconsin.

Artwork © University of Wisconsin Sea Grant Institute/State Historical Society of Wisconsin

BURNING
OF THE
STEAMER NIAGARA!
Of The Collingwood Line.

NEARLY 100 LIVES LOST!

Boat and Cargo a Total Loss.

We are pained to be obliged to record another dreadful lake disaster, in the loss by fire of the steamer *Niagara*, of the Collingwood Line, last night, off Port Washington, about 20 miles north of this city.

We are indebted to Mr. Wm. Snow, of the firm of Snow & Williams, of this city, who came up on the *Traveler* last night, for the following particu-

Milwaukee Sentinel, Sept. 26, 1856. AUTHOR'S COLLECTION

The *Niagara* site displays vast piping, an upright paddlewheel, and the flat anchor for the marker buoy provided by the State of Wisconsin. PHOTOS BY JON ZEAMAN.

4. BYRON

LORAN: 32736.4/48929.0	**LAT 43° 36.29′ LON 087° 41.29′**
DEPTH: 135 feet	**LEVEL: Technical**

LOCATION: This wreck lies off Sheboygan, Wisconsin.

The small schooner, *Byron,* only about 40′ long, sank after a collision with the larger schooner, *Canton,* on May 8, 1867. This wreck is difficult to locate because it rises only 3′ off the lake floor. Do not drag an anchor into any shipwreck to locate it, particularly this fragile little beauty. Anchors cause damage. Using a knowledgeable dive charter to visit this site is preferred. This wreck lies intact, with centerboard, fallen mast, attached tiller and a capstan just off the wreck.

5. ATLANTA

LORAN:	**LAT 45° 45.454′ LON 075° 45.454′**
DEPTH: 90 feet	**LEVEL: Advanced**

LOCATION: This wreck lies just offshore from the town of Cedar Grove, Wisconsin.

The wooden passenger and freight steamer, *Atlanta* (200′ x 32′2″ x 13′6″), launched at

The *Atlanta.* MPL/WMHS

Cleveland on April 25, 1891, burned to a total loss on March 18, 1906, with one life lost (a fireman from the *Atlanta's* crew fell into the lake and drowned while attempting to enter a lifeboat). The fire spread quickly, assisted by the large cargo of wooden furniture and pianos. The tug, *Tessler,* under the command of Captain G.H. Smith, came to the rescue and removed most of the passengers and crew, later returning to the burning wreck and towing it to shore.

This shipwreck lies about 450′ off shore, and rises 3′ to 5′ off the bottom, with the bow pointing north. This vast site sits in a busy boating area; stay close to your dive flag.

6. ADVANCE

LORAN: 32741.2/48919.3	**LAT 43°36.71′ LON 087° 49.91′**
DEPTH: 83 feet	**LEVEL: Advanced**

LOCATION: This wreck lies about 9 miles southeast of Sheboygan, 2.5 miles off shore.

The two-masted schooner, *Advance* (117′ x 25′ x 9′), built in 1853 at Milwaukee and heading to Chicago with a cargo of tan bark, foundered in a storm on September 8, 1885, with all five men on board, including Captain M. Paulson and his son, George.

The wreck, located accidentally by sport fishermen in 1983, is surprisingly, for this depth, broken up, with most of it sitting on sand in a large pile, with pieces scattered nearby.

7. HETTY TAYLOR

LORAN: 32700.9/48885.5	**LAT 43° 40.89′ LON 087° 39.30′**
DEPTH: 97 to 107 feet	**LEVEL: Advanced**

LOCATION: This wreck lies southeast off Sheboygan, Wisconsin.

The 85-gross-ton, two-masted schooner, *Hetty Taylor* (84′ + bowsprit x 22′6″ x 8′), built in 1874 at Milwaukee, capsized on August 26, 1880, in a storm because her lumber cargo on deck made her topheavy. The crew reached shore in a lifeboat. A salvage crew steamed out immediately in the tug, *Messenger,* in an attempt to tow in the overturned ship before she sank, but upon arriving at the site, they found only the top 8′ of a mast above water. She was already on the bottom. Today she makes an excellent dive site.

Artwork © University of Wisconsin Sea Grant Institute/State Historical Society of Wisconsin

The schooner,
Hetty Taylor

The *Hetty Taylor,* buoyed annually by the State Historical Society of Wisconsin, lies upright and considerably intact, with her photogenic bow (bowsprit and chains in place, windlass and anchor chain on deck) and portside in excellent condition. The pilothouse, in good shape, sits off the broken starboard side, and the rudder sits in the damaged stern.

8. PHOENIX

LORAN:	LAT	LON
DEPTH: 8 feet	LEVEL: Novice	

LOCATION: This wreck lies just north of the Sheboygan city boat ramp.

The wooden passenger and freight sidewheel steamer, *Phoenix* (144′ x 26′ x 11′), built in 1845 at Cleveland, was fated to become another of the worst tragedies in Great Lakes history. In the middle of the night on November 21, 1847, the ship, loaded with package freight and almost 250 people (mostly Dutch immigrant families), caught on fire from an overheated boiler and burned to a total loss, with about 180 to 200 men, women and children being lost. The ship carried only two lifeboats which saved a total of 43 lives, including the captain's. The tug, *Delaware,*

The burning of the *Phoenix,* from *Lloyd's Steamboat Directory.* AUTHOR'S COLLECTION

rescued three sailors who clung to the *Phoenix's* steering chains at the stern, and also towed in the burnt out hulk to Sheboygan, where burnt bodies (plus coins and machinery) were recovered and the hull was allowed to sink. Relocated in modern times in 1982 by Jim Brotz, Jim Jetzer and Bill Wangemann, the *Phoenix's* hull lies mostly buried in a soft bottom.

9. HELVETIA

LORAN: 32650.7/48824.2	LAT 43° 47.31′ LON 087° 36.49′
DEPTH: 165 feet	LEVEL: Technical

LOCATION: About 10 miles northeast of Sheboygan.

This old ship's bare hull was purposely burned on Lake Michigan on September 10, 1921. She had outlived her usefulness after almost half a century of hauling bulk cargoes such as lumber around the Great Lakes. Built at Tonawanda, New York, in 1873, the large schooner, *Helvetia* (204′5″ x 35′6″ x 13′8″), was located in 1975. Beware of commercial fishing nets snagged onto this deep hull.

The *Helvetia.* MPL/WMHS

10. SELAH CHAMBERLAIN

> **LORAN: 32670.7/48828.0**   **LAT 43° 46.12'   LON 087° 34.47'**
> **DEPTH: 75 to 88 feet**   **LEVEL: Advanced**

LOCATION: This wreck lies two miles north of Sheboygan Point, Wisconsin.

Th wooden steam barge, *Selah Chamberlain* (212' x 34' x 14'), built at Cleveland in 1873, sank in a collision in dense fog and heavy seas with the steamer, *John Pridgeon, Jr.,* on Wednesday, October 13, 1886, with the loss of 5 lives when the 16 crew rushed for the lifeboat. The *Chamberlain* was bound light from Milwaukee to Escanaba, Michigan. The *Pridgeon,* having turned around in an unsuccessful attempt to locate the sinking ship in the fog, continued to Chicago and reported the matter.

This is one of Wisconsin's most popular dive sites. The wreck of the *Selah Chamberlain,* sitting upright on a sand bottom, displays her engine and boiler, the site's highlights. Other items include the propeller and tools lying around the deck. Shifting sands cover and uncover portions of the wreck steadily, so each new visit will yield new things to see.

11. SILVER LAKE

> **LORAN: 32637.5/48819.5**   **LAT 43° 48.39'   LON 087° 34.65'**
> **DEPTH: 209 feet**   **LEVEL: Technical**

LOCATION: This wreck lies about 8.5 miles northeast of Sheboygan, Wisconsin.

A 337' steel Pere Marquette Railroad carferry ran down and sank the small, two-masted scow schooner, *Silver Lake* (95' x 20' x 7'6"), on May 28, 1900, in a heavy fog. The lumber-laden Silver Lake was struck midship port side, cutting her almost in two. The cook, Henry Eastman, 45 and single, lost his life. The ship, valued at $1,500, carried no insurance. Located by John Steele and his team (Bill Cohrs, Steve Radovan, Jim Brotz and Wally Bissonnette) on May 22, 1977, this wreck sits upright and mostly intact, with the foremast rising to 138'.

12. WALTER B. ALLEN

> **LORAN: 32637.3/48748.0**   **LAT 43° 53.08'   LON 087° 41.01'**
> **DEPTH: 158 to 170 feet**   **LEVEL: Technical**

LOCATION: This wreck lies about 9 miles northeast of Sheboygan, Wisconsin.

The twin-masted, 137' schooner, *Walter B. Allen,* built at Ogdensburg, NY, in 1866, foundered in a fierce storm on April 16, 1880, with no lives lost. Located by Kent Bellrichard in May, 1975, this upright wreck has both masts still standing 70' above the deck. Her bowsprit, a windlass and a cargo steam engine behind the first hold remain in place.

13. MCMULLEN & PITZ DREDGE

> **LORAN: 32632.6/48746.5**   **LAT 43° 53.52'   LON 087° 40.31'**
> **DEPTH: 85 feet**   **LEVEL: Advanced**

LOCATION: This wreck lies about halfway between Sheboygan and Manitowoc.

Located by Steve Radovan in 1984, this work dredge sank in a storm off Cleveland, Wisconsin, on November 18, 1919, with no lives lost. Features include a full-length crane boom, a boiler and huge cleats. Penetration is possible for the trained and experienced.

14. FLORETTA

> **LORAN: 32576.4/48732.4**   **LAT 43° 57.02'   LON 087° 32.13'**
> **DEPTH: 181 feet**   **LEVEL: Technical**

LOCATION: This wreck lies about 11 miles southeast of Manitowoc, Wisconsin.

The schooner, *Floretta* (134' x 26' x 11'), constructed at Detroit in 1868, foundered with her iron ore cargo on September 18, 1885. No lives were lost. The wreck is mostly intact, with three anchors at the bow, but the visibility is usually poor and commercial fishing nets are snagged on the wreck, posing serious danger to the diver.

15. HOME

LORAN: 32585.5/48732.4	LAT 43° 56.83' LON 087° 33.28'
DEPTH: 165 feet	LEVEL: Technical

LOCATION: This wreck lies about 10 miles southeast of Manitowoc, Wisconsin.

The small, two-masted schooner, *Home* (84' x 23'), built in Lower Sandusky, Ohio, in 1843, sank after a collision with another ship on October 23, 1858. Located by Steve Radovan in April, 1981, this site is infrequently visited due to her depth, usually poor visibility and the potentially dangerous commercial fish nets draped over most of the wreck.

16. HENRY GUST

LORAN: 32501.1/48619.9	LAT LON
DEPTH: 80 feet	LEVEL: Advanced

LOCATION: This wreck lies about three miles east of Two Rivers, Wisconsin.

The steam-powered fishing tug, *Henry Gust,* was built in 1893 at Milwaukee. After 1929, this aging ship was shortened by ten feet (from 72' to 62') to bypass mandatory inspection requirements for vessels over 65' in length. But the vessel was already on her last legs, and in 1935, she was stripped of her reusable brass and copper items, towed into Lake Michigan and scuttled. Her boiler, propeller and other machinery remain in place.

Left to right: The fishing tug, *Henry Gust* and the steamers, *S.C. Baldwin* and *Vernon.* All MPL/WMHS

17. S. C. BALDWIN

LORAN: 32487.3/48597.3	LAT 44° 10.90' LON 087° 29.10'
DEPTH: 80 feet	LEVEL: Advanced

LOCATION: North of Two Rivers, about 2.3 miles southeast of Rawley Point.

One life was lost when the wooden steamer-converted-to-a-bulk-freight-barge, *S.C. Baldwin,* (160' x 30' x 11'), with a stone cargo, capsized and sank on August 27, 1908. She was built in 1871 at Detroit. She sits upright and quite intact. Avoid snagging on wire rigging.

18. VERNON

LORAN: 32461.6/49598.9	LAT 44° 11.96' LON 087° 24.81'
DEPTH: 210 feet	LEVEL: Technical

LOCATION: This wreck lies about 6 miles east of Rawley Point Lighthouse.

Built in 1886 at Chicago, the wooden steamer, *Vernon* (158'7" x 25'5" x 18'8"), was lost in a gale on Oct. 29, 1887, with 41 lives lost; a sole survivor clung to a raft for two days. Kent Bellrichard located this wreck, which is upright and intact, on July 12, 1969.

19. Rouse Simmons

LORAN: 32437.7/48550.7	LAT 44° 16.51′ LON 087° 24.94′
DEPTH: 155 to 168 feet	LEVEL: Technical

LOCATION: This wreck lies east-northeast of Two Rivers Point, Wisconsin.

The three-masted schooner, *Rouse Simmons* (123′5″ x 27′6″ x 8′4″), launched at Milwaukee in August, 1868, is the famous "Christmas Tree Ship," so-named because her final runs of each season traditionally consisted of northern Michigan evergreen trees packed into her holds and on deck for the Christmas Chicago market. She was carrying just such a cargo when she foundered in a fierce blizzard off Kewaunee, Wisconsin, on November 23, 1912. All 16 people on board perished. This wreck, upright and intact, was located by Kent Bellrichard in October, 1971. Many needle-less evergreen trees remain in position in her hold. Mast stumps, about 10′ tall, remain on deck, and rails around the ship remain intact.

The "Christmas Tree Ship," the schooner, *Rouse Simmons,* loaded with evergreen trees. Both MPL/WMHS

20. Pathfinder

LORAN: 32473.5/48552.3	LAT 44° 14.69′ LON 087° 30.68′
DEPTH: 10 feet	LEVEL: Novice

LOCATION: This wreck lies about 2.5 miles north of Two Rivers Point, Wisconsin.

The three-masted schooner, *Pathfinder* (188′ x 31′), built in Detroit in 1869, attempted to ride out heavy seas with her anchors set, but they failed to hold and she stranded with her cargo of 1,053 tons of iron ore on November 19, 1886. No lives were lost. This notorious storm sank or stranded at least 29 other Great Lakes vessels, a few of which were recovered. Among those total losses was, at Marquette, Michigan, the schooner, *Florida* (which is also in this book). The *Pathfinder's* anchors and other items were salvaged, but the wreck lies scattered where she broke up.

21. Continental

LORAN: 32476.8/48561.2	LAT 44° 13.83′ LON 087° 30.52′
DEPTH: 25 feet	LEVEL: Novice

LOCATION: One mile north of Rawley Point.

The wooden steamer, *Continental* (244′7″ x 36′4″ x 19′2″), stranded in a severe snow storm on December 13, 1904, enroute to Manitowoc to pick up a cargo. None of the 20 lives was lost. The ship, built at Cleveland in 1882, broke up over the winter.

Today, wooden ribs (framing) and decking emerge from the sandy bottom of the lake. Her upright engine rises very close to the surface (boaters: beware!).

Left: The *Continental.* GLHS

22. *Francis Hinton*

> **LORAN: 32548.9/48614.3** **LAT 44° 06.67' LON 087° 37.88'**
> **DEPTH: 20 feet** **LEVEL: Novice**

LOCATION: This wreck lies about 4.5 miles north of Two Rivers, Wisconsin.

Built at Manitowoc, Wisconsin, in 1889, the wooden steamer, *Francis Hinton* (152'2" x 30'9" x 10'8"), bound for Chicago from Manistique, Michigan, with a heavy cargo of lumber (Norway pine), ultimately stranded and broke in two on November 16, 1909. Captain John Campbell (who was 86 years old) had anchored his leaking ship offshore, but ordered the line cut so his vessel, which he knew was doomed, would sink in shallow water. Once it drifted west and stranded, he and his crew reached shore safely in their lifeboat.

This shipwreck lies somewhat broken and scattered, but not flattened as badly as other wrecks in such shallow water. The propeller is in place and the boiler rises to within 10' of the surface. This site is buoyed annually by the State Historical Society of Wisconsin.

The *Francis Hinton*, with a cargo of lumber on her deck (as well as in her hold), exactly like the day she sank. MPL/WMHS

Two Rivers, Wisconsin
7/1994

Artwork © University of Wisconsin Sea Grant Institute/State Historical Society of Wisconsin

23. *America*

> **LORAN: 32423.1/48498.5** **LAT 44° 21.01' LON 087° 26.84'**
> **DEPTH: 112 to 130 feet** **LEVEL: Advanced**

LOCATION: This wreck lies about 9 miles north of Two Rivers Light, Wisconsin.

Heading to Escanaba, Michigan, from Chicago, empty in order to pick up an iron ore cargo destined for Michigan City, Indiana, the three-masted schooner, *America* (137' x 26' x 11'), built at Port Huron, Michigan, in 1873, collided at full speed the night of September 28, 1880, with the braided steel towline between an unlighted tug and her equally unlighted towbarge. The impact put a large hole in the schooner's bow and she went down within minutes, but with her stern floating for several days afterwards. The strain of salvage tugs towing her in caused her to sink totally. Her crew had escaped to shore in their yawlboat.

The wreck, located on Sept. 3, 1977, by John Steele, Jim Brotz, Kent Bellrichard, Rich Zaleski and Jim Jetzer, faces east, upright and relatively intact, with her open deck and cargo holds inviting exploration. Beware of snagged lines at this popular fishing spot. The wheel was recovered several years ago and is now in the Manitowoc Maritime Museum.

24. *Daniel Lyons*

> **LORAN: 32283.5/48329.1** **LAT 44° 40.22' LON 087° 17.71'**
> **DEPTH: 95 feet** **LEVEL: Advanced**

LOCATION: Several miles northeast of Algoma, Wisconsin, and 3 miles off shore.

Built at Oswego, NY, in 1873, the three-masted, 318-ton, grain-laden schooner, *Daniel Lyons,* sank after the schooner, *Kate Gillett,* sliced halfway through the *Lyons'* starboard side on October 18, 1878. No lives were lost. This wreck is quite broken up.

37. Door County

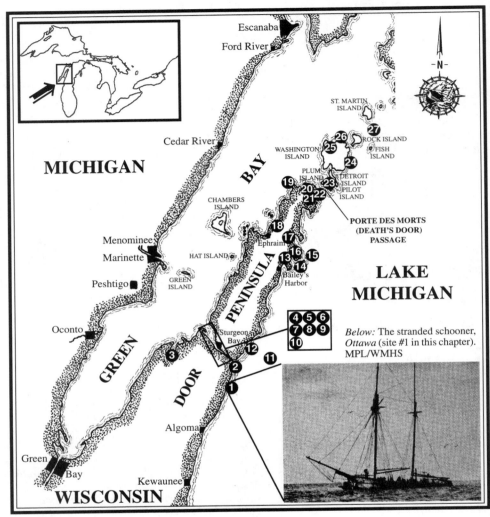

Below: The stranded schooner, *Ottawa* (site #1 in this chapter). MPL/WMHS

1. *Ottawa*	10. *J.S. Williams*	19. *Fleetwing*
2. Coast Grd. breakwall	11. *Lakeland*	20. Table Bluff
3. Little Sturgeon Bay	12. *City of Glasgow*	21. Wisconsin Bay
4. *Adriatic*	13. Moonlight Bay	22. *Resumption*
5. *Joys*	14. *Michael J. Bartelme*	23. Pilot Island wrecks
6. *Fountain City*	15. *Frank O'Connor*	24. *Winfield Scott*
7. *Mueller*	16. *Boaz*	25. *Louisiana*
8. *Joseph L. Hurd*	17. *Cherubusco*	26. *Pride*
9. Bullhead Pt. wrecks	18. Sister Bay wreck	27. Steam barge & tug

1. OTTAWA

LORAN: 32395.6/46144.5	LAT 46° 52.84′ LON 090° 46.25′
DEPTH: 20 feet	LEVEL: Novice

LOCATION: This wreck lies about 6 miles north of Algoma, Wisconsin.

The two-masted schooner, *Ottawa* (113′ x 25′ x 7′6″), built at Grand Haven, Michigan, in 1874, stranded on her first trip of the season less than a mile off shore in heavy fog and building seas while bound from Manistique, Michigan for Chicago with a lumber cargo on Thursday, April 13, 1911. The crew of five lost their lives when they attempted to reach shore in a yawl boat. They should have remained with their ship, which stayed so intact that the decks had to be dynamited later so salvagers could remove the cargo.

Hull framing and some planking remain of this shipwreck, flattened by time and nature in the shallows where she hit the rocks.

2. COAST GUARD BREAKWALL

DEPTH: To 35 feet	LEVEL: Novice

LOCATION: The northern breakwall close to the navigation light at the eastern entrance of the Sturgeon Bay Canal.

Many fish tend to congregate here, including burbots, carp, alewives and, in the autumn when there are also many fishermen in this area, salmon. The bottom is sand and the visibility is generally good.

3. LITTLE STURGEON BAY

DEPTH: To 20 feet	LEVEL: Novice

LOCATION: Off Claflin Memorial Park at the end of Lime Kiln Road near the west entrance to Little Sturgeon Bay.

Fish life and the broken remains of a small, wooden ship are found at this site.

4. ADRIATIC

DEPTH: 10 to 20 feet	LEVEL: Novice

LOCATION: This wreck lies south of the yacht club and north of the docks northwest of the old railroad bridge on the east side of the bay, on the southeasterly end of the old Leatham Smith Co. dock.

Built at West Bay City, Michigan, in 1889, the three-masted schooner, *Adriatic* (202′ x 34′7″ x 16′6″), worked as a stone barge all of her life. She was laid up at the dock in 1927 and sank in 1930 where she lies today. This wreck consists basically of her ribs. Beware of boating traffic here, as well as low visibility and snagged fishing line.

The *Adriatic.* AUTHOR'S COLLECTION

5. JOYS

DEPTH: 10 to 20 feet	LEVEL: Novice

LOCATION: This wreck lies next to the remains of the *Adriatic* (see site #4).

Built for the lumber trade at Milwaukee in 1884, the wooden steamer, *Joys* (131′ x 28′2″ x 9′9″), burned to a total loss at Sturgeon Bay on Christmas Day, 1898. The wreck lies flat and broken. Be cautious of boating traffic and fishing lines.

The *Joys.* MPL/WMHS

6. FOUNTAIN CITY

DEPTH: 10 to 30 feet — **LEVEL: Novice**

The Fountain City, after the fire.
AUTHOR'S COLLECTION

LOCATION: This wreck lies off Sunset Park on the north side of Sturgeon Bay.

Built at Cleveland in 1857, the old wooden steamer, *Fountain City* (209'11" x 30'3" x 13'6"), caught on fire at the coal dock in Sturgeon Bay on May 5, 1896, was cut loose to save the dock, stranded and had her fire extinguished by the fire department, but she was still declared a total loss. Wreckage, mainly ribs and planks, is spread over a large area in a busy boating portion of the bay known for generally low visibility (5' to 8')

7. MUELLER

DEPTH: 9 to 13 feet — **LEVEL: Novice**

LOCATION: This wreck lies about 50' off shore in the northern part of Sturgeon Bay, off one of the old stone quarry pits along county highway "B," near the *J. Hurd* (site #8).

Launched as the *Edwin S. Tice* at Manitowoc, Wisconsin, in 1887, the wooden bulk freight steamer, *Mueller* (160' x 32' x 12'--1915 Chicago remeasurement), received her new name on May 6, 1901, after her rebuild. She was abandoned in 1933. Usually visible from shore, this stone-filled, abandoned ship rises about 5' at the bow. Her stern is at the Sturgeon Bay Museum off Sunset Park North.

Right: The steamer, *Mueller.* AUTHOR'S COLLECTION

8. JOSEPH L. HURD

DEPTH: 30 feet — **LEVEL: Novice**

LOCATION: This wreck lies near the *Mueller* (site #7), about 100' off the stone quarry, and just to the north of the new cement fishing dock.

The wooden steamer, *Joseph L. Hurd* (128'5" x 24'5" x 12'5"), launched on September 1, 1869 at Detroit, stranded with a cargo of crushed stone 9 miles northwest of the Sturgeon Bay Ship Canal on September 23, 1913, but was released and towed to the old Leatham Smith quarry dock at the northwest end of Sturgeon Bay, where the ship was scuttled. The *Joseph L. Hurd* is perhaps most (in)famous for her collision with the steamer, *Cayuga,* (which is also in this book) near the Straits of Mackinac in 1895.

The bow half of the wreck is fairly intact, but the stern has broken off. Visibility is usually good, but boating traffic is steady. Use a dive flag.

The *Joseph L. Hurd.* MPL/WMHS

9. BULLHEAD POINT WRECKS

DEPTH: 10 to 15 feet   LEVEL: Novice

LOCATION: Three abandoned wooden ships rest at the foot of the old Sawyer Quarry dock at Bullhead Point, Sturgeon Bay, in a busy boating and fishing area:

❶ The three-masted schooner, *Oak Leaf* (final measurements 160′ x 31′2″ x 10′7″), built at Cleveland in 1866 and converted to a barge in 1917, was abandoned in 1928.

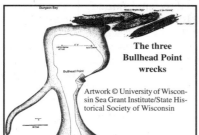

The three
Bullhead Point
wrecks

Artwork © University of Wisconsin Sea Grant Institute/State Historical Society of Wisconsin

❷ The wooden barge, *Ida Corning* (168′ x 31′3″ x 10′9″), launched in 1881 at East Saginaw, Michigan, was abandoned in 1928.

❸ The wooden steamer, *Empire State* (212′ x 33′ x 18′6″), constructed at Buffalo, New York, in 1862, spent her first 44 years carrying passengers before being reduced to a barge; she was abandoned in 1916.

All three ships worked together in the stone trade in the final years of their careers. Their hulls offer excellent exploration opportunities.

❶ The *Oak Leaf*. GLHS

The remains of the *Oak Leaf*
Artwork © University of Wisconsin Sea Grant
Institute/State Historical Society of Wisconsin

❷ The *Ida Corning* MPL/WMHS

The remains of the *Ida Corning*
Artwork © University of Wisconsin Sea Grant
Institute/State Historical Society of Wisconsin

The *Empire State*. Author's Collection ❸

The remains of the *Empire State*
Artwork © University of Wisconsin Sea Grant
Institute/State Historical Society of Wisconsin

10. J.S. WILLIAMS

DEPTH: 15 to 20 feet   LEVEL: Novice

The *J.S. Williams* in tow. MPL/WMHS

LOCATION: These vessel remains lie about one mile south of the large quarries on County Highway "B," off a small access road to the water. In the water, to the south, a sand and concrete finger runs into the bay. The remains of three unidentified ships lie scattered together here. Go further. There is a second finger, off which you will find the *J.S. Williams*.

Launched as the three-masted schooner, *Phoenix*, in 1868 at Henderson, Minnesota and renamed the *J.S. Williams* (121' x 26') in 1896, this vessel toiled mainly in the lumber and stone trades before being abandoned in the spring of 1902. Flattened wooden framing and planking are all that remain of this once-beautiful sailing ship.

11. LAKELAND

LORAN: 32219.3/48274.5   LAT 44° 47.57'   LON 087° 11.49'
DEPTH: 210 to 235 feet   LEVEL: Technical

LOCATION: This wreck lies about 9 miles north-northeast of Algoma, Wisconsin, just northeast of the Sturgeon Bay Ship Canal.

Contemporary newspaper ad for sailing on the *Lakeland*.
AUTHOR'S COLLECTION

Launched as the *Cambria* in 1887 at Cleveland, the iron-hulled ship was renamed *Lakeland* (280' x 40' x 20') in 1910. She was one of the first three steamers on the Great Lakes to have a triple expansion engine. Converted from a bulk freighter to a combination passenger and package freight steamer in 1910, she sprang a leak and foundered on

The sinking *Lakeland*. MPL/WMHS

December 3, 1924. None of the 30 lives on board was lost, but the thirty 1924 automobiles all went to the bottom. One auto, a Rollins, was raised in 1979, with considerable damage done to the vehicle. The *Lakeland* lies upright, intact -- and deep!

12. CITY OF GLASGOW

DEPTH: 8 to 10 feet   LEVEL: Novice

LOCATION: About 400' off the community of Lily Bay, 3 miles north of the canal.

City of Glasgow. MPL/WMHS

The wooden steamer, later a barge, *City of Glasgow* (297' x 41' x 24'2"),was built at West Bay City, Michigan, in 1891. It was after she burned off Green Bay on December 3, 1907, that her hull was converted to a barge. She stranded during a strong southern gale at her final resting place, where she broke in two, on October 6, 1917. Her anchors and chain were salvaged. Her broken hull lies in two large sections some distance apart.

13. MOONLIGHT BAY

DEPTH: 25 feet	LEVEL: Novice

LOCATION: On the north side of Moonlight Bay, south off Highway "Q."
Interesting rock formations, old net stakes and fish make up the highlights of a dive near the boat ramp.

14. *MICHAEL J. BARTELME*

DEPTH: 15 feet	LEVEL: Novice

LOCATION: This wreck lies at the south end of Cana Island.

Launched on April 20, 1895 at West Bay City, Michigan, as the *John J. McWilliams* (and renamed *Central West* in 1916 and given her last name in the final year of her life) the huge, steel steamer, *Michael J. Bartelme* (128'5" x 24'5" x 12'5"), named after a dock superintendent who lived from 1881 to 1970, stranded in a storm on Cana Island on October 4, 1928, and was declared a total loss. The wreck was partly scrapped in 1929. The site today consists of steel, rigging, valves, cables and pumps, plus much machinery, all of which

The stranded *Michael J. Bartelme.* MPL/WMHS

makes for good underwater photography in an area of generally good visibility. Take a boat, as it is a long walk on shore and the privately-owned lighthouse property is off limits.

15. *FRANK O'CONNOR*

LORAN: 32078.7/48115.9	LAT 45° 06.87' LON 087° 00.73'
DEPTH: 50 to 67 feet	LEVEL: Intermediate-Advanced

LOCATION: This wreck lies about two miles off Cana Island.

The steel-strapped, wooden steamer, *Frank O'Connor* (301' x 42'5" x 22'8"), launched on September 17, 1892, at West Bay City, Michigan, as the *City of Naples* (she was renamed in 1916), burned with a cargo of coal on October 2, 1919. Her crew safely abandoned the blazing ship after her seacocks were ordered opened to hasten her sinking.

Located by divers Sam Mareci and Tom Beaudwin in 1990, the *Frank O'Connor* sits upright with most of her artifacts and much machinery in

In drydock, Aug. 14, 1917. MPL/WMHS

A diver examines the *Frank O'Connor's* engine controls. PHOTO BY JON ZEAMAN.

place, including her 20'-tall triple expansion steam engine, two large scotch boilers, a steam windlass, a capstan, much bow chain, a rudder and steering quadrant lying flat and a large four-bladed propeller. An anchor illegally removed by Chicago divers in 1991 outraged local divers to the point where an out-of-court settlement was reached: the anchor today resides at the Cana Island Lighthouse overlooking the site where the ship met its end. This site, likely the most popular in Door County, is buoyed annually at both bow and stern by the State Historical Society of Wisconsin.

16. BOAZ

LORAN: 32082.4/48093.8	LAT 45° 08.31' LON 087° 03.10'
DEPTH: 15 feet	LEVEL: Novice

LOCATION: In North Bay in a small cove southwest of Marshall's Point.

Launched at Sheboygan, Wisconsin, in 1869, the three-masted, oak-hulled schooner, *Boaz* (118'9" x 22' x 7'), sailing from Pierpont, Michigan, towards Racine, Wisconsin with a load of lumber, sought shelter from a strong gale in this bay on November 9, 1900. She anchored safely and her crew, having little faith in the 31-year-old wooden vessel, abandoned ship, boarding a steamer which had also taken shelter there. Her cargo was removed and the *Boaz* sank shortly afterwards. Her centerboard and trunk, plus two pump shafts and much of the hull, form the highlights of this site.

The *Boaz*. AUTHOR'S COLLECTION

WISCONSIN HISTORICAL SOCIETY
Underwater Archaeology Program

The Wisconsin Historical Society (WHS) conducts underwater archaeological research and public education to preserve and protect the over 700 shipwrecks located in the state. Through public programs, publications, Web Sites, and museum exhibits, the WHS is dedicated to enhancing our appreciation and understanding of Wisconsin's maritime history, as well as increasing access to shipwrecks.

Wisconsin Maritime Trails and Shipwreck Moorings
Winding above and below the waves, the Maritime Trails will link maritime properties such as shipwrecks, lighthouses, docks, and ships. A major component of the this initiative are the seasonal shipwreck moorings placed on some of state's most popular shipwrecks, making the sites easier to find and protecting them from anchor damage.

Wisconsin's Great Lakes Shipwrecks: www.seagrant.wisc.edu/shipwrecks
The Web site features detailed information on various Wisconsin shipwrecks. It also includes underwater video and images, archaeological maps and illustrations, a maritime history overview, searchable databases, and historic photos.

Waterproof Guides to Wisconsin's Historic Shipwrecks
The WHS and the University of Wisconsin Sea Grant have produced visitors' guides for popular Wisconsin Lake Superior and Lake Michigan shipwrecks. The rugged, waterproof guides are designed to go along on dives and feature site maps, schematics, diving information, and vessel data and histories. The 9.5" x 6.5" slates allow divers to take a self-guide tour of the wrecks.

For more information, including public programs or to order publications, call 608/ 271-8172 or visit www.seagrant.wisc.edu/shipwrecks. Please help protect Wisconsin's maritime history. Keep shipwrecks intact for future divers to explore. Wisconsin law prohibits unauthorized disturbance or removal of artifacts, structure, cargo or human remains. Report shipwreck looting at (800) TIP-WDNR.

17. CHERUBUSCO

> **LORAN: 32084.5/48090.2**   **LAT 45° 08.46′   LON 087° 03.72′**
> **DEPTH: 8 to 10 feet**   **LEVEL: Novice**

LOCATION: This wreck lies in the middle of North Bay, Door Peninsula, Wisconsin. This old vessel, built in Milwaukee in 1848, was a bark-rigged scow named the *Cherubusco* (144′ x 27′ x 9′4″). After a career in the lumber business, she was beached in a

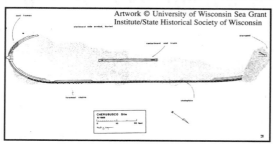

Artwork © University of Wisconsin Sea Grant Institute/State Historical Society of Wisconsin

waterlogged condition considerably north of her destination while enroute from Chicago to Manitowoc with a lumber cargo in November, 1872, and was abandoned in place.

Most of the *Cherubusco's* lower hull lies intact, with the bow, centerboard and trunk, and sternpost in place. The port side is in good condition, but the starboard side lies buried in the sand.

18. SISTER BAY WRECK

> **DEPTH: 10 to 20 feet**   **LEVEL: Novice**

LOCATION: Southwest of the boat launch at the end of Country Lane, at the base of Sister Bay. An unidentified wooden vessel, about 50′ long, lies in these shallow waters, with wreckage lying on shore marking the site. Use a dive flag; traffic can get busy here.

19. FLEETWING

> **LORAN: 32041.11/48006.22**   **LAT 45° 17.25′   LON 087° 02.99′**
> **DEPTH: 10 to 30 feet**   **LEVEL: Novice**

LOCATION: This wreck lies in the southwest part of Garrett Bay, Door County.

The three-masted schooner, *Fleetwing* (136′ x 29′ x 12′), built in 1867 at Manitowoc, Wisconsin, was enroute with a cargo of lumber from Menominee, Michigan, to Chicago, when, on the night of September 26, 1888, heading into a northwest gale, Captain Andrew McGraw mistook another bluff for Table Bluff, and sailed at full speed into Garrett Bay instead of the open waters into Lake Michigan through Death's Door Passage. In the darkness, he hit a dead end, grinding his vessel's wooden hull upon the rocky beach with such force that a mast sheared off. Fortunately, the crew all

The *Fleetwing*. MPL/WMHS

reached land safely, but their ship soon broke in two. This site, buoyed annually by the State Historical Society of Wisconsin, consists of several sections of hull, scattered over an area

Artwork © University of Wisconsin Sea Grant Institute/State Historical Society of Wisconsin

500′ long. Four sections, from the hull and decking, lie broken 200′ to 300′ east-northeast of the boat landing at Garrett Bay Road, while the fifth section lies about 500′ north-northeast of the boat launch.

20. TABLE BLUFF

DEPTH: 10 to 110 feet	LEVEL: Novice to Advanced

LOCATION: Along the northern wall of Table Bluff.

Geologic formations (steep walls, boulders, outcroppings) form the highlights of any underwater exploration here. This is a boat dive, unless you happen to be staying at the lodge which adjoins the cliff. Caution: the ferry to Washington Island passes close by.

21. WISCONSIN BAY

DEPTH: 25 to 55 feet	LEVEL: Novice to Intermediate

LOCATION: Off Shastal's dock, at the end of Timberline Road, just northwest of the boat launch. The dock itself is private property, so a boat is required to dive here. This bay offers quite a lot: schools of fish, submerged dock cribbing in 25', a 34' commercial gill net fishing boat in 55' of water about 200' in front of Shastal's dock, and a 40' fishing tug in 55' of water about 400' 70 degrees off Shastal's dock.

22. *RESUMPTION*

DEPTH: 5 to 15 feet	LEVEL: Novice

LOCATION: This wreck lies off the southeast side of Plum Island in Death's Door.

The schooner, *Resumption* (143'4" x 29' x 10'3"), built at Milwaukee in 1879, stranded here on Nov. 7, 1914 and became a total loss. Only portions of the hull's bottom remain.

23. PILOT ISLAND WRECKS

LORAN: 32006.5/48032.3	LAT 45° 37.64' LON 086° 55.31'
DEPTH: 20 to 50 feet	LEVEL: Novice-Intermediate

LOCATION: These wrecks lie off the northwest side of Pilot Island, Death's Door.

The broken remains of three wooden ships rest at this site:

1. The scow-schooner, *Forest* (115'6" x 23', after 1880 rebuild), built in 1857 at Newport (later Marine City), Michigan, stranded here in a gale on October 28, 1891. All 5 crew rowed to the safety of the lighthouse.

2. The schooner, *J.E. Gilmore* (137'7" x 25'4"), constructed at Three Mile Bay, NY, in 1867, was blown onto the reef on October 17, 1891. No lives were lost.

Artwork © University of Wisconsin Sea Grant Institute/State Historical Society of Wisconsin

Pilot Island

U.S. Lighthouse Service Mooring Block

Hull Fragments

Large Debris Field

Chainplate

Loading Port

Nichols' Port Side & Stern Deadwood

Nichols' Bilge

Forest's Port Side & Bow

Mast Steps

0 10 20 feet

N

Centerboard

This photo, taken on October 29 or 30, 1891, shows the *A.P. Nichols* on the right and a broadside view of the *J.E. Gilmore*, left. The sunken *Forest* lies between them. MPL/WMHS

3. The schooner, *A.P. Nichols* (145′2″ x 30′2″ x 11′9″), launched at Madison Dock, Ohio, in 1861, was driven onto the island in the gale of Oct. 28, 1891. No lives were lost.

This group site consists of a large debris field near a cement dock. The sand and gravel bottom turns silty the deeper it gets. This jumble of wreckage from three ships is worth the effort to get out there. A boat capable of handling unexpectedly bad weather, usually from the northwest, is needed. Currents can sometimes be moderate.

24. WINFIELD SCOTT

> **LORAN: 31968.5/48000.2**   **LAT 45° 21.75′   LON 086° 51.39′**
> **DEPTH: 10 feet**   **LEVEL: Novice**

LOCATION: Off Hog Island, about 2000′ to the east of Washington Island.

The two-masted, 213-ton schooner, *Winfield Scott,* sometimes called the *General W. Scott,* built in Cleveland in 1852, capsized while enroute from Menominee, Michigan, to Chicago with a lumber cargo on August 30, 1871. Her crew clung to her overturned hull for 13 hours until rescued by a passing steamer. This wreck, sitting on shifting sands, lies broken and scattered, with the main section displaying its bilge, keelson and centerboard trunk.

25. LOUISIANA

> **LORAN: 31975.7/47964.7**   **LAT 45° 23.98′   LON 086° 55.36′**
> **DEPTH: 10 to 25 feet**   **LEVEL: Novice**

LOCATION: At the north end of Washington Island on the southeast side of the harbor.

The *Louisiana.* MPL/WMHS

Launched on May 12, 1887, at Marine City, Michigan, the wooden steamer, *Louisiana* (267′ x 39′ x 20′), was driven ashore during the Great Storm of 1913, on Nov. 10th. She caught on fire and was a total loss; no lives were lost.

A boat is needed to reach this site; the property adjacent to the wreck is private. This site, buoyed annually by the State Historical Society of Wisconsin, features most of this ship's hull and some decking sitting on a rock and sand bottom. Most of the machinery was salvaged in 1920, but much of interest remains here.

Artwork © University of Wisconsin Sea Grant Institute/State Historical Society of Wisconsin

Louisiana's remains. PHOTO BY JON ZEAMAN

26. PRIDE   (Loran: 31975.1/47963.5   Lat 45° 29.77′ Lon 086° 38.76′)

LOCATION: N. end of Washington I., broken and scattered in about 40′. This site, like the nearby *Louisiana,* offers superb visibility. The two-masted schooner, *Pride* (87′ x 20′), built at Sandusky, OH, in 1849, stranded in a storm on Nov. 29, 1901. No lives were lost.

27. STEAM BARGE & TUG   (Loran: 31885.0/47967.7   Lat 45° 28.70′ Lon 086° 40.20′)

LOCATION: 2.8 miles south of the old Poverty Island Lighthouse, in 75′ to 110′.

The tug and steam barge owned by modern-day salvager John Roen sank in a storm in 1956. The upside-down steambarge is supported by its crane. Penetration is possible, but only for the trained and experienced. Tools lie scattered at this site.

38. Green Bay

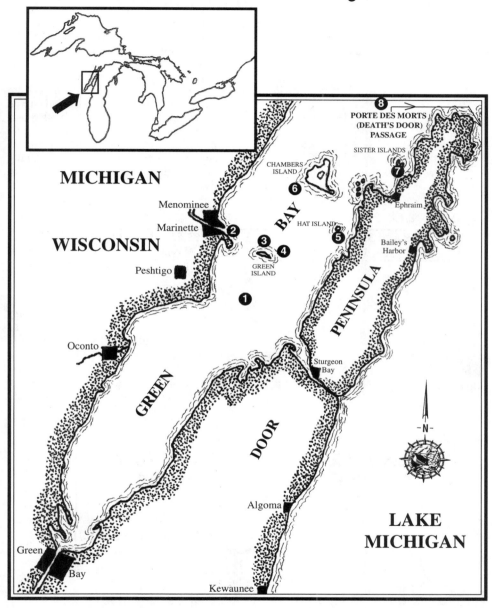

1. *W. L. Brown*
2. *Sidney O. Neff*
3. *Wisconsin*
4. *Erie L. Hackley*
5. *Carrington*
6. *Jennibell*
7. *Meridian*
8. *R. J. Hackett*

1. W. L. BROWN

LORAN: 32261.6/48096.8	LAT 44° 57.96' LON 087° 33.05'
DEPTH: 80 feet	LEVEL: Advanced

LOCATION: This wreck lies near the middle of Green Bay off Peshtigo, Wisconsin. Launched at Oshkosh, Wisconsin, in 1872 as the *Neptune,* and, in 1880, renamed the *W.L. Brown* (140' x 28' x 13'), this wooden steamer sprang a leak and foundered about one

The *W. L. Brown.* MPL/WMHS

mile off Peshtigo Reef in Green Bay on October 21, 1886. The vessel was carrying an iron ore cargo from Escanaba, Michigan, to De Pere, Wisconsin, and no lives were lost. The boiler, anchors, chain and engine were salvaged, but today's divers will see both masts still standing, bilge pumps and other artifacts on deck, rudder and propeller tips at the stern, and intact wooden railings on this upright wreck. This is usually a low-visibility (4' to 8') site in orange water, so penetration diving is not recommended here.

2. SIDNEY O. NEFF

LORAN: 32233.2/48015.2	LAT 45° 05.55' LON 087° 34.69'
DEPTH: 15 feet	LEVEL: Novice

The *Sidney O. Neff* in later years. MPL/WMHS

LOCATION: About one-quarter mile south of the Marinette lighthouse.

Launched as a schooner-barge at Manitowoc, Wisconsin, in 1890, the *Sidney O. Neff* (149'6" x 30'2" x 10'4"), was converted to a bulk freight steamer in 1897 and worked mainly in the lumber trade until she was scuttled in June, 1940, due to age. The wreck lies broken and scattered over a large area. Highlights include the windlass and other machinery.

3. WISCONSIN

LORAN: 32213.4/48040.2	LAT 45° 04.95' LON 087° 29.30'
DEPTH: 85 feet	LEVEL: Advanced

LOCATION: This wreck lies just to the north of Green Island.

The wooden steamer, *Wisconsin* (187' x 30'5" x 12'2" after 1918), launched at Detroit in 1882 as the *F. & P. M. No. 1* (Flint and Pere Marquette Railroad No. 1), received her new name in 1906. When she grew old, she was converted to a schooner-barge in 1918. Finally, she was abandoned at Marinette in 1935. The government paid to have her removed, and a local entrepreneur set up a spectacular show with many people ferried to Green Island to watch this ship burn to the waterline and sink.

The *Wisconsin* in early years. MPL/WMHS

Steel frames around the hull give a rib cage effect to this upright shipwreck. Her bilge pumps and other machinery lie inside her hull, while the anchor chain sits at the bow and her rudder is in place. Take a dive light, as it is usually dark with only 5' to 10' of visibility.

4. *Erie L. Hackley*

LORAN: 32209.5/48058.2	LAT 45° 03.71' LON 087° 27.37'
DEPTH: 99 to 112 feet	LEVEL: Advanced

The *Erie L. Hackley.* MPL/WMHS

LOCATION: This wreck lies to the northeast of Green Island, Green Bay.

The small, wooden steamer, *Erie L. Hackley* (79' x 17'4" x 5'2"), foundered in a storm on October 3, 1903, with 11 lives lost (8 passengers and 3 crew, including the captain) from the 19 on board. The ship had been launched on August 11, 1882, at Muskegon, Michigan. Located by Frank Hoffman in 1980, the *Erie L. Hackley* sits upright and is mostly intact. In place are her engine, boiler, the cargo of red bricks, some decking and her hull. Take along a light, as it is dark at this poor-visibility site.

5. *Carrington*

LORAN: 32167.4/48067.4	LAT 45° 05.58' LON 087° 19.32'
DEPTH: 35 to 55 feet	LEVEL: Intermediate

LOCATION: This wreck lies about 3/4 of a mile south-southwest of Hat Island.

The two-masted, 215' schooner, *Carrington,* running between Green Bay and Chicago with a cargo of pig iron and shingles, stranded on Hat Island Reef due to confusion about lights. The crew was safely removed, but a storm arose and destroyed the *Carrington.* The wreck lies broken in two, with much framing and decking. Beware of the adjacent boulder.

6. JENNIBELL

> **LORAN: 32176.1/48013.3**   **LAT 45° 09.04'   LON 087° 25.11'**
> **DEPTH: 125 feet**   **LEVEL: Advanced**

LOCATION: This wreck lies about 1.5 miles southwest of Chambers Island.

Laden with lumber products, the two-masted, 110' schooner, *Jennibell* (sometimes spelled *Jenny Bell*), capsized in a squall on Oct. 10, 1881, but stayed afloat. She sank only after becoming waterlogged while under tow in a salvage attempt. Frank Hoffman located this wreck in the mid-1960's. His colleagues attempted to raise her (as he had done with the *Alvin Clark* in 1969) but they succeeded only in breaking her in two. She sits upright with deadeyes, winches, windlass and chain in place. Visibility is poor, usually only 5' to 10'.

7. MERIDIAN

> **LORAN: 32084.1/48030.2**   **LAT 45° 12.80'   LON 087°085.57'**
> **DEPTH: 28 to 45 feet**   **LEVEL: Intermediate**

LOCATION: This wreck lies just south of the Sister Islands.

The twin-masted schooner, *Meridian* (120'3" x 23'), built in 1848 at Black River, Ohio, stranded and broke up on Oct. 23, 1873. The wreck is broken and scattered over a wide area on a sand and clay bottom. Much framing and considerable decking comprise this site.

8. R. J. HACKETT

> **LORAN:**   **LAT 45° 45.454' LON 075° 45.454'**
> **DEPTH: 10 to 15 feet**   **LEVEL: Novice**

LOCATION: On the east side of Whaleback Shoal, about 7 miles from the mainland.

The wooden *R. J. Hackett* (211'2" x 32'5" x 19'2") was the first of a new kind of Great Lakes ship: the bulk freight steamer, with continuous cargo holds, 24-foot hatch centers, the engine as far aft as possible and the pilothouse right on the bow. Launched at Cleveland in 1869, she became the first steamer to deliver iron ore to that city on August 14, 1871. On November 12, 1905, she caught on fire and was purposely stranded on Whaleback Shoal, but she became a total loss. The crew escaped in two yawlboats.

Much decking and machinery lies scattered on the white sand and pebbles bottom, with highlights being the engine, boilers, and propeller. Be careful here; this is a remote site.

The *R.J. Hackett*. GLHS

Artwork © University of Wisconsin Sea Grant
Institute/State Historical Society of Wisconsin

The schooner, *Alvin Clark:* In July, 1969, Frank Hoffman successfully raised a completely intact wooden schooner named the *Alvin Clark* from 100' of Green Bay (Lake Michigan) water. For several years, it operated as a museum. But then the vessel began to deteriorate quickly, massive conservation being prohibitively expensive, and Hoffman unable to locate any sources of funding. The ship which had stayed perfectly preserved for 105 years on the lake bottom crumbled in fewer than 20 years on the surface. The broken remains were trucked to the local garbage dump.

39. Sites near Lake Michigan

1. Heart Lake
2. Hardy Dam Pond
3. Murray Lake
4. Gull Lake
5. Lake Cora
6. Paw Paw Lake
7. Diamond Lake
8. Stone Lake
9. France Park

10. Haigh Quarry
11. Pearl Lake
12. Geneva Lake
13. Racine Quarry
14. Lannon Quarry
15. Devils Lake
16. Green Lake
17. Red Granite Quarry
18. Gilbert Lake

1. HEART LAKE

LOCATION: One mile north of the town of Waters, Michigan, which is west of exit #270 on I-75 between Gaylord and Grayling, Michigan. Access on the lake's south side.

Heart Lake, small at only 62.5 acres but with a maximum depth of about 123', is known for incredible visibility, a mostly sand bottom, and large numbers of bass (both largemouth and smallmouth). Sunken logs which were on their way to the sawmill at the water's edge years ago are another of the visual treats here. Look out for boaters and water skiers.

2. HARDY DAM POND

LOCATION: In Newaygo State Park, Newaygo County, 7 miles west of exit #125 on Highway 131, and 40 miles northeast of Muskegon, Michigan.

The huge, 4,000-acre Hardy Dam Pond, created in 1932 by the damming of the Muskegon River, reaches a maximum depth of 110'. Many fish and sunken logjams, as well as a steel bridge in 60', attract scuba divers. Beware of entanglement on monofilament line.

3. MURRAY LAKE

LOCATION: About 12 miles east-northeast of Grand Rapids, 7 miles north of Lowell.

Murray Lake, covering 320 acres in a horseshoe shape, reaches a depth of about 72' and offers considerable aquatic life to see, such as perch, bluegills, bass and sunfish. This lake is also popular for night diving and ice diving. Lalley Avenue at the south end of Murray Lake will take you to Causeway Drive, which leads to public access.

4. GULL LAKE

LOCATION: Straddling Kalamazoo County and Barry County, 10 miles northwest of Battle Creek, Michigan, and 12 miles northeast of Kalamazoo, Michigan.

The 2,030-acre Gull Lake, often used for diving charity events, is known for its excellent visibility and has a maximum depth of about 110', with considerable aquatic life plus old, unwanted farm equipment and automobiles which were placed on the ice in early spring and allowed to sink as the ice melted, located in 10' to 40'. Streets circle this lake, allowing access to its waters. There are also two parks where divers can suit up, enter and exit the lake: Ross Township Park near the town of Yorkville at the southwest corner of Gull Lake, and Prairieville Township Park at the north end. Beware of much boating traffic in summer.

5. LAKE CORA

LOCATION: Five miles west of Paw Paw, Michigan; public access is via 46th Street and West Street on this circular lake's west side. Lake Cora, covering 197 acres with a maximum depth of 59', is used for diver checkouts, as well as recreational exploration.

6. PAW PAW LAKE

LOCATION: This 900-acre lake in Berrien County, near Lake Michigan 10 miles northeast of Benton Harbor, Michigan, is not to be confused with the 126-acre lake of the same name only a few miles to the east in Kalamazoo County near Kalamazoo, Michigan.

The large Paw Paw Lake, just north of Watervliet, Michigan, has a maximum depth of 90'. The best public access for scuba diving is at the northeastern end of the lake off North Watervliet Road. This old resort lake, busy on weekends, is good for bottle diving.

7. DIAMOND LAKE

LOCATION: Southeast of Cassopolis, Michigan, east-northeast of Niles, Michigan.

The 1,020-acre Diamond Lake has historic Diamond Isle, popular with Chicago people in the 1890's as a vacation destination complete with a large hotel, in the middle of it. A twin-decked 65' excursion steamer, the *South Bend,* from that era, lies broken in several large pieces, including her boiler, at a depth of about 40′ off the northeast side of the island. Located in the 1970's by Zoltan and Diane Tiser, the pieces of this wreck were moved closer together by them and other divers for easier diver exploration in April, 1989. The wreck site is usually buoyed. Diamond Lake reaches maximum depths of 42′ off Diamond Isle's west side, 50′ off its north side, and 64′ off its east side. Public access is from the southwest end of the lake. A boat is necessary to reach the wreck of the *South Bend*.

8. STONE LAKE

LOCATION: At Middlebury, Indiana, just east of Elkhart, Indiana.

Stone Lake, maximum depth: 26′, contains much which has been placed specifically for scuba divers to explore: small boats, a car, a swing set and many other fun items.

9. FRANCE PARK

LOCATION: 4 miles east of Logansport, Indiana, about 60 miles south of South Bend.

This stone quarry, maximum depth: 35′, offers good visibility (10′ to 25′) in early spring and fall when swimmers are absent, and views of rare paddlefish and freshwater jellyfish.

10. HAIGH QUARRY

LOCATION: About 35 miles south-southwest of Chicago, in Kankakee, Illinois.

This 12-acre, spring-fed quarry teems with catfish, perch, bluegill, sunfish, crappie, bass and rare paddlefish, as well as mining equipment left behind when the quarry flooded. Visibility is usually excellent, with east access to the water. Land features include change houses, bbq grills and picnic tables in a park-like setting. There are five scuba training platforms in the shallows, as well as five in the deep area.

At Haigh Quarry, a 33′ cabin cruiser, fully explorable, is one of the many underwater sights. PHOTO BY JIM JARECKI.

11. PEARL LAKE

LOCATION: Off Highway 251, South Beloit, Illinois, just south of Wisconsin.

This small lake, with a maximum depth of 85′, has had numerous items, such as small boats and several vehicles, placed in it for diver exploration. There are also training platforms.

12. GENEVA LAKE

LOCATION: In the center of the triangle formed by Chicago-Madison-Milwaukee.

Geneva Lake, popular with scuba divers, is very large: 5,262 acres, with a maximum depth of 144'. No night-diving or shore-diving are allowed, but boats and motors can be rented. Divers must register with the Water Safety Patrol in Lake Geneva or Fontana. The lake offers gamefish, old tools, bottles and shipwrecks (all the manmade items are protected by the State of Wisconsin; please do not remove them). The shipwrecks include the excursion steamers, *Lady of the Lake* (93' x 22'), which sank in 1893 and lies in 35' of water in Buttons Bay at the southeast end of Geneva Lake, and the 115' *Lucius Newberry,* which sank in 1891, the wreckage of which was located in 1981 in 65' of water 300' off Geneva Bay Estates in the northeast part of the lake. The lake also has cribs and an old hotel dump.

13. RACINE QUARRY

LOCATION: Just outside the northwest corner of Racine, Wisconsin.

This spring-fed quarry, with an average depth of 45' to 60', but with a deep, sulphur-layered hole in 85', offers a couple of cars and a former city dump in the far corner.

14. LANNON QUARRY

LOCATION: Just outside Menomonee Falls, WI, just west of Milwaukee.

This 8-acre limestone quarry in a park system has a maximum depth of 50. Quarry machinery, fish and snagged monofilament line (take a knife!) are found here.

15. DEVILS LAKE

LOCATION: Off Highway 123, northwest of Madison, and southeast of Baraboo, WI.

Devils Lake State Park is perhaps the most popular inland dive site in Wisconsin, open year round and offering camping and picnicking. Rock formations and gamefish are common in this 45' maximum depth lake. This spring-fed lake has a silty bottom.

16. GREEN LAKE

LOCATION: About 40 miles southwest of Appleton, WI, off highway 23.

Four boat launches provide access to Green Lake; shore diving is restricted.

17. RED GRANITE QUARRY

LOCATION: About 30 miles west of Oshkosh, in the town of Red Granite, WI.

Although most divers stay in 30' to 90', this deep quarry descends to 238'! The water is cold, clear, and full of game fish but little vegetation. Open water dive classes are held here.

18. GILBERT LAKE

LOCATION: In Waushara County off County Road K near 22nd Street.

Lush aquatic vegetation coats the bottom (in a max. of 60') of this clear-water lake.

40. Whitefish Point

Whitefish Point is one of Michigan's ten Underwater Preserves, and every shipwreck in this chapter, with the exception of the recently discovered *A.A. Parker,* lies within that Preserve's boundaries.

1. *Sagamore*
2. *Samuel Mather*
3. *Panther*
4. *Comet*
5. *Superior City*
6. *Zillah*
7. *Sadie Thompson*
8. *Vienna*
9. *Ora Endress*
10. *John B. Cowle*
11. *Myron*
12. *Miztec*
13. *M. M. Drake*
14. *Niagara*
15. *John Mitchell*
16. *Eureka*
17. *Indiana*
18. *John M. Osborne*
19. *Alex. Nimick*
20. *A. A. Parker*

1. SAGAMORE

LORAN: 31072.9/47771.8	LAT 46° 31.089′ LON 084° 37.927′
DEPTH: 42 to 63 feet	LEVEL: Intermediate-Advanced

LOCATION: This wreck lies at the entrance to the St. Mary's River, Whitefish Bay.

The uniquely-designed whaleback steamer-barge, *Sagamore* (308′ x 38′ x 24′), launched at Superior, Wisconsin, on July 23, 1892, sank nine years and six days later, on July 29, 1901, after a collision with the steamer, *Northern Queen*. Three of the eight lives on board the *Sagamore* were lost that foggy day. The wreck sits upright and mostly intact. The wide open hatches provide easy access for a swim throughout the wreck, and the collision damage

The "pigboat," *Sagamore*. MPL/WMHS

Examining the *Sagamore's* towrings. PHOTO BY CRIS KOHL.

Artwork ©Tim Reed
Copyright © 1998 by Tim Reed
Vr. 1. 4

is clear near the stern. The triple bow towrings are impressive, as is the sheer size of this wreck. This excellent site lies in the shipping lane directly out of the Sault locks, with immense freighters pouring out of there almost non-stop. Call the U.S. Coast Guard at the Soo (Sault Ste. Marie, MI) at 906-635-3273 or VHF 16 to let them know you will be anchored at this site. Maybe they can get the freighters to go around your boat, but don't count on it.

2. SAMUEL MATHER

LORAN: 31086.7/47734.8	LAT 46° 34.308' LON 084° 42.325'
DEPTH: 172 feet	LEVEL: Technical

LOCATION: This wreck lies 16 miles southeast of Whitefish Point, Michigan.

Launched at Cleveland on April 9, 1887, the wooden steamer, *Samuel Mather* (246' x 40' x 19'3"), was sunk in a collision with the new steel steamer, *Brazil*, on November 22, 1891, while downbound with a cargo of wheat. No lives were lost.

The *Samuel Mather,* located by Tom Farnquist and his team in May, 1978, is one of the best preserved and most intact shipwrecks off Whitefish Point. The wreck sits upright, intact and penetrable. The stern mast towers high off the deck, and the rudder, four-bladed propeller, trumpet-shaped dorades (air vents), the engine and much rigging are of interest. Use caution: this is a deep dive far away from help.

The steamer, *Samuel Mather.* AUTHOR'S COLLECTION

A coffee mug sits atop the *Mather's* engine. PHOTO BY CRIS KOHL

Gary Elliott examines the smoke-stack opening. PHOTO BY CRIS KOHL

3. PANTHER

LORAN: 31105.8/47685.9	LAT 46° 38.40' LON 084° 48.29'
DEPTH: 88 to 110 feet	LEVEL: Advanced

The *Panther.* AUTHOR'S COLLECTION

LOCATION: Off Parisienne Island, about 10 miles southeast of Whitefish Point.

The wooden steamer, *Panther* (247'6" x 35'8" x 22'2"), built at West Bay City, Michigan, in 1890, sank with a wheat cargo on June 26, 1916, in a collision with the steamer, *James J. Hill.* No lives were lost. Upright and reasonably intact, the *Panther's* decks have collapsed, but interesting items may be viewed on deck: tools, dishes and portholes. The more intact stern offers the engine, smokestack, boiler, winch, stove and much of the cargo.

Toppled bollards are only a small part of the interesting collection of shipwreck parts at the *Panther's* stern. Other items include the rudder post, engine, steering quadrant and a stove. PHOTO BY CRIS KOHL

Artwork ©Tim Reed

4. COMET

LORAN: 31111.4/47638.1	LAT	LON
DEPTH: 210 to 230 feet	LEVEL: Technical	

LOCATION: This deep wreck lies 4.6 miles southeast of Whitefish Point, Michigan.

The wooden, twin-arched steamer, *Comet* (182′ x 29′2″ x 11′2″), built in Cleveland in 1857, sank in a collision with the Canadian sidewheel steamer, *Manitoba*, on August 26, 1875, with the loss of 10 of the 20 lives on board and the cargo of pig iron ingots and copper and silver ore.

Located in the summer of 1980 by the Great Lakes Shipwreck Historical Society, this site lies in the main shipping channel. The bow is detached and partially buried, while the exposed engine has the ship's name ornately painted on it. The large debris field is interesting.

The *Comet*. ONTARIO ARCHIVES

5. SUPERIOR CITY

LORAN: 31112.0/47633.5	LAT 46° 43.51′	LON 084° 52.37′
DEPTH: 210 to 270 feet	LEVEL: Technical	

LOCATION: This wreck lies 4.0 miles southeast of Whitefish Point, Michigan.
Launched at Lorain, Ohio, on April 13, 1898, the steel steamer, *Superior City* (429′ x

50' x 24'7"), sank in a collision with the 580' steamer, *Willis L. King,* on August 20, 1920, with the loss of 29 of her 33 crew (the four survivors were blown clear of the ship when her boilers exploded) and her iron ore cargo. Located by John Steele in 1972, this deep wreck shows explosion damage in her stern area. Use extreme caution at this site.

The *Superior City.* MPL/WMHS

6. ZILLAH

LORAN: 31123.6/47624.3	LAT	LON
DEPTH: 230 to 250 feet	LEVEL: Technical	

LOCATION: This wreck lies 2.8 miles south-southeast of Whitefish Point, Michigan.

Launched as the *Edward Smith* at West Bay City, Michigan, on March 31, 1890, and renamed the *Zillah* (201'7" x 37' x 13') in 1901, this wooden steamer foundered on August 29, 1926, with no lives lost. Carrying a cargo of limestone at the time of her loss, the *Zillah* sits upright and mostly intact in very deep water. Use every precaution here.

The *Zillah.* MPL/WMHS

7. SADIE THOMPSON

LORAN: 31150.1/47619.8	LAT 46° 42.537' LON 084° 59.878'
DEPTH: 85 to 116 feet	LEVEL: Advanced

LOCATION: This wreck lies 4.1 miles west-southwest of Whitefish Point, Michigan.

The old barge, *Sadie Thompson,* built in the 1890's, broke from her moorings in a storm in the early 1950's while involved in the construction of the breakwall and pier at Whitefish Point Harbor of Refuge while under contract to the U.S. Army Corps of Engineers.

Located by the Great Lakes Shipwreck Historical Society (Tom Farnquist's group) and contracted wreckhunter Dave Trotter in August, 1992, the *Sadie Thompson* rests almost upside-down and displays her steam crane, huge gears, spindle and a large bell, among many other items. Penetration is possible for trained, experienced and prepared divers. This relatively protected site lies in the lee of Whitefish Point.

Ohio diver Steve Whitman explores under the nearly-overturned barge, *Sadie Thompson,* to view her massive gears, winches and bitts. PHOTO BY CRIS KOHL.

8. VIENNA

LORAN: 31135.8/47610.2	LAT 46° 44.46' LON 084° 57.91'
DEPTH: 118 to 148 feet	LEVEL: Advanced-Technical

LOCATION: This wreck lies 1.6 miles west-southwest of Whitefish Point, Michigan. The wooden steamer, *Vienna* (191'4" x 33'8" x 14'1"), launched at Cleveland on June 19, 1873, carried a cargo of iron ore when she collided with the steamer, *Nipigon*, on September 17, 1892. No lives were lost. Following the collision, the *Nipigon* was towing the *Vienna* towards shore when the latter ship sank.

The *Vienna*. MPL/WMHS

The *Vienna's* rudder and deck tools. PHOTOS BY CRIS KOHL.

Joyce Hayward prepares to photograph a winch. PHOTO BY CRIS KOHL

Scuba divers Kent Bellrichard and Tom Farnquist located the *Vienna* in 1974. She sits upright, rising 30' off the lake bottom. From her artistic, curved stern railing to the collision damage at her bow, the *Vienna* offers much to see, including a lifeboat near midship and tools strewn about the deck. Penetration is possible for the trained and experienced. This site is buoyed annually, as are most of the wrecks in the Whitefish Point Underwater Preserve.

9. ORA ENDRESS

LORAN: 31133.8/47592.8	LAT LON
DEPTH: 13 to 15 feet	LEVEL: Novice

LOCATION: This wreck lies about one mile west of Whitefish Point, Michigan.

The *Ora Endress*. AUTHOR'S COLLECTION

The 56-net-ton fishing tug, *Ora Endress* (58' x 15' x 6'), built at Manitowoc, Wisconsin, in 1910, capsized on September 13, 1914, with the Whitefish Point lighthouse keeper and two other men rescuing all 11 crewmembers. The wreck, uncovered when sands shifted in early 1997, lies with her hull intact (but the cabin is missing) with much machinery in and around the hull. Sands continue to shift around this wreck.

10. JOHN B. COWLE

LORAN: 31125.1/47579.4   LAT 46° 44.435′ LON 084° 57.875′
DEPTH: 180 to 220 feet   LEVEL: Technical

LOCATION: This wreck lies 2.3 miles north-northwest of Whitefish Point, Michigan.

The *John B. Cowle* MPL/WMHS

The steel steamer, *John B. Cowle* (420′ x 50′2″ x 24′), loaded with iron ore, sank on July 12, 1909, in a tragic collision in thick fog with the steel steamer, *Isaac M. Scott* (which did not sink in this episode, but rather four years later in Lake Huron; that wreck is also in this book), with 14 of the 24 on the *Cowle* perishing. The *John B. Cowle*, launched in September, 1902, at Port Huron, Michigan, was located by Kent Bellrichard and his team in the summer of 1972 (he also found the *Isaac M. Scott*). This wreck, angled on a slope, offers an intact pilothouse at the shallowest point.

11. MYRON

LORAN: 31142.9/47566.5   LAT 46° 48.463′ LON 085° 01.646′
DEPTH: 42 to 52 feet   LEVEL: Intermediate

LOCATION: 4.2 miles NW of Whitefish Point.

The wooden steamer, *Myron* (186′ x 32′6″ x 13′), launched as the *Mark Hopkins* in 1888 at Grand Haven, Michigan, was renamed in 1902 and foundered in a severe storm on November 22, 1919, with the loss of 17 of the 18 lives on board (only the captain survived). The wreck lies broken in basically two clusters: the bow with its anchor chain tapestry, and the stern, with its propeller and engine (with the boiler lying nearby).

The *Myron*. MPL/WMHS

Left: Diver Gary Elliott examines the *Myron's* bow. *Above:* Joan Forsberg takes a close look at the *Myron's* boiler. PHOTOS BY CRIS KOHL

A huge chain mound on the nearby *Miztec* attracts Steve Whitman. PHOTO BY CRIS KOHL

12. MIZTEC

LORAN: 31156.9/47561.2	LAT 46° 48.073' LON 085° 04.500'
DEPTH: 45 to 50 feet	LEVEL: Intermediate

LOCATION: This wreck lies 5.5 miles west-northwest of Whitefish Point, Michigan.

The *Miztec*. MPL/WMHS

The schooner-barge, *Miztec* (194'1" x 34'6" x 14'), built at Marine City, Michigan, in 1890, carried heavy bulk cargoes, usually towed by the steamer *Myron* (see site #11). She survived the storm which sank the *Myron* in 1919. However, as if responding to some powerful summons to be with her old partner, the *Miztec* foundered in a severe gale on May 15, 1921, not far from where the *Myron* sank. All seven people on the *Miztec* perished. Today, the wreck lies broken, but with much hardware and many tools still to explore and examine.

13. M. M. DRAKE

LORAN: 31167.5/47569.3	LAT 46° 46.75' LON 085° 05.87'
DEPTH: 42 to 50 feet	LEVEL: Intermediate

LOCATION: This wreck lies 6.0 miles west of Whitefish Point.

The wooden steamer, *M. M. Drake* (201' x 34'5" x 14'6"), built at Buffalo, New York, in 1882, attempted to remove the crew of the sinking barge, the 213' *Michigan,* which she was towing, when an enormous wave crashed the wooden vessels together on October 2, 1901. Both ships sank, with the loss of the *Michigan's* cook. The *Michigan* remains to be located. The *Drake,* although broken and scattered, offers a photogenic boiler, a propeller shaft (but the prop is gone), wooden hull and a variety of tools.

The *M. M. Drake*. MPL/WMHS

The *Drake's* rudder at Whitefish Point. PHOTO BY CRIS KOHL

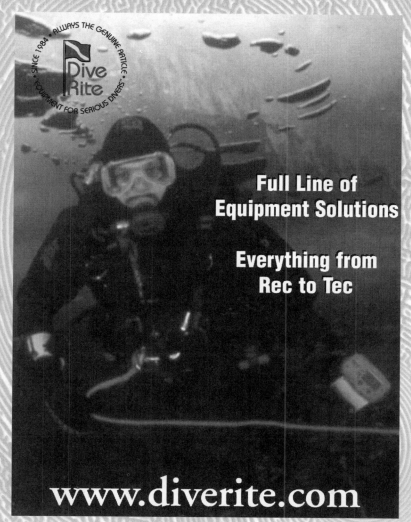

14. NIAGARA

> **LORAN: 31168.3/47543.9**   **LAT 46° 49.173′ LON 085° 07.488′**
> **DEPTH: 96 to 108 feet**   **LEVEL: Advanced**

A *Niagara* anchor adorns the Superior College campus in nearby Sault Ste. Marie, MI. PHOTO BY CRIS KOHL

LOCATION: 7.8 miles WNW of Whitefish Point.
Built at Tonawanda, New York, in 1873, the schooner-barge, *Niagara* (204′6″ x 34′ x 14′), with a cargo of iron ore, foundered on September 7, 1887, with her entire crew (9 lives) in a severe gale after breaking her tow line from the steamer, *Australasia*. Today, that iron ore cargo forms the highest point of this broken shipwreck. The sides of the hull lie alongside the cargo, with numerous bits of equipment lying scattered.

15. JOHN MITCHELL

> **LORAN: 31153.6/47545.6**   **LAT 46° 50.05′   LON 085° 04.81′**
> **DEPTH: 120 to 150 feet**   **LEVEL: Advanced-Technical**

LOCATION: This wreck lies 6.6 miles northwest of Whitefish Point, Michigan.
The steeel steamer, *John Mitchell* (420′ x 52′ x 23′), constructed at St. Clair, Michigan,

The *John Mitchell*. MPL/WMHS

in 1907, sank within five minutes of colliding with the 354′ steel steamer, *William H. Mack*, on July 9, 1911. Three lives were lost from the 34 on board. This wreck, located in 1972 by John Steele and his crew (Bill Cohrs, Kent Bellrichard and Tom Farnquist), lies upside-down, the bow buried in the sand and the propeller and rudder in about 120′. Inside, porcelain toilets hang from above, while the engine room and crew quarters are penetrable for trained, experienced and prepared divers.

16. EUREKA

> **LORAN: 31181.2/47524.4**   **LAT 46° 50.15′   LON 085° 10.76′**
> **DEPTH: 48 to 54 feet**   **LEVEL: Intermediate**

LOCATION: This wreck lies 10.3 miles west-northwest of Whitefish Point, Michigan.
This 138′ schooner-barge foundered with all six lives on board and a cargo of iron ore on October 20, 1886. Her rudder box stands upright in the midst of broken planking.

17. INDIANA

> **LORAN: 31215.1/47520.3**   **LAT 46° 48.66′   LON 085° 17.16′**
> **DEPTH: 103 to 118 feet**   **LEVEL: Advanced**

LOCATION: This wreck lies 14.1 miles west-northwest of Whitefish Point, Michigan.
Launched at Vermilion, Ohio, in 1848, the early propeller-driven steamer, *Indiana* (146′6″ x 23′ x 10′10″), laden with iron ore, foundered on June 6, 1858, with no lives lost.

THE *INDIANA* WRECK SITE

Drawing by David S. Robinson, Smithsonian Institution

Located in 1972 by John Steele and his team mates, Bill Cohrs and Kent Bellrichard, this historic shipwreck was extensively salvaged by museums, including Washington's Smithsonian, which raised the engine and boiler. Much remains here, e.g. prop shaft, stem and sternposts with Roman numeral markings, and iron ore scattered on deck.

18. JOHN M. OSBORNE

> **LORAN: 31149.5/47528.2**   **LAT 46° 52.14'   LON 085° 05.13'**
> **DEPTH: 150 to 170 feet**   **LEVEL: Technical**

LOCATION: This wreck lies 8.3 miles northwest of Whitefish Point, Michigan.

The wooden steamer, *John M. Osborne* (178'1" x 32'1" x 14'), sank in dense fog after being struck by the 305' steel steamer, *Alberta,* on July 27, 1884, with the loss of four lives (three from the *Osborne* and one from the *Alberta*). The *John M. Osborne,* upright and quite intact, was located in 1984 by the Great Lakes Shipwreck Historical Society and the Odyssey Foundation of Lansing, Michigan. Both bow anchors are in place, as are a capstan and winches, and the cargo holds are open for penetration. The stern offers the boiler and engine.

The *John M. Osborne.* MPL/WMHS

An anchor and the pristine bow of the *John M. Osborne.* PHOTO BY CRIS KOHL

19. ALEX. NIMICK

> **LORAN: 31203.3/47555.2**   **LAT   LON**
> **DEPTH: 15 to 22 feet**   **LEVEL: Novice**

LOCATION: This wreck lies 11.2 miles west of Whitefish Point, Michigan.

Launched on January 25, 1890, at West Bay City, Michigan, the wooden steamer, *Alex. Nimick* (298'4" x 40' x 21'), stranded in a strong gale on September 20, 1907, with the loss of six lives. Pounded to pieces, the wreck lies scattered in shallow water.

20. A. A. PARKER

> **DEPTH: About 250 feet**   **LEVEL: Technical**

LOCATION: This wreck lies in deep water off the harbor town of Grand Marais, Michigan, about 52 miles to the west of Whitefish Point.

The wooden steamer, *A. A. Parker* (246'9" x 38'2" x 20'9"), launched as the *Kasota* at Cleveland in 1884 (name changed in 1892), foundered with a cargo of iron ore after springing a leak in a northwest gale on September 19, 1903. All on board were rescued by the U.S. Life Saving crew. This long-sought wreck was located, upright and intact, on June 28, 2001, by Tom Farnquist and his team.

The *A.A. Parker.* AUTHOR'S COLLECTION

41. Munising

Munising, Michigan, is the hub of activity for the Alger Underwater Preserve, one of the state's ten special areas recognized as encompassing a high concentration of shipwrecks.

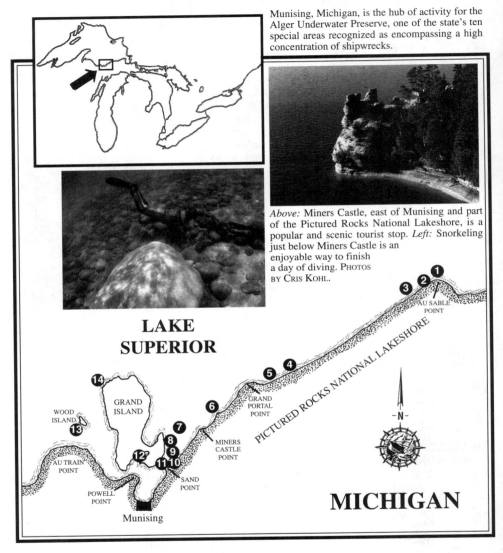

Above: Miners Castle, east of Munising and part of the Pictured Rocks National Lakeshore, is a popular and scenic tourist stop. *Left:* Snorkeling just below Miners Castle is an enjoyable way to finish a day of diving. PHOTOS BY CRIS KOHL.

LAKE SUPERIOR

MICHIGAN

1. *Gale Staples*	8. *Herman H. Hettler*
2. **Au Sable shore wrecks**	9. *Manhattan*
3. *Kiowa*	10. **Sand Point wrecks**
4. *Superior*	11. *Smith Moore*
5. *Wabash*	12. *Bermuda*
6. *George*	13. *Chenango*
7. *Steven M. Selvick*	14. *F. Morrell*

1. GALE STAPLES

LORAN:	LAT 46° 40.80' LON 086° 09.10'
DEPTH: 20 feet	LEVEL: Novice

LOCATION: This wreck lies about 3/4 mile to the northwest of the Au Sable lighthouse.

The wooden bulk freight steamer, *Gale Staples* (277'2" x 42' x 24'7"), launched as the *William B. Morley* at Marine City, Michigan, in 1888, stranded off Au Sable light on October 1, 1918, with no lives lost. She is broken up in a widely scattered debris field which includes both boilers, visible from the surface, about 250' apart, with most of the wreckage around the more westerly boiler: propeller, folding anchor, iron-sheathed wooden rudder, capstan, tools and much miscellaneous machinery and fittings.

The *Gale Staples*. MPL/WMHS

2. AU SABLE SHORE WRECKS

LORAN:	LAT 46° 40.15' LON 086° 10.08'
DEPTH: To 6 feet	LEVEL: Landlubber to Novice

LOCATION: These two wrecks lie 0.5 and 1.25 miles west of the Au Sable Lighthouse.

The remains of the *Sitka* and the *Mary Jarecki* lie along shore. PHOTO BY CRIS KOHL

Two wooden shipwrecks lie badly broken up along the shoreline and out a bit into very shallow water. The remains of the steamer, *Sitka* (272'5" x 40'5" x 19'4"), built at West Bay City, Michigan, in 1887, and stranded and broken up here on October 4, 1904, with no lives lost, rest closer to the lighthouse. The steamer, *Mary Jarecki* (179'6" x 32'7" x 13'2"), built at Toledo, Ohio, in 1871, stranded with an iron ore cargo on July 4, 1883, and broke to pieces with no lives lost. Chunks of her hull lie 200' east of the Hurricane River; the above co-ordinates are for her broken boiler in 6' of water.

3. KIOWA

LORAN: 31499.78/47425.19	LAT 46° 38.71' LON 086° 13.21'
DEPTH: 25 to 35 feet	LEVEL: Novice

LOCATION: This wreck lies 3.8 miles southwest of the Au Sable Lighthouse.

The steel freighter, *Kiowa* (251' x 43'6" x 22'2"), resembles a "salty" (an ocean-going ship) with her midship bridge and masts, cranes and booms. In fact, she was built for World War I in Europe, but she slid down the Detroit launch-ramp too late (May 18, 1920). On November 30, 1929, she stranded in a severe gale with 5 lives lost. Partially salvaged for World War II, much remains here: pieces of steel hull, pumps, generators, piping and valves.

The *Kiowa*. AUTHOR'S COLLECTION

National Park Service (Submerged Cultural Resources Unit)

The *Kiowa*

4. SUPERIOR

LORAN: 31577.1/47429.1	LAT 46° 33.45′ LON 086° 24.91′
DEPTH: 6 to 33 feet	LEVEL: Novice

LOCATION: This wreck lies 7.3 miles northeast of Miners Castle Point.

The sidewheel passenger steamer, *Superior* (191′ x 27′8″ plus 22′ for the paddlewheels x 11′2″), became the most tragic, in terms of lives lost, shipwreck in Lake Superior when she stranded in heavy seas and broke up on October 30, 1856, with the loss of 35 lives from the 50 on board. Captain Hiram Jones, who had lost three ships earlier (the *Ben Franklin* in 1850, the *Albany* in 1853 and the *E.K. Collins* in 1854) reportedly made no effort to save himself this time. The *Superior* was built at Perrysburg, Ohio, in 1845. The wreck lies broken and scattered around the base of Spray Falls, with her boilers visible from the surface.

5. WABASH

LOCATION: This wreck lies 6.0 miles northeast of Miners Castle Point.

The schooner-barge, *Wabash* (140′ x 26′ x 12′), built at Toledo, Ohio, in 1873, stranded and broke up with a cargo of coal and no lives lost in a storm on Nov. 16, 1883. Keelson and frames lie in 8′ of water (**LAT 46° 32.86′ LON 086° 26.80′**), sometimes hidden by shifting sands, while hull pieces and coal cargo lie in 16′ to 48′ (**LAT 46° 33.65′ LON 086° 26.30′**)

6. GEORGE

LORAN: 31604.48/47430.63	LAT 46° 30.96′ LON 086° 31.25′
DEPTH: 15 feet	LEVEL: Novice

LOCATION: About 150′ off shore, 1.9 miles northeast of Miners Castle Point.

Launched as the *George Murray* at Manitowoc, Wisconsin, in 1873, the large, three-masted schooner, *George* (202′8″ x 34′ x 13′8″), stranded in a severe gale on broke up with a coal cargo and no lives lost on October 24, 1893. Much equipment was later salvaged. The ship's bare frames remain.

The *George*. AUTHOR'S COLLECTION

7. STEVEN M. SELVICK

LORAN: 31629.3/47427.0	LAT 46° 29.53′ LON 086° 35.87′
DEPTH: 45 to 65 feet	LEVEL: All levels

LOCATION: Between Grand Island and Miners Castle Point, 6 miles north-northeast of Munising.

The tug, *Steven M. Selvick* (68′7″ x 17′ x 11′), launched in 1915 at Cleveland as the *Lorain,* was purposely scuttled to create a new scuba dive site on June 1, 1996. This tug aided in the construction of the Mackinac Bridge in 1957, and Mr. Steven M. Selvick was married on board this vessel on June 19, 1982. Her exterior is impressive and, with caution, the inside of the pilot house, engine room, galley, messroom and crew quarters can be explored. Take a light.

The *Lorain*. MPL/WMHS   Exploring the *Selvick:* deck railing and pilothouse. PHOTOS BY PETE TOMASINO

8. HERMAN H. HETTLER

> **LORAN: 31632.18/47431.39** **LAT 46° 29.03' LON 086° 35.98'**
> **DEPTH: 20 to 36 feet** **LEVEL: Novice**

LOCATION: This wreck lies two miles north of Sand Point.

Built in 1890 at West Bay City, Michigan, as the *Walter Vail*, the wooden steamer, *Herman H. Hettler* (210' x 34'7" x 13'2"), renamed in 1913, was driven ashore at Grand Island in a blizzard on November 23, 1926, and broke in two with no lives lost. Today, the wooden hull and decking, broken into large pieces, sit on the rocky lake bottom. The huge boiler is also on site, along with much piping and a bathtub. An anchor raised in 1961 by local divers was returned to the site in 1996.

Left: The Herman H. Hettler. AUTHOR'S COLLECTION. *Below: An anchor from the Hettler, recently returned to the site.* PHOTO BY PETE TOMASINO. *Right:* A diver studies the hull. PHOTO BY CRIS KOHL.

9. MANHATTAN

> **LORAN: 31638.20/47438.13** **LAT 46° 28.02' LON 086° 36.56'**
> **DEPTH: 20 to 40 feet** **LEVEL: Novice**

LOCATION: 0.8 mile north of Sand Point.

Burned after stranding off the south end of Grand Island with a cargo of wheat on October 26, 1903, with no lives lost, the wooden steamer, *Manhattan* (252'3" x 38' x 19'3"), built in 1887 at Wyandotte, Michigan, today offers aquatic visitors views of hull timbers, some machinery and her rudder. Much of this wreck was salvaged shortly after her loss, but she remains interesting (see the underwater photos on the next page).

Left: The Manhattan. MPL/WMHS

Views of the *Manhattan* shipwreck: *left,* a portion of the propulsion system; *center,* chains, cables and hull timbers which, *right,* are fairly extensive. PHOTOS LEFT AND CENTER BY PETE TOMASINO, RIGHT BY CRIS KOHL.

10. SAND POINT WRECKS

LOCATION: These wreck remains lie in the shallows just north and east of Sand Point. Remnants of at least three shipwrecks lie in these shifting sands:

1. The schooner, *Mary M. Scott* (138'6" x 26'6" x 11'8"), built at Conneaut, Ohio, in 1857, stranded and broke up with a cargo of iron ore on November 2, 1870, with no lives lost. What is likely the *Mary M. Scott's* centerboard trunk, keelson, frames and mound of iron ore in the middle of her hull lie in 15' of water at **LAT 46° 27.54' LON 086° 36.37'**.

2. The schooner-barge, *Elma* (165'2" x 30' x 11'), launched in 1873 at Marine City, MI, stranded in immense seas at Miners Castle on Sept. 29, 1895, with one life lost. Her hull, it is believed, drifted down to Sand Point and broke up. An anchor and chain in 43' of water off Miners Castle, believed to be from the *Elma,* lie at **LAT 46° 29.55' LON 086° 33.74'**.

3. The lumber-laden steam barge, *Michael Groh* (120'4" x 23'8" x 8'6"), built at Cleveland in 1867, stranded in a storm on Nov. 22, 1895 at Miners Castle, drifted down to Sand Point, broke up and lies in two sections in 10' to 12' of water at **LAT 46° 27.74' LON 086° 35.59'** and at **LAT 46° 27.73' LON 086° 35.86'**. She was extensively salvaged.

11. SMITH MOORE

LORAN: 31642.2/47442.1	LAT 46° 27.33' LON 086° 37.06'
DEPTH: 91 to 105 feet	LEVEL: Advanced

LOCATION: 2.9 miles northeast of Munising, between Grand Island and Sand Point. Launched on July 29, 1880 at Cleveland, the wooden steamer, *Smith Moore* (223'4" x

The *Smith Moore*
Artwork ©Pat Labadie

Right: A diver takes a close look at the *Smith Moore's* bitts. PHOTO BY CRIS KOHL.

35′ x 18′2″), carrying iron ore, sank after a collision with the _James Pickands_ (which is also in this book). No lives were lost. The wreck sits upright, with her engine, boiler and deck hardware increasingly threatened and covered by shifting sands from Sand Point.

12. _BERMUDA_

LORAN: 31647.8/47431.2	**LAT 46° 27.89′ LON 086° 38.81′**
DEPTH: 12 to 30 feet	**LEVEL: Novice**

LOCATION: This wreck lies in protected Murray Bay at southern Grand Island.

The two-masted schooner, _Bermuda_ (136′ x 26′ x 11′9″), launched in April, 1860, at Oswego, New York, foundered in a storm in Munising Bay on October 15, 1870, with the loss of three lives and her iron ore cargo. In October, 1883, she was raised and towed into Murray Bay, where her chains slipped and she again sank. Much of her iron ore cargo was salvaged. This well-preserved, intact shipwreck is one of the most visited sites in all the Great Lakes. Explorable above, beside and below deck, this wreck features a bow samson post, three hatches, railing and rudder post.

The _Bermuda_ (two views)
Artwork ©Pat Labadie

Diver and bass on the _Bermuda_. PHOTOS BY CRIS KOHL

13. _CHENANGO_ LORAN: 31665.2/47391.1 LAT 46° 30.10′ LON 086° 44.76′

This iron ore-laden schooner-barge stranded on November 20, 1875; no lives were lost. The bottom of the hull and the rudder lie in 15′ about 1,000′ southwest of Wood Island.

14. _F. MORRELL_ LAT 46° 32.85′ LON 086° 42.88′ Depth: 15′

This 144′, 369-ton schooner stranded with iron ore on Nov. 7, 1874, off the northwest edge of Grand Island. No lives were lost. Sights include capstans, chains and iron ore.

42. Marquette

The Marquette Underwater Preserve, one of ten such designations created by the State of Michigan, was established in 1990 to promote conservation of the area's submerged historical resources.

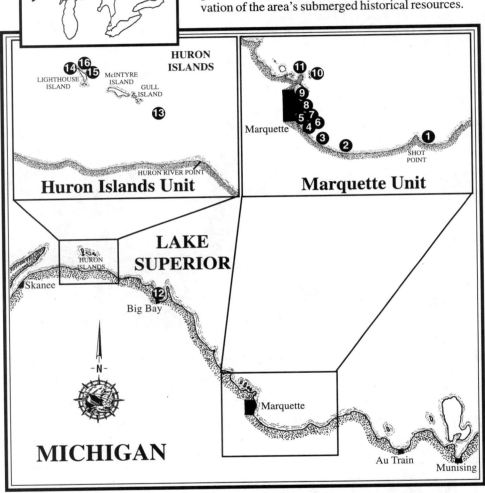

1. *George Sherman*
2. *Queen City*
3. *Charles J. Kershaw*
4. *DeSoto*
5. *Florida*
6. *F-106B parts*
7. *Superior* and *Marion L.*
8. *D. Leuty*
9. *J.H. Sheadle* parts & "Iron Man"
10. "Gold Mine" pinnacle
11. Black Rocks
12. Big Bay lumber dock
13. *Southwest*
14. *Huron Island*
15. *Arctic*
16. *George Nestor*

1. GEORGE SHERMAN

LORAN:	LAT 46° 29.89' LON 087° 09.63'
DEPTH: 10 to 12 feet	LEVEL: Novice

LOCATION: About 12 miles east-southeast of Marquette, just east of Shot Point.
The 323-ton schooner, *George Sherman* (139'8" x 26'2" x 11'6"), built at Cleveland in 1862, stranded at Shot Point with a coal cargo in a blinding snowstorm which destroyed or stranded many other vessels in the Great Lakes on October 23, 1887. No lives were lost, but the ship quickly broke up. Basically three portions of the wooden hull remain amidst a scattered debris field to be explored in shallow water.

2. QUEEN CITY

LORAN:	LAT 46° 29.42' LON 087° 18.64'
DEPTH: 10 to 13 feet	LEVEL: Novice

LOCATION: 150' off Chocolay Beach, about 5 miles southeast of Marquette.
The 368-ton, two-masted schooner, *Queen City* (137' x 25'7" x 11'3"), constructed at Vermilion, Ohio, in 1855, lost her anchors while trying to ride out a gale and stranded on November 18, 1864 with a cargo of firebricks. The crew was saved, but the vessel broke up. The remains, when not covered by sand, include the port side of the hull, plus the neatly-stacked bricks in the cargo hold just aft of the high-profile centerboard trunk.

3. CHARLES J. KERSHAW

LORAN:	LAT 46° 30.56' LON 087° 21.81'
DEPTH: 25 feet	LEVEL: Novice

LOCATION: This wreck lies about two miles south-southeast of Marquette.
The wooden steamer, *Charles J. Kershaw* (223' x 37'3" x 19'9"), built at Bangor, Michigan, in 1874, was towing the schooner-barges, *Henry A. Kent* and *Moonlight,* on Sept.

The *Charles J. Kershaw.*
AUTHOR'S COLLECTION

29, 1895, when the steamer lost power and all three were stranded by the high seas. Members of Marquette's U.S. Life Saving Service made daring rescues of the *Kershaw's* crew, while the schooners' crews simply jumped onto land. The *Detroit Free Press* of Oct. 10, 1895, reported that "The recent gale removed the last trace of the *Kershaw,* which broke its spinal column on Chocolay reef...." The two

This widely-reproduced photograph dramatically shows the stranded schooner-barges, *Henry A. Kent* and *Moonlight,* while salvage ships work on the *Kershaw.* MPL/WMHS

schooners were recovered and returned to service eight months later. This wreck lies broken and scattered, with the huge boiler being the site's highlight.

4. DESOTO

LORAN:	LAT 46° 32.07' LON 087° 23.55'
DEPTH: 8 to 10 feet	LEVEL: Novice

LOCATION: About 1000' north of the Shiras Generating Plant, inside an old dock.
Launched on April 10, 1856 at Cleveland, the bark, *DeSoto* (160'10" x 33'8" x 11'7"), stranded and broke up on Dec. 4, 1869. Some framing and planking make up this site.

5. *FLORIDA*

LORAN:	LAT 45° 45.454' LON 075° 45.454'
DEPTH: 90 feet	LEVEL: Advanced

LOCATION: South of Whetstone Brook and just north of the *DeSoto* wreck site.

The two-masted schooner, *Florida* (139' x 26' x 11'), built at Oswego, New York, in 1868, was dashed against the Marquette docks during a blizzard on November 17, 1886, with the loss of one life. Partly buried in the sand are framing and planking just outside the cribs of an old dock.

Left: The stranded schooner, *Florida*. MPL/WMHS

6. F-106B PARTS

LORAN:	LAT 46° 31.71' LON 087° 23.75'
DEPTH: 20 to 22 feet	LEVEL: Novice

LOCATION: Near the Shiras Generating Plant, Marquette, Michigan.

This F-106B fighter plane from the nearby K.I. Sawyer Air force Base lost power and crashed after the pilot bailed out safely on June 12, 1974. The engine and most of the fuselage were recovered, but pieces of this aircraft remain lodged in the shifting sands.

7. *SUPERIOR* AND *MARION L.*

LORAN:	LAT 46° 32.50' LON 087° 23.35'
DEPTH: 18 to 22 feet	LEVEL: Novice

LOCATION: Inside the Lower Harbor at Marquette, Michigan.

These two abandoned fish tugs lie in an area of heavy boating traffic; caution must be used here, including the use of a dive flag. The *Marion L.* lies along the south side of Thill's dock, while the *Superior* rests across the slip on the north side of the Association dock.

8. *D. LEUTY*

LORAN:	LAT 46° 32.76' LON 087° 22.44'
DEPTH: 5 to 40 feet	LEVEL: Novice-Intermediate

LOCATION: This wreck lies about 800' off Lighthouse Point near downtown Marquette.

The wooden steamer, *D. Leuty* (179' x 33'6" x 12'6"), stranded in a snowstorm while trying to enter Marquette harbor on October 31, 1911, with a cargo of logs. No lives were lost, but the ship broke up. Her engine, boiler and machinery were salvaged. Three large sections of wooden hull remain at this site, which is one of the area locations usually buoyed. The huge rudder lies in 40', with tools, fasteners and piping scattered in more shallow water. Unfortunately, this is not a shore dive, as the nearest public access is about 1/4 mile from the wreck. That's a long swim; use a boat instead.

D. Leuty. AUTHOR'S COLLECTION

9. *J.H. SHEADLE* PARTS AND "IRON MAN"

The steamer, *J.H. Sheadle,* left behind her rudder and a propeller blade when she backed into the rocky reef on Nov. 20, 1920. These items lie in 15' of water at **LAT 46° 34.08' LON 087° 23.17'**. The *Sheadle* was repaired and remained in service until scrapped in 1980. The "Iron Man" is the human-shaped water intake for the long-defunct charcoal plant.

10. "GOLD MINE" PINNACLE

This finger of granite rises from the sandy lake bottom at 150′ to about 12′ from the surface, and features steep walls and overhangs. Divers named it "Gold Mine" because of snagged fishing equipment they found on it. The controllable depth makes diving experience level variable. The pinnacle, marked on charts, is just east of the Presque Isle Point Rocks.

11. BLACK ROCKS

This site, at the northernmost tip of Presque Isle Park north of Marquette and featuring unusual geological formations, is accessible from shore with depths from 10′ to 50′.

12. BIG BAY LUMBER DOCK

This all-weather site, about 800′ north of the Big Bay Harbor of Refuge, offers interesting artifacts among the old timber cribs, ballast stones and an old railroad car from the old dock.

13. *SOUTHWEST*

LORAN: 31851.9/46890.0	LAT 46° 56.42′ LON 087° 56.11′
DEPTH: 88 to 110 feet	LEVEL: Advanced

LOCATION: This wreck lies one mile southeast of Gull Island in the Huron Islands.

The schooner, *Southwest* (137′2″ x 26′1″ x 11′), built at Ogdensburg, New York, in 1866, stranded and eventually sank in deep water on September 19, 1898, while upbound light. No lives were lost. The forest fire smoke which the captain blamed for the disaster also caused the loss of the steamer, *Colorado*, (which is also in this book) off the Keweenaw at about the same time. Discovered by divers in 1978, the remains of the *Southwest* are broken up, but there is much to see that is of interest. This wreck, usually buoyed, can be reached by boat from either the Big Bay Harbor of Refuge or the marina at Skanee.

14. *HURON ISLAND*

LOCATION: This wreck lies just north of the rocks on the north side of the channel between Lighthouse Island and the small island immediately next to it. The 40′ wooden launch, *Huron Island,* lying on her side and collapsed in about 15′ of very clear water, was used as the lighthouse launch until it sank in 1922. Sand partially covers the engine.

15. *ARCTIC*

LORAN:	LAT 46° 57.74′ LON 087° 59.85′
DEPTH: 5 to 100 feet	LEVEL: Variable (Advanced)

LOCATION: Off the middle of the eastern side of Lighthouse Island in the Hurons.

The sidewheel steamer, *Arctic* (236′6″ x 30′ x 12′), launched at Newport (later Marine City), Michigan, in late April, 1851, stranded in thick fog on May 29, 1860. No lives were lost. The main wreckage field contains many artifacts, such as broken china and wooden timbers, with the ship's bow located in the shallow channel between Lighthouse Island and the small island at the south end. Part of her engine and hull lie in 20′ on the west side.

16. *GEORGE NESTOR*

LORAN:	LAT 46° 57.99′ LON 088° 00.20′
DEPTH: 20 to 100 feet	LEVEL: Advanced

LOCATION: 1/4 mile north of the *Arctic,* near the northern tip of Lighthouse Island.

The schooner-barge, *George Nestor* (207′ x 35′ x 14′), built at Baraga, Michigan, in 1887, stranded in a storm on April 30, 1909, with 6 lives lost. The wreck is very scattered.

43. Keweenaw

The stranding and loss of the U.S. Coast Guard cutter, *Mesquite* (pictured, IGLR; see site #3 in this chapter) on December 4, 1989, at the tip of the Keweenaw Peninsula, and the subsequent decision to scuttle her in deeper water in July, 1990 for the creation of a new scuba dive site, set the final impetus for approving the creation, in 1991, of the Keweenaw Underwater Preserve, one of Michigan's ten specially designated areas with a high concentration of shipwrecks.

LAKE SUPERIOR

MICHIGAN

1. **The Canal wrecks (8 sites)**
2. *Langham*
3. *Mesquite*
4. *Scotia*
5. *Wasaga*
6. *City of Superior*
7. *John Jacob Astor*
8. *John L. Gross*
9. *Traveller*
10. *City of St. Joseph* and *Transport*
11. *Tioga*
12. *James Pickands*
13. *Colorado* and *Fern*
14. *William C. Moreland*
15. *Maplehurst*
16. *Panama*

1. THE CANAL WRECKS (8)

The Portage Ship Canal, also called the Keweenaw Waterway, encompasses a lake, a pond, two rivers and some manmade canal work to provide convenient marine access across the base of the long Keweenaw Peninsula. This lengthy waterway contains both natural and abandoned shipwrecks. Here are eight of them, from east to west:

1. The wooden steamer, *Alfred P. Wright* (286' x 41'5" x 22'3"), built at Cleveland in 1888, burned with a wheat cargo on Nov. 16, 1915, at the canal's lower entry. She lies in 10' to 15' of water. **LORAN: 31954.2/46749.5   LAT 46° 57.96' LON 088° 26.41'**

2. Also lying at the lower entry, the wooden passenger steamer, *International* (80'8" x 26'4" x 7'4"), burned on Nov. 2, 1913, with no one aboard. Built at Buffalo, NY, in 1889, she lies in 3' to 10' of water. **LORAN: 31948.3/46743.0 LAT 46° 58.97' LON 088° 25.84'**

3. The wooden steamer, *Charles H. Bradley* (201' x 37' x 13'6"), built at West Bay City, Michigan, in 1890, grounded then burned in lower Portage Lake on October 9, 1931, with no lives lost. She lies in 2' to 5' of water.   **LAT 47° 02.14' LON 088° 29.02'**

4. The wooden steam yacht, *Sea Fox* (101'6" x 16' x 6'8"), launched as the *Azalea* at Detroit in 1895, was abandoned in about 1930. She lies in 5' to 15' of water across from the Michigan Tech water plant. Site sights: engine, boiler, rudder, sink, bathtub and head.

5. The schooner-barge, *Mediator* (127'3" x 27'5" x 10'), built at Cape Vincent, NY, in 1862, stranded in a storm on Sept. 18, 1898. Towed to Houghton, the damaged ship was abandoned. She lies in 20'. **LORAN: 31942.4/46640.1 LAT 47° 07.30' LON 088° 33.00'**

6. The small, wooden steam yacht, *Morgan* (64'6" x 12'4" x 6'1"), built in 1891 at Rome, NY, was abandoned in about 1928. She lies in 4' to 15' of water about 100' east of the Houghton Super 8 Motel (let's hope they never change names!) just off the south shore.

7. The iron passenger steamer, *Uarda* (95'3" x 12'5" x 8'3"), built at Buffalo, NY, in 1881, burned on June 4, 1912, with no lives lost. She lies in 15' to 20' of water near the wreck of the *Sailor Boy* (see next site).   **LAT 47° 07.42' LON 088° 35.30'**

8. The wooden excursion steamer, *Sailor Boy* (91' x 24' x 6'5"), launched on January 6, 1891 at West Bay City, Michigan, burned on May 12, 1923 and drifted to 300' east of Osceola Point., where she lies in 10' to 20' of water about 30' off shore.

2. LANGHAM

LORAN: 31758.1/46675.8	LAT 47° 22.37' LON 087° 55.53'
DEPTH: 90 to 106 feet	LEVEL: Advanced

LOCATION: In Bete Grise Bay, 2.0 miles east of the entrance to Lac La Belle.

Launched as the *Tom Adams* at West Bay City, Michigan, in 1888, the wooden steamer, *Langham* (281'1" x 41'4" x 20'), burned to a total loss with a coal cargo but with no lives lost on October 23, 1910. Features include the ship's two boilers, engine and much machinery still in place. The *Langham* is the identical sister ship to the *Robert L. Fryer* (which is also in this book).

The *Langham*. MPL/WMHS

A burbot explores the upright remains of the steamer, *Langham*. PHOTO BY PETE TOMASINO.

3. MESQUITE

LORAN: 31714.6/46712.8	LAT 47° 22.38' LON 087° 55.55'
DEPTH: 82 to 112 feet	LEVEL: Advanced

LOCATION: This wreck lies in Keystone Bay, southwest of Keweenaw Point.

The U.S. Coast Guard cutter/buoy tender, *Mesquite* (180' x 37' x 14'), built at Duluth, Minnesota, in 1942, stranded on Keweenaw's notorious rocks on December 4, 1989, and became a total loss, with no lives lost (see archival photo on page 364). The wreck was moved into deeper water on July 14, 1990, as a dive site. Almost everything, excluding most Coast Guard insignia, was left on board! There is much to see on deck and along the hull. Penetration diving should be done only by trained and experienced divers. As with all Great Lakes shipwrecks, please leave all (repeat: ALL) items in place on the *Mesquite*.

Sights at the *Mesquite*: a davit, a below-deck filing cabinet (full!), and a porthole. PHOTOS BY PETE TOMASINO.

4. SCOTIA

LORAN: 31697.8/46710.5	LAT 47° 25.86' LON 087° 42.28'
DEPTH: 15 to 25 feet	LEVEL: Novice

LOCATION: About 150' off the old rocket launch platform at High Rock Point.

Lost in a blinding blizzard on October 24, 1884, the iron package freighter, *Scotia* (231' x 35'6" x 25'), ran hard aground on Keweenaw's tip and broke up. A passing steamer saved the crew. Built at Buffalo, New York, in 1873, the *Scotia's* engine and boiler were salvaged shortly after her loss. More recently, one of her propellers was placed on exhibit at nearby Fort Wilkins State Park. Today, the wreck lies broken and scattered. A rough terrain roadway runs 7 miles from US 41 to the shore, but boat access would be easier.

5. WASAGA

LORAN:	LAT 47° 28.22' LON 087° 52.93'
DEPTH: 25 to 36 feet	LEVEL: Novice

The *Wasaga* MPL/WMHS

LOCATION: In the harbor at Copper Harbor, Michigan.

While taking shelter from a storm at Copper Harbor on November 6, 1910, the wooden steamer, *Wasaga* (238'2" x 35'6" x 14'8"), launched as the *Wissahickon* on July 1, 1876 at Buffalo, New York, caught on fire and burned to a total loss with no lives lost. She sank with a cargo of farm implements bound for Canada. Salvage efforts recovered the engine, boiler and much machinery and cargo. Although this wreck (the keel and some cargo) lies just off Harbor Haus Restaurant in Copper Harbor, it is best accessed by boat.

6. CITY OF SUPERIOR

LORAN:	LAT 47° 28.40′ LON 087° 51.72′
DEPTH: 15 to 35 feet	LEVEL: Novice

LOCATION: This wreck, accessible from shore, lies off the Copper Harbor lighthouse.
Launched on July 18, 1857, at Cleveland, the wooden steamer, *City of Superior* (187′8″ x 29′3″ x 11′1″), was lost in her first year. She struck a reef off Copper Harbor on November 10, 1857, and became a total loss, including her cargo of barrelled copper, but with no lives lost. Much of this ship and her cargo were salvaged at that time, so today, only small pieces of her hull remain to be explored.

7. JOHN JACOB ASTOR

LORAN: 31725.4/46643.3	LAT 47° 28.34′ LON 087° 51.88′
DEPTH: 10 to 35 feet	LEVEL: Novice

LOCATION: This shore-dive wreck lies directly off the old Fort Wilkins dock.
The 112-gross-ton, two-masted, wooden brig, *John Jacob Astor* (77′8″ x 21′8″ x 7′7″), is the oldest known shipwreck site in Lake Superior. Constructed at Black River, Ohio, and shipped in pieces to Sault Ste. Marie where she was launched in August, 1834, the first U.S. commercial vessel on the big lake. The *Astor* stranded and broke up in strong winds on September 21, 1844. Her machinery and rigging were recovered, but the broken and scattered remains are interesting. Artifacts from this wreck are on exhibit at Fort Wilkins State Park and the Copper Harbor Lighthouse Museum.

8. JOHN L. GROSS

LORAN: 31789.2/46575.5	LAT 47° 27.58′ LON 088° 09.30′
DEPTH: 20 to 30 feet	LEVEL: Novice

LOCATION: This wreck lies just inside the entrance to Eagle Harbor, on the west side.
The two masted schooner, *John L. Gross* (131′5″ x 25′7″ x 10′1″), built in 1857 at Vermilion, Ohio, stranded in a storm on October 30, 1873, and was pounded to pieces with a coal cargo but no lives lost. Originally thought to be the sidewheeler, *Gazelle* (which grounded here on Sept. 8, 1860, but was mostly removed), the *John L. Gross* site features ribs, keel, much coal and some of the hull still standing.

9. TRAVELLER

LORAN: 31788.7/46577.0	LAT 47° 27.53′ LON 088° 09.09′
DEPTH: 15 to 30 feet	LEVEL: Novice

LOCATION: This wreck lies just inside the entrance to Eagle Harbor, on the east side.
Built in 1852 at Newport (now Marine City), Michigan, the sidewheel steamer, *Traveller* (199′1″ x 29′ x 10′1″), burned to a complete loss on August 17, 1865. This flattened wreckage, off the old Eagle Harbor Life Saving Station, sits on a shifting sand bottom, broken but nonetheless an interesting and enjoyable shore dive. This site is often buoyed.

10. CITY OF ST. JOSEPH AND TRANSPORT

LORAN: 31777.6/46581.4	LAT 47° 28.20′ LON 088° 06.75′
LORAN: 31777.5/46582.2	LAT 47° 28.10′ LON 088° 06.58′
DEPTH: 25 to 35 feet	LEVEL: Novice

LOCATION: About 1/4 mile off Little Grand Marais harbor, east of Eagle Harbor.
Near the terrible beginning of World War II, two barges were lost off the Keweenaw on

September 21, 1942. The steel barge, *City of St. Joseph* (254′ x 34′ x 16′6″), built as the passenger steamer, *City of Chicago,* in 1890 at West Bay City, Michigan, renamed in 1915, was converted to a barge in 1938. The iron barge, *Transport* (254′1″ x 45′9″ x 14′), launched as a steamer on January 24, 1880 at Wyandotte, Michigan, and working mainly as a railroad car ferry on the Detroit River, was reduced to a barge in 1933. Both pulpwood-laden barges were towed by the tug, *John Roen,* which survived. However, one life, the *City of St. Joseph's* captain's wife, was lost when the barges stranded.

The wrecks lie about 300′ apart, with the *Transport* closer to shore. Much machinery remains at the *City of St. Joseph* site, which is usually marked with a buoy.

The *City of St. Joseph.* MPL/WMHS

The *Transport.* MPL/WMHS

11. *TIOGA*   (LORAN: 31817.3/46556.3   LAT 47° 26.31′ LON 088° 16.21′)
LOCATION: This wreck lies three miles east of Eagle River, Michigan.

The iron package steamer, *Tioga* (285′5″ x 38′9″ x 25′7″), built at Buffalo, NY, in 1884, stranded with a wheat cargo on Nov. 26, 1919, and broke up with no lives lost. This popular wreck lies in 28′ to 35′ of water, with her boilers, machinery and hull pieces scattered.

12. *JAMES PICKANDS*   (LORAN: 31825.1/46553.2   LAT 47° 25.46′ LON 088° 18.02′)
Located today on Sawtooth Reef in 10′ to 30′ of water, the wooden steamer, *James Pickands* (232′6″ x 40′ x 19′2″), built at Cleveland in 1886, stranded and broke up with her iron ore cargo on Sept. 22, 1894. No lives were lost. Her boilers and rudder are the highlights. This popular wreck lies scattered with the *Colorado* and the *Fern* (see site #13).

13. *COLORADO/FERN*   (LORAN: 31824.5/46553.4   LAT 47° 25.72′ LON 088° 17.95′)
The wooden steamer, *Colorado* (254′6″ x 35′ x 13′), built in 1867 at Buffalo, NY, stranded in smoky conditions on Sept. 19, 1898, with a flour cargo and no lives lost. The 65′ tug, *Fern,* lost with all 5 hands in a storm while salvaging the *Colorado* on June 29, 1901, lies nearby. Both these wrecks lie scattered with the *James Pickands* in 10′ to 30′ of water.

14. *WILLIAM C. MORELAND*   (LORAN: 31832.9/46551.0   LAT 47° 25.07′ LON 088° 19.61′) LOCATION: In 25′ to 40′, on Eagle River Shoals off Eagle River, Michigan
This steel steamer (580′ x 58′ x 32′), left only her unsalvaged bow half after stranding and breaking up on Oct. 18, 1910. Flattened by nature, this wreck offers interesting machinery.

15. *MAPLEHURST*   (LAT 47° 13.90′ LON 088° 38.05′)
In 15′ to 20′ of water 225′ west of the North Entry, this steel steamer (235′1″ x 36′8″ x 15′4″), grounded in a fierce storm and broke up with 11 lives lost on December 1, 1922.

16. *PANAMA*   (LORAN: 32200.8/46518.9   LAT 46° 50.17′ LON 089° 32.89′)
LOCATION: In 5′ to 20′ of water off Mineral Point, 14 miles west of Ontanagon, MI.

Launched as the *John Craig* at Trenton, MI, on May 19, 1888, the wooden steamer, *Panama* (290′ x 41′ x 25′), coal-laden, stranded and broke up in heavy seas on Nov. 21, 1906.

44. Apostle Islands

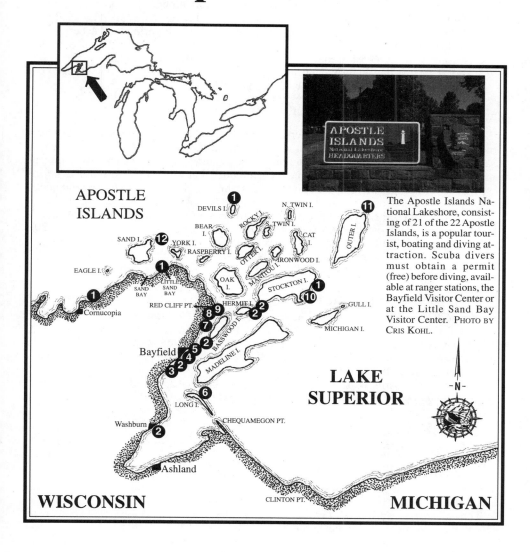

APOSTLE ISLANDS

The Apostle Islands National Lakeshore, consisting of 21 of the 22 Apostle Islands, is a popular tourist, boating and diving attraction. Scuba divers must obtain a permit (free) before diving, available at ranger stations, the Bayfield Visitor Center or at the Little Sand Bay Visitor Center. PHOTO BY CRIS KOHL.

LAKE SUPERIOR

WISCONSIN

MICHIGAN

1. "Caves" (4 sites)
2. Dock ruins (5 sites)
3. *Charlotte* and barge
4. *Fin McCool*
5. Pickup truck
6. *Lucerne*

7. *Fedora*
8. *H. D. Coffinberry*
9. *Ottawa*
10. *Noquebay*
11. *Pretoria*
12. *Sevona*

1. "CAVES"

That which scuba divers call the "caves" here are nothing at all like cave-diving in Florida, for example. These are caverns, overhangs, short tunnels and other interesting geological formations that are about the closest thing to real caves in the Great Lakes. In the Apostle Islands, there are four recommended "cave" areas, all requiring boat access:

1. **Little Sand Bay** (north and west of), with depths to 30', usually with 50'+ of visibility.
2. **Squaw Bay**, northeast of the town of Cornucopia, with depths to 35'.
3. **Devils Island** (north end), depths to 30', stratified sandstone extending 60' back.
4. **Stockton Island** (east end of), with depths to 35'.

2. DOCK RUINS

Dock ruins usually consist of submerged cribs (timber boxes with rocks in them) which formed the solid foundations for docks, and pilings, short, thick telephone poles to which vessels were often docked with ropes. Not only are the interesting tools and other equipment from a long-gone era viewable here (please remember that it is illegal to remove any of these non-renewable submerged cultural resources), but the fish life around these old docks is often prolific. There are five recommended historic docks to explore underwater:

1. **Washburn** (at the south end, off the point in Vandeventer Bay), with depths to 40'.
2. **Bayfield** (south of; the dock is often marked with a green buoy), with depths to 80'.
3. **Basswood Island** (south end, LORAN 32406.7/46176.0), depths to 35'.
4. **Hermit Island** (southeast end, LORAN 32381.4/46171.0), depths to 30'.
5. **Stockton Island** (southwest end; LORAN 32367.7/46170.8), depths to 35'.

3. *CHARLOTTE* AND BARGE

LOCATION: This wreck lies near the marine railroad in Pikes Bay south of Port Superior.

The 28-net-ton tug, *Charlotte* (62' x 17'6" x 6'6"), built in Erie, Pennsylvania, in 1912, worked mainly in Lake Superior towing and commercial fishing before being abandoned due to age and condition in 1943. She lies in 3' to 6' of water, with parts of her frames and stem protruding from the water.

An unknown barge or scow, believed to have been abandoned in the 1930's and subsequently gutted by fire, lies in shallow water near the *Charlotte*.

4. *FIN McCOOL*

LORAN: 32423.3/46171.4	LAT	LON
DEPTH: 10 to 20 feet	LEVEL: Novice	

LOCATION: This wreck lies just down the hill from the Seagull Bay Motel, at the south end of the Apostle Islands Yacht Club Harbor, in Bayfield harbor.

The oak barge, *Fin McCool* (135' x 34' x 7'7"), built at nearby Ashland, Wisconsin, in 1926, worked in the local lumber trade until it sank in Bayfield harbor in 1964 and was abandoned. It lies in what is today a private marina. In years of low levels in the Great Lakes, parts of this wreck will appear above water. Often this wreck, which features most of its original deck equipment, such as steam winches and cable drums, is buoyed by local divers. It is also a popular ice diving location.

5. PICKUP TRUCK

Off the Bayfield harbor breakwall, in 65' of water, rest the remains of a 1932 Ford pickup truck in relatively good condition (the chrome still shines and a door still opens). Parking for this shore dive is available inside the marina near Bayfield's city park. Huge, flat concrete slabs on the lake side of the breakwall mark the entry point. At a depth of 6', a yellow polypropylene line is secured to a wooden part of the breakwall. The truck, lying on its side, lies at the end of this line about 150' off shore.

6. LUCERNE

> **LORAN: 32434.6/46234.9**   **LAT 46° 43.389′ LON 090° 46.035′**
> **DEPTH: 15 to 24 feet**   **LEVEL: Novice**

LOCATION: This wreck lies off the northeast side of Long Island, Wisconsin.

The three-masted schooner, *Lucerne* (195′ x 34′ x 14′), built in 1873 at Tonawanda,

The *Lucerne*. MPL/WMHS

Lucerne artifacts in the Canal Park museum in Duluth. PHOTO BY CRIS KOHL.

New York, sank with a large cargo of iron ore while attempting to ride out a severe snowstorm on November 19, 1886. Her anchor slipped and her centerboard hit the lake bottom, snapping the keel. Later, a nearby lighthouse keeper spied the ship's masts standing out of the water. Upon closer examination, he saw that three of the crew had lashed themselves to the rigging to keep from being swept overboard. Their lifeless bodies were coated with several inches of ice. All ten men on board the *Lucerne* perished.

Artwork © University of Wisconsin Sea Grant Institute/State Historical Society of Wisconsin

This site, which features the centerboard and trunk, an amazingly intact bow with a capstan, windlass, samson post and chain, intact starboard railing and a large ore cargo field, is buoyed annually by the State Historical Society of Wisconsin.

7. FEDORA

> **LORAN: 32403.3/46153.5**   **LAT 46° 51.588′ LON 090° 46.709′**
> **DEPTH: 0 to 10 feet**   **LEVEL: Novice**

LOCATION: Just south of Red Cliff Point.

The composite (iron frame, ribs and keel with oak planking) bulk freight steamer, *Fedora* (282′2″ x 41′5″ x 20′1″), built at West Bay City, Michigan, in 1889, burned to a complete loss on September 20, 1901 with no lives lost. A kerosene lamp had started the fire in the engine room. Her machinery was salvaged, but some boiler plates and the immense hull, with its engine beds, remain in place.

The *Fedora* then. MPL/WMHS. The *Fedora* now. PHOTO BY CRIS KOHL

Artwork © University of Wisconsin Sea Grant Institute/State Historical Society of Wisconsin

8. H. D. COFFINBERRY

LORAN: 32395.8/46144.4	LAT 46° 52.978' LON 090° 45.814'
DEPTH: 3 to 6 feet	LEVEL: Novice

The *H.D. Coffinberry.* MPL/WMHS

The remains today. PHOTO BY CRIS KOHL

LOCATION: This wreck lies along the shore in Red Cliff Bay, Wisconsin.

The wooden bulk freight steamer, *H.D. Coffinberry* (191'4" x 33'5" x 13'4"), launched at East Saginaw, Michigan, in 1874, was abandoned at Ashland in 1912 after a long career hauling coal, grain, iron ore and lumber. Her hull was towed to its present site in 1917 and stripped of its machinery. Only the lower portion of the wooden hull remains to be seen today.

Artwork © University of Wisconsin Sea Grant Institute/State Historical Society of Wisconsin

9. OTTAWA

LORAN: 32395.8/46144.4	LAT 46° 52.978' LON 090° 45.814'
DEPTH: 12 to 20 feet	LEVEL: Novice

The *Ottawa* working on the wreck of the *Sevona.* AUTHOR'S COLLECTION

Artwork © University of Wisconsin Sea Grant Institute/State Historical Society of Wisconsin

LOCATION: This wreck lies next to the *H.D. Coffinberry* in Red Cliff Bay, Wisconsin.

Launched as the *Boscobel* at Chicago in 1881 and renamed in 1903 when it changed to Canadian ownership, the large, wooden tug, *Ottawa* (151' x 28'4" x 13'7"), burned to a complete loss with no lives lost on November 29, 1909. The fire had begun in the coal bunker. She was one of the most powerful tugboats in the world when she was built, and worked at salvaging many lost ships, including the *Sevona,* for famous Great Lakes wreckers Jim and Tom Reid of Sarnia, Ontario. Her machinery was recovered, but the large, wooden hull remains in place.

10. NOQUEBAY

LORAN: 32351.3/46184.6	LAT 46° 55.568' LON 090° 32.717'
DEPTH: 10 to 15 feet	LEVEL: Novice

LOCATION: This wreck lies 300' off Stockton Island in Julian Bay.

The huge schooner-barge, *Noquebay* (205'2" x 34'7" x 12'5"), built at Trenton, Michigan, in 1872, caught fire on October 8, 1905, with a lumber cargo while in tow of the steamer, *Lizzie Madden.* The *Noquebay* was beached, where she burned to a total loss. No lives were lost. Her lumber cargo and anchors were salvaged. Shifting sands continually change this site, which includes the ship's wheel and steering gear, and many interesting scattered parts.

The *Noquebay.* MPL/WMHS

Artwork © University of Wisconsin Sea Grant Institute/State Historical Society of Wisconsin

Depth draft markings on the *Noquebay.* PHOTO BY CRIS KOHL

11. PRETORIA

LORAN: 32288.0/46141.1	LAT 47° 05.36′ LON 090° 23.66′
DEPTH: 55 feet	LEVEL: Intermediate

LOCATION: This wreck lies one mile off the northeast shore of Outer Island.

The three-masted schooner-barge, *Pretoria* (338′4″ x 44′ x 23′), launched at West Bay City, Michigan, on July 28, 1900, foundered with the loss of five of the ten lives on board and her iron ore cargo in the fierce gale of September 2, 1905. The *Pretoria* was one of the largest sailing vessels ever to ply Great Lakes waters. Her two huge anchors were recovered in the summer of 1961 for exhibit at the Madeline Island Historical museum. The wreck is broken and scattered, with no penetration possibilities, but the site yields views of the iron-reinforced keelson, bollards, hanging knees, cargo, much planking and a hatch cover.

Pretoria's launching. MPL/WMHS

Artwork © University of Wisconsin Sea Grant Institute/State Historical Society of Wisconsin

Both the *Pretoria* and the *Sevona* sites, among others in the Apostle Islands, are buoyed annually by the State Historical Society of Wisconsin.

12. SEVONA

LORAN: 32388.1/46032.9	LAT 47° 00.410′ LON 090° 54.520′
DEPTH: 16 to 20 feet	LEVEL: Novice

LOCATION: This wreck lies on Sand Island Reef, northeast of Sand Island.

The tragic loss of the steel steamer, *Sevona* (372′5″ x 41′ x 24′6″), resulted in 7 of the 24 people on board losing their lives when the ship stranded during a severe storm on Sept. 2, 1905. Launched as the *Emily P. Weed* in 1890 at West Bay City, Michigan, the *Sevona* today lies scattered (from nature and salvage attempts), with steel and iron ore cargo covering a wide area.

Artwork © University of Wisconsin Sea Grant Institute/State Historical Society of Wisconsin

The *Sevona.* MPL/WMHS

45. Minnesota's Superior Shore

1. *Thomas Wilson*
2. **Duluth breakwall**
3. *Onoko*
4. **Stony Point**
5. *Niagara*
6. **Knife River ruins**
7. *Samuel P. Ely*
8. **Agate Bay merchant dock**
9. **Flood Bay wayside**
10. *Lafayette*
11. **Gooseberry Falls State Park**
12. *Madeira*
13. *Hesper*
14. *Amboy* **and** *George Spencer*

1. THOMAS WILSON

LORAN: 32605.3/45820.1	LAT	LON
DEPTH: 54 to 70 feet	LEVEL: Advanced	

LOCATION: This wreck lies about 7/8 mile off the Duluth harbor entrance.

The whaleback steamer, *Thomas Wilson* (308′ x 38′ x 24′), launched on April 30, 1892, at West Superior, Wisconsin, was the 19th vessel built of this particular and uniquely-Great-Lakes design. The *Thomas Wilson* sank within 3 minutes with 9 lives lost after a collision with the wooden steamer, *George G. Hadley*, on June 7, 1902. The *Hadley*, which also sank, was later recovered and returned to service as the *William P. Rend,* only to sink at Alpena, Michigan, in 1917 (her story is also in this book).

Left: The whaleback steamer, *Thomas Wilson.* MPL/WMHS. *Right:* The *Meteor* is the only one of the 44 whalebacks ever constructed which remains intact above water, as a museum in Superior, Wisconsin, examined by diver Don Edwards. Eight whalebacks lie wrecked in the Great Lakes (three remain missing); the others were either scrapped or lie in saltwater seas. PHOTO BY CRIS KOHL.

The *Thomas Wilson,* dynamited shortly after her sinking as a hazard to navigation, lies with her bow and stern somewhat intact, but her midship area destroyed. Visibility is often bad, reduced even more after a storm, but increased if the wind has been out of the northwest for a couple of days. Penetration diving is possible with almost zero visibility to be expected because of the silt and cave-diving techniques and precautions mandatory. Two anchors from the *Thomas Wilson,* raised in 1973 and 1978, are exhibited at the Canal Park Museum.

Of the 44 whalebacks ever constructed, the first 6 were built at Duluth, Minnesota, the next 34 at West Superior, Wisconsin, then one at Everett, Washington, two in Brooklyn, New York, and one in England. Several "near-whalebacks" were constructed by various shipyards in both the U.S.A. and England.

2. DULUTH BREAKWALL

LOCATION: About 600′ off the Fitger Inn Complex on Lake Superior.

With depths from 5′ to 45′, this novice dive offers views of the old, submerged docks, cribs, tools, chains and other artifacts from the 1800's. Please do not remove these items.

3. ONOKO

DEPTH: 220 feet	LEVEL: Technical

LOCATION: This deep shipwreck lies about 13.5 miles east of Duluth and 6.5 miles south of Knife Island.

The *Onoko* (287′3″ x 38′8″ x 20′7″), launched at Cleveland on Feb. 16, 1882, as the first iron-hulled steam freighter on the Great Lakes, sprang a leak and sank on Sept. 14, 1915, with a wheat cargo and no lives lost. Found by Jerry Eliason and Kraig Smith in June, 1988, the *Onoko* lies upside down.

The *Onoko.* MPL/WMHS

4. STONY POINT

LOCATION: Take Stony Point Rd. for 3/4 mile off U.S. 61, 11 miles n. of Lester River.

This novice shore-dive site, popular among those divers interested in geology, runs from 10′ to 40′ deep along very old lava ledges, with interesting lava crevices and boulders along the northeast side in 15′ of water. You will also see agates embedded in the lava.

5. NIAGARA

LORAN:	LAT	LON
DEPTH: 65 to 95 feet	LEVEL: Advanced	

DOWNWARD SLOPE ⇩

LOCATION: This wreck lies 500′ due south of the middle of Knife Island.

Launched in 1872 at Detroit, the tug, *Niagara* (130′ x 24′7″ x 8′7″), stranded along Knife Island during a heavy northeast gale on June 4, 1904, and broke in two. No lives were lost, as the 13 people on board were removed by a tug dispatched to the scene. The engine, boiler and other machinery were salvaged soon afterwards.

The wreckage of the wooden hull consists of the bow section lying in four slabs on a rocky slope, with the stern still missing.

Artwork: Minnesota Historical Society/Legislative Commission on Minnesota Resources.

The tug, *Niagara*. MPL/WMHS

6. KNIFE RIVER RUINS

LOCATION: Just off the mainland to the northwest of the *Niagara* site and Knife I.

This old pulpwood dock at the mouth of the Knife River, owned by the Alger Smith logging railroad which ceased operations in about 1919, offers a shore dive in about 5′ to 25′ of water. Avoid any northern rivers in the spring or early summer, as the run-offs produce strong currents and poor visibility. Divers can park at the end of the river's mouth road.

7. SAMUEL P. ELY

DEPTH: 20 to 35 feet	LEVEL: Novice

LOCATION: Along the inner west breakwall halfway between shore and the light.

The schooner-barge, *Samuel P. Ely* (200′ x 31′6″ x 13′8″), built as a three-masted schooner at Detroit in 1869, stranded and sank along the breakwall with no cargo or lives lost on October 30, 1896.

A boat is required to reach this site, which is one of the most popular shipwreck dives along this north shore. The wreck, sitting on sand, is easily penetrated because of the missing hatch covers. The bow and stern ends are broken, but wooden railings, the deck, a bilge pump and a winch greet visiting divers. The site is often marked with a buoy, or paint along the breakwall. Recently,

Samuel P. Ely. AUTHOR'S COLLECTION

conservation work has been done here by the Great Lakes Shipwreck Preservation Society.

8. AGATE BAY MERCHANT DOCK AND FISHING TUGS

LOCATION: Northwest of the public boat launch at Agate Bay.

The old dock lies in about 10′ of water, with the remains of 3 abandoned fishing tugs in about 25′ of water approximately 70′ off shore. This shore dive is suitable for novice divers.

9. FLOOD BAY WAYSIDE

LOCATION: About one mile northeast of Two Harbors, immediately off shore from the parking area in 2′ to 20′ of water lies an assortment of artifacts from the old mining days (chains, railroad spikes, nails, axles, gears and rails). Please leave these items in place.

10. *LAFAYETTE*

DEPTH: 6 to 30 feet	LEVEL: Novice

LOCATION: A boat is required to reach this site four miles northeast of Two Harbors.

The large, steel steamer, *Lafayette* (454′ x 50′ x 28′5″), along with several other ships, succumbed to one of the worst storms in Great Lakes history. On November 28, 1905, the light *Lafayette,* buffetted by strong gales and lashing waves, collided with her equally empty barge consort, the *Manila,* before stranding and breaking in two on the inhospitable rocky shoreline near

The wrecked *Lafayette* bow. MPL/WMHS

Encampment Island. One life was lost. The *Manila* was later recovered, and the *Lafayette's* stern half was refloated and taken to Duluth, with the bow half deemed a total loss and left in place. Scrap iron salvage during the two World Wars left little of the *Lafayette's* bow other than some steel plates, railing and pipes to the south and east of Lafayette Bluff. The large steamer had been launched at Lorain, Ohio, on May 31, 1900.

11. GOOSEBERRY FALLS STATE PARK

LOCATION: Off U.S. 61 at Gooseberry Falls State Park.

This novice shore dive to 30′ will be of interest to geology and shipwreck buffs alike,

as there are massive lava formations, as well as portions of the wooden steamer, *Belle P. Cross* (146′ x 26′ x 12′), built at Trenton, Michigan, in 1870, and stranded at the mouth of the Gooseberry River in a blinding snowstorm on April 29, 1903. The ship broke up with her lumber cargo and no lives lost, and the pulverized remains lie scattered over a wide area.

The *Belle P. Cross.* AUTHOR'S COLLECTION

12. *MADEIRA*

DEPTH: 30 to 110 feet **LEVEL: Intermediate-Advanced**

LOCATION: This wreck lies at the base of Golden Cliff, NE of Split Rock Point.

The *Madeira*. MPL/WMHS

Exploring the *Madeira's* angled steel pieces. PHOTOS BY CRIS KOHL

The three-masted, schooner-rigged, steel barge, *Madeira* (436′ x 50′2″ x 24′2″), built at Chicago in 1900, was wrecked in the same storm that destroyed the nearby *Lafayette* (site #10). On November 28, 1905, this huge barge stranded and broke up with the loss of the First Mate.

There is a small parking area along U.S. 61, and a short trail down to the water's edge, where divers can suit up and swim a few hundred feet over to the wreck site. The wreck of the *Madeira,* usually buoyed at the base of the cliff, lies basically in three large sections of steel. The bow is upside-down in 40′ to 50′ of water, while the stern, with its steam winch and open hatches, rests on its starboard side in 65′. A small, roof-less pilot house sits at 75′. In spite of being torn apart as with a giant can opener, this shipwreck offers interesting scuba diving and exploration.

Artwork: Minnesota Historical Society/Legislative Commission on Minnesota Resources.

13. *HESPER*

DEPTH: 30 to 48 feet **LEVEL: Novice-Intermediate**

LOCATION: This wreck lies along the west breakwall of Silver Bay harbor, Minnesota.

Built at Cleveland in 1890, the wooden bulk freight steamer, *Hesper* (250′3″ x 41′6″ x 20′2″), stranded during a severe gale on May 3, 1905, and slid into deeper water in two main pieces in the harbor at Silver Bay. No lives were lost. The large machinery was salvaged that year. Located in August, 1961 by divers Don Franklin and Curtis Anderson, the *Hesper* was further salvaged of smaller pieces, including the name-plate, bell and compass bin-nacle. A boat is needed to reach this site, and the wreck lies near

The *Hesper*. MPL/WMHS

the midway point along the breakwall from shore. The site features the large, wooden hull, with the sides collapsed, and the rudder.

Artwork © Great Lakes Shipwrecks Preservation Society.

14. *AMBOY* AND *GEORGE SPENCER*

LOCATION: 1 mile southwest of Sugar Loaf Cove, in 3′ to 20′ of water 50′ from shore.

The wooden steamer, *George Spencer* (230′5″ x 37′2″ x 18′8″), built at Cleveland in 1884, and her tow, the schooner-barge, *Amboy* (209′3″ x 34′2″ x 14′4″), also from Cleveland in 1874, stranded in the storm of Nov. 28, 1905. A keelson part of the *Amboy* lies on shore.

46. Isle Royale

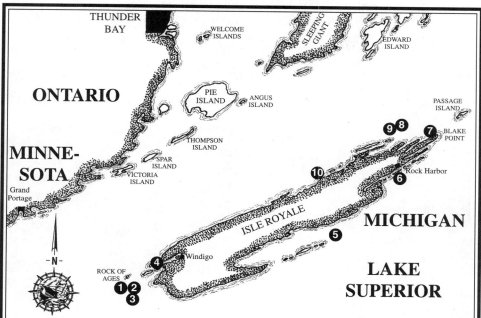

Isle Royale, the largest island in the largest Great Lake, with its wilderness remoteness and tempting inaccessibility, is the Mecca of Great Lakes diving, beckoning scuba divers from afar with its handful of legendary shipwrecks. It offers the most challenging shipwreck diving and post-diving conditions in the world. Converted to National Park status in 1940, Michigan's Isle Royale lies only a few miles off Minnesota and Ontario. All the shipwreck sites except the *Kamloops* have surface buoys provided by the Park Service. The main rules at present are:

1. Boats from Canada must clear customs.
2. Scuba divers must register at a ranger station before diving and obtain a free permit.
3. A standard dive flag must be used.
4. Disturbance or removal of anything underwater is prohibited.
5. Compressor use is restricted to certain locations and hours. (There are no airfill stations on the island, so you have to bring your own.)
6. There is a daily use fee for anyone visiting the island. Campers need a camping permit.
7. The shipwreck *America* is closed to diving during certain hours (presently noon to 2:00 PM) to allow visitors on the passenger ferry to view the wreck.

Plan this trip of a lifetime carefully. Contact Isle Royale National Park at (906) 482-0986.

1. *Cumberland*
2. *Henry Chisholm*
3. *George M. Cox*
4. *America*
5. *Glenlyon*
6. *Algoma*
7. *Monarch*
8. *Emperor*
9. *Chester A. Congdon*
10. *Kamloops*

1. CUMBERLAND

> **LORAN: 31927.24/46066.70   LAT 47° 52.73'   LON 089° 18.33'**
> **DEPTH: 20 to 90 feet   LEVEL: Advanced**

LOCATION: This wreck lies intermingled with the remains of the *Henry Chisholm* (see site #2 below) near Rock of Ages Reef and Light, off the western end of Isle Royale.

The wooden sidewheel steamer, *Cumberland* (204'5" x 26' x 10'7"), launched on August 9, 1871, at Port Robinson, Ontario, stranded on the Rock of Ages Reef on July 23, 1877, and finally broke and sank several weeks later during storms after salvage attempts failed. No lives were lost in the stranding.

The wreck site is a jumble of timber slabs and machinery, such as engine boilers, rudder, paddlewheel and propeller.

The paddlewheel steamer, *Cumberland,* was wrecked at Isle Royale in 1877. AUTHOR'S COLLECTION

The wooden steamer, *Henry Chisholm,* joined the wreck of the *Cumberland* in 1898. GLHS

2. HENRY CHISHOLM

> **LORAN: 31927.24/46066.70   LAT 47° 52.73'   LON 089° 18.33'**
> **DEPTH: 20 to 90, and 140 feet LEVEL: Advanced-Technical**

LOCATION: This wreck lies intermingled with the remains of the *Cumberland* (see site #1 above) near Rock of Ages Reef and Light, off the western end of Isle Royale.

This wooden steamer (256'5" x 39'3" x 20'3"), launched on Aug. 28, 1880, at Cleveland, stranded and sank at Rock of Ages Reef on Oct. 21, 1898, with no lives lost. Her engine lies on the reef's other side in 145' at **LORAN: 31936.1/46068.0   LAT 47° 54.35' LON 089° 21.49'**

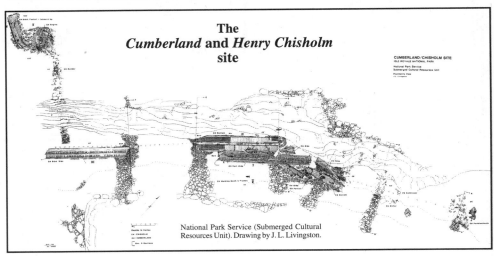

The
Cumberland and *Henry Chisholm*
site

CUMBERLAND/CHISHOLM SITE
ISLE ROYALE NATIONAL PARK
National Park Service
Submerged Cultural Resources Unit
Planimetric View

National Park Service (Submerged Cultural Resources Unit). Drawing by J. L. Livingston.

380

3. GEORGE M. COX

LORAN: 31934.9/46069.8	LAT 47° 51.56' LON 089° 19.52'
DEPTH: 12 to 97 feet	LEVEL: Intermediate-Advanced

LOCATION: This wreck lies along Rock Island Reef, near the Rock of Ages Light.

The wooden steamer, *George M. Cox* (259' x 40'5" x 26'6"), launched as the *Puritan* on May 1, 1901, at Toledo, Ohio, and renamed by wealthy new owner George M. Cox in honor of himself in early 1933, ran hard aground on her first trip of the season with 121 people on board on May 27, 1933. Fortunately, all were safely removed. Salvage efforts failed and the ship broke up, but much of her machinery and equipment had been recovered.

The *George M. Cox,* the second-most visited shipwreck at Isle Royale (after the popular *America* nearby), lies within a mile of the *Cumberland/Henry Chisholm* site. The highlights of this shipwreck site are the four (!) large boilers (she was a fast ship!), the rudder lying flat, and the vast amount of broken steel. Much scattered steel debris, mainly from the bow, lies in the shallows, but the bulk of the shipwreck (and the most interesting part, which happens to be the stern half) rests between 50' and 97'.

bow

Above: The *George M. Cox* failed to complete her maiden voyage under her new name, opting instead to pose for another one of the more dramatic Great Lakes shipwreck photos. MPL/ WMHS. *Above right:* Diver Don Edwards examines the several boilers at the site. PHOTO BY CRIS KOHL. Artwork: National Park Service (Submerged Cultural Resources Unit). Drawing by J. Livingston and L. Nordby.

stern

4. AMERICA

LORAN: 46082.2/31909.2	LAT 47° 53.39′ LON 089° 13.15′
DEPTH: 4 to 85 feet	LEVEL: Intermediate-Advanced

LOCATION: This wreck lies just outside Washington Harbor at western Isle Royale. The steel-hulled passenger and freight steamer, *America* (182′6″ x 31′ x 11′), launched on April 2, 1898, at Wyandotte, MI, struck a rocky reef in the darkness of night and became

The active *America.*
MPL/WMHS

The passive *America.* MPL/WMHS

an unsalvageable total loss on June 7, 1928. Fortunately, there were no lives lost, as all 47 passengers and crew took to the lifeboats. Unfortunately, a dog tied to the stern went down with the ship. Today, the wreck of the *America* is the most visited divesite at Isle Royale. She sits on a 45-degree angle on the incline and a 30-degree list to port. Her bow in the shallows offers tantalizingly photogenic visuals with a windlass, pump and bollards. Narrow passageways into the wreck offer access to the galley, the dining salon, various staterooms with several below-deck corridors, and the engine room. Don't get snagged on any of the debris below deck. The pride of the *America's* crew remains evident where, years ago, they painted the American flag, still visible today, onto the side of the engine. At the stern, the deepest part of the wreck, the propeller and taffrail are of interest.

The *America* in profile

Artwork: National Park Service (Submerged Cultural Resources Unit). Drawings by (left) H. Thom McGrath, and (right) Jerry Livingston.

America site map. Drawing by Jerry Livingston.

Left: Diver Karen Della-Mattia ventures below deck in the *America.* PHOTO BY JOE LARK. *Below:* Don Edwards explores the bow. PHOTO BY CRIS KOHL. *Right:* Karen at the propeller. PHOTO BY JOE LARK.

5. GLENLYON

> **LORAN: 31808.65/46188.57**   **LAT 47° 57.21′   LON 088° 45.01′**
> **DEPTH: 10 to 100 feet**   **LEVEL: Novice to Advanced**

LOCATION: On Isle Royale's south side, at Glenlyon Shoal north of Menagerie Island. The steel freighter, *Glenlyon* (328′ x 42′5″ x 20′5″), launched as the *William H. Gratwick* at West Bay City, Michigan, in 1893, headed for Siskiwit Bay seeking shelter from a storm,

but instead stranded on a reef on November 1, 1924, with a cargo of wheat. No lives were lost in this mishap. Broken wreckage, such as the triple expansion engine, rudder, capstan and spare propeller blades, lies widely scattered in 10′ to 50′ of water, with parts of the separated stern cabin sitting in 100′.

AUTHOR'S COLLECTION

The freighter, *Glenlyon*

Diver Karen Della-Mattia explores the *Glenlyon's* components. PHOTOS BY JOE LARK.

National Park Service (Submerged Cultural Resources Unit). Drawing by J. Livingston and L. Nordby.

6. ALGOMA

> **LORAN: 31748.36/46187.83**   **LAT 48° 06.46′   LON 088° 31.54′**
> **DEPTH: 15 to 100 feet**   **LEVEL: Intermediate-Advanced**

LOCATION: On the south side of Mott Island, southwest of Rock Harbor, Isle Royale. Built in Glasgow, Scotland in 1883, the steel passenger steamer, *Algoma* (262′8″ x 38′2″ x 23′3″), stranded on Nov. 7, 1885, with the loss of 45 lives from the 59 on board. Those lost were on the bow when the ship broke in half and that part of the wreck was swept into deep water. It has not yet been located. Engine, boiler and other machinery were salvaged in 1886. Today's divers explore the stern half, broken and scattered in three gullies.

Views of the *Algoma* wreck.
MPL/WMHS

National Park Service (Submerged Cultural Resources Unit) Drawing by Larry Nordby.

7. MONARCH

> **LORAN: 46171.3/31702.4** **LAT 48° 11.44' LON 088° 26.03'**
> **DEPTH: 10 to 150 feet** **LEVEL: All levels possible here**

LOCATION: This wreck lies on the north side of Blake Point, eastern Isle Royale.

The wooden passenger and freight steamer, *Monarch* (240' x 35' x 14'8"), launched at Sarnia, Ontario, in 1890, grounded hard onto the inhospitable and uninhabited shoreline called the Palisades during a blinding snowstorm on December 6, 1906. One man reached shore with a rope, which he tied to a tree so the other 60 people could escape the sinking ship hand over hand along that line. One life was lost when a young crewman slipped from the rope.

Massive pieces of hull and decking, as well as some scattered machinery (the engine and boiler were salvaged), comprise this site, which is extensive in shallow water (to 70'), but less so in deeper water.

Above: The regal *Monarch* proudly underway. MPL/WMHS. *Below:* The *Monarch* dethroned at the Palisades, December, 1906. AUTHOR'S COLLECTION.

Monarch

National Park Service (Submerged Cultural Resources Unit). Drawing by Jerry Livingston.

deeper water

8. EMPEROR

> **LORAN: 46150.6/31711.8** **LAT 48° 12.39' LON 088° 29.47'**
> **DEPTH: 30 to 175 feet** **LEVEL: Intermediate-Technical**

LOCATION: This wreck lies off the Canoe Rocks, eastern Isle Royale.

Launched on December 17, 1910, at Collingwood, Ontario, the huge, steel, bulk freight steamer, *Emperor* (525' x 56'1" x 27'), carrying a cargo of iron ore, struck the rocks and sank on June 4, 1947, with the loss of 12 of the 33 people on board. At the time of her launching, she was the largest ship ever built in Canada.

The hull, although split, forms a long line of massive, cracked steel running down a rocky slope, with her propeller and rudder sitting at the deep end. This wreck is so enormous that you cannot see it all in one dive (or even a few!). Fortunately, the shallow bow and the deep stern are buoyed separately. At the bow, the large anchor and open holds are impressive, while the stern offers the ship's galley, crew's quarters (with bunkbeds), skylights and large dorades, or air vents. Penetration is only for specially trained and experienced divers.

Above: Emperor. REV. PETER VAN DER LINDEN COLLECTION. *Below:* Crew's quarters. PHOTO BY JOYCE HAYWARD

The freighter, *Emperor*

National Park Service (Submerged Cultural Resources Unit). Drawing by Jerry Livingston.

Don Edwards studies the *Emperor's* engine. PHOTO BY JOE LARK

9. CHESTER A. CONGDON

LORAN: 46147.8/31717.5	LAT 48° 11.37′ LON 088° 30.51′
DEPTH: 60 to 212 feet	LEVEL: Advanced-Technical

LOCATION: Off Congdon Shoal near the Canoe Rocks, northeastern Isle Royale.

The steel freighter, *Chester A. Congdon* (532′ x 56′2″ x 26′5″), launched as the *Salt Lake City* at Chicago on August 29, 1907, and renamed in 1912, stranded in thick fog on the rocks with her huge cargo of wheat and broke in two over the reef on November 6, 1918. No lives were lost in this simple but costly accident.

The *Congdon* site is in two parts, with the bow and its intact (but empty) pilot house resting in 70′ to 111′ of water, with the forward mast being less deep. The stern section on the other side of the reef, not usually buoyed as the Park does not encourage diving this deep, sits on a steep angle in 60′ to 212′ of water; the engine room and stern cabins are here.

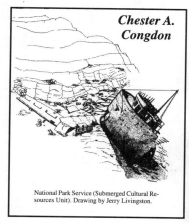

Chester A. Congdon

National Park Service (Submerged Cultural Resources Unit). Drawing by Jerry Livingston.

Above: The wrecked *Chester A. Congdon.* MPL/WMHS. *Below:* The *Congdon's* pilot house. PHOTO BY JOE LARK.

stern

National Park Service (Submerged Cultural Resources Unit). Drawing by Jerry Livingston.

Chester A. Congdon

bow

10. KAMLOOPS

LORAN: 46124.5/31786.1	LAT 48° 05.24′ LON 088° 46.14′
DEPTH: 178 to 255 feet	LEVEL: Technical

LOCATION: About 300′ off Twelve O'Clock Point, north shore of Isle Royale.

The *Kamloops* story is one of the more tragic Isle Royale shipwreck tales. Built in England in 1924, this steel freighter (250′ x 42′9″ x 24′3″) foundered in a severe early winter storm on December 6, 1927, alongside rocky Isle Royale. Not all of the crew of 20 men and 2 women perished immediately; some reached the island by lifeboat and froze or starved to death slowly. One woman left a heart-wrenching note to her parents in a bottle. The bodies were found the following spring.

The *Kamloops* was located in 1977, with diver Ken Merryman being the first to explore and identify her. She lies on her starboard side, bow deeper than stern, and very intact, with the perfectly preserved ship's wheel chain-and-padlocked in place so it won't get lost. The Park does not encourage diving this deep site, so there is no surface buoy here.

Artwork ©Robert McGreevy

47. North Shore Superior

Left: The *James Whalen* was the first tugboat to go to the *Gunilda's* assistance. PHOTO BY CRIS KOHL.

If you were a millionaire and this were your luxury yacht, would you be too cheap to hire a second tugboat to help get it off the rocks? Read about the *Gunilda* (site #15) in this chapter. MPL/WMHS

Nipigon
Schreiber
ONTARIO
Rossport
Terrace Bay
Marathon
ST. IGNACE ISLAND
PIC ISLAND
SLATE ISLANDS
THUNDER BAY
PIE ISLAND
LAKE SUPERIOR
ISLE ROYALE
-N-

1. *Howard*	10. *W. J. Emerson*
2. *Monkshaven*	11. *St. Andrew*
3. *Gray Oak*	12. *Neebing*
4. *Green River*	13. *Mary E. McLachlan*
5. *Robert L. Fryer*	14. *Ontario*
6. *Puckasaw*	15. *Gunilda*
7. "Wally Sank Six Boats"	16. *Rappahannock*
8. *Gordon Gauthier*	17. *Judge Hart*
9. Thunder Bay ships' graveyard	18. Whaleback *Barge 115*

1. *Howard*

LORAN:	LAT 48° 04.871′ LON 089° 21.794′
DEPTH: 40 to 120 feet	LEVEL: Inetermediate-Advanced

LOCATION: Off the south end of Victoria Island, south-southwest of Thunder Bay.

One of the oldest vessels active on Lake Superior, the 195-ton wooden tug, *Howard* (114′5″ x 22′2″ x 10′), launched at Wilmington, Delaware, in 1864 as the gunrunner *Admiral D.D. Porter,* received her last name in 1889. On June 13, 1921, she stranded on Victoria Island, caught fire and burned to a total loss with no lives lost.

The tug, *Howard.* Rev. Peter Van der Linden Collection

The main wreckage of the *Howard,* including her 300 horsepower steeple compound engine, lies between 40′ and 60′, with her propeller at 50′. The fact that a barge lies in 90′ to 100′ lends truth to the rumor of two wrecks at this site, one almost atop the other. Divers can suit up on Victoria Island at the navigation light and walk out into the lake along the shallow reef. The wreck lies on the right side of the reef facing the mainland.

Don Edwards and *Howard's* propeller. Photo by Joe Lark.

Don examining the *Howard's* fire-box door. Photo by Joe Lark.

2. *Monkshaven*

DEPTH: 3 to 70 feet	LEVEL: Intermediate-Advanced

LOCATION: This wreck lies off the south side of Angus Island.

The steel steamer, *Monkshaven* (249′ x 36′1″ x 17′5″), a canaler-type freighter built in England in 1882, stranded for the second time in as many years in the Thunder Bay area on October 10, 1906, when she broke free from her moorings and impaled herself on the rocks of Angus Island. Fall weather completed her destruction. Although much steel was salvaged during World War II, there are areas of interest at this broken and scattered site.

The demise of the *Monkshaven.* Author's Collection

3. *Gray Oak*

LORAN: 31800.7/45915.7	LAT	LON
DEPTH: 108 feet	LEVEL: Advanced	

LOCATION: This wreck lies about two miles southeast of the Welcome Islands.

The flat-bottomed, blunt-nosed scow-schooner, *Gray Oak* (133′7″ x 31′7″ x 9′), launched at Bayfield, Wisconsin, on June 20, 1885, was scuttled in about 1911. The hull and glass in the windows are intact. White letters on the hull clearly spell out the name *GRAY OAK*, with additional lettering obliterated.

Right: The *Gray Oak's* wheel. Photo by Joe Lark.

4. ROBERT L. FRYER

LORAN: 31801.7/45902.4	LAT	LON
DEPTH: To 35 feet	LEVEL: Novice-Intermediate	

LOCATION: This wreck lies at "B" Island, in the Welcome Islands, Thunder Bay.

The wooden steamer, *Robert L. Fryer* (290' x 41'6" x 20'), built in 1888 at West Bay City, Michigan, became a display of spectacular entertainment when it was towed to the Welcome Islands and set on fire on July 29, 1930. Part of the island burned as well. It is easy to locate this wreck, since a piece of the hull breaks the surface. Highlights include the boiler, propeller and rudder. A small unidentified wreck lies next to the *Fryer,* while portions of 3 other scuttled wrecks lie nearby.

The *Robert L. Fryer.* AUTHOR'S COLLECTION

SPECIAL EXCURSION to Silver Islet and the burning of the Str. Robert L. Fryer

The steamer *Fryer* will be burned tomorrow evening, July 29, in the bay.

By going to Silver Islet tomorrow you may spend the day at the Islet and witness the burning of the ship on the way in. The Islet Prince will stop alongside the burning vessel and you may have a broadside view.

Round trip fare, including the burning $1.00 return. Children Half Fare

Islet Prince leaves Port William tomorrow morning at 9.30.

This will be a Sight of a Lifetime

DAILY MAIL SERVICE

Newspaper ad for the *Robert L. Fryer's* burning. AUTHOR'S COLLECTION

5. GREEN RIVER

DEPTH: 50 to 80 feet	LEVEL: Advanced

LOCATION: This wreck lies 450' north of the *Robert L. Fryer* wreck (site #4).

The wooden steamer, *Green River* (275' x 40' x 22'), launched on October 1, 1887, at West Bay City, Michigan, as the *Gogebic,* was reduced to a barge and renamed *Green River* in 1921. She was dismantled and scuttled at the Welcome Islands on November 5, 1932. The deck (at 50') and rudder are intact, and penetration is possible; training and a dive light are necessary.

Right: The *Green River.* MPL/WMHS

6. PUCKASAW

LORAN: 31801.4/45901.3	LAT	LON
DEPTH: 55 to 80 feet	LEVEL: Advanced	

Lying very close to the *Green River* (site #5), the tug, *Puckasaw,* (96' x 26' x 12'4"), built at Sturgeon Bay, WI, in 1910, as the *John Hunsader* (renamed in 1921), was scuttled in 1934. Several old boilers weighed down this intact, upright hull when she was scuttled.

Left: The tug, *Puckasaw,* is a penetrable shipwreck today. MPL/WMHS

7. "WALLY SANK SIX BOATS"

In the early 1990's, Wally Peterson of Thunder Bay arranged for the sinking of six boats, including a decrepit, old 32' Chris Craft named *Sho-Nuff,* as a dive training site. They sit in 20' to 47' of water off the conservation area at Silver Harbour. A short trail runs from the parking lot to the water; in between are picnic tables, outhouses and tables. All the boats are roped together underwater, with the first boat being about 50' offshore. Fly a dive flag!

8. GORDON GAUTHIER

The 26-ton wooden tug, *Gordon Gauthier* (52'7" x 13'9" x 6'4"), built at Wallaceburg, Ontario, in 1884, burned at a quarry dock at Port Arthur harbor on Oct. 8, 1911. Today, she sits in 15' of water at Mary Island, off Silver Harbour, ON. The propeller was removed in 1974 by divers who would have received $25 for its scrap metal value; instead, they sold it to an appreciative diver for the same amount. Today, it is displayed in a dive shop.

9. THUNDER BAY SHIPS' GRAVEYARD

DEPTH: 190 to 250 feet   LEVEL: Technical

In the 1920's and '30's, various levels of government in both Canada and the U.S.A. allocated funds for harbor clean-ups to eliminate the eyesores created by the half-submerged hulks of ships abandoned due to age and condition. The most famous of these ships' graveyards lie off Kingston, Ontario; Sarnia, Ontario; Sturgeon Bay, Wisconsin; and Thunder Bay, Ontario. The latter place recently added vastly to its numbers when Ryan LeBlanc, to prove his historical research, sidescanned Thunder Bay with colleagues Gerry Buchanan, Ken Engelbrecht and Dan Kuss in July, 2001, and located 26 to 30 scuttled ships in deep water just to the west of the known ships' graveyard in the Welcome Islands.

Among the many scuttled vessels in this newly-located site are:

❶ The steamer, *Corunna* (241' x 34'1" x 21'), built at Leith, Scotland, in 1891, with its "saltie" characteristic of a midship pilothouse, was dismantled and scuttled in 1938. the *Corunna* and the *Niagara* are the only two metal-hulled ships known to be in this graveyard.

❷ The iron steamer, *Niagara* (159' x 21'1" x 10'4"), launched at Glasgow, Scotland, in 1856 as the *Druid,* was used early in her career by the Nova Scotia government as a lighthouse supply ship for lonely Sable Island in the North Atlantic. Converted from a paddlewheeler to a propeller-driven vessel in 1894, she was sold in 1900 by the Canadian government to a private company in Quebec for $2,150; she was already an old ship then. Renamed *Niagara* in 1901, she operated as an excursion steamer on Lake Ontario until 1911, when she was sold for freight use at Port Arthur, Ontario. She was scuttled on October 1, 1936.

❸ The wooden tugboat, *Mary Ann,* believed to be the first vessel registered in the new country called Canada after the Confederation of 4 British colonies on July 1, 1867.

All three: AUTHOR'S COLLECTION

10. *W. J. EMERSON*

LOCATION: Off distant Bennett Island, at the old Number 10 Light, in 30' of water. This 19-ton, 70' tug, built in 1910, sank on Oct. 9, 1933. The wreck lies broken.

11. *ST. ANDREW*

LOCATION: This wreck lies off the rocks at the south end of tiny Bachand Island.

The wooden steamer, *St. Andrew* (192'6" x 41' x 12'4"), built at St. Catharines, Ontario, in 1885, as the *W.B. Hall,* changed her name after her 1897 rebuild. She stranded at Bachand Island and slipped into deeper water (40' to 60'). No lives were lost. Her machinery was salvaged and she lies broken, with her many parts forming a sizeable debris field.

Right: The *St. Andrew. Below:* The *Neebing* with crane. Both: AUTHOR'S COLLECTION

12. *NEEBING*

LORAN: LAT 48° 39.80'   LON 088° 07.80'
DEPTH: 60 to 100 feet   LEVEL: Advanced

Five lives were lost when the gravel carrier, *Neebing* (193' x 40'5" x 12'3"), built in 1892 at Toledo, Ohio, as the *John B. Ketcham II,* foundered on Sept. 24, 1937, off the north tip of Moss Island in the Nipigon Straits. The ship and crane are intact.

13. *MARY E. MCLACHLAN*

> **LORAN: 31454.5/46053.0**   **LAT 48° 54.66'**   **LON 087° 48.06'**
> **DEPTH: 16 to 33 feet**   **LEVEL: Novice-Intermediate**

LOCATION: This wreck lies about one mile off the mainland in Mountain Bay.

The huge 4-masted schooner, *Mary E. McLachlan* (251' x 41' x 16'2"), launched on March 2, 1893, at West Bay City, Michigan, foundered on Nov. 7, 1921, with no loss of life. Located on May 16, 1981, by Ryan LeBlanc, this wreck is loaded with interesting items, but the visibility here is often reduced because of the outflow from two nearby rivers.

Left: The schooner, *Mary E. McLachlan.* MPL/WMHS

14. *ONTARIO*

> **LORAN: 31426.7/46178.0**   **LAT 48° 45.20'**   **LON 087° 31.99'**
> **DEPTH: 10 to 40 feet**   **LEVEL: Novice-Intermediate**

LOCATION: Around the most eastern peninsula on Battle Island, 7 miles south of Rossport, Ontario.

Built at Chatham, Ontario, in 1874, the wooden steamer, *Ontario* (181' x 35' x 12'2"), smashed onto the rocks in the shallows off Battle Island on August 10, 1899, with a cargo of coal. No lives were lost. Located by Ryan LeBlanc in 1977, this wreck lies broken and scattered on a rock and sand bottom. One boiler sits on shore (great landmark!), while the other lies nearby in 10' of water.

The *Ontario.* MPL/WMHS

Below: Joyce Hayward and Ryan LeBlanc explore the *Ontario's* shorebound boiler.
Below right: Ryan examines the *Ontario's* planking. PHOTOS BY CRIS KOHL

15. *GUNILDA*

> **DEPTH: 257 feet**   **LEVEL: Technical**

LOCATION: This wreck lies just north of McGarvey Shoal near Rossport, Ontario.

The palatial steam yacht, *Gunilda* (195'--with her bowsprit-- x 24'7" x 14'2"), built at Leith, Scotland, in 1897, was owned by multi-millionaire William Harkness of Cleveland. He was entertaining his family and a number of friends when the *Gunilda* scraped hard aground on McGarvey Shoal. Nonplussed, Harkness arranged for the tug, *James Whalen*, to release his yacht. When told that a second tug would be required to keep the *Gunilda* upright, Harkness balked. The *Whalen* pulled, and the *Gunilda* capsized and sank in deep water. Harkness and his party returned home by train and he bought himself another boat.

Proclaimed "the most beautiful shipwreck in the world" by the 1980 Cousteau expedition, the *Gunilda* sits upright, intact, deadly, controversial, and carefully watched by the locals.

16. *RAPPAHANNOCK*

DEPTH: 35 to 85 feet   LEVEL: Advanced

LOCATION: This wreck lies in Jackfish Bay, near Schreiber, Ontario.

The wooden steamer, *Rappahannock* (308'1" x 42'5" x 21'2"), launched on June 6, 1895, at West Bay City, Michigan, was beached in a 70-mile-per-hour gale in Jackfish Bay on July 25, 1911. No lives were lost as the ship sank along the steep underwater incline.

Located by Ryan LeBlanc in 1979, the *Rappahannock* is in excellent shape, with an intact hull, capstan, and a unique covered walkway held up by carved wooden supports. Below, there is a carpenter's bench, a stove with utensils, and much machinery, including the engine. To reach this usually-buoyed site, launch an inflatable boat (anything bigger won't fit) at Jackfish Lake, head towards Lake Superior, and go through an extremely narrow channel under the Jackfish Bay railway culvert into Jackfish Bay.

Below: The *Rappahannock.* AUTHOR'S COLLECTION. *Below left:* Diver Joe Lark explores the *Rappahannock's* intact stern cabin. PHOTO BY JOYCE HAYWARD. *Right:* Ryan LeBlanc glides past the ship's wheel lying flat on the deck. PHOTO BY CRIS KOHL.

17. *JUDGE HART*

DEPTH: 180 to 210 feet   LEVEL: Technical

LOCATION: This wreck lies at Fitzsimmons Rocks and Barclay Island, close to Simon's Reef in Ashburton Bay, west of Neys Provincial Park, north shore of Lake Superior, Ontario.

Built in England in 1923, the steel steamer, *Judge Hart* (252'2" x 43'2" x 17'8"), carried grain for most of her Great Lakes career, which ended its activity on Nov. 27, 1942, when she stranded with a grain cargo and sank. No lives were lost.

The *Judge Hart,* located on June 16, 1990, by divers Jerry Eliason and Kraig Smith, sits upright and incredibly intact, including all equipment, like the wheel, in the pilot house.

The *Judge Hart.* MPL/WMHS

18. WHALEBACK *BARGE 115*

DEPTH: 40 to 80 feet   LEVEL: Intermediate-Advanced

LOCATION: This wreck lies off the middle west side of Pic Island, Lake Superior.

The whaleback *Barge 115* (256' x 36'1" x 18'9"), built at Superior, Wisconsin, in 1891, stranded with her iron ore cargo on Pic Island on Dec. 18, 1899, becoming the last Great Lakes shipwreck of the 1800's. After struggling for several days, the 8 crew reached safety.

Located by Ryan LeBlanc in 1980, *Barge 115* sits broken on the rocky bottom, with only her bow and its deckhouse intact. A windlass lies among the large sheets of steel.

Left: Whaleback *Barge 115.* MPL/WMHS. *Right:* This little nook on Pic Island's rocky shoreline near the wreck offers a safe harbor. PHOTO BY CRIS KOHL. *Far right:* Examining machinery from *Barge 115.* PHOTO BY JOE LARK.

48. Eastern Lake Superior

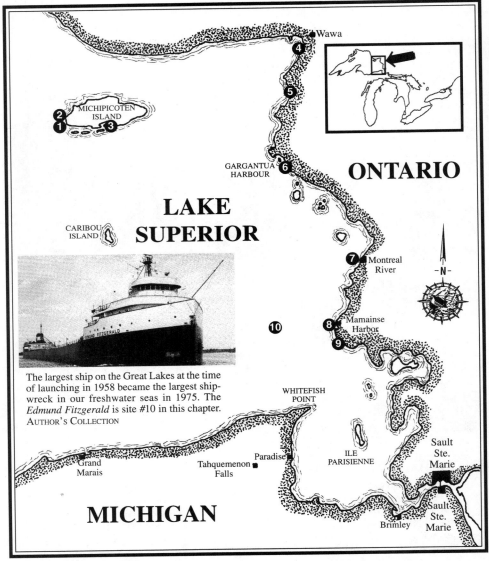

ONTARIO

LAKE
SUPERIOR

MICHIGAN

The largest ship on the Great Lakes at the time of launching in 1958 became the largest shipwreck in our freshwater seas in 1975. The *Edmund Fitzgerald* is site #10 in this chapter.
AUTHOR'S COLLECTION

1. *Chicago*
2. *Strathmore*
3. *Hiram R. Dixon*
4. *Acadia*
5. *Golspie*

6. *Columbus*, dredge and cribs
7. **Montreal River harbor**
8. **William O. Brown**
9. **Batchawana**
10. **Edmund Fitzgerald**

1. CHICAGO

LORAN:	LAT 47° 43.84' LON 085° 57.91'
DEPTH: 10 to 70 feet	LEVEL: Intermediate-Advanced

LOCATION: This wreck lies in Schafer Bay at the western end of Michipicoten Island.
The steel package freighter, *Chicago* (324'2" x 44' x 14'), launched on Sept. 28, 1901, at Buffalo, New York, with a cargo of zinc ingots and steel fence posts, stranded at this remote location 35 miles off the mainland on October 23, 1929, with no lives lost from the 31 crew.

The wreck lies on her port side on a slope with visual treats that include the stern deck capstan, the zinc ingots cargo, two chains running down a stern hawsepipe, a chain locker, her propeller and hub, and a stream anchor. The broken bow in the shallows displays a windlass and other interesting nautical items.

The *Chicago*.
AUTHOR'S COLLECTION

2. STRATHMORE

LORAN:	LAT 47° 44.64' LON 085° 57.36'
DEPTH: 5 to 35 feet	LEVEL: Novice-Intermediate

LOCATION: This wreck lies a bit north of the *Chicago* (site #1) in Schafer Bay.
Launched in 1871 at Detroit as the *Gordon Campbell* and given her last name in 1906,

The *Strathmore*.
AUTHOR'S COLLECTION

the wooden freight steamer, *Strathmore* (207' x 33' x 21'), ran onto the rocks at Michipicoten Island while downbound with a grain cargo on Nov. 14, 1906, caught on fire and sank, with no harm to her crew. An underwater photographer's delight resting on a rock and sand bottom, this wreck displays big eccentric rods and a propulsion system with the propeller. At Quebec Harbour on southern Michipicoten Island, a set of *Strathmore* bollards sit on a dock and her rudder reclines on a lawn.

3. HIRAM R. DIXON

LOCATION: In 10' - 15' at the e. end of Quebec Harbour, on the s. side of Michipicoten I. The wooden steamer, *Hiram R. Dixon* (147'2" x 20'6" x 9'), built at Mystic, Connecticut in 1883, burned to a total loss on August 18, 1903. Her hull was damaged during the salvage of her machinery. Cribs and the remains of another small wreck lie nearby.

The *Hiram W. Dixon*.
AUTHOR'S COLLECTION

4. ACADIA

LOCATION: This wreck lies in 10' to 30', at the mouth of the Michipicoten River.

The steamer, *Acadia* (177' x 26' x 12'3"), built of early composite hull construction and launched at Hamilton, Ontario, on May 1, 1867, exactly 2 months before Canada became a country, stranded with a grain cargo on November 5, 1896, while seeking shelter. No lives were lost, but the ship was pounded to pieces, which today lie scattered over a wide area between boulders and include hull pieces, steam fittings and tools.

The *Acadia*. ONTARIO ARCHIVES

5. GOLSPIE

LOCATION: This wreck lies at the mouth of Old Woman River in Old Woman Bay.
The wooden steamer, *Golspie* (183'6" x 34' x 22'), launched as the *Osceola* in 1882 at West Bay City, MI, stranded in a blizzard on Dec. 4, 1906 and broke up. Her boiler remains.

6. *COLUMBUS,* DREDGE AND CRIB

LOCATION: These submerged cultural resources lie in Gargantua Harbour, Ontario.

A rough, adventurous dirt road runs 9 long miles from the main highway to a parking lot, from which it is only a couple more miles of hiking with your scuba gear to reach pretty Gargantua Harbour. It's rough, but it's worth it. The harbor is lined with scenic submerged cribs and an abandoned dredge, while the wreck of the wooden steamer, *Columbus* (136'2" x 25'2" x 11'8"), launched as the *John Owen* in 1874 at Detroit and burned to a total loss with no lives lost on Sept. 10, 1909, lies in 0' to 27' of water near the harbor's center. The wreck features the towering engine, propeller, boiler, a capstan, and much interesting debris.

The *Columbus.* IGLR   *Columbus'* angled Fore & Aft Compound engine, left, and her toppled boiler, approached by diver Joan Forsberg, right, are highlights. PHOTOS BY CRIS KOHL

7. MONTREAL RIVER HARBOR

LOCATION: A boat is necessary to reach the mouth of the harbor, where two unidentified tugs lie in 24' to 35' of water. Keep someone on board to watch for boating traffic.

8. *WILLIAM O. BROWN*

LOCATION: In 30' of water at Mamainse Point lie the remains of the 400-ton, two-masted schooner, *William O. Brown,* lost in a ruthless west-southwest snow-battering gale which also sank 3 other ships on Nov. 28, 1872. The *Brown* stranded and broke up with the loss of 6 of her 9 crew and her wheat cargo. Pieces of this ship lie scattered over a wide area.

9. *BATCHAWANA*

LOCATION: In 4' to 35' on the north side of Rousseau Island off Coppermine Point.

Launched as the *Robert A. Packer* in 1881 at Bay City, MI, burned in 1902, and rebuilt and renamed in 1906, the wooden steamer, *Batchawana* (209' x 33'8" x 16'1"), burned to a final total loss on June 26, 1907, with no lives lost. Divers with stamina have done this as a shore dive from the mainland, but a small boat is much preferred. Spikes and bolts lie in the shallows, with slabs of hull and pieces of machinery scattered in the slightly deeper water.

Diver Frank Troxell takes a good look at the *Batchawana's* damaged, four-bladed propeller. PHOTO BY CRIS KOHL

10. *EDMUND FITZGERALD*

LORAN:	LAT 46° 59' 9" LON 085° 06' 6" (old system)
DEPTH: 529 feet	LEVEL: VERY Technical

Lying just inside Canadian waters is the most famous Great Lakes shipwreck of them all, thanks in large part to Gordon Lightfoot's popular, tough ballad about her. This steel freighter (729'3" x 75' x 39'), built in 1958 at River Rouge, MI, foundered in a storm with all 29 lives on Nov. 10, 1975. Broken in half, this controversial wreck has been visited by submersibles, but only once by a pair of trimix divers (1995). The wreck victims' families have asked that no further visitations take place to the largest shipwreck in the Great Lakes.

49. St. Mary's River

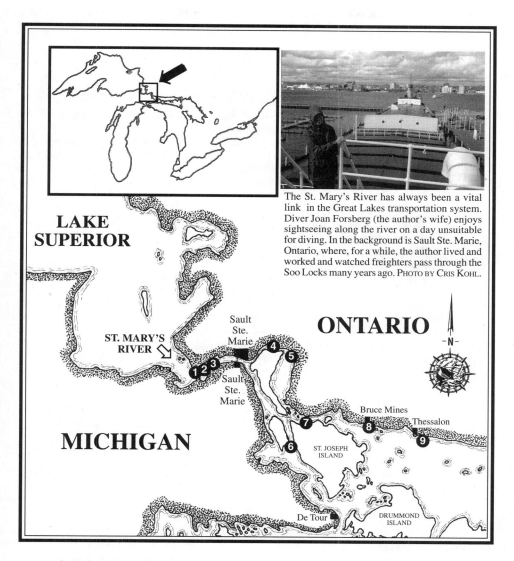

The St. Mary's River has always been a vital link in the Great Lakes transportation system. Diver Joan Forsberg (the author's wife) enjoys sightseeing along the river on a day unsuitable for diving. In the background is Sault Ste. Marie, Ontario, where, for a while, the author lived and worked and watched freighters pass through the Soo Locks many years ago. PHOTO BY CRIS KOHL.

LAKE SUPERIOR

ST. MARY'S RIVER

Sault Ste. Marie

Sault Ste. Marie

ONTARIO

-N-

MICHIGAN

Bruce Mines

Thessalon

ST. JOSEPH ISLAND

De Tour

DRUMMOND ISLAND

1. Pointe aux Pins
2. *L. J. Farwell* and memorial
3. Beechcraft airplane
4. Garden River drift dive
5. Squirrel Island

6. *B. F. Bruce*
7. St. Joseph Island
8. *Premier*
9. *Oregon*

1. POINTE AUX PINS

DEPTH: To 45 feet	LEVEL: Intermediate-Advanced

LOCATION: A few miles west of Sault Ste. Marie, Ontario.

Pointe aux Pins is famous for being the first shipyard on Lake Superior, used by early explorers and settlers from 1730 to 1836. One can drift dive from Pointe Louise to Furkey's Marina searching for old bottles. The diver should have some experience in current diving. Since boating traffic is heavy, use of a dive flag is strongly recommended.

2. *L. J. FARWELL* AND PEER MEMORIAL

LORAN: 31030.4/47820.5	LAT	LON
DEPTH: To 43 feet	LEVEL: Intermediate-Advanced	

LOCATION: This wreck lies west of Sault Ste. Marie, Ontario, off Pointe aux Pins, downstream from the dock and the navigation buoy.

The *L.J. Farwell*. MPL/WMHS

The oak-hulled, two-masted schooner, *L.J. Farwell* (136' x 26' x 10'), built in 1856 at Black River, Ohio, worked mainly in the lumber trade until 1903 when she was abandoned due to her age and poor hull condition. Once thought to be a wreck named the *Russell* (which was the previous name of the *Checotah,* which lies in Lake Huron and is also in this book), the *L.J. Farwell* sits upright with her hull intact, but her deck has collapsed.

Positioned just off this schooner's photogenic bow is a concrete and brass plaque memorial to David Eric Peer, a Master Scuba Instructor who had been in the business in the Canadian Sault for many years, and who had passed away from illness on August 28, 1990. The 2,400-pound memorial, provided by the Lake Superior Tridents Dive Club, was placed on August 28, 1991. Among many other things he did for diving, David Peer had served on the Executive Board of the Ontario Underwater Council at the same time as the author.

This site can be done as a shore or a boat dive.

3. BEECHCRAFT AIRPLANE

DEPTH: 42 feet	LEVEL: Intermediate-Advanced

LOCATION: About 1,100' downstream from the *L.J. Farwell* (see site #2).

Local scuba divers purposely planted this vintage Beechcraft 18 airplane in the St. Mary's River on June 5, 1982, about 75' upstream of the schooner, *L.J. Farwell,* but a huge "seiche" (an inland lake tidal-like wave) swept the plane downstream on July 15, 1988, leaving a trail of scattered wreckage. The plane finally came to rest upside-down more than 1,000' away. This can be done as a shore or a boat dive.

4. GARDEN RIVER DRIFT DIVE

DEPTH: To 30 feet	LEVEL: Novice-Intermediate

LOCATION: The community of Garden River is east of Sault Ste. Marie, Ontario.

This drift dive is usually done along the steep underwater clay bank, or the "drop-off," Old bottles have been seen here. Near the former site of a late 19th century cookhouse is the underwater area known as the "boneyard" where cattle bones and horns lie in abundance. Divers can also appreciate seeing discarded cooking utensils, axes, saws and other broken garbage. There is current and boating traffic here. Fly a dive flag.

5. SQUIRREL ISLAND

Squirrel Island, just east of Garden River (see site #4), is a good bottle site. A boat is required to reach the island, but once there, virtually any area is good to dive.

6. *B. F. BRUCE*

DEPTH: 30 feet	LEVEL: Advanced

LOCATION: This wreck lies off Sailor's Encampment in the lower St. Mary's River, at channel marker C "15." The schooner, *B.F. Bruce,* sank in October, 1895. It was located on August 8, 1969 by five scuba divers from the Sault area. The usually very poor visibility and the fast speed of the river's current make this site an advanced dive for experienced divers. Beware of boating traffic, too.

7. ST. JOSEPH ISLAND

DEPTH: To 30 feet	LEVEL: Novice-Intermediate

St. Joseph Island is rich with history, commencing with the strategic fort at Old Fort St. Joe Point on the southern portion of the island during the War of 1812. Most waterfront communities on this large island have (or had) their own docks, and exploring around those areas can be rewarding. Beware of boating traffic and fly a dive flag.

8. *PREMIER*

DEPTH: 10 to 20 feet	LEVEL: Novice

LOCATION: This wreck lies at the old government dock just east of Bruce Mines, ON.

The wooden combination passenger and package freight steamer, *Premier* (139'3" x 35' x 9'), launched as the *Greyhound* at Hamilton, Ontario, in 1888, and renamed *Lincoln* in 1899 before being given her final name in 1906 (didn't anyone tell these people what it means to change a ship's name?) was destroyed by fire on Nov. 13, 1920. No lives were lost. The engine and boiler were salvaged, but the hull with charred timbers inside remains quite intact, bow nestled into a crib pointing towards open water, rudder lying off the port side. Access is from shore or boat. Identification of this mystery wreck was made by Hugh and Glenna Wyatt in 1996.

The *Premier*. MPL/WMHS

9. *OREGON*

LORAN:	LAT 46° 14.765' LON 083° 31.838'
DEPTH: 15 to 45 feet	LEVEL: Novice

LOCATION: This wreck lies just west of Dyment Rock, east of Thessalon, Ontario.

The wooden steam barge, *Oregon* (197' x 33' x 13'9"), launched on September 20, 1882, at West Bay City, MI, grounded with a pulpwood cargo on Dyment Shoals on August 22, 1908, caught fire and burned to a complete loss, with no lives lost.

Divers are impressed by the large, 4-bladed propeller and the anchor wedged between a rock and the ship. So large is the boiler that divers can swim through it. Massive hull portions, wood with iron bracing, bollards, cleats, a windlass and a winch remain at this site. A hardhat diver explored it long ago, but Hugh Wyatt of Sault Ste. Marie, Ontario, rediscovered the *Oregon* on August 12, 1993.

The *Oregon*. MPL/WMHS

50. Sites near Lake Superior

There are literally thousands of unmentioned places (anywhere where there is water!) to go scuba diving around the Great Lakes. The following sites are located near Lake Superior in Wisconsin and Ontario:

1. LAKE OWEN, WISCONSIN

LOCATION: About 20 miles east of the community of Hayward in Bayfield County and about three miles south of Drummond. Access to the lake is via Highway 63 and county roads. Long, narrow Lake Owen covers 2,250 acres and reaches a maximum depth of 95′. The lake bottom is a mixture of sand and gravel, plus large boulders. The 24 miles of shoreline offer two boat launches at the north end. Divers here will encounter fish, such as bass, bluegills, crappies, walleye and pike, and an underwater railroad station at the north end.

2. RED CEDAR LAKE, WISCONSIN

LOCATION: Two miles south of Birchwood, Wisconsin, on Highway 48.

This long, narrow lake with a maximum depth of 60′ features a sunken boathouse and old bottles. Ice diving is popular here.

3. BOND LAKE, WISCONSIN

LOCATION: About 60 miles south of Duluth, off County Road "T," which runs west off Highway 53 in Douglas County, about 10 miles north of Minong, Wisconsin.

This lake, with a maximum depth of about 80′, offers views of several types of freshwater fish among the thick aquatic vegetation (avoid entanglement!).

4. OLIVER LAKE, ONTARIO

LOCATION: About 16 miles southwest of Thunder Bay, Ontario (the largest city on Lake Superior). This northern Ontario lake is reputed to be the clearest of the many inland lakes in this area. visibility of 20′ to 30′ can be expected, with views of bass, pickerel, northern pike and lake trout. Depths can exceed 100′ in this lake, so be cautious of your depth and bottom time.

5. SILVER LAKE, ONTARIO

LOCATION: About 35 miles northeast of Thunder Bay, Ontario, this lake is about 1.5 miles long and 0.5 mile wide. Near the eastern shore, a reef runs the entire length of the lake at a depth of 20′. At the base of this reef, the depth is 60′, with the middle of the lake dropping to the deepest point at over 100′. This lake abounds with lake trout and bass.

6. LAKE SHEBANDEWAN

LOCATION: West of the city of Thunder Bay, Ontario.

This deep lake demands that divers use lights if they venture deeper than 50′ because of the darkness. Bass, pickerel (walleye), and northern pike are the main features at this site.

The Hunt for Great Lakes Shipwrecks

The Great Lakes are gifted with a rich endowment of maritime history, one that easily rivals the saltwater heritage of the East Coast or any other parts of the world. With the voluminous shipping traffic covering our freshwater seas in the past two centuries, it is little wonder that we have over 5,000 shipwrecks in the Great Lakes, with only a third located.

A century ago, shipwrecks in the Great Lakes were sought for their commercial value in recovery. The old profession of "wrecking" has changed considerably since then, primarily because they're not making shipwrecks like they used to. In 1987, one Great Lakes historian and commercial fishing expert, Frank Prothero of St. Thomas, Ontario, said, "I can't think of a quicker way to go bankrupt than to become a commercial salvager in the Great Lakes today." The very few who have pursued Great Lakes shipwrecks with a goal of financial gain have found it to be a costly experience in this more heritage-conscious modern age.

Early Great Lakes shipwreck hunters John Steele and Kent Bellrichard patiently study the sidescan sonar for signs of any object which could be a shipwreck. PHOTO BY CRIS KOHL

But the hunt for Great Lakes shipwrecks continues, mainly for the satisfaction of locating another "needle in the haystack" which will add one more piece to that enormous patchwork quilt of Great Lakes Maritime History: the tapestry of lost ships and the stories behind them. Up until the Second World War, hardhat divers still pursued commercial shipwreck salvage utilizing the equipment which was prohibitively expensive for mere weekend aquatic warriors. However, since the advent of scuba (self-contained underwater breathing apparatus) after World War II, the barrier of costly and cumbersome equipment was eliminated. Also available in the 1950's were surplus "pingers," or electronic submarine detectors. Crude by comparison to today's sophisticated sidescan sonar units which offer color, high resolution digitized printouts of precisely what the shipwreck looks like so far underwater, these early machines nonetheless worked. Great Lakes explorers in search of shipwrecks, men like John Steele and Dick Race, were on their way by the late 1950's to locating long-lost history at the bottom of our inland seas.

The list is long, the adventures are many, and the hunters' research and discoveries have made us all richer with dramatic tales and material history from our maritime past. We go in quest of shipwrecks, to paraphrase Sir Edmund Hillary, who was the first person to reach the summit of Mount Everest, "because they are there." Just as technology had reached the point where it could be used for man to climb successfully to the highest point on earth in the 1950's, so too has technology developed in leaps and bounds in the last two decades to allow man to plumb the lowest depths on the planet, including our Lakes. With sensitive sidescan sonar, the global positioning system, remote-operated vehicles equipped with strong lights and sensitive cameras,

The stern deck of the Great Lakes Shipwreck Society's research ship, *David Boyd,* from Whitefish Point, shows only some of its sophisticated shipwreck-hunting equipment. This high-tech vessel located the wreck of the *A.A. Parker* in June, 2001. PHOTO BY CRIS KOHL

and exotic mixed gases which let divers go deeper and stay longer than ever before, technology has come a long way in a scant 20 years. Goverments set controls; in Canada, a permit is required to do a sidescan search. Despite such controls, we ourselves are reaching the point where we can responsibly manage that which technology is allowing us to discover.

Today's shipwreck hunters are adventurers who were born a couple of centuries too late. But even in modern times, those who find shipwrecks, like the first people to climb Mt. Everest, are making history. The hunt for Great Lakes shipwrecks continues....

Here is the top ten countdown of the most hunted Great Lakes shipwrecks:

10 *Andaste* (Lake Michigan, 1929)

The steel, semi-whaleback freighter, *Andaste* (246'9" x 38'1" x 17'9"), built in 1892 at Cleveland, foundered somewhere southwest of Grand Haven, Michigan, on September 9, 1929, with the loss of all 25 lives.

The *Andaste*. REV. PETER VAN DER LINDEN COLLECTION

9 *Hydrus* (Lake Huron, 1913)

One of the many victims of the Great Storm of November 9-12, 1913, the steel steamer, *Hydrus* (416' x 50' x 28'), foundered with all 24 hands somewhere off Southampton, Ontario, where bodies and wreckage washed ashore. The ship was built in 1903 at Lorain, Ohio. She could be the last to be discovered of the 8 steel freighters lost with all hands in lower Lake Huron in that overwhelmingly tragic 1913 storm.

The *Hydrus*. GLHS

8 *Speedy* (Lake Ontario, 1804)

The historic schooner, *Speedy* (about 128' x 24' x 8'), constructed at Kingston, Ontario (then called Upper Canada) in 1798, sank with all hands, estimated to be from 20 to 27 persons, in a storm four miles off Presqu'ile, Ontario, on October 8, 1804, with the loss of prominent people and an accused murderer in chains. Claims to this wreck's discovery have not yet been substantiated.

The *Speedy*, in a 1913 C.H.J. Snider depiction. AUTHOR'S COLLECTION.

7 *Kent* (Lake Erie, 1845)

The much-sought 122-ton paddlewheel steamer, *Kent* (122' x 20' x 7'), built at Chatham, Ontario (then called Canada West) in 1841, sank in about 67' of water after a collision with the steamer, *London,* somewhere to the east of Point Pelee on August 12, 1845, with the loss of about 10 lives and most of the personal effects of the 75 passengers. This wreck may be embedded in mud.

PUBLIC ARCHIVES OF CANADA

6 *Cerisoles* and *Inkerman* (Lake Superior, 1918)

The cannon-mounted warships, *Cerisoles* and *Inkerman* (each 135'6" x 26'2" x 12'7"), built at the end of WW I at Fort William (today Thunder Bay), ON, foundered with all 76 people on them in a storm on Nov. 24, 1918, on their maiden voyages to France.

AUTHOR'S COLLECTION

5 *Alpena* (Lake Michigan, 1880)

The wooden sidewheel passenger steamer, *Alpena* (175' x 35' x 12'), built at Marine City, Michigan, in 1867, foundered with all 73 people on board reportedly about 20 miles off Kenosha, WI, on Oct. 16, 1880, in fierce gales. Wreckage washed ashore near Holland, MI.

The *Alpena*. MPL/WMHS

4 *Asia* (Lake Huron, 1882)

The wooden steamer, *Asia* (136' x 23'4" x 11'), built at St. Catharines, ON, in 1873, foundered in one of the worst losses in Great Lakes history in Georgian Bay off Byng Inlet, ON, on Sept. 14, 1882, with 123 lives lost and only two survivors. Several parties are actively searching for this wreck, with a recent tip that some of it lies in 83'.

The *Asia*. MPL/WMHS

3 *Marquette & Bessemer #2* (Lake Erie, 1909)

Long-elusive, much-hyped, and prematurely claimed as found, this steel railroad car ferry (338' x 54' x 19'5"), built at Cleveland in 1905, disappeared with all hands (31 to 38) between Port Stanley, ON, and Conneaut, OH, in a severe blizzard on Dec. 8, 1909. I told wreckhunter Roy Pickering where I think it is, but he hasn't found it yet (so he says).

The *M & B #2*. MPL/WMHS

2 *Bannockburn* (Lake Superior, 1902)

Only a lifeboat oar was recovered 18 months after the steel steamer, *Bannockburn* (245' x 40'1" x 18'4"), foundered with all 22 hands on November 22, 1902. Built in England in 1893, this ship has become the Great Lakes' "Flying Dutchman," reportedly seen afloat several times since she disappeared.

AUTHOR'S COLLECTION

1 *Griffon* (Lake Michigan? Lake Huron? 1679)

The fabled, elusive 45-ton brig, *Griffon* (about 55' x 16' x 8'), the dream of marine archaeologists, disappeared with all 5 hands, 5 cannons and cargo of furs on her return maiden voyage in September, 1679, to become the first shipwreck in the upper Great Lakes. The waters off western Manitoulin Island offer the most credible of the 16 claims in the quest for this holy grail of freshwater shipwrecks.

The *Griffon* being built at Niagara, 1679. AUTHOR'S COLLECTION

BIBLIOGRAPHY

Books

Amos, Art, and Patrick Folkes. *A Diver's Guide to Georgian Bay*. Toronto, Ontario: Ontario Underwater Council, 1979.

Arlov, Gary. *Divers Guide to the Shipwrecks of Lake Michigan*. Milwaukee, Wisconsin: The Arlov Company, 1987.

Bennett, Dale. *The Captain's Shipwreck Book of South-West Lake Michigan*. Wheeling, Illinois: Captain Dale's, Inc., 2000.

Berent, John. *Diving the Lake Erie Island Wrecks*. Marblehead, Ohio: John Berent, 1992.

Bors, Brian J., ed. *New York State Dive Site Directory*. Niagara Falls, New York: The New York State Divers Association, 1993 and 2000 editions.

Club Poseidon. *The St. Clair River...a sport diver's guide*. Port Huron, Michigan, June, 1983.

Cooper, David J. ed., *By Fire, Storm, and Ice: Underwater Archaeological Investigations in the Apostle Islands*. Madison, WI: State Historical Society of Wisconsin, 1991, revised 1996.

.... with John O. Jensen. *Davidson's Goliaths, Underwater Archaeological Investigations of the Steamer Frank O'Connor and the Schooner-Barge Pretoria*. Madison, WI: State Historical Society of Wisconsin, 1995.

.... *Survey of Submerged Cultural Resources in Northern Door County, 1988 Field Season Report*. Madison, WI: State Historical Society of Wisconsin, 1989.

Creviere, Paul J., Jr. *Wild Gales and Tattered Sails*. Paul John Creviere, Jr., 1997.

Engman, Elmer. *In the Belly of a Whale, Duluth's Shipwreck Tragedy*. Duluth, Minnesota: Innerspace, 1976; revised 1988.

.... *Shipwreck Guide to the Western Half of Lake Superior*. Duluth, Minnesota: Innerspace, 1976.

Feltner, Dr. Charles E., and Jeri Baron. *Shipwrecks of the Straits of Mackinac*. Dearborn, Michigan: Seajay Publications, 1991.

Frederickson, Arthur C. and Lucy F. *Ships and Shipwrecks in Door County, Wisconsin, Volume One*. Frankfort, Michigan: Arthur C. and Lucy F. Frederickson, 1961.

.... *Ships and Shipwrecks in Door County, Wisconsin, Volume Two*. Frankfort, Michigan: Arthur C. and Lucy F. Frederickson, 1963.

Frimodig, Mac. *Shipwrecks off Keweenaw*. The Fort Wilkins Natural History Association in cooperation with the Michigan Department of Natural Resources.

Gibbs, Barry L. *Quarry Quest, The Diver's Guide to the Midwest*. Crawfordsville, IN: Palmer Publishing, 1987.

Greenwood, John O. *Namesakes 1900-1909*. Cleveland, Ohio: Freshwater Press, Inc., 1987.

.... *Namesakes 1910-1919*. Cleveland, Ohio: Freshwater Press, Inc., 1986.

.... *Namesakes 1920-1929*. Cleveland, Ohio: Freshwater Press, Inc., 1984.

.... *Namesakes 1930-1955*. Cleveland, Ohio: Freshwater Press, Inc., 1978.

.... *Namesakes 1956-1980*. Cleveland, Ohio: Freshwater Press, Inc., 1981.

Halsey, John R. *Beneath the Inland Seas: Michigan's Underwater Archaeological Heritage*. Lansing: Bureau of History, Michigan Department of State, 1990.

Hammer, Patrick. *Lake Michigan Shipwrecks*. Alsip, Illinois: Scuba Emporium, 1996 (5th edition).

Harold, Steve. *Shipwrecks of the Sleeping Bear*. Traverse City, Michigan: Pioneer Study Center, 1984.

Harrington, Steve. *Divers Guide to Michigan*, Mason, Michigan: Maritime Press, 1990; rev. ed., 1998.

.... with David J. Cooper. *Divers Guide to Wisconsin, including Minnesota's North Shore*. Mason, Michigan: Maritime Press, 1991.

Heyl, Eric. *Early American Steamers, Volumes I-VI*. Buffalo, New York: Eric Heyl, 1953-1969.

Hirthe, Walter M. and Mary K. *Schooner Days in Door County*. Minneapolis: Voyageur Press, Inc., 1986.

Holden, Thom. *Above and Below, A History of Lighthouses and Shipwrecks of Isle Royale*. Houghton, Michigan: Isle Royale Natural History Association. 1985.

Keatts, Henry C., and George C. Farr. *Dive Into History, Volume 3: U-Boats*. Houston, Texas: Pisces

Books, 1994.

Keller, James M. *The "Unholy" Apostles, Tales of Chequamegon Shipwrecks.* Bayfield, Wisconsin: Apostle Island Press, 1984.

Kohl, Cris. *The 100 Best Great Lakes Shipwrecks, Volume I.* West Chicago, Illinois: Seawolf Communications, Inc., 1998.

.... *The 100 Best Great Lakes Shipwrecks, Volume II.* West Chicago, Illinois: Seawolf Communications, Inc., 1998.

.... *Dive Ontario! The Guide to Shipwrecks and Scuba.* Chatham, Ontario: Cris Kohl, 1990, revised 1995.

.... *Dive Ontario Two! More Ontario Shipwrecks Stories.* Chatham, Ontario: Cris Kohl, 1994.

.... *Dive Southwestern Ontario!* Chatham, Ontario: Cris Kohl, 1985.

.... *Shipwreck Tales: The St. Clair River (to 1900).* Chatham, Ontario: Cris Kohl, 1987.

.... *Titanic, The Great Lakes Connections.* West Chicago, Illinois: Seawolf Communications, Inc., 2000

.... *Treacherous Waters: Kingston's Shipwrecks.* Chatham, Ontario: Cris Kohl, 1997.

Lane, Kit. *Chicora, Lost on Lake Michigan.* Douglas, Michigan: Pavilion Press, 1996.

.... *Shipwrecks of the Saugatuck Area.* Saugatuck, MI: Saugatuck Commercial Record, 1974.

Lauer, Richard, compiler. *Freshwater Vision, A Guide to Diving in Ohio, Pennsylvania, and West Virginia.* Reynoldsburg, Ohio: Sub-Aquatics, Inc., 1989.

Lenihan, Daniel *Shipwrecks of Isle Royale National Park.* Duluth, Minnesota: Lake Superior Port Cities, Inc., 1996.

Mansfield, J. B., ed. *History of the Great Lakes, Volumes I and II,* Chicago, IL: J. H. Beers & Co, 1899

Marshall, James R. *Shipwrecks of Lake Superior.* Duluth, MN: Lake Superior Port Cities, Inc., 1988

McKenney, Jack. *Dive to Adventure.* Vancouver: Panorama Publications, Inc., 1983.

Metcalfe, Willis. *Canvas & Steam on Quinte Waters.* South Bay, Ontario: the South Marysburgh Marine Society, 1979.

Neel, Robert, ed. *Diving in Ohio.* Ohio Council of Skin and Scuba Divers, Inc., 1979.

Roberts, Mark and Kathy. *An Underwater Guide to Lake Superior's Keweenaw Peninsula.* Houghton, Michigan: Mark and Kathy Roberts, 1991.

Salen, Rick. *The Tobermory Shipwrecks.* Tobermory, Ontario: The Mariner Chart Shop, 1996 edition.

Stabelfeldt, Kimm A. *Explore Great Lakes Shipwrecks, Volume I Covering Wrecks on Part of the Lower Lake Michigan.* Wauwatosa, Wisconsin: Stabelfeldt & Associates, Inc., 1992 (sixth edition, 1996).

.... *Explore Great Lakes Shiwprecks, Volume II Covering Wrecks on the Upper Part of Lake Michigan and Green Bay off the Coasts of Wisconsin and Michigan.* Wauwatosa, Wisconsin: Stabelfeldt & Associates, Inc., 1993 (fourth edition, 1996).

.... *Explore Great Lakes Shipwrecks, Volume III, Known Wrecks around Whitefish Point and the Surrounding Area.* Wauwatosa, Wisconsin: Adventure Diving, Inc., 1998.

Stanton, Samuel Ward. *American Steam Vessels.* New York: Smith & Stanton, 1895.

Stayer, Pat and Jim. *Shipwrecks of Sanilac.* Lexington, Michigan: Out of the Blue Productions, 1995.

Stonehouse, Frederick. *Isle Royale Shipwrecks.* Au Train, Michigan: Avery Color Studios, 1983.

.... *Keweenaw Shipwrecks.* Au Train, Michigan, Avery Color Studios, 1988.

.... *Lake Superior's Shipwreck Coast.* Au Train, Michigan: Avery Color Studios, 1985.

.... *Marquette Shipwrecks.* Au Train, Michigan: Avery Color Studioes, 1974.

.... *Munising Shipwrecks.* Au Train, Michigan: Avery Color Studios, 1983.

.... *Shipwreck of the Mesquite.* Duluth, Minnesota: Lake Superior Port Cities, Inc., 1991.

.... *Short Guide to the Shipwrecks of Thunder Bay, A.* Alpena, MI: B&L Watery World, 1986.

.... with Daniel R. Fountain. *Dangerous Coast: Pictured Rocks Shipwrecks.* Marquette, Michigan: Avery Color Studios, 1997.

Van der Linden, Rev. Peter J., ed. and the Marine Historical Society of Detroit. *Great Lakes Ships We Remember.* Cleveland, Ohio: Freshwater Press, 1979; revised 1984.

.... *Great Lakes Ships We Remember II.* Cleveland, Ohio: Freshwater Press, 1984.

.... *Great Lakes Ships We Remember III.* Cleveland, Ohio: Freshwater Press, 1994.

Wachter, Georgann & Michael. *Erie Wrecks East, A Guide to Shipwrecks of Eastern Lake Erie.* Avon Lake, Ohio: Corporate*Impact,* 2000.

.... *Erie Wrecks West, A Guide to Shipwrecks of Western Lake Erie.* Avon Lake, Ohio: Corporate*Impact,* 2001 (second edition; originally published in 1997).

Washburn, Nancy. *Snorkeling Guide to Michigan Inland Lakes.* East Lansing, Michigan: Nanmar International, Inc., 1997.

Wolff, Julius F., Jr., *Lake Superior Shipwrecks.* Duluth, MN: Lake Superior Port Cities, Inc., 1990.

Wrigley, Ronald. *Shipwrecked, Vessels That Met Tragedy on Northern Lake Superior.* Cobalt, Ontario: Highway Book Shop, 1985.

Periodicals

Alford, Terry. "Kingston's Newest Wreck Dive (*Wolfe Islander II*)." *Diver Magazine.* Vol. 12, No. 1 (March, 1986), 18-21.

.... "Time Capsule in Kingston, Queen of Kingston's Wrecks (*Wolfe Islander II*)." *Diver Magazine.* Vol. 14, No. 1 (March, 1988), 19-20.

Armbruster, Peter. "Verano Found After 48 Years." *Great Lakes Diving Magazine* (Oct/Nov,1994) 26

Bailey, Dan Holden. "Mackinac Straits." *Diver Magazine.* Vol. 25, No. 6 (September, 1999), 18-19.

.... "Time in Tobermory." *Diver Magazine.* Vol 24, No. 2 (April, 1998), 20-22.

.... "Wrecks of the St. Lawrence." *Diver Magazine.* Vol. 23, No. 1 (April, 1997), 36-37.

Bellefeuille, Monique and Mike. "*Lillie Parsons.*" *Diver Magazine.* Vol. 16, No. 7 (Nov., 1990) 18-19

Bowen, Curt. "*Vienna, 1873-1892.*" *Advanced Diver Magazine.* Issue 1 (Spring, 1999), 44-46.

Boyd, Ellsworth. "The *Regina.*" *Skin Diver.* Vol. 37, No. 10 (October, 1988), 78. 150-152.

Coplin, Larry, and Bruce McLaughlan. "A Shipwreck Shrouded in Mystery (*Kamloops*)." *Diver Magazine.* Vol. 10, No. 9 (December, 1984), 15-19.

Drew, Richard C. "Chicago's Most Popular Dive (*Material Service*)." *Skin Diver.* Vol. 39, No. 1 (January, 1990), 12, 146-150.

Emering, Ed. "The Fated Lady (*Wisconsin*)." *Scuba Times.* Vol. 14, No. 3 (May-June 1993), 48-49.

Feltner, Charles. "*Cedarville* Tragedy." *Diving Times* (June/July, 1981).

.... "*Eber Ward.*" *Diver Magazine.* Vol. 7, No. 6 (September, 1981), 18-22. Reprinted from the November/December, 1980, issue of *Diving Times* of Royal Oak, Michigan.

.... "Raise the *Cayuga.*" *Diving Times* (April/May, 1981).

.... "Strange Tale of Two Ships (*Maitland* and *Northwest*). *Diving Times* (Feb./March, 1981).

.... "Wreck of the *Col. Ellsworth.*" *Diving Times* (June/July, 1980).

.... "Wreck of the Brig *Sandusky.*" *Diving Times* (October/November, 1981).

.... "Wreck of the *William H. Barnum.*" *Diving Times* (August/September, 1980).

Forsberg, Joan. "Sea Storyteller, Cris Kohl." *Immersed.* Vol. 5, No. 3 (Fall, 2000), 20-25.

Garn, Myk. "Return to the *Emperor,* The Pride of Canada." *Skin Diver.* Vol. 35, No. 4 (Apr., 1986), 30

Gilchrist, David. "Diving Weekend at Port Colborne, Ontario (the Wreck of the Steamer, *Raleigh*)." *Diver Magazine.* Vol. 20, No. 5 (August, 1994), 14-15.

.... "Lake Erie Wreck Dive (*Carlingford*)." *Diver Magazine.* Vol. 20, No. 1 (Mar., 1994) 22-23

.... "Shipwreck Discovery in Lake Ontario (*Henry Clay?*)." *Diver Magazine.* Vol. 25, No. 5 (July/August, 1999), 25.

.... "Wrecks of Lower Georgian Bay." *Diver Magazine.* Vol. 26, No. 3 (May, 2000), 17-19.

Golding, Peter. "Fathom Five Park." *Diver Magazine.* Vol. 5, No. 6 (August/September, 1979), 24-27.

.... "Inner Space Adventure, *Comet* in Lake Ontario." *Diver Magazine.* Vol. 5, No. 4 (June, 1979), 21 -24.

.... "Innerkip Quarry, An Unusual Experience." *Diver Magazine.* Vol. 5, No. 2 (February/March, 1979), 22-23, 44, 45.

.... "Lady of Muskoka, The *Waome.*" *Diver Magazine.* Vol. 6, No. 4 (June, 1980), 20-21.

.... "*Maple Dawn* (sic)." *Diver Magazine.* Vol. 6, No. 4 (April-May, 1980), 36-37.

.... "*Michigan's* Muscle Machines." *Diver Magazine.* Vol. 5, No. 4 (June, 1979), 20-21.

.... "The *Price* Adventure." *Diver Magazine.* Vol. 4, No. 8 (Nov.-Dec., 1978), 34-38.

.... "Tale of Two Wrecks, *Sweepstakes--City of Grand Rapids.*" *Diver Magazine.* Vol. 6, No. 1 (January/February, 1980), 24-25.

.... "Tobermory Tug." *Diver Magazine.* Vol. 7, No. 2 (March, 1981), 38-39.

.... "Tobermory's Limestone Grottos." *Diver Magazine.* Vol. 5, No. 3 (April/May, 1979) 28-31

.... "Wreck of the *George A. Marsh.*" *Diver Magazine.* Vol. 5, No. 8. (Nov.-Dec., 1979), 38-40

Halsey, John R., and Scott M. Peters. "Resurrection of a Great Lakes Steamer (*Three Brothers*)." *Michigan History Magazine.* (November-December, 1996), 22-25.

Hector, Bruce. "Kingston Wrecks." *Diver Magazine.* Vol. 17, No. 1 (March, 1991), 32-33.

Holland, Sean. "A Deep Freshwater Adventure, *Roy A. Jodrey.*" *Immersed.* Vol. 5, No. 3 (Fall, 2000), 46-52.
Jalbert, Andrew. "The Wreck of the *Niagara* (paddlewheeler)." *Diver Magazine.* Vol. 26, No. 9 (January-February, 2001), 24-25.
Jensen, John Odin. "The History and Archaeology of the Great Lakes Steamboat, *Niagara.*" *Wisconsin Magazine of History.* Vol. 82, No. 3 (Spring, 1999), 198-230.
Johnson, Ken. "Graveyard of Lake Superior, Whitefish Point and Whitefish Bay." *Diver Magazine.* Vol. 11, No. 1 (January-February, 1985), 16-19.
.... "Strange Story of the Steamer, *Myron.*" *Diver Magazine.* Vol. 10, No. 6 (Sept., 1984) 20-21
.... "The Controversial Loss of the Motorship *Material Service.*" *Diver Magazine.* Vol. 11, No. 8 (December, 1985), 16-19.
Kemp, Bruce. "Lake Huron Mystery (*Charles S. Price*)." *Diver Magazine.* Vol. 8, No. 2 (March, 1981), 7-20.
.... "Shipwrecks of the St. Clair River." *Diver Magazine.* Vol. 9, No. 8 (Dec., 1983), 18-20.
Kohl, Cris. "12-Fathom Maiden: Lake Erie's *Willis.*" *Diver Magazine.* Vol. 25, No. 5 (July-August, 1999), 26-27.
.... "*America,* the Beautiful---Shipwreck." *Diver Magazine.* Vol. 23, No. 8 (Dec., 1997), 25-28
.... "Backwoods Secret (*Columbus*)." *Diver Magazine.* Vol. 17, No. 5 (August, 1991), 33-35.
.... "*Barge 115*--Last Shipwreck of the 1800's." *Diver Magazine.* Vol. 25, No. 8 (December, 1999), 6-8.
.... "Battle for the *Atlantic.*" *Diver Magazine.* Vol. 19, No. 3 (May, 1993), 36-37.
.... "Beautiful, Tragic *Myron,* The." *Diver Magazine.* Vol. 24, No. 8 (December, 1998), 25-27.
.... "Broken Lady of Driftwood Cove, the *Caroline Rose.*" *Diver Magazine.* Vol. 24, No. 2 (April, 1998), 26-27.
.... "Current Diving on the *Conestoga.*" *Diver Magazine.* Vol. 24, No. 1 (March, 1998), 26-27.
.... "Deep Dive in Superior (*Samuel Mather*)." *Diver Magazine.* Vol. 25, No. 1 (March, 1999), 26-28.
.... "Dredge *Munson.*" *Diver Magazine.* Vol. 23, No. 6 (September, 1997), 26-27.
.... "*Fleur Marie.*" *Diver Magazine.* Vol. 23, No. 7 (October-November, 1997), 26-27.
.... "Gargantua Harbor: Lake Superior's Secret." *Great Lakes Diving Magazine.* (December, 1994/January, 1995), 16-19.
.... "*George A. Marsh* Mystery, The." *Diver Mag.* Vol. 24, No. 5 (July-August, 1998), 26-28.
.... "Georgian Bay's *Jane McLeod.*" *Diver Magazine.* Vol. 22, No. 5 (July/Aug., 1996), 24-25.
.... "Georgian Bay's *Mapledawn.*" *Diver Magazine.* Vol. 24, No. 9 (Jan.-Feb. 1999), 16-17.
.... "Ghost Fleet of the St. Clair River." *Diver Magazine.* Vol. 22, No. 3 (May, 1996), 24-25.
.... "Great Lakes Report Card." *Diver Magazine.* Vol. 24, No. 7 (Oct.-Nov., 1998), 26-28.
.... "Honeymoon Wreck: Lake Huron's *Joyland.*" *Diver Magazine.* Vol. 22, No. 2 (April, 1996), 30-31.
.... "Kingston's Newest Shipwreck: the Tug, *Frontenac.*" *Diver Magazine.* Vol. 23, No. 3 (May, 1997), 18-19.
.... "Lake Erie Shipwreck Discovery." *Diver Magazine.* Vol. 15, No. 8 (Dec., 1989), 18-22.
.... "Lake Erie's Lost Steamer, *Colonial.*" *Diver Magazine.* Vol. 20, Vol. 4 (June, 1994), 22-23; modified and printed in *Great Lakes Diving Magazine* (April/May, 1995), 19-21.
.... "Lake Huron Gem: *Emma E. Thompson.*" *Diver Mag.* Vol. 23, No. 4 (June, 1997), 18-19.
.... "Lake Huron's Narrow Island Shipwreck: *B. B. Buckhout.*" *Diver Magazine.* Vol. 22, No. 8 (December, 1996), 14-15.
.... "Lake Huron's *Sport.*" *Diver Magazine.* Vol. 25, No. 2 (April, 1999), 24-25.
.... "Lake Huron's Tobermory." *Discover Diving.* Vol. 17, No. 2 (April, 1999), 68-72.
.... "Lake Ontario's Lost Team: *Condor* and *Atlasco.*" *Diver Magazine.* Vol. 22, No. 7 (November, 1996), 24-25.
.... "Lake Superior's Wreck of the *Batchawana.*" *Diver Mag.* Vol. 22, No. 1 (Mar., 1996), 26.
.... "Lost with All Hands--the *Olive Branch.*" *Diver Mag.* Vol. 25, No. 3 (May, 1999), 24-25.
.... "*Manola*--Half a Shipwreck." *Diver Magazine.* Vol. 21, No. 9 (February, 1996), 28.
.... "The Once-Mighty *Metamora.*" *Diver Magazine.* Vol. 23, No. 5. (July/Aug., 1997), 18-19.
.... "Shipwrecks Threatened by Freshwater Barnacles." *Diving Times.* Vol. 12, No. 2 (Summer, 1989).
.... "Sleepless on the *Seattle.*" Diver *Magazine.* Vol. 23, No. 2 (April, 1997),
.... "Steamer *Canisteo.*" *Diver Magazine.* Vol. 24, No. 6. (September, 1998), 26-28.

.... "Steamer *Northern Indiana*, Lake Erie Tragedy." *Diver Magazine*. Vol. 22, No. 9 (February, 1997), 20-22.

.... "Steamer *Philip Minch*." *Diver Magazine*. Vol. 23, No. 9 (Feb., 1998), 24, 26.

.... "Tobermory: Shipwreck Waters!" *Great Lakes Cruiser Magazine*. (November, 1995), 6-8.

.... "Tobermory's Forgotten Shipwrecks." *Diver Magazine*. Vol. 22, No. 4 (June, 1996), 24-26

.... "Tragic Wreck on Lake Erie (*Merida*)." *Diver Mag*. Vol. 24, No. 3 (May, 1998), 26-27.

.... "Three Strikes Against the *Burlington*." *Diver Magazine*. Vol. 21, No. 8 (Dec., 1995), 26.

.... "Whitefish Point." *Diver Magazine*. Vol. 23, No. 1 (March, 1997), 18-19, 26.

.... "Wreck of the *William H. Wolf*." *Ontario Diver's Digest*. August, 1990.

.... and Sharon Hamilton. "*City of Genoa*." *Diving Times*. Vol. 10, No. 4 (Winter, 1987-88), 14

.... (Photos by Cris Kohl) Pierce Hoover, "Shipwreck City" (Kingston, Ontario). *Sport Diver*. Vol. 9, No. 3 (April, 2001), 56-61.

Kozmik, Jim. "*Arabia*. Fathom Five's Deep Lady." *Diver Mag*. Vol. 7, No. 2 (March, 1981), 28-29.

.... "Diving the Flowerpots of Georgian Bay. *Diver Mag*. Vol. 8, No. 3(April/May, 1982)34-35

.... "Stokes Bay for Wreck Diving Enthusiasts." *Diver Mag*. Vol. 6, No. 2 (March, 1980) 14-15

Kuss, Dan. "Wreck of the *Rappahannock*." *Diver Magazine*. Vol. 16, No. 8 (December, 1990), 19-21.

.... ""Lake Superior's Storm to Remember." *Diver Magazine*. Vol. 10, No. 7 (October-November, 1984), 12-14.

Labadie, C. Patrick. "Lake Superior's *Bermuda*." *Skin Diver*. Vol. 39, No. 10 (October, 1990), 12-13, 154-155.

Laughrey, Chris. "Great Lakes Freighter, *Dean Richmond*." *Immersed*. Vol.3, No.3 (Fall, 1998) 46-50

.... "Lake Erie's Mystery Schooner X, *Saint James*." *Advanced Diver Magazine*. Issue 3 (Fall, 1999), 43-46.

Lewis, Steve. "Discovery of Lake Huron's Elusive *Wexford*?" *Advanced Diver Magazine*. Issue 7 (Fall, 2000), 30-31.

Mack, Robert. "Ten Dives in Eastern Ontario." *Diver Magazine*. Vol. 16, No. 3 (May, 1990), 14-15.

Marshall, James R. "Isle Royale's Most Unusual Tragedy, The *George M. Cox*." *Lake Superior Magazine*. (March-April, 1988), 62-64.

.... "Farewell *Mesquite*." *Lake Superior Magazine*. (December-January, 1991), 24-28.

McDaniel, Neil. "Fathom Five's Deep Treasure, the Barque *Arabia*." *Diver Magazine*. Vol. 13, No. 3 (May, 1987), 22-23.

.... Tobermory, Ontario's Wreck Diving Capital." *Diver Mag*. Vol. 12, No. 8(Dec.,1986) 24-31

.... "Tobermory's Wreck of the Steam Barge, *Wetmore*." *Diver Magazine*. Vol. 13, No. 5 (July/August, 1987), 14-15.

.... "Wreck Diving at the Tip of the Bruce in Canada's First National Marine Park: Fathom Five." *Diver Magazine*. Vol. 15, No. 5 (July/August, 1989), 26-29.

McLaughlin, Bruce. "Lake Huron's Five-Mile-Long Shipwreck (*Daniel J. Morrell*)." *Diver Magazine*. Vol. 10, No. 4 (June, 1984), 32-34.

Mullings, Ken. "The Fate of the *Falconer*." *Diver Magazine*. Vol. 18, No. 6 (Sept., 1992), 18-19.

Neilsen, Rick. "Hat Trick at Kingston, *George T. Davie*." *Diver Magazine*. Vol. 27, No. 1 (March, 2001), 18-19.

.... "*R. H. Rae*, Lake Ontario." *Diver Magazine*. Vol. 24, No. 1 (March, 1998), 28-29.

.... "Sidewheeler, *Cornwall*." *Diver Magazine*. Vol. 17, No. 4 (June, 1991), 32-33.

Orr, Dan. "The Barque *Arabia*: 1853-1884." *Diver Magazine*. Vol. 11, No. 6 (Sept. 1985), 30-32.

Orth, Darryl, and Rick Skoryk. "Flagship of the Muskokas." *Diver Magazine*. Vol. 19, No. 9 (February, 1994), 30-32.

Remick, Teddy. "Wreck of the *S. S. Wisconsin.*" *Skin Diver*. Vol. 14, No. 9 (September, 1965), 55, 66.

Schmitt, Paul J. "Lake Huron's *Sport*." *Skin Diver*. Vol. 38, No. 10 (October, 1989), 16, 58.

Soegtrop, Michael. "Bruce Peninsula National Park." *Diver Mag*. Vol. 14, No. 2 (April, 1988), 14-17

.... "Deep or Shallow, Tobermory Has It All." *Diver Mag*. Vol. 19, No. 1 (March, 1993), 26-29

.... "Killarney, Ontario." *Diver Magazine*. Vol. 14, No. 3 (May, 1988), 28-31.

.... "Killarney, Diving Georgian Bay's N. Shore." *Diver Mag*. Vol. 11, No. 4 (June,1985)20-21

.... "Killarney Wrecks." *Diver Magazine*. Vol. 17, No. 1 (March, 1991), 25-27.

.... "*Mapledawn,* Wreck in Southern Georgian Bay." *Diver Magazine*. Vol. 18, No. 4 (June, 1992), 20-21.

.... "The *Mayflower*." *Diver Magazine*. Vol. 17, No. 3 (May, 1991), 36-37.

.... "Tobermory's Classic Shipwreck, *City of Cleveland*." *Diver Magazine*. Vol. 13, No. 1

(March, 1987), 24-29.
.... "Twice Lost by Fire (*Atlantic*)." *Diver Magazine,* Vol. 7, No. 3 (April-May, 1981), 27-29.
.... with Eva Woloszciuk. "Kingston." *Diver Magazine.* Vol. 7, No. 1 (Jan./Feb., 1981), 23-24.
Steinborn, Bill. "Lake Michigan's *Milwaukee.*" *Skin Diver.* Vol. 40, No. 5 (May, 1991), 30, 66.
.... "Lake Michigan's *Norland* (sic)." *Skin Diver.* Vol. 39, No. 3 (March, 1990), 8, 56-57.
.... "Lake Superior's *Smith Moore.*" *Skin Diver.* Vol. 40, No. 7 (July, 1991), 188-190.
.... "Milwaukee's *Prins Willem V.*" *Skin Diver.* Vol. 39, No. 7 (July, 1990), 16, 18-19.
.... "Wisconsin's *S. S. Wisconsin.*" *Skin Diver.* Vol. 40, No. 4 (April, 1991), 24, 182-183.
Swierczewski, John. "Isle Royale, Lake Superior's Shipwreck Mecca." *Diver Magazine.* Vol. 10, No. 2 (March, 1984), 34-35.
Tomasi, Bettey. "Sinking of the *Wisconsin.*" *Diver Magazine.* Vol. 7, No. 8 (Dec., 1981), 26-27, 38-39
Triebe, Richard. "*Milwaukee* Car Ferry." *Skin Diver.* Vol. 36, No. 1 (Jan., 1987), 110, 113-114, 120.
.... "*S. S. Wisconsin.*" *Skin Diver.* Vol. 36, No. 5 (May, 1987), pp. 142-147.
.... "The Burning of the *Niagara,* Gold & Goodies, Sizzle & Sink." *Skin Diver.* Vol. 37, No. 5 (May, 1988), 184-188.
Trotter, David. "The Discovery of the *John McGean.*" *Diver Magazine.* Vol. 13, No. 6 (September, 1987), 30-33.
VandenHazel, Besel. "Lake Nipissing Shipwreck, the Story of the *John Fraser.*" *Diver Magazine.* Vol. 8, No. 7 (October/November, 1982), 26-27.
Wachter, Mike, and Darin Cowhardt and Mike King. "*Oxford,* Lake Erie." *Advanced Diver Magazine.* Issue 8 (Winter, 2000), 16-17, 48.
Wachter, Mike and Georgann. "Lake Erie's Schooner *C.B. Benson.*" *Advanced Diver Magazine.* Issue 8 (Winter, 2000), 60-61.
Weir, Stephen. "Bottle Mania, The Collecting Bottle Story: Ten Tips for Beginners." *Diver Magazine.* Vol. 16, No. 3 (May, 1990), 30-32.
.... "*City of Sheboygan,* The." *Diver Magazine.* Vol. 26, No. 2 (April, 2000), 18-19.
.... "Double Dip Kingston's *Marsh* and *Comet.*" *Diver Magazine.* Vol. 26, No. 7 (October-November, 2000), 8-9.
.... "Dyer Bay." *Diver Magazine.* Vol. 9, No. 2 (March, 1983), 20-22.
.... "Hunting for Bottles." *Diver Magazine.* Vol. 7, No. 6 (September, 1981), 35-39.

Miscellaneous

Ackerman, Paul. Chicago, Illinois: Midwest Explorers League. "Lake Erie Dive Chart" (1998 edition), "Lake Huron Dive Chart" (1999 edition), "Lake Michigan Dive Chart" (1992 edition), "Lake Michigan Shipwrecks, South Shores" (1988 edition), "Lake Ontario Dive Chart" (1990 edition), "Lake Superior Dive Chart" (1990 edition).
Collections of Archival Materials available at: Center for Archival Collections, Bowling Green State University, Bowling Green, Ohio (formerly named the Institute for Great Lakes Research): Great Lakes Historical Society, Vermilion, Ohio; Cris Kohl Collection, Great Lakes Shipwrecks and Maritime History; Marine Historical Collection of the Milwaukee Public Library, Milwaukee, Wisconsin; Wisconsin Marine Historical Society, Milwaukee, Wisconsin.
Explore Michigan's Underwater Preserves 2001. (Booklet) Lexington, Michigan: Out of the Blue Productions, for the Michigan Underwater Preserve Council, Inc., 2001.
Guyer, Capt. Jerry. *Jerry's Shipwreck Charts. Lake Michigan Shipwrecks from North of Port Washington to the Illinois State Line.* April 1996, fifth edition.
Newspapers: 72 different Great Lakes newspapers on microfilm were accessed at 29 different locations, such as state historical libraries and municipal libraries, with dates ranging from 1834 to the present.
Olson, Valerie, ed. *The Goshawk Project, A Reconnaissance Survey of the Great Lake's Oldest Schooner.* February, 1995.
S. S. Regina, 1987 Report to the State of Michigan. Marysville, Michigan: Commercial Diving and Marine Service, 1987.

INDEX

Ships' names are in *italics*. Caption material is excluded.

ADVERTISERS' INDEX

We thank the following advertisers for their support of, and faith in, this project:

ABOUT THE AUTHOR

CRIS KOHL has spent his life around water, whether crossing the Atlantic Ocean by ship a number of times, or exploring his beloved Great Lakes in his sailboat or powerboat. He has taken and taught Power Squadron classes for safe boating. An intrepid explorer, he has spent time scuba diving on hundreds of shipwrecks in three oceans and all five Great Lakes during the past two-and-a-half decades. He has a Master of Arts degree in History, specializing in Great Lakes Maritime History, an important element which has helped him research, locate and identify numerous Great Lakes shipwrecks. He is also a certified Divemaster, Nitrox and Full Cave diver.

A prolific writer and prize-winning underwater photographer, Cris Kohl's work has appeared in the *Washington Post, Immersed* Magazine, *Diver* Magazine, *Sport Diver* Magazine, *Discover Diving* Magazine, *Great Lakes Cruiser* Magazine, *Inland Seas* and many others.

Cris Kohl is a popular speaker at history conferences and annual scuba shows such as Our World--Underwater (Chicago), Underwater Canada (Toronto), Beneath the Sea (New York City), Seaspace (Houston), and the Sea Rovers Scuba Show (Boston). He has often been interviewed on radio and television where he is able to promote the maritime history and the scuba diving potential of the Great Lakes which, from his experiences and in his opinion, contain the world's best-preserved submerged cultural resources, particularly shipwrecks.

He is presently on the Executive Board of the Underwater Archaeological Society of Chicago, and on the Technical Advisory Committee of the Lake Erie Shipwreck Research Center in Vermilion, Ohio. In the past, he has served in the capacity of scuba club President (3 years), Executive Board member of the Ontario Underwater Council (9 years), and Executive Board member of a branch of Save Ontario Shipwrecks (6 years).

His nine published books include the popular two-volume *The 100 Best Great Lakes Shipwrecks,* the *Dive Ontario!* books, *Treacherous Waters: Kingston's Shipwrecks,* and *TITANIC, The Great Lakes Connections.*

Raised in Windsor, Ontario, he now resides with his wife and partner, Joan Forsberg, at High Lake, Illinois, outside Chicago.

Cris Kohl and Jim Stayer (right) appear elated after identifying one of their Lake Huron shipwreck discoveries.   PHOTO BY PAT STAYER.

EMERGENCY CONTACTS

D.A.N.
Diver Alert Network
(919) 684-8111

If you're a scuba diver, and you aren't a D.A.N. member, you should be. Look into it.

VHF Emergency Radio Contact: Channel 16
Emergency Telephone: dial 911
In Ontario, for the Ontario Provincial Police, dial "0" and request ZENITH 50,000 and for the Ontario Ambulance Service, dial "0" and request ZENITH 90,000.

Hyperbaric Chambers

Chicago, Illinois, Edgewater Medical Center: (773) 878-6000, extension 3583
Detroit, Michigan, Henry Ford Hospital: (313) 916-3929
Kalamazoo, Michigan, Bronson Methodist Hospital: (616) 341-7654 or (616) 341-7778.
Marquette, Michigan, Marquette General Hosital: (906) 225-3560.
Milwaukee, Wisconsin, St. Luke's Hospital: (414) 649-6577.
Minneapolis, Minnesota, Hennepin County Hospital: (612) 347-3131
Tobermory, Ontario, Hyberbaric Facility: (519) 596-2306
Toronto, Ontario, General Hyperbaric: (416) 340-4131. After hours: (416) 340-3155
     NOTE: Only Toronto and Milwaukee have the capability of handling trimix cases.

U.S. Coast Guard: Traverse City, Michigan, Air Station: (231) 922-8214
To report thefts of artifacts from shipwrecks in Michigan: 1-800-292-7800

The End